TAKING SIDES

Clashing Views on

Psychological Issues

FOURTEENTH EDITION

TAKING SIDES

Clashing Views on
Psychological Issues
FOURTEENTH EDITION

Selected, Edited, and with Introductions by

Brent Slife
Brigham Young University

Mc Graw Hill **Contemporary Learning Series**
A Division of The McGraw-Hill Companies

To my three garrulous sons, Conor, Nathan, and Jacob

Photo Acknowledgment
Cover image: David Toase/Getty Images

Cover Acknowledgment
Maggie Lytle

Copyright © 2006 by McGraw-Hill Contemporary Learning Series
A Division of The McGraw-Hill Companies, Inc., Dubuque, Iowa 52001

Manufactured in the United States of America

Fourteenth Edition

123456789DOCDOC98765

Library of Congress Cataloging-in-Publication Data
Main entry under title:
Taking sides: clashing views on controversial psychological issues/selected, edited, and with introductions by Brent Slife.—14th ed.
Includes bibliographical references and index.
1. Psychology. 2. Human behavior. I. Slife, Brent, *comp.*
150

0-07-354558-9
ISSN: 1098-5409

Printed on Recycled Paper

Preface

Critical thinking skills are a significant component of a meaningful education, and this book is specifically designed to stimulate critical thinking and initiate lively and informed dialogue on psychological issues. In this book I present 36 selections, arranged in pro and con pairs, that address a total of 18 different controversial issues in psychology. The opposing views demonstrate that even experts can derive conflicting conclusions and opinions from the same body of information.

A dialogue approach to learning is certainly not new. The ancient Greek philosopher Socrates engaged in it with his students some 2,400 years ago. His point-counterpoint procedure was termed a *dialectic*. Although Socrates and his companions hoped eventually to know the "truth" by this method, they did not see the dialectic as having a predetermined end. There were no right answers to know or facts to memorize. The emphasis in this learning method is on how to evaluate information—on developing reasoning skills.

It is in this dialectical spirit that *Taking Sides: Clashing Views on Psychological Issues* was originally compiled, and it has guided me through this 13th edition as well. To encourage and stimulate discussion and to focus the debates in this volume, each issue is expressed in terms of a single question and answered with two points of view. But certainly the reader should not feel confined to adopt only one or the other of the positions presented. There are positions that fall between the views expressed or totally outside them, and I encourage you to fashion your own conclusions.

Some of the questions raised in this volume go to the very heart of what psychology as a discipline is all about and the methods and manner in which psychologists work. Others address newly emerging concerns. In choosing readings I was guided by the following criteria: the readings had to be understandable to newcomers to psychology; they had to have academic substance; and they had to express markedly different points of view.

Plan of the book Each issue in this volume has an issue *introduction,* which defines each author's position and sets the stage for debate. Also provided is a set of point-counterpoint statements that pertain to the issue and that should help to get the dialogue off the ground. Each issue concludes with *challenge questions* to provoke further examination of the issue. The introduction and challenge questions are designed to assist the reader in achieving a critical and informed view on important psychological issues. Also, at the beginning of each part is a list of Internet site addresses (URLs) that should prove useful as starting points for further research. At the back of the book is a listing of all the *contributors to this volume,* which gives information on the psychologists, psychiatrists, philosophers, professors, and social critics whose views are debated here.

In the interest of space, the reference lists of many of the original articles have been omitted or severely curtailed. Although I welcome further scholarly investigations on these issues, I assume that readers who engage in such investigation will want to look up the original articles (with the original reference lists) anyway. Furthermore, many of the articles have been heavily edited.

Changes to this edition This edition represents a considerable revision. There are seven completely new issues: "Should Psychological Treatments Be Empirically Supported?" (Issue 1); "Does Giving Praise Harm Children?" (Issue 6); "Are Human Cognitive and Behavioral Activities Determined?" (Issue 9); "Does ADHD Exist?" (Issue 11); "Does Taking Antidepressants Lead to Suicide?" (Issue 12); "Should Psychologists Be Able to Prescribe Medicine?" (Issue 14); and "Do Video Games Lead to Violence?" (Issue 16). In addition, for Issue 4 on whether or not humans are naturally violent and Issue 8 on whether or not divorce harms children, one side of the issue has been replaced to bring the debate up to date. In all, there are 16 new selections.

A word to the instructor An *Instructor's Manual With Test Questions* (multiple-choice and essay) is available through the publisher for the instructor using *Taking Sides* in the classroom. A general guidebook, *Using Taking Sides in the Classroom*, which discusses methods and techniques for integrating the pro-con approach into any classroom setting, is also available. An online version of *Using Taking Sides in the Classroom* and a correspondence service for *Taking Sides* adopters can be found at http://www.mhcls.com/usingts/.

Taking Sides: Clashing Views on Psychological Issues is only one title in the Taking Sides series. If you are interested in seeing the table of contents for any of the other titles, please visit the Taking Sides Web site at http://www.mhcls.com/takingsides/.

Acknowledgments In working on this revision I received useful suggestions from many of the users of the previous edition, and I was able to incorporate many of their recommendations for new issues and new readings.

In addition, special thanks to the McGraw-Hill staff for their support and perspective.

Brent Slife
Brigham Young University

Contents In Brief

Contents

participants were subjected to a research design that caused undue psychological stress that was not resolved after the study. Social psychologist Stanley Milgram, in response to Baumrind s accusations, asserts that the study was well designed, the stress caused to participants could not have been anticipated, and the participants anguish dissipated after a thorough debriefing.

psychology Phillip S. Strain and assistant research professor Gail E. Joseph contend positive reinforcement is a time-tested and scientifically sound way to teach children the difference between good and bad behavior and to help them develop a healthy sense of self-worth.

Child developmentalists Jeanne Brooks-Gunn, Wen-Jui Han, and Jane Waldfogel assert that their findings show many types of negative effects from maternal employment on the later cognitive and educational outcomes of children. Professor of sociology and anthropology Thomas M. Vander Ven and his colleagues argue that their studies show that the qualities or quantities of a mother working have relatively little or no influence on the social, emotional, and behavioral functioning of her children.

Clinical psychologist Judith S. Wallerstein and professor of psychology Julia Lewis argue their research indicates that the vast majority of children from divorced families are harmed in many subtle and obvious ways at various times and stages of their lives. Developmental psychologist E. Mavis Hetherington and writer John Kelly do not deny that divorce can have some harmful effects, especially in the short term, but they maintain that most of these children eventually become well adjusted.

Psychologists John A. Bargh and Tanya L. Chartrand assert that people are controlled not by their purposeful choices and intentions but by the environment through automatic cognitive processes. In response, psychologist Amy Fisher Smith agrees that people do, in fact, have automatic behaviors but she believes these behaviors can be explained by mental processes akin to a free will.

Psychologist Howard Gardner argues that humans are better understood as having eight or nine different kinds of intelligence rather than as having one general intelligence. Psychologist Linda S. Gottfredson contends that despite some popular assertions, a single factor for intelligence can be measured with IQ tests and is predictive of success in life.

PART 5   MENTAL HEALTH   203

Russell A. Barkley, a professor in the department of psychiatry and neurology, leads a team of researchers who claim that current scientific evidence, particularly evidence provided by heritability and neuro-imaging studies, points unarguably toward ADHD's validity and existence. Another group of researchers, led by psychiatrist Sami Timimi, claims the current ADHD epidemic is the result of unrealistic expectations for today's children and the pharmaceutical companies' desire to sell more drugs.

Psychiatrist David Healy and statistician Chris Whitaker argue that psychological research reveals a significant number of suicidal acts by individuals taking antidepressants and, thus, recommend stricter controls on these drugs. In response, psychiatrist Yvon D. Lapierre maintains that the research on suicidality and antidepressants is unconvincing, recommending that conclusions from these findings should be severely limited.

Developmental psychologist Douglas A. Gentile and department of psychology chair Craig A. Anderson assert that violent video games cause several physiological and psychological changes in children that lead to aggressive and violent behavior. Cheryl K. Olson, a professor of psychiatry, contends that further research is needed because there is so little current evidence of a substantial connection between exposure to violent video games and serious real-life violence.

Issue 17.   Does the Internet Have Psychological Benefits?   318

Research scientist James E. Katz and Philip Aspden, executive director of the Center for Research on the Information Society, contend that the Internet has positive effects on the lives of its users. They also maintain that the Internet creates more opportunities for people to foster relationships with people, regardless of their location. Robert Kraut, a professor of social psychology and human computer interaction, and his colleagues at Carnegie Mellon University question how beneficial Internet use really is. They argue that Internet use reduces the number and quality of interpersonal relationships that one has.

Issue 18.   Is Pornography Harmful?   336

Sociology professor Diana E. H. Russell argues that pornography is profoundly harmful because it predisposes men to want to rape women and undermines social inhibitions against acting out rape fantasies. Michael C. Seto, Alexandra Maric, and Howard E. Barbaree, of the Centre for Addiction and Mental Health, contend that evidence for a causal link between pornography use and sexual offense remains equivocal.

Introduction

Unresolved Issues in Psychology

Brent Slife
Stephen C. Yanchar

Eminent psychologist Edward Bradford Titchener (1867–1927) once stated that although psychology has a short history, it has a long past. He meant that even though the science of psychology is of relatively recent origin, the subject matter of psychology extends back to ancient history. Unfortunately, this dual history—the short and the long—is rarely treated in psychology texts; most texts focus almost exclusively on the shorter history. This shorter history is thought to be guided by the scientific method, so texts are generally filled with the scientific facts of the discipline. However, we cannot fully understand psychology without also understanding its longer intellectual history, a history of age-old questions that have recently been addressed by science but rarely been completely answered. Some history texts portray this longer intellectual history, but they do not deal with its contemporary implications. *Taking Sides: Clashing Views on Controversial Psychological Issues* is dedicated to the unresolved issues that still plague psychologists from this longer history.

Why Are There Unresolved Issues?

The subject matter of psychology is somewhat different from the subject matter of the natural sciences. In fact, psychology has been termed a "soft" science because it deals with neither the "hard" world of observable entities and physical elements—like zoology, biology, physiology, and chemistry—nor the rigorous computational analyses of mathematics, physics, and astronomy. These hard sciences are disciplines in which the crucial questions can usually be answered through scientific observation and experimentation.

Psychologists, on the other hand, deal with the warm, "soft" world of human beings—the thoughts, attitudes, emotions, and behaviors of people interacting with other people. Psychologists are therefore concerned with many of the philosophical questions that seem so central and unique to humanity. These questions have no quick and simple answers. Indeed, these questions have occupied thinkers—scientists and philosophers alike—since at least the time of the ancient Greeks.

For example, psychologists regularly deal with the topic of mind and matter, or what is sometimes referred to as the mind-body problem. The mind-body problem essentially asks, Does the mind (which is often viewed as *not* being entirely composed of matter) control the body (which *is* entirely composed of matter), or does the brain control the mind? Yet the essence of what we mean by the mind-body problem has been a topic of debate since at least the time of the Greek philosopher Aristotle (Robinson, 1989). Aristotle (384–322 B.C.) believed that the human mind had to be distinct from the crude matter of the human body. While the human body would eventually die and decay, the human mind (or soul) was imperishable. Aristotle accounted for much of human psychology on biological grounds (i.e., in terms of matter), but he still considered the higher rational activities of a human to be aspects of a mind that are independent of the body (Robinson, 1986). However, what is left out of his and other accounts is a precise explanation of how mind and body are connected. That is, if we assume that the mind is *not* composed of matter and is thus intangible, then how can it connect or interact with something material and tangible like the body? If, on the other hand, we decide that the mind *is* tangible and material, then we inherit a host of other problems associated with reductionism (see Slife & Williams, 1995, for details).

The point is that these and other such questions may not be resolved merely through scientific observation and experimentation. Scientific method is helpful for answering certain empirical questions, but its benefits are limited for many philosophical questions. And, for better or worse, psychology is infused with philosophical questions as well as empirical questions. There are basically two reasons for this infusion: the complexity of psychology's subject matter and the methods that psychologists use to study their subject matter.

Human beings—the primary subject matter of psychology—appear to operate with wills of their own within a hopelessly complex network of situations and relationships. This, it would seem, hinders the ability of scientists to attain the kind of certainty with people that they can attain with inanimate objects. Perhaps more important, it is difficult to know *why* people act in a particular manner because we cannot directly observe their intentions, thoughts, and desires. Thus, there are some aspects of human beings that elude the traditional methods of natural science.

The scientific method itself provides no irrefutable verification of an explanation. This is because data alone do not provide answers. Scientists sometimes talk as if the data from their experiments "tell" them what to believe or "give" them results, but this is somewhat misleading. Data are meaningless until they have been interpreted by the scientist (Slife & Williams, 1995). That is, scientists have a lot to do with their findings. Because there are a number of possible interpreters, there are, in principle, a number of possible interpretations. As some of the issues in this volume show, results that seem to supply indubitable proof for one interpreter might appear quite dubious to another. The reason for this is that the scientific method is set up in a manner that requires interpretation. As many who have studied this method have noted (e.g., Popper, 1959; Rychlak, 1988), the scientific method basically takes the form of a logical if-then statement: *If* my theory is correct, *then* my data will come out as I predict. However, problems can occur when we use this logic inappropriately. What if we know, for example, that we have the "then" portion of our statement, that the data did come out as I predicted? Do we then know that my theory is correct? Of course we cannot know this, because there can be an alternative theory (or many alternatives) that could explain the same data.

Unfortunately, however, this is the way in which science is conducted. We do not know the "if" portion of our logical statement—that my theory is correct; we can only know the "then" portion—that my data came out as I predicted. And our knowledge of our data cannot tell us that our theory is correct. All we can ever do is *interpret* what our data mean because our data can always mean something else.[1]

So, as a little logic has shown, data from human subjects can always be interpreted in different ways. In fact, because of these possible interpretations, there can never be a final and definitive experiment to determine what is really true about human beings (Slife & Williams, 1995). This is what scientists mean when they say that they cannot *prove* a theory but can only *support* it. Unfortunately, this simple distinction leaves many important questions unresolved, such as the mind-body problem. Still, this lack of resolution does not mean that scientists can ignore these issues. Just because certain issues are not amenable to scientific methods does not mean they go away. The issue of whether or not the mind controls matter, for example, is vital to cancer patients who wonder whether or not positive mental attitudes will alter the course of their disease. Such issues require exploration and debate regardless of the state of scientific knowledge. Whatever scientific information is available is important, and the lack of a complete scientific answer cannot prevent us from debating what information we do have, particularly when we may never get a complete scientific answer.

A Dialectical Approach

This volume introduces some of the most important contemporary debates in psychology as well as some classical issues that remain unresolved. As mentioned, this volume is different from texts that focus exclusively on what is known scientifically. Most texts with an exclusive scientific focus adopt a "banking conception" of education.

The banking conception of education assumes that students are essentially "banks" in which scientific facts are "deposited." Because psychology is considered a science, there are presumably many scientific psychological facts, derived from experiments, that need to be deposited in students' minds. The banking conception makes teachers and textbooks fact distributors or information transmitters. Lectures are monologues through which the facts of experiments or the findings of method are distributed and transmitted into the mental "banks" of students. At test time, then, teachers make information "withdrawals" to discern how well students have maintained the deposits of educational currency referred to as knowledge.

Since the time of the Greek philosopher Socrates (470–399 B.C.), the banking conception of education has not been considered effective for learning about unresolved conceptual issues. One reason for this is that nestled within the banking conception lies the assumption that knowledge is above reasonable criticism and that the facts of a scholarly discipline are approximations of truth—distilled and ready for distribution to students. This is the notion of education that considers knowledge to be strictly objective. Students are thought to acquire a clear and objective picture of reality—the way things really are. As we have observed, however, it is questionable whether teachers of the "soft" sciences have access to clear and objective facts only. In many cases, the "facts" are not so clear and objective but rather puzzling and debatable. Indeed, interpretations of data are always debatable, in principle.

An alternative to the banking tradition of education is the *dialectical* tradition of education. In this tradition, there can be no meaning (and thus no knowledge) without opposition. For example, there is no way to understand what "beauty" or "upness" means without implicitly understanding what "ugliness" or "downness" is, respectively. To judge the beauty of a work of art, one must have some notion of the contrast to beauty. In other words, opposing notions only make sense when considered at the same time, one complementing the other and together forming a complete concept. In this Greek conception of the dialectic, there are no quick and easy answers to difficult questions, and there are few incontestable facts to present. Instead, there are at least two sides to every issue.

Socrates taught his students that we may begin in error or falsity, but we will eventually arrive at truth if we continue our dialectical conversation. This is because truth, for Socrates, involves uncovering what is already there. Because all conceptions—true or false—supposedly have their dialectical complements implicit within them, truth is itself already implicit and waiting to be revealed. Truth, then, according to Socrates, is uncovered by a rational analysis of the relevant (and perhaps even false) ideas and arguments already under discussion.

The discipline of psychology is often considered to be dialectical, at least in part. Any student who has studied the many different theories of human behavior (e.g., humanism, behaviorism, psychoanalysis) can attest to this. Psychology frequently consists of two or more voices on the same psychological issue. Consequently, many of the ideas of psychology develop through conversation that takes place among psychologists or among the students of psychology. Although this is understandable when we consider the complexity of psychology's subject matter, it can create problems for the banking approach to education. What can be deposited in a mental bank when two or more voices are possible and the conversation among the voices is ongoing? Some information distribution is certainly important. However, information distribution alone cannot capture this type of knowledge in the discipline, because that knowledge is dialectical in nature.

Benefits of a Dialectical Approach

The dialectical approach is the focus of this volume: Psychological issues are presented in true dialectical fashion, with two distinct sides. Students are asked to familiarize themselves with both sides of an issue, look at the supporting evidence on both sides, and engage in constructive conversation about possible resolutions. This approach to education requires students to take an active role in making sense of the issues. In so doing, students benefit in several ways.

First, students come to a richer understanding of the subject matter of psychologists. It is important to understand that there is a dialectical, or humanities, side of psychology as well as an informational, or scientific, side of psychology. As necessary as data may be, there will always be a human interpreter of the data that will never permit psychology to dispense with humanities entirely.

Second, students develop a healthy respect for both sides of a debate. There is a natural tendency to underestimate reasonable arguments on one side or the other of a debate. Often, of course, the side one favors is the "most reasonable." Without exception, the issues in this book have reasonable people and reasonable arguments *on both sides*. That is, these issues are issues in psychology precisely because they have reasonable arguments and evidence on either side. This is not to say that both sides are correct (although this too is possible). It is to say, rather, that a proper appreciation of both sides is necessary to understanding what is at issue and thus to begin to find a resolution.

A third benefit of this dialectical approach is that students better understand the nature of psychological knowledge in general. Although contemporary psychologists have taken up the scientific challenge of exploring behavior and mind, many questions are still far from being answered. Psychology's parent, like all sciences, is philosophy. Hence, philosophical (or theoretical) issues always lurk behind the activities of psychologists. Issues such as mind versus body, free will versus determinism, nature versus nurture, and the philosophy of science are both philosophical and psychological questions. Students will necessarily have to entertain and explicate these types of issues as they learn about and advance the discipline.

Fourth, students become more aware of alternative views on controversial psychological issues. People often do not even realize that there is another point of view to an issue or evidence to the contrary. This realization, however, can help students to be more cautious in their knowledge. As the dialectician Socrates once noted, this caution is sometimes the first step toward true wisdom—knowing what it is that you don't know.

Finally, the dialectical approach promotes critical thinking skills. As authorities on critical thinking have noted (e.g., Brookfield, 1987), thinking skills require an awareness of what one *does* believe and a knowledge of alternatives regarding what one *could* believe. *Taking Sides: Clashing Views on Controversial Psychological Issues* provides both elements. Finely honed critical skills give students a better position from which to examine the psychological literature critically and to select or develop their own positions on important psychological issues.

Note

1. Unfortunately, falsifying the consequent—the "then" portion of our logical statement—does not prevent us from needing to interpret either, as Slife and Williams (1995) have shown.

References

Brookfield, S. (1987). *Developing critical thinkers: Challenging adults to explore alternative ways of thinking.* San Francisco: Jossey-Bass.

Popper, K. (1959). *The logic of scientific discovery.* New York: Basic Books.

Robinson, D. (1986). *An intellectual history of psychology.* Madison, WI: University of Wisconsin Press.

Robinson, D. (1989). *Aristotle's psychology.* New York: Columbia University Press.

Rychlak, J. F. (1988). *The psychology of rigorous humanism* (2d ed.). New York: New York University Press.

Slife, B. D., & Williams, R. N. (1995). *What's behind the research: Discovering hidden assumptions in the behavioral sciences.* Thousand Oaks, CA: Sage Publications.

Anthro.Net: Evolutionary Psychology

This site contains links and references for the study of the evolution of human behavior.

> http://home1.gte.net/ericjw1/evpsych.html

Center for evolutionary Psychology

This is the Web site of the Center for Evolutionary Psychology, which is based at the University of California, Santa Barbara. Here you will find and evolutionary psychology primer, recent research in evolutionary psychology, other places to study evolutionary psychology, and more.

> http://www.psych.ucsb.edu/research/cep/
> index.html

The Psi Cafe: A Psychology Resource Site

This site discusses different aspects of psychological research and provides helpful links to other sites that discuss research methods and popular ethical issues.

> http://www.psy.pdx.edu/PsiCafe/Research/
> Ethics.htm

Legal, Ethical, and Professional Issues in Psychoanalysis and Psychotherapy

This site's home page offers a wealth of information about different research issues in psychology. This particular link provides access to different papers that discuss the empirically support treatment (EST) movement.

> http://www.academyprojects.org/est.htm

PART 1

Research Issues

*R*esearch methods allow psychologists to investigate their ideas and subject matter. However, the way in which psychologists perform their research is sometimes the subject of controversy. Indeed, some have accused psychologists of conducting their research without being aware of their scientific biases. For example, could it be that some psychologists' bias toward empirically supported treatments has closed the door to other possibly effective treatments? In addition, researchers have a responsibility to act ethically toward the participants in their studies. To this end, animals are often used to test experimental procedures before they are applied to humans. Is this right? Should animals be experimented upon—and sometimes subjected to pain or even killed—in the service of psychological investigation? Similarly, what limits, if any, should be placed on psychological research that is conducted on humans? Are there some studies that are so potentially dangerous that they should not be performed?

- Should Psychological Treatments Be Empirically Supported?

- Should Animal Research in Psychology Be Eliminated?

- Classic Dialogue: Was Stanley Milgram's Study of Obedience Unethical?

ISSUE 1

Should Psychological Treatments Be Empirically Supported?

YES: Georgios K. Lampropoulos, from "A Reexamination of the Empirically Supported Treatments Critiques," *Psychotherapy Research* (Winter 2000)

NO: Arthur C. Bohart, from "Paradigm Clash: Empirically Supported Treatments Versus Empirically Supported Psychotherapy Practice," *Psychotherapy Research* (Winter 2000)

ISSUE SUMMARY

YES: Psychologist Georgios K. Lampropoulos argues that the identification of scientifically proven, manualized treatments is the only way to provide safe and effective therapy to the public.

NO: Psychologist Arthur C. Bohart disagrees with Lampropoulos and explains that empirically supported treatments stifle the therapeutic process by limiting the ability of the therapist and client to generate their own solutions.

If you went in to see a therapist or counselor, would you want to know if the treatment you were receiving was scientifically proven? Currently, many psychological treatments have not been fully investigated scientifically, leading some psychologists to fear that certain therapies do more harm than good. This fear has led to the development of empirically supported treatments, or ESTs for short. ESTs are typically manualized, step-by-step procedures for providing effective therapy, according to therapy research. ESTs seem to make a lot of sense to consumers of therapy because they want to know that their treatment is, as they say on the drug commercials, "safe and effective."

The problem is that some psychologists have noticed that only certain types of therapies make it to EST status. In fact, some researchers contend that those therapy techniques that fit the way science does things are the only ones that become "empirically supported." From this perspective, science is not the transparent and objective revealer of which techniques are effective and which are not. Science is based on a world view or paradigm that could influence which therapies are considered effective. If this is true, then there is a hidden bias in the scientific method that could mislead us in deciding counseling effectiveness.

Psychologist Georgios K. Lampropoulos, in the first selection, would clearly disagree with this notion. He sees the scientific method as an objective instrument of investigation and feels that a therapy's effectiveness should be proven by science in order to protect public welfare. Indeed, Lampropoulos asserts that ESTs are more humane and sensitive because they allow therapists to treat their clients more efficiently. He also addresses concerns about the use of manuals in clinical training. He explains that a step-by-step procedure for doing therapy is a better teaching tool than talking about general principles and theories that are often inconsistent and confusing. At least with manuals, therapists are provided with a standard technical language they can use in any therapeutic situation.

In the second selection, psychologist Arthur C. Bohart replies to Lampropoulos by noting that his arguments are based on a particular way of viewing the world—a world view or paradigm. Bohart explains that the EST movement understands therapy from within the medical model. This paradigm focuses almost exclusively on decreasing symptoms rather than getting to the root of problems. Bohart describes an alternative approach in which clients are considered unique rather than instances of general laws. Lampropoulos, by contrast, views therapy techniques as akin to a Newtonian clock where all the parts are step-by step, interchangeable, and can be examined independently. From Boharts perspective, these manuals and techniques are inadequate because they constrain therapists to act in ways that might not fit the needs of the client.

POINT

- Not all therapies are effective.
- ESTs can handle individual differences because they are proven to be effective for specific situations.
- Manuals and techniques help novice therapists because they give form and shape to abstract theories.
- ESTs allow therapists to treat clients more humanely.

COUNTERPOINT

- We cannot truly know if a therapy is effective because different therapies work with different people.
- ESTs provide little room for the therapist to meet a client's individual and unique needs.
- Solutions in therapy should emerge out of therapist and client interaction, rather than being determined beforehand.
- Treatments that are dictated by research findings miss the importance of a changing and unique therapeutic relationship.

Georgios K. Lampropoulos  **YES**

A Reexamination of the Empirically Supported Treatments Critiques

. . . Several years have passed since psychotherapy demonstrated its value and effectiveness as a mental health treatment, with many schools of therapy reaching a compromised decision that they are more or less equally effective (i.e., the Dodo bird verdict). Recently, an old antagonist (biological psychiatry) with the help of a new ally (managed health care) has created a new challenge, that of cost-effectiveness. A new horse race has begun, with cognitive-behavioral therapies leading the competition. While cognitive-behavioral treatments try to compete with drug therapies, psychodynamic and humanistic treatments have just started, screaming "unfair!"

A gloves-off fight has erupted again in psychotherapy. In the empirically supported treatments (EST) debate over the last ten years, the majority of opposition comes from psychodynamic and humanistic researchers and practitioners who refuse to play with the unfair rules that their rivals made in some sort of agreement (based on the medical model) with their major antagonist (psychiatry). Accusations of violation, politics, and conflicts of interest regarding ESTs have proliferated. Indeed, most of the opposition, repeatedly expressed through the years, is largely justified.

Nevertheless, calmer voices have called for the avoidance of extremities. Psychodynamic and experiential researchers have started to develop manuals and empirically support their therapies. In some countries, psychodynamic and humanistic therapies are already considered empirically supported and enjoy equal status with cognitive-behavioral therapies.

To enhance progress in this positive direction, this paper considers recent critiques of ESTs and attempts to pinpoint positive aspects of ESTs that their critics may have overlooked. Specifically, this article is a response to the 1998 special section of *Psychotherapy Research* on the topic of ESTs, in which substantial supportive arguments for the EST project were missing. The article also discusses similar criticism on the ESTs that has recently appeared in the literature. My hope is that psychodynamic and experiential researchers will get more actively involved in the EST movement, fighting for appropriate changes they have already identified, and conducting research to support their psychotherapies.

From *Psychotherapy Research,* vol. 10, issue 4, 2000, pp. 474–477, 480–487. Copyright © 2000 by Taylor & Francis Journals. Reprinted by permission. References omitted.

Although the EST project (and the Diagnostic and Statistical Manual [DSM] taxonomy on which ESTs are based) originated in the United States and are not necessarily followed by the rest of the world, the issues discussed in this paper go beyond specific diagnostic systems and treatment lists. Beyond any potential uses that EST-related research may have for clinicians and researchers who follow other diagnostic and treatment systems, it is the underlying methodological and research principles of the EST project that are most important. These principles have universal value and can be generalized to any alternative systems, lists, and projects around the world.

This article will not focus on criticisms related to possible dangers from the pressure of third-party payers and possible misuse of the movement's findings. Nor will I discuss problems related to the criteria used to determine the ESTs. All of these concerns are important, and recommendations for improvement are promising.

Most of the justified criticism focuses on the *process* of determining the ESTs (e.g., inconsistent, invalid, strict, or lenient criteria, lack of statistical power, nonconsideration of effect sizes and clinical significance, inadequate outcome measures and targeted areas of improvement, limited length of research, lack of long-term follow-up data, high relapse rates, inadequate control for protocol adherence and investigator allegiance, discrimination against specific therapies and populations, and paucity of external validity). But it is difficult to argue against the *goals* of the EST movement (e.g., adequately controlled empirical research, evidence-based treatment, explicit guidance in clinical practice, replicable practice and research, dissemination of empirical findings, improvement of therapy training). Independent of the technical problems in the process, it is important that we should not miss the ESTs' essence, as well as the benefits that they have to offer in the areas of treatment selection, psychotherapy research, and the training of the psychotherapists. What follows is a discussion of some major points of criticism concerning the goals of the EST movement and an attempt to show how these perceived weaknesses might actually be strengths under certain conditions.

The Dodo Bird Verdict and Empirically Invalid Treatments

One major concern is that efficacy research might be abandoned in the name of the Dodo bird verdict. The Dodo bird verdict on the equivalency of therapies and the common factors hypothesis is responsible for a great deal of the criticism on ESTs. Although common factors might explain the largest part of the rough equivalence of therapies, they are not the only explanation. While acknowledging the potency of common factors, Norcross has summarized reasons to critically question the Dodo verdict and to support, in some instances, differential effects of the psychotherapies.

Two good examples of such differential treatment effects can be found in the areas of the anxiety disorders and the sexual dysfunctions and are useful in the deconstruction of a universal outcome equivalence belief. In addition to differences found in main effects of treatments, aptitude-treatment interaction (ATI) research also occasionally shows differential therapeutic outcomes (particularly when aptitude is a clinically meaningful psychological variable.

Although the degree of real outcome equivalence between therapies cannot be easily determined, a few important limitations of the verdict to keep in mind are: (a) It is based on horse-race outcome studies, almost half of which lack adequate statistical power to detect differential effects; (b) The outcome equivalence finding involves at best only a few types of therapy (i.e., those that have been tested, usually well-developed ones), but not all therapeutic practices; (c) Equivalent outcomes are usually based on self-reported symptom reduction out of many possible areas of change—that is, outcome measures might be insensitive or unsuitable to detect some meaningful differences; (d) In therapeutic practice, "the Dodo bird verdict is intuitively and clinically wrong . . . and defies clinical reality" "seriously doubt that any psychotherapy researcher (or clinician) ever seriously believed in universal equivalence."

Two recent major studies that support the Dodo bird verdict were also immediately subject to similar and multiple criticisms. For example, [one] study confirmed the Dodo bird verdict mainly between cognitive and behavioral therapies or, at best, other "bona fide" treatments that are either included in the ESTs list or could be in the future. [Another] study was criticized for lack of adequate power and appropriate client variables to be tested for ATI effects. All these methodological critiques should not allow therapists to rest exclusively on the therapeutic relationship, powerful placebos, and other ill-defined common factors, which seems to be a major assumption shared by most of the EST opponents. In concluding their sophisticated review of the Dodo bird verdict, Elliott et al. clearly advocated "the need for continued disorder- or problem-focused treatment outcome research, coupled with more intensive investigation of client and therapist individual differences and in-therapy processes."

Some have argued that searching for ESTs is a case of blanket validation of psychotherapy per se, since EST inclusion criteria are too lenient and since almost every therapy could be validated. Instead, they suggest that a list of empirically invalid treatments would be more useful. Although the lenient criteria of ESTs makes it quite possible that they will lead to another form of Dodo bird verdict, this is certainly beneficial, since (a) the first one is obviously limited, and (b) the second Dodo bird verdict will be more problem-specific this time (and increasingly become more specific with the progressive development and validation of ESTs for comorbid disorders and other client characteristics). As Howard et al. (1997) pointed out, even in the medical field there is often more than one intervention that produces equivalent results in the treatment of an illness, but this does not mean that all kinds of medical treatments are effective for a specific disorder. The same should be assumed to be true in psychotherapy. Even if only a few treatments were proved invalid and nonefficacious, this would be an important gain for the field and the protection of the public. We should not forget that there are 400 forms of therapies out there and that only seven or eight of them have been tested and contributed to the Dodo verdict in the first place. There are serious reasons to believe that not all of the existing treatments will finally make the EST list (especially since it is disorder-specific), while some specific treatments will probably never be tested for specific problems, due to the fact that they lack anecdotal or preliminary effectiveness. That is, an empirically invalid treatments list (official or unofficial) could be potentially devised parallel to the EST list. . . .

Are ESTs Inhumane and Insensitive in Clinical Practice?

Developing Empirical Treatment Selection

ESTs represent one form of eclectic practice, that is, specific treatments for specific disorders. In this respect, arguments that ESTs are insensitive to client variability seem somewhat unjustified. Empirically supported treatment is more humane and sensitive than any procrustean application of theoretically pure therapies that claim to be equally effective for all clients and all problems, or "anything goes" practices based on the therapeutic equivalence paradox. Symptoms and problems are very specific, meaningful, and important client characteristics, among many other client variables. Symptoms and problems are undeniably a serious aspect of clients' realities and a central characteristic of their case formulation. That is, ESTs in their present form are at least partially sensitive to client individual differences.

However, the insensitivity criticism has a sound basis when it comes to problem subtypes, comorbidity, and nondiagnostic personality variables. Two proposals to deal with these important concerns follow.

A gradual demonstration of ESTs for complex clinical realities.   Using ATI research designs, ESTs could be determined for more complex clinical situations, client characteristics and comorbid disorders. Findings from personality-matched treatments might also be very helpful here. However, official practice guidelines may be somewhat premature at this point, which explains why the EST Task Force has not issued more specific eclectic recommendations yet. It is likely that specific differential EST recommendations might be issued in the future for client variables like those studied by Beutler and associates. My integrative hope is that in the distant future, through painstaking research in empirically dismantling, adding, comparing, and matching specific techniques with individual realities, we will be able to create a database of empirically supported components from different orientations to be used in different situations in building optimally effective individualized case formulations.

A flexible and individualized application of manualized ESTs, especially for complex cases.   In addition to identifying and matching ESTs to comorbid disorders and client personality variables, flexible applications of these ESTs will individualize them even further. That is, we should rely on empirical ATI research to advance eclectic practice as far as possible in terms of optimal therapies for meaningful clinical subpopulations (i.e., the big decisions) and leave clinical wisdom and expertise to complete the prescriptive matching task (i.e., the small decisions). The combination of these two proposals will make clinical practice as empirically individualized as possible, resembling the ideal individualized practice described in Stiles' *responsiveness theory.*

The slowly but steadily accumulated EST-based ATI findings will allow therapists to treat clients more humanely (i.e., sensitively but also empirically supported). This empirically supported approach to client individuality might be necessary, since early research shows that clinicians' individualized case formulations, compared with manualized treatments, may actually reduce therapeutic effectiveness on average. This is particularly applicable with trainees and inexperienced therapists who may believe that their clinical experience is adequate to identify important client variables and match them with the appropriate intervention.

What is being advocated here is some form of empirical humanism, as opposed to an idiosyncratic and unsystematic way of approaching clients' multidimensional and complex realities. ESTs are, by definition, empirical means toward humanistic ends; the most respectful way to treat people is effectively and efficiently, and this requires empirical research. Thus, the argument that ESTs are inhumane and insensitive can be reversed and stated in the form that treating clients with empirically supported interventions according to their diagnostic (and other individual) differences is a sublime version of humanistic practice.

A related major point of criticism is that diagnostic specificity dehumanizes clients because it deemphasizes the relationship variables in therapy. Although clinical diagnosis alone is not adequate for a humane treatment, it is definitely important, and does not preclude an effective therapeutic relationship. Training therapists in techniques does not mean that the therapeutic relationship and important common factors must be neglected. After all, when efficacious ESTs are applied to naturalistic settings, we should expect both the therapeutic alliance and subsequently the clinical utility of ESTs to increase, at least comparing to efficacy research conditions. This is due to the fact that random assignment of clients to therapists in RCTs may compromise the relationship and the final outcome, thus underrepresenting the real effectiveness of an EST in the free market (where clients actively look for the therapist and treatment most suitable for them.

Is Training in ESTs Potentially Harmful?

The Art and the Science in Therapy

Parts of the scientific community have expressed concerns about the use of manuals in clinical training and the emphasis on techniques. Is therapy a science of an art? Many believe it is both. Whether we like it or not, some of the basic human and relationship qualities preexist training, and might be difficult to be taught. That is, therapists might be partly born and partly bred.

In that case, what is the role of graduate training? Obviously, its role is to take these naturally equipped individuals and teach them the best way to enhance, complement, and transform their interpersonal qualities into practice. This is the technical and scientific part of therapy training. We get the talent and the art, and add scientific training. This suggests that most of our concern with therapists' interpersonal qualities should move to the pretraining level (i.e., the selection process). Of course, training in interpersonal skills might also be useful. For example, Henry has been developing a CD-ROM for therapist training in interpersonal behavior, based on the Structural Analysis of Social Behavior (SASB) system.

Admission committees should ensure that they accept "humans," and use manualized and other training to make them scientists. ESTs are manualized, step-by-step explanatory processes of how to do therapy. This might be the best way to teach therapy, rather than talking in general about principles and theories. Even if trainees do not always follow the manual step by step (and they should not), they have a great opportunity to be exposed to and educated in the way theoretical principles are operationalized in clinical practice.

Some evidence of negative therapeutic outcomes associated with manualized training came from a data set of 16 clinicians trained in brief psychodynamic treatment. In this study, a subgroup of "therapists with hostile introjects were found to be largely responsible for the posttraining increase in negative and complex interpersonal communications." However, "it appears that training did not make them more hostile per se. Rather, the greater activity level might simply have provided more opportunities to display baseline rates of problematic interpersonal behavior." This points toward issues of therapist preexisting qualities and trainee selection, as well as additional interpersonal training. Training in techniques through the use of manuals does not mean that interpersonal effectiveness training must be neglected.

In any case, research findings showing that manualization may interfere with therapist's interpersonal skills should receive attention. However, such findings might be transient and reflect trainee difficulties in assimilating new knowledge while using their interpersonal skills effectively at the same time, a problem that may gradually disappear as trainees become more experienced and flexible in applying manualized ESTs. Although manuals are not panacea for psychotherapy training, their value and benefits for novice therapists have been recognized.

Manuals as the Common Language for Training, Practice, and Research

The development of manuals is not just a necessary evil for the validation of treatments; it specifies the content of often abstractly described interventions and gives form and shape to sometimes inconsistent theories. In this sense, manuals may provide a standard language in terms of techniques that can enhance understanding, communication, and comparisons in the field, both between the same theoretical orientation and between orientation. The problem of a common language and standard frames of reference has been long considered as one major obstacle for psychotherapy integration and rapprochement between therapies. The manualization part of the ESTs movement seems to represent an improvement in this direction. This standard technical language can facilitate the quest for commonalities and differences between therapies, at least at the lower level of techniques.

Conclusions

To conclude, ESTs seem to have advanced our knowledge about therapy one step further. Slowly but steadily, we move from "does therapy work" to Paul's "*What* treatment, by *whom,* is most effective for *this* individual with *that* specific problem, and under *which* set of circumstances." These developments have been recently advanced to include the identification of efficacious and cost-effective psychological ESTs in areas that have been traditionally dominated by pharmacotherapy, such as severe, chronic, and resistant nonpsychotic disorders.

In the EST effort and through constructive criticism, we will hopefully be able to detect and overcome weaknesses, improve our research, protect clients' welfare from economic pressures, and capitalize on the products of the EST movement. The identification of empirically supported, manualized treatments seems necessary in order to proceed, and arguments on *how to do it* should not cancel the decision to *do it*, as some may suggest. On the other hand, premature decisions should be avoided on mendatory practice guidelines, while plenty of time and equal opportunity should be given to therapies to join research trials, especially since RCTs need time and effort to be completed. As we move to the next EST-related generation of psychotherapy research, insurance companies, licensing procedures, accreditation bodies, and professional regulations should be careful and fair.

NO

Arthur C. Bohart

Paradigm Clash: Empirically Supported Treatments Versus Empirically Supported Psychotherapy Practice

. . . Lampropoulos presents a good case for how empirically supported treatments (ESTs) could address opponents' concerns. However, he does not address a deeper problem: a paradigm conflict that mitigates against this kind of solution. Kuhn has noted that it is difficult for those from different paradigms to understand one another. The EST approach is based on one paradigm of psychotherapy and research. From the perspective of that paradigm, the EST approach seems so logical that its advocates have difficulty grasping the objections of those of us who do not subscribe to the paradigm.

When confronted with objections, EST proponents typically respond in two ways. First, they assume that the motivation of their opponents is to inappropriately defend "unscientific" practice. Therefore, these opponents should manualize and conduct the randomized clinical trials (RCTs) that show that their approaches work. Second, they argue that the remaining objections can be satisfied by the EST paradigm. This, however, is a little like a Republican telling Democrats that all their concerns (e.g., gun control, poverty) can be handled within a Republican framework. This is true. In a restricted sense, all issues and ideas can be handled from within any paradigm. However, substantive conflicts are framed and handled differently in separate paradigms. So, in another sense, it is not true.

In this rejoinder I will (a) make a brief paradigmatic comment on the Dodo verdict, (b) present what I perceive from within my paradigm as the implicit logic of the EST paradigm, and (c) briefly present the rationale of an alternative paradigm. Ultimately, my argument is that there are other ways to construe evidence-based practice and that it is paradigmatic imperialism to force both research and practice into an EST framework.

From *Psychotherapy Research,* vol. 10, issue 4, 2000, pp. 488–492. Copyright © 2000 by Taylor & Francis Journals. Reprinted by permission. References omitted.

The Dodo: An Example of Paradigm Clash

Perhaps no issue is more pivotal in highlighting the difference between competing paradigms of psychotherapy than the Dodo verdict that all therapies, for the most part, are equally effective for most disorders. For proponents of the EST paradigm, the Dodo verdict, if true, would be instant death. There would be no point in developing and studying different treatments for different disorders. The EST paradigm views specific technology and standardized treatment as the primary cause of behavior change. Therefore, it is not surprising that EST advocates are quick to conclude that the Dodo verdict is "flawed" or that it has been superseded. For proponents of some alternative paradigms, therapy is fundamentally an emergent interpersonal/dialogical process, with technology secondary. Therefore, we are likely to accept the Dodo verdict in terms of techniques, and if we contest it, see different relationship working better for different people (as opposed to different treatments for different disorders).

Because the willingness with which one accepts the Dodo verdict is at least partially paradigm-based, it is unlikely this issue will ever be resolved until one or the other paradigm (or some new paradigm) triumphs. Therefore, I object to Lampropoulos's comment that therapists such as myself should not be allowed to "rest exclusively on the therapeutic relationship, powerful placebos and other ill-defined common factors, which seems to be a major assumption shared by most of the EST opponents." I will simply make this point: The opposite of the Dodo verdict, the contention that differential treatment effects have been demonstrated, has equally been criticized. Wampold has pointed out that the number of such findings does not exceed chance. Additionally, findings of investigator allegiance effects cast further doubt on differential treatment findings. A conservative scientific conclusion concerning the idea of differential treatment effects is a weak version of the Dodo, in that there is still no compelling evidence for them in the vast majority of cases. Accordingly, those of us who choose to pursue an alternative view of psychotherapy and to rest that view on "ill-defined common factors" are on as solid ground as is Lampropoulos.

The EST Paradigm from the Perspective of a Nonbeliever

I will briefly sketch from within my perspective the underlying logic of the EST paradigm. The EST paradigm is based on an analogy to medical practice. The focus is on treatment and treatment packages, which are viewed as analogous to drugs. The treatment is applied to the problem and is believed to be the curative agent. As in medicine, the more specifically tailored the treatment is to the problem, the more likely it is to be effective. Because there is an a priori belief that specific treatment must be more effective than "nonspecific" treatment, research becomes a matter of discovering and demonstrating differential treatment effects.

This paradigm makes perfect sense if psychotherapy is administration of a treatment analogous to a drug. In medicine, one wants to control as tightly as possible the independent variable (e.g., the purity of the drug). In psychotherapy, one wants to manualize. In medicine, one wants to identify the active ingredients in medication. In psychotherapy research, one wants to perform dismantling studies. Traditional experimental logic is the cornerstone of the research methodology, along with its emphasis on internal validity (to rigorously establish "cause") and manualization (to specify or "operationalize" the treatment as the independent variable). To empirically study therapy, the treatment becomes the independent variable, which is applied to the dependent variable, the client or the client's problem. Underlying this model is the assumption that the best way to practice is to discover general laws and then to treat individual cases as specific instances of these general laws.

Even with manuals, psychotherapy cannot be as standardized as a drug trial. However, it is assumed that further research will take care of this, specifying more and more tightly the linear causal relationship between specific therapeutic "ingredients" and specific outcomes, including aptitude by treatment interactions (ATIs). According to Lampropoulos, "[W]e should rely on empirical ATI research to advance eclectic practice as far as possible in terms of optimal therapies for meaningful clinical subpopulations (*i.e., the big decisions*) and leave clinical wisdom and expertise to complete the prescriptive matching task (*i.e., the small decisions*)" (italics mine). The endpoint of this paradigmatic project would theoretically be an immensely complex manual, where the therapy process could be schematized in a series of decision rules, at least for all the "big decisions."

Underlying this model is a traditional Newtonian world view of the universe as a giant clock. The clock is, in principle, completely knowable. It can be dismantled and the contribution of all parts figured out.

An Alternative Paradigm

The alternative paradigm I present is my interpretation of principles in both client-centered therapy and strategic/solution-focused therapy. Both client-centered and strategic therapy view therapy holistically: The therapist engages in a dialogue with a whole person to help that person remove obstacles to living a better life. Second, the therapist relies on clients' own capacities for self-healing, and works within the client's frame of reference. The client's generativity is an integral part of the process. Solutions emerge out of therapist and client interaction, rather than being dictated a priori by a cookbook list of treatments matched up to problems or diagnoses. Third, while the practitioner is guided by a set of principles, these can be embodied or actualized by different practitioner in interaction with different clients in widely different ways. The resultant therapy may, therefore, look quite different from one therapist-client pair to another. Fourth, each client is treated as unique and not as an instance of a category. Fifth, since therapy relies crucially on clients' active creative intelligence to fashion solutions, there will be no guarantee of a one-to-one relationship between "intervention" and outcome. Finally, for both client-centered and solution-focused therapy, interactive responsiveness is the core of therapy, and not a "small detail" to be added within a manualized framework.

Because of all this, these approaches are incompatible with "manual-ized, step-by-step explanatory processes of how to do therapy." However, Lampropoulos claims that strategic/solution-focused therapy can be man-ualized. Spokespersons for this point of view would disagree. To quote Rosenbaum, "Therapy requires a constant, ongoing process where the thera-pist adjusts to the client, and the client adjusts to this adjustment. This makes the manualizing of therapy precisely the wrong strategy for psychotherapy research." While versions of client-centered therapy and solution-focused ther-apy can be manualized, practitioners of these approaches, such as myself, would not consider these manuals as truly representative of these approaches because of the philosophical incompatibility with the concept of manual-drive practice. Rather, these manuals are analogues mapped into a different intellectual universe.

The relationship of science to practice is also different in this paradigm. ESTs are based on what Schön calls "technical rationality"—finding general laws and then treating individual cases as instances of general categories to which these laws are applied. In contrast, my alternative paradigm is compat-ible with Schon's view of the "reflective practitioner," derived from studies of practice in many domains. Psychotherapy is conceived of as *science-informed practice,* rather than as a science in its own right. According to Schon, practi-tioners treat each new case as unique, and develop a new theory of each case. Science-based principles are incorporated. This is compatible with the view of Goldfried and Wolfe, who have said about the relationship of therapy research to practice: "Although we strongly believe that clinical practice should be informed by outcome research, it is quite another thing for it to be dictated by such findings. Group designs, in which patients are randomly assigned to treatment conditions, simply do not generalize to how we prac-tice clinically."

In my model, there is no independent variable being applied to a depen-dent variable. Manualizing a treatment provides the illusion that something standardized is being applied to a disorder, with improvement coming out the other end of the process as a product. However, in my alternative paradigm, psychotherapy is a conversation or dialogue between two intelligent beings. It is an ongoing, responsive, self-corrective process. The "independent variable" is constantly being made and remade through the dialogue. Therapy is more properly conceived of as the interaction of two complex systems, which them-selves from a complex system, with complex recursive processes happening both within each system and between the two. RCTs would not be the "gold standard" for research in this paradigm. Rather, RCTs would be one of many useful methods, including qualitative ones, for discovering how to be thera-peutically useful.

For practice, what becomes more important than some standardized starting point such as a manual is sensitive and responsive utilization of princi-ples of learning and change as the process unfolds. Research should therefore focus on exploring useful principles and processes of change upon which the practitioner can draw. I do not have the space to review the empirical base for examples of such principles in this brief rejoinder, but suggest, based on the reviews of others, that the following principles may qualify. First, a good therapeutic relationship is associated with change. Tailoring the relationship to individual clients may even be more important than tailoring treatments to their disorders. Second, promoting client involvement is important. A major way to promote involvement is to take the client's frame of reference seriously. Third, Grawe has based his "research-informed" approach to therapy practice on the following empirically supported principles: clarification/insight, problem actuation, and provision of mastery experiences. Therefore, a practitioner could be said to be practicing in an empirically supported manner if he or she works to provide and maintain a good relationship, works with or within the client's frame of reference, fosters clarification and insight, works when the problem is actuated, and works to provide mastery experience. The therapist and client together may then design widely different solutions to the client's problems, with a good chance of them being effective, based on utilization of these principles, just as an architect could utilize principles of science to design widely differing viable buildings.

Conclusion

The EST criteria for therapeutic effectiveness and practice represent on paradigmatic approach to the problem. However, contrary to what EST proponents have asserted, the issue is not whether to practice in an empirically supported way or not, with those who follow the EST approach identifying themselves with science, and those who do not being identified as antiscience. Rather, the issue is: What is empirically supported therapy practice? I have tried to suggest in this reply that there are alternative paradigms of what psychotherapy is which are antithetical to the EST paradigm. Following from this, there are alternative ways of construing empirically supported or empirically corroborated therapy practice. It is paradigmatic hegemony to assert that all research and practice ought to be conducted within the EST paradigm.

CHALLENGE QUESTIONS

Should Psychological Treatments Be Empirically Supported?

1. Bohart contends that ESTs are part of the medical model. Find out what this model is, and form your own, informed opinion about its relevance or irrelevance to psychotherapy. Support your answer.
2. Many people think that they would feel safer if their therapist used techniques that have been validated by science. Explain what it is about science that would lead them to feel this way.
3. Explain why you, as a potential client of a psychotherapist, might not want ESTs used on you.
4. Research the EST movement and describe its history leading up to the present. What do you predict the discipline of psychology will do about ESTs and why?
5. Why do you think that ESTs have met with such resistance in psychology? Feel free to find articles that help you to answer this question.

ISSUE 2

Should Animal Research in Psychology Be Eliminated?

YES: Peter Singer, from *Animal Liberation* (Ecco, 2002)

NO: R. G. Frey, from "Justifying Animal Experimentation: The Starting Point," in Ellen Frankel Paul and Jeffrey Paul, eds., *Why Animal Experimentation Matters: The Use of Animals in Medical Research* (Transaction, 2001)

ISSUE SUMMARY

YES: Bioethicist Peter Singer asserts that to engage in animal research is to commit speciesism (similar to racism), often without any important research findings at all.

NO: Professor of philosophy R. G. Frey expresses support for the similarity that Singer and others note between animals and humans but ultimately argues that animals should be used for research because their quality of life is lower than that of most humans.

Many students assume that psychologists deal with humans exclusively. Psychotherapy, for example, is rarely thought to be relevant to animals. However, a large portion of psychological research does involve animals of all types—monkeys, pigeons, rats, dogs, etc. Psychologists often believe they need animals to perform the experiments that cannot be ethically conducted with humans. These experiments illuminate or test concepts that could be helpful to humans, such as in psychotherapy and education. Also, many psychologists are interested in the animals themselves. Understanding the behaviors and functioning of such animals is itself a goal of many researchers.

The problem is that many such experiments entail a treatment of animals that some might regard as harmful or painful. Indeed, this harm or pain is often the primary reason that animals are used instead of humans; no one would reasonably allow what happens to the animals to happen to humans. Researchers have shocked animals with electrical current, subjected them to painful situations, and injected them with harmful drugs, to name but a few of the research practices to which some people have objected. Why is this treatment of animals in research permitted? Why would researchers subject animals to situations and treatments that they would never condone with humans?

Peter Singer is often credited with first sensitizing people to these types of issues. A bioethicist of considerable notoriety, Singer penned a book in 1975 entitled *Animal Liberation* that formalized the arguments against the subjugation of animals to psychological and medical research. In the following selection from his 2002 update of this book, he continues to press the arguments he originally formulated. For example, Singer describes in some detail many different types of animal research in psychology but finds none that justifies the suffering of the animals involved. He also continues to refute the notion that lower animals are absolutely different from higher animals (humans). Consequently, when animals are subjected to harmful procedures, they are unjustifiably discriminated against (speciesism) in the same way that other races might be unjustifiably discriminated against (racism).

In the second selection, R. G. Frey replies with perhaps a surprising tack. Although he agrees with Singer that animals cannot be absolutely differentiated from humans, Frey argues that animals generally (though not without exception) have a lower quality of life than humans. He then brings to bear a second argument with respect to the consequences of animal experiments. He regards such consequences as almost indisputably positive and beneficial, especially for medical research. Also, Frey notes, university and government committees do attempt to safeguard the use of animals in psychological research, looking specifically at whether or not the significance of the studies proposed is substantial enough to warrant the animals used. The reason that so much animal research is approved, Frey concludes, is that the benefits clearly outweigh the quality of life of the animals involved.

POINT

- Lower and higher animals (humans) do not absolutely differ on any factor relevant to their suffering in psychological experimentation.
- Many psychological experiments using animals are conducted for insignificant reasons.

- The members of many animal-use committees are biased toward the use of animals in questionable experiments.
- Experimenters have been trained to ignore or overlook the incredible suffering of animals in psychological research.

COUNTERPOINT

- Lower and higher animals do differ in their quality of life, which justifies the use of animals in experiments of significance.
- Animal-use committees are specifically charged with examining whether or not the significance of such experiments are sufficient to justify the use of animals.
- There is no reason to suspect that the members of these committees have unchangeable biases in favor of animal use.
- The benefits of much research is rarely disputed.

YES

Peter Singer

Animal Liberation

Most human beings are speciesists. The following [descriptions] show that ordinary human beings—not a few exceptionally cruel or heartless humans, but the overwhelming majority of humans—take an active part in, acquiesce in, and allow their taxes to pay for practices that require the sacrifice of the most important interests of members of other species in order to promote the most trivial interests of our own species. . . .

Many of the most painful experiments are performed in the field of psychology. To give some idea of the numbers of animals experimented on in psychology laboratories, consider that during 1986 the National Institute of Mental Health [NIMH] funded 350 experiments on animals. The NIMH is just one source of federal funding for psychological experimentation. The agency spent over $11 million on experiments that involved direct manipulation of the brain, over $5 million on experiments that studied the effects drugs have on behavior, almost $3 million on learning and memory experiments, and over $2 million on experiments involving sleep deprivation, stress, fear, and anxiety. This government agency spent more than $30 million dollars on animal experiments in one year.

One of the most common ways of experimenting in the field of psychology is to apply electric shocks to animals. This may be done with the aim of finding out how animals react to various kinds of punishment or to train animals to perform different tasks. In the first edition of [my] book I described experiments conducted in the late Sixties and early Seventies in which experimenters gave electric shocks to animals. Here is just one example from that period:

O. S. Ray and R. J. Barrett, working in the psychology research unit of the Veterans Administration Hospital, Pittsburgh, gave electric shocks to the feet of 1,042 mice. They then caused convulsions by giving more intense shocks through cup-shaped electrodes applied to the animals' eyes or through clips attached to their ears. They reported that unfortunately some of the mice who "successfully completed Day One training were found sick or dead prior to testing on Day Two."

Now, nearly twenty years later, . . . experimenters are still dreaming up trifling new variations to try out on animals: W. A. Hillex and M. R. Denny of the University of California at San Diego placed rats in a maze and gave them electric shocks if, after one incorrect choice, on their next trial they failed to choose which way to go within three seconds. They concluded that the "results are clearly reminiscent of the early work on fixation and regression in the rat, in which the animals were typically shocked in the stem of the T-maze just preceding the choice point. . . ." (In other words, giving the rats electric shocks at the point in the maze at which they had to choose, rather than before that point—the novel feature of this particular experiment—made no significant difference.) The experimenters then go on to cite work done in 1933, 1935, and other years up to 1985. . . .

Experiments in conditioning have been going on for over eighty-five years. A report compiled in 1982 by the New York group United Action for Animals found 1,425 papers on "classical conditioning experiments" on animals. Ironically, the futility of much of this research is grimly revealed by a paper published by a group of experimenters at the University of Wisconsin. Susan Mineka and her colleagues subjected 140 rats to shocks that could be escaped and also subjected them to shocks that could not be escaped in order to compare the levels of fear generated by such different kinds of shocks. Here is the stated rationale for their work:

> Over the past 15 years an enormous amount of research has been directed toward understanding the differential behavior and physiological effects that stem from exposure to controllable as opposed to uncontrollable aversive elements. The general conclusion has been that exposure to uncontrollable aversive events is considerably more stressful for the organism than is exposure to controllable aversive events.

After subjecting their rats to various intensities of electric shock, sometimes allowing them the possibility of escape and sometimes not, the experimenters were unable to determine what mechanisms could be considered correct in accounting for their results. Nonetheless, they said that they believed their results to be important because "they raise some question about the validity of the conclusions of the hundreds of experiments conducted over the past 15 years or so."

In other words, fifteen years of giving electric shocks to animals may not have produced valid results. But in the bizarre world of psychological animal experiments, this finding serves as justification for yet more experiments giving inescapable electric shock to yet more animals so that "valid" results can finally be produced—and remember, these "valid results" will still only apply to the behavior of trapped animals subjected to inescapable electric shock.

An equally sad tale of futility is that of experiments designed to produce what is known as "learned helplessness"—supposedly a model of depression in human beings. In 1953 R. Solomon, L. Kamin, and L. Wynne, experimenters at Harvard University, placed forty dogs in a device called a "shuttlebox," which consists of a box divided into two compartments, separated by a barrier. Initially the barrier was set at the height of the dog's back. Hundreds of intense electric shocks were delivered to the dogs' feet through a grid floor. At first the dogs could escape the shock if they learned to jump the barrier into the other compartment. In an attempt to "discourage" one dog from jumping, the experimenters forced the dog to jump one hundred times onto a grid floor in the other compartment that also delivered a shock to the dog's feet. They said that as the dog jumped he gave a "sharp anticipatory yip which turned into a yelp when he landed on the electrified grid." They then blocked the passage between the compartments with a piece of plate glass and tested the dog again. The dog "jumped forward and smashed his head against the glass." The dogs began by showing symptoms such as "defecation, urination, yelping and shrieking, trembling, attacking the apparatus, and so on; but after ten or twelve days of trials dogs who were prevented from escaping shock ceased to resist. The experimenters reported themselves "impressed" by this, and concluded that a combination of the plate glass barrier and foot shock was "very effective" in eliminating jumping by dogs.

This study showed that it was possible to induce a state of hopelessness and despair by repeated administration of severe inescapable shock. Such "learned helplessness" studies were further refined in the 1960s. One prominent experimenter was Martin Seligman of the University of Pennsylvania. He electrically shocked dogs through a steel grid floor with such intensity and persistence that the dogs stopped trying to escape and "learned" to be helpless. In one study, written with colleagues Steven Maier and James Geer, Seligman describes his work as follows:

> When a normal, naive dog receives escape/avoidance training in a shuttle-box, the following behavior typically occurs: at the onset of electric shock the dog runs frantically about, defecating, urinating, and howling until it scrambles over the barrier and so escapes from shock. On the next trial the dog, running and howling, crosses the barrier more quickly, and so on, until efficient avoidance emerges.

Seligman altered this pattern by strapping dogs in harnesses and giving them shocks from which they had no means of escape. When the dogs were then placed in the original shuttlebox situation from which escape was possible, he found that

> such a dog reacts initially to shock in the shuttlebox in the same manner as the naive dog. However in dramatic contrast to the naive dog it soon stops running and remains silent until shock terminates. The dog does not cross the barrier and escape from shock. Rather it seems to "give up" and passively "accept" the shock. On succeeding trials the dog continues to fail to make escape movements and thus takes 50 seconds of severe, pulsating shock on each trial. . . . A dog previously exposed to inescapable shock . . . may take unlimited shock without escaping or avoiding at all.

In the 1980s, psychologists have continued to carry out these "learned helplessness" experiments. At Temple University in Philadelphia, Philip Bersh and three other experimenters trained rats to recognize a warning light that alerted them to a shock that would be delivered within five seconds. Once they understood the warning, the rats could avoid the shock by moving into the safe compartment. After the rats had learned this avoidance behavior, the experimenters walled off the safe chamber and subjected them to prolonged periods of inescapable shock. Predictably, they found that even after escape was possible, the rats were unable to relearn the escape behavior quickly. . . .

⁕

How can these things happen? How can people who are not sadists spend their working days driving monkeys into lifelong depression, heating dogs to death, or turning cats into drug addicts? How can they then remove their white coats, wash their hands, and go home to dinner with their families? How can taxpayers allow their money to be used to support these experiments? How did students carry on protests against injustice, discrimination, and oppression of all kinds, no matter how far from home, while ignoring the cruelties that were—and still are—being carried out on their own campuses?

The answer to these questions lies in the unquestioned acceptance of speciesism. We tolerate cruelties inflicted on members of other species that would outrage us if performed on members of our own species. Speciesism allows researchers to regard the animals they experiment on as items of equipment, laboratory tools rather than living, suffering creatures. In fact, on grant applications to government funding agencies, animals are listed as "supplies" alongside test tubes and recording instruments.

In addition to the general attitude of speciesism that experimenters share with other citizens, some special factors also help to make possible the experiments I have described. Foremost among these is the immense respect that people still have for scientists. Although the advent of nuclear weapons and environmental pollution has made us realize that science and technology are not as beneficial as they might appear at first glance, most people still tend to be in awe of anyone who wears a white coat and has a Ph.D. In a well-known series of experiments Stanley Milgram, a Harvard psychologist, demonstrated that ordinary people will obey the directions of a white-coated researcher to administer what appears to be (but in fact is not) electric shock to a human subject as "punishment" for failing to answer questions correctly, and they will continue to do this even when the human subject cries out and pretends to be in great pain. If this can happen when the participants believe they are inflicting pain on a human being, how much easier is it for students to push aside their initial qualms when their professors instruct them to perform experiments on animals? What Alice Heim has rightly called the "indoctrination" of the student is a gradual process, beginning with the dissection of frogs in school biology classes. When the future medical students, psychology students, or veterinarians reach the university and find that to complete the course of studies on which they have set their hearts they must experiment on living animals, it is difficult for them to refuse to do so, especially since they know that what they are being asked to do is standard practice. Those students who have refused to engage in such studies have found themselves failing their courses and are often forced to leave their chosen field of study.

The pressure to conform does not let up when students receive their degrees. If they go on to graduate degrees in fields in which experiments on animals are usual, they will be encouraged to devise their own experiments and write them up for their Ph.D. dissertations. Naturally, if this is how students are educated they will tend to continue in the same manner when they become professors, and they will, in turn, train their own students in the same manner. . . .

When are experiments on animals justifiable? Upon learning of the nature of many of the experiments carried out, some people react by saying that all experiments on animals should be prohibited immediately. But if we make our demands as absolute as this, the experimenters have a ready reply: Would we be prepared to let thousands of humans die if they could be saved by a single experiment on a single animal?

This question is, of course, purely hypothetical. There has never been and never could be a single experiment that saved thousands of lives. The way to reply to this hypothetical question is to pose another: Would the experimenters be prepared to carry out their experiment on a human orphan under six months old if that were the only way to save thousands of lives?

If the experimenters would not be prepared to use a human infant then their readiness to use nonhuman animals reveals an unjustifiable form of discrimination on the basis of species, since adult apes, monkeys, dogs, cats, rats, and other animals are more aware of what is happening to them, more self-directing, and, so far as we can tell, at least as sensitive to pain as a human infant. (I have specified that the human infant be an orphan, to avoid the complications of the feelings of parents. Specifying the case in this way is, if anything, overgenerous to those defending the use of nonhuman animals in experiments, since mammals intended for experimental use are usually separated from their mothers at an early age, when the separation causes distress for both mother and young.)

So far as we know, human infants possess no morally relevant characteristic to a higher degree than adult nonhuman animals, unless we are to count the infants' potential as a characteristic that makes it wrong to experiment on them. Whether this characteristic should count is controversial—if we count it, we shall have to condemn abortion along with experiments on infants, since the potential of the infant and the fetus is the same. To avoid the complexities of this issue, however, we can alter our original question a little and assume that the infant is one with irreversible brain damage so severe as to rule out any mental development beyond the level of a six-month-old infant. There are, unfortunately, many such human beings, locked away in special wards throughout the country, some of them long since abandoned by their parents and other relatives, and, sadly, sometimes unloved by anyone else. Despite their mental deficiencies, the anatomy and physiology of these infants are in nearly all respects identical with those of normal humans. If, therefore, we were to force-feed them with large quantities of floor polish or drip concentrated solutions of cosmetics into their eyes, we would have a much more reliable indication of the safety of these products for humans than we now get by attempting to extrapolate the results of tests on a variety of other species. The LD50 tests, the Draize eye tests, the radiation experiments, the heatstroke experiments, and many others described [elsewhere] could have told us more about human reactions to the experimental situation if they had been carried out on severely brain-damaged humans instead of dogs or rabbits.

So whenever experimenters claim that their experiments are important enough to justify the use of animals, we should ask them whether they would be prepared to use a brain-damaged human being at a similar mental level to the animals they are planning to use. I cannot imagine that anyone would seriously propose carrying out the experiments described [here] on brain-damaged human beings. Occasionally it has become known that medical experiments have been performed on human beings without their consent; one case did concern institutionalized intellectually disabled children, who were given hepatitis. When such harmful experiments on human beings become known, they usually lead to an outcry against the experimenters, and rightly so. They are, very often, a further example of the arrogance of the research worker who justifies everything on the grounds of increasing knowledge. But if the experimenter claims that the experiment is important enough to justify inflicting suffering on animals, why is it not important enough to justify inflicting suffering on humans at the same mental level? What difference is there between the two? Only that one is a member of our species and the other is not? But to appeal to that difference is to reveal a bias no more defensible than racism or any other form of arbitrary discrimination. . . .

We have still not answered the question of when an experiment might be justifiable. It will not do to say "Never!" Putting morality in such black-and-white terms is appealing, because it eliminates the need to think about particular cases; but in extreme circumstances, such absolutist answers always break down. Torturing a human being is almost always wrong, but it is not absolutely wrong. If torture were the only way in which we could discover the location of a nuclear bomb hidden in a New York City basement and timed to go off within the hour, then torture would be justifiable. Similarly, if a single experiment could cure a disease like leukemia, that experiment would be justifiable. But in actual life the benefits are always more remote, and more often than not they are nonexistent. So how do we decide when an experiment is justifiable?

We have seen that experimenters reveal a bias in favor of their own species whenever they carry out experiments on nonhumans for purposes that they would not think justified them in using human beings, even brain-damaged ones. This principle gives us a guide toward an answer to our question. Since a speciesist bias, like a racist bias, is unjustifiable, an experiment cannot be justifiable unless the experiment is so important that the use of a brain-damaged human would also be justifiable.

This is not an absolutist principle. I do not believe that it could never be justifiable to experiment on a brain-damaged human. If it really were possible to save several lives by an experiment that would take just one life, and there were no other way those lives could be saved, it would be right to do the experiment. But this would be an extremely rare case. Certainly none of the experiments described in this [selection] could pass this test. Admittedly, as with any dividing line, there would be a gray area where it was difficult to decide if an experiment could be justified. But we need not get distracted by such considerations now. As this [selection] has shown, we are in the midst of an emergency in which appalling suffering is being inflicted on millions of animals for purposes that on any impartial view are obviously inadequate to justify the suffering. When we have ceased to carry out all those experiments, then there will be time enough to discuss what to do about the remaining ones which are claimed to be essential to save lives or prevent greater suffering.

In the United States, where the present lack of control over experimentation allows the kinds of experiments described in the preceding pages, a minimal first step would be a requirement that no experiment be conducted without prior approval from an ethics committee that includes animal welfare representatives and is authorized to refuse approval to experiments when it does not consider that the potential benefits outweigh the harm to the animals. . . . [S]ystems of this kind already exist in countries such as Australia and Sweden and are accepted as fair and reasonable by the scientific community there. [However], such a system falls far short of the ideal. The animal welfare representatives on such committees come from groups that hold a spectrum of views, but, for obvious reasons, those who receive and accept invitations to join animal experimentation ethics committees tend to come from the less radical groups within the movement. They may not themselves regard the interests of nonhuman animals as entitled to equal consideration with the interests of humans; or if they do hold such a position, they may find it impossible to put it into practice when judging applications to perform animal experiments, because they would be unable to persuade other members of the committee. Instead, they are likely to insist on proper consideration of alternatives, genuine efforts to minimize pain, and a clear demonstration of significant potential benefits, sufficiently important to outweigh any pain or suffering that cannot be eliminated from the experiment. An animal experimentation ethics committee operating today would almost inevitably apply these standards in a speciesist manner, weighing animal suffering more lightly than potential comparable human benefit; even so, an emphasis on such standards would eliminate many painful experiments now permitted and would reduce the suffering caused by others.

In a society that is fundamentally speciesist, there is no quick solution to such difficulties with ethics committees. For this reason some Animal Liberationists will have nothing to do with them. Instead they demand the total and immediate elimination of all animal experimentation. Such demands have been put forward many times during the last century and a half of antivivisection activity, but they have shown no sign of winning over the majority of voters in any country. Meanwhile the number of animals suffering in laboratories continued to grow, until . . . recent breakthroughs. . . . These breakthroughs resulted from the work of people who found a way around the "all or nothing" mentality that had effectively meant "nothing" as far as the animals were concerned.

R. G. Frey    **NO**

Justifying Animal Experimentation: The Starting Point

Introduction

If the use of animals in scientific and medical research is justified, it seems reasonably clear that it is justified by the benefits that this research confers upon humans. The benefits involved here are understood to include such things as advances in knowledge as well as things more commonly regarded as benefits, such as improvements in disease diagnosis and treatment. Even were we to concede in a particular case that we may be unclear whether something is a benefit or whether the extreme costs we propose to exact from some animal are worth an envisaged benefit, some version of this *argument from benefit* appears to underlie all attempts to justify animal experimentation in science and medicine. This is not to ignore the fact that many of our efforts in fact benefit animals themselves, but I take it that no one would dispute the claim that the vast bulk of research has human benefit, not animal benefit, as its goal. Moreover, we must not think only of the short term: much research does not lead to immediate benefit. Often, it is only later, when the results of the research are put together with the results of other pieces of research (usually done by other researchers), that their long-term import can be detected. More often than not, science and medicine work by accretion rather than by individual instances of dramatic breakthrough.

Benefit and Abolitionism

The argument from benefit is a consequentialist argument: it maintains that the consequences of engaging in animal research provide clear benefits to humans that offset the costs to animals involved in the research. This is an empirical argument and so could be refuted by showing that the benefits of research are not all that we take them to be. This is not the place to undertake an examination of the costs and benefits of the myriad uses that we make of animals in science and medicine, nor am I the person to undertake such an examination. Instead, I want to look at another aspect of the argument from benefit.

Therefore, I shall simply assume that, either in the short or long term (or both), the benefits of research are substantive, an assumption that is quite compatible with it also being true that some alleged benefits of research are spurious.

I myself accept some version of the argument from benefit, as do, I think, most people. Those who favor the abolition of animal experiments may dispute that the benefits of these experiments are all that substantial, but I often encounter in argument "abolitionists" who do not dispute this fact. They simply maintain that human gain can never be used to justify animal loss, while conceding that many human advances in medicine have come at the cost of animal suffering and loss of animal life.

There is another position, the *3R approach,* that shares some of the abolitionists' concerns about animal research, but still accepts the argument from benefit, at least at our current state of scientific knowledge. Those who favor the 3R approach to animal research usually support a pro-research position, suitably qualified. The 3R approach seeks (1) to *refine* experiments in order to diminish animal suffering and/or loss of life; (2) to *reduce* the number of animals used and the number of experiments performed to obtain or confirm a particular result; and, ultimately, (3) to *replace* animal subjects with nonanimal models or replace "higher" animals with "lower" ones. In fact, the 3R approach typically is thought today to help define a humane research position, even if and when adopting the approach might require that some piece of research be curtailed on the ground that it is incompatible with one strand or more of the 3R approach.

A humane research position is not an abolitionist position. While abolitionists may themselves be concerned with refinement, reduction, and replacement in animal experimentation, so long as present practices continue, abolitionists cannot be satisfied. They will still object that the 3R approach permits animal research to continue.

Moreover, an abolitionist will not be concerned with exactly how far along a piece of research is, or how likely we are to be able to come up with a nonanimal model for conducting this research in the immediate future. The thought that we may be able to replace animal models with nonanimal models for studying certain diseases is a pro-research thought, if it is also held that this replacement must await the development of nonanimal models for these diseases. Abolitionists reject this conditional approach because it would hold replacement hostage to scientific advances that may lie a considerable period into the future.

If an abolitionist had the opportunity to shut down all animal research now—whatever the potential for human benefit, however far along the research, and whatever the state of development of nonanimal models—I take it that the abolitionist would do so. Why a complete shutdown now? Why not a progressive shutdown over a much longer period, during which some experiments would be allowed to run their course, realize some benefit, or evolve into a nonanimal model? The abolitionist's reason is that a progressive shutdown of animal research would perpetuate animal suffering and/or loss of life. Therefore, a progressive shutdown, while it may appeal to those of a more practical disposition, is not typically proposed by abolitionists.

While it is obvious that abolitionists oppose the argument from benefit, it is not evident that many others do so. It is ironic, to say the least, that abolitionism has received so much attention in the media of late at the very time that scientific and medical research seems on the threshold of revolutionary discoveries that will greatly alleviate human suffering. Genetic research involving animals promises new treatments for diseases that previously were thought to be intractable defects in the human condition. AIDS research proceeds apace, with animal research playing a crucial role. One aspect of genetic engineering that is likely to have an impact in the near future involves transforming animals to become carriers of human organs for human transplants. Cross-species transplants—xenografts—that should result from these efforts will benefit the thousands of people who die each year while waiting on queues for human organs. Cloning of animals is another scientific breakthrough that holds out the prospect of genetic replacement as the solution to some presently incurable medical disorders. An enormous amount of genetic engineering in animals is presently underway with the goal of advancing human health care (quite apart from any genetic engineering in animals that has to do with food or meat-eating).

With the prospect of such remarkable discoveries on the horizon, I do not think it likely that very many people will embrace abolitionism. The benefits, real and potential, of animal research appear too considerable for us to turn away from them. Yet, lab break-ins, disturbances, and assaults upon scientists by abolitionist fringe groups are already of grave concern to researchers, and these incidents may increase. It is unlikely that such acts will win many converts to the abolitionist cause. In fact, it seems likely that acts of intimidation may well alienate moderates who strive for observance of the 3R approach, who otherwise might see themselves as allies of the abolitionists on some policy proposals. On the whole, then, I doubt that abolitionism is going to capture the day. The argument from benefit will continue to predominate.

Animals or Humans?

The argument from benefit requires closer philosophical scrutiny. For example, with many uses of the argument, the individual who bears the costs is also the individual who benefits; this is not true in the case of animal experimentation. Yet there are plenty of instances in which we impose costs on some to benefit others, as in the cases of conscription or the progressive income tax.

The feature of the argument from benefit that I want to discuss is this: Whatever benefits animal experimentation is thought to hold in store for us, those very same benefits could be obtained through experimenting upon humans instead of animals. Indeed, given that problems exist because scientists must extrapolate from animal models to humans, one might hold that there are good scientific reasons for preferring human subjects.

Accordingly, any reliance upon the argument from benefit, however hedged and qualified that reliance may be, has to be accompanied by a further argument establishing that while we may use animals as means to the ends of scientific and medical inquiry, we may not use humans to these ends. I do not mean that we may never use humans as research subjects; obviously, a good deal of research involves experiments on humans. I mean, rather, that we may not do to humans all the things that we presently do to animals. For example, we may not induce amyotrophic lateral sclerosis in a perfectly healthy human in order to study the pathology of the disease. Furthermore, we may not do this even if the human in question were to consent to be treated in this way.

The argument from benefit, then, needs to be supplemented by a further argument, one that strikes a deeper note than any obvious appeal to discernible benefit. This further argument must answer the question: what justifies using animals in science and medicine in ways that would be considered improper to use humans, even humans who consented to the treatment? This question can be asked regardless of whether the research is applied or pure (that is, whether or not the research has practical use), whether the techniques involved in it are invasive or noninvasive, or whether it involves pain or is entirely painless. In fact, what this question is asking of us is how we distinguish the human from the animal case. I have discussed this issue in a number of other places. In this essay, I want to distill from these other discussions how it is that this issue of separating humans from animals forms the starting point of any justification of animal experimentation.

The Appeal to Similarity

The appeal to similarity between ourselves and animals (or, in any event, the "higher" animals) has come to be thought of as one important barrier to animal experimentation. . . .

An Assumption About Humans

It is true, of course, that the appeal to similarity depends upon a crucial assumption, an assumption that those who make use of the appeal nevertheless seem justified in making. This is the assumption (which might be called the *characteristics claim*) that, for any characteristic around which one formulates the appeal, humans will be found who (1) lack the characteristic altogether, (2) lack it to a degree such that they are not protected from being used in scientific/medical experiments, or (3) lack it to a degree such that some animals have it to a greater degree. For example, it seems undeniably true that chimps give evidence of being more intelligent than many severely mentally subnormal humans, more sentient than anencephalic infants (infants born without a brain), and more able to direct their lives than humans in the final stages of Alzheimer's disease or senile dementia. Indeed, depending upon the characteristics selected and the humans under consideration, many animals, of many different species, will display levels of the characteristics higher than those found in some humans.

The only characteristic that seems unquestionably to favor humans, no matter what their condition or quality of life, is that of having had two human parents (in the near future, cloning may well call this characteristic into question). It is unclear, however, why this characteristic would be relevant. Having human parents could matter in one sense, at least if they objected to what was to be done to their offspring, but it is hard to see why having human parents matters in any deeper sense. The nature of one's parentage says nothing about one's present quality of life; one's intelligence; one's capacity for pain, distress, and suffering; one's ability to direct one's own life; etc. These characteristics seem more like the things that could serve to distinguish a human life as something that may not be treated in the way that we presently treat animal lives. This is because these characteristics say something not about what produced a life, but rather about the life being lived, about the nature and quality of that life. Thus, while it is true that anencephalic infants have human parents, the nature and quality of their lives nevertheless seem, by all reasonable standards, to be far worse than the lives of numerous ordinary animals. The same seems true of people in the final throes of AIDS, Alzheimer's disease, Lou Gehrig's disease, Huntington's disease, and so on.

In short, the appeal to similarity depends upon an assumption that, though it can be overturned, nevertheless appears to be very plausible. If we pick any characteristic around which to formulate the appeal, we seem inevitably doomed to come across some humans who lack that characteristic and some animals who, to a greater or lesser degree, have it. The result is a dilemma of a painful, unhappy kind: either we use humans as well as animals in order to obtain the benefits of research—since some humans fall outside the class of those having the relevant characteristic—or we use neither humans nor these animals that possess the characteristic and fall into the class of the protected. Given this dilemma, the case for opposing experimentation in science and medicine that uses the typical animal subjects is stronger than usually imagined, and it is salutary to be aware of this. However, if the benefits of scientific/medical research are everything we think them to be, then we can see how the first option, allowing the use of some humans as well as animals, is bound to seem the lesser of the two evils to some people. Those to whom this occurs are not Hitlers in the making; rather, they are simply those who employ the argument from benefit but are unable to separate human cases from animal cases in a morally significant way. . . .

Use and Quality of Life

I have argued elsewhere that . . . animals are indeed members of the moral community, they have moral standing in their own right, and their lives do indeed have significant value (though not the value of normal adult human life). If it is thought that the argument in favor of experimentation starts by denying animals moral standing or by denying that their lives have value, then I think that this strategy must be rejected. I see no way of denying either proposition. How, then, does the argument for experimentation get underway?

. . . [I]n our secular age, our problem is that we can find nothing that ensures that all human life (whatever its condition and quality), but no animal life (whatever its condition and quality), falls into the preferred class of nonuse. Secular attempts to replace God as the guarantor of the preferred status of humans have not proved successful. They inevitably involve us, yet again, in the search for some magical characteristic that can both separate humans from animals and be a plausible candidate upon which to hang a difference in treatment.

Suppose one can save either one's faithful dog, who has rendered long and valuable service, or some human whom one does not know. If one saves the dog, has one done something wrong? Is there a sense in which one *must* prefer human beings over animals, if one is to be moral? Suppose further that the human being suffers from a series of terrible maladies that give him a very low quality of life and a prognosis of a much-reduced life span: must one still prefer him to the dog? What if the human were an anencephalic infant? In these latter two cases, the questions seem to be asking us for the characteristic or set of characteristics upon which we can decide which life to save, whether human or animal, in circumstances in which it may be the dog, rather than the human, who best exemplifies that characteristic or set of characteristics.

Our central problem should now be obvious. Suppose someone were to claim that all human lives, whatever their condition or quality, possess equal worth. This comforting thought, which encapsulates the claim that two lives of massively different quality are nevertheless of the same worth, lies, I am sure, at the base of many attempts to provide a secular analog to the religious claim that all human lives are equal in the eyes of God. But if not in its condition or quality, in what does the worth of a life consist? How do we assess and recognize the worth of a life? What criteria do we use to determine such worth?

It is obvious that not all human lives are of the same quality: no one in the final stages of amyotrophic lateral sclerosis or pancreatic cancer would say otherwise. From the Judeo-Christian perspective, however, such lives are equal in worth to ordinary human lives because they are held to be equal in the eyes of God. If God is taken out of this picture, then what underpins the claim that all human lives are of equal worth? The notion of worth here does not pick out any actual features of the lives in question. Rather, what we are left with is simply the *quality* of the lives being lived, whether human or animal, and the implicit recognition that, in some cases, an animal will have a higher quality of life than a human. . . .

Experience and Quality of Life

As far as I can see, then, defending animal experimentation by means of the argument from benefit, which I think most people want to do, leaves us with a problem not about animals, but about humans. If there is nothing that shows that humans always, without exception, have a higher quality of life than any animal, then the cost of permitting experiments upon animals may have to be a preparedness to envisage similar uses of humans. For it seems inevitable, given that we know of nothing that always gives human life a higher quality, that on some occasions an animal will have a higher quality of life than a human to whom it is compared. To avoid the conclusion that humans may be used we might be forced to accept one of two claims: that we just do not know what an animal's quality of life is, or that animals have no quality of life whatsoever.

The claim of not knowing what an animal's quality of life is, while an important claim, does not seem to be a decisive refutation of the human-use conclusion. It might simply dictate that we should make greater efforts to learn about the quality of life of the animal. To say that we can never really know what it is like to be a rat is not to say that we can never know a good deal about what a better quality of life is like for a rat. Indeed, veterinary text-books are filled with discussions of subjects that directly refer to or imply something about the inner states of animals. Difficulty is not the same thing as impossibility, and in the case of the higher primates, I think that we have already begun to overcome the difficulties of assessing quality of life. More-over, to say that we do not know what an animal's quality of life is may well be taken as a reason for *not* using the animal, on the basis of some "play-safe" principle. The second claim then becomes crucial. But the claim that animals do not have a quality of life seems to me to be simply false.

Animals are *experiential subjects,* with an unfolding series of experiences that, depending upon their quality, can make an animal's life go well or badly. A creature of this sort has a welfare that can be enhanced or diminished by what we do to it; with this being the case, such a creature has a quality of life. To deny that rats, rodents, rabbits, and chimps are experiential subjects is to deny that they have subjective experiences at all. It is to deny that their lives are lived, just as ours are, in terms of unfolding sets of experiences, of a kind such that what we do to these animals can affect the quality of those experi-ences. Today, however, it is increasingly the case that scientific journals, peer review committees, Institutional Animal Care and Use Committees, and gov-ernment funding agencies demand that it be clearly stated what sorts of tech-niques will be used on research animals and what sorts of impacts these techniques are likely to have on them. The scientists involved do this regu-larly. It cannot be the case, therefore, that these groups and scientists think that they are dealing with nonexperiential creatures, creatures that do not reg-ister anything at all with respect to what is done to them. So I doubt very much whether any party to the experimentation debate will argue that ani-mals do not have a quality of life. . . .

Conclusion: Experimentation and the Argument From Benefit

How is my argument a pro-research position? I accept some version of the argument from benefit and hold that the benefits of scientific/medical research are sizable. I accept that animals may be used in such research. I believe that I have deployed arguments that show that normal adult human lives have a higher quality than animal lives. Animals, then, will remain the creatures of preferred use. However, I have not been able to find an argument that ensures always and inevitably that all human lives will exceed all animal lives in value; hence, I have not been able to come up with an argument that ensures that humans can never be used in experiments. When a human life is of lower quality than an animal life, it will not be right to use the animal rather than the human.

Mine is not a position that advocates the use of humans in experiments. Indeed, the adverse side effects of any such use, especially on those humans who are the weakest among us, are likely to be considerable, and my position would be strongly sensitive to these concerns. Yet however sensitive to these side effects we may be, the fact remains that the argument from benefit, if the benefits in question are all that science and medicine would have us believe and are as desired by the public as the media suggests, seems to demand that we proceed with experimentation and obtain the benefits. My doubt about the argument from benefit, then, is precisely this: I want to realize the benefits, just as other people do, but I can see no way of doing so without it coming into plain view that some humans will be put at risk as potential experimental subjects. In other words, I have found nothing to take the place that God played in the traditional argument: nothing to provide the comforting assurance that humans are the preferred creatures on Earth whose lives are the only ones that are morally considerable and valuable.

I am well aware, of course, that most people will find this starting point for the justification of animal experimentation to be very unpalatable. But I know of nothing that enables us to avoid it if we rely upon the argument from benefit. Failing to find some justification for why it is that the preferred class of nonuse includes any and all humans but no animals, my position is ineluctable, however unappealing it might be.

Finding my view extremely distasteful, many may respond by renewing the search for what makes us unique, for what confers on us the preferred status that we enjoyed under the traditional argument. But how, exactly, will they do this? As far as I can see, their only recourse is to generate yet more abstractions in the search for one that gives us the desired result. It remains to be seen whether or not the next generation of abstractions will be any more tenable than their predecessors.

Some will conclude that my position vis-à-vis impaired humans is so objectionable that my argument is tantamount to a rejection of animal experimentation. I don't see it that way. For me, the crucial question is: will we decide to forgo the benefits that scientific and medical research promise? It is hard to imagine that we will. Hence, we are faced with the problem over humans.

Notice another ploy that might be tried to evade my argument, and how it too goes astray. It might be argued that there are not enough anencephalic infants, or enough people in the final throes of devastating illnesses, to provide anything like the total number of research subjects that we can presently find in the animal kingdom. But the issue posed by my position is not about replacement of animals by humans; instead, it is about our need to come to terms with the issue of human use. It is a moral question, not a practical one. If we are going to use animals, the argument that I have raised in this essay seems to require that we at least be prepared to use certain humans as well, depending upon their respective qualities of life. Can we bring ourselves to do this?

One final ploy might be devised. It might be said that if a quality-of-life argument lands us at my unpalatable conclusion, then I have inadvertently discredited quality of life as the determiner of the value of a life. Yet every hospital in the land uses quality-of-life considerations in making all kinds of judgments, including life-or-death judgments. Hospitals use such considerations constantly in human health care, including situations in which they decide who will receive treatment and of what sort, who will be saved, and who left to nature's course. If quality-of-life is ubiquitous in making health care decisions for humans, how can it be sundered from medicine's bedrock—experimentation? Clearly, it cannot.

CHALLENGE QUESTIONS

Should Animal Research in Psychology Be Eliminated?

1. Read Singer's book and discuss why it has been so effective in galvanizing support for eliminating animal research.
2. Frey's article is part of an anthology of chapters that support the use of animals in scientific research. Read two other chapters from the book, and report what other arguments are used to justify animal experimentation.
3. Why might some people distinguish between medical and psychological research regarding the justification of animal research? Are there subject matter and philosophy of science differences between the two disciplines? Support your answer.
4. Do you agree with Frey's argument that animals cannot be distinguished from humans absolutely (i.e., without some exceptions)? Why, or why not?
5. Do you find Frey's emphasis on quality of life pertinent to the debate over animal research? What is this quality, and how might it be relevant to committees that approve the use of animals for experimentation?

ISSUE 3

Classic Dialogue:
Was Stanley Milgram's
Study of Obedience Unethical?

YES: Diana Baumrind, from "Some Thoughts on Ethics of Research: After Reading Milgram's 'Behavioral Study of Obedience,'" *American Psychologist* (vol. 19, 1964)

NO: Stanley Milgram, from "Issues in the Study of Obedience: A Reply to Baumrind," *American Psychologist* (vol. 19, 1964)

ISSUE SUMMARY

YES: Psychologist Diana Baumrind argues that Stanley Milgram's study of obedience did not meet ethical standards for research, because participants were subjected to a research design that caused undue psychological stress that was not resolved after the study.

NO: Social psychologist Stanley Milgram, in response to Baumrind's accusations, asserts that the study was well designed, the stress caused to participants could not have been anticipated, and the participants' anguish dissipated after a thorough debriefing.

$\mathbf{A}$re there psychological experiments that should not be conducted? Is the psychological distress that participants experience in some studies too extreme to justify the experimental outcomes and knowledge gained? Or is it sometimes necessary to allow participants to experience some anguish so that a researcher can better understand important psychological phenomena? These questions lie at the heart of ethical considerations in psychological research. They have traditionally been answered by the researcher, who attempts to weigh the costs and benefits of conducting a given study.

The problem is that a researcher's ability to accurately anticipate the costs and benefits of a study is severely limited. Researchers are likely to have an investment in their studies, which may lead them to overestimate the benefits and underestimate the costs. For these and other reasons, in 1974 the U.S. Department of Health, Education, and Welfare established regulations for the protection of human subjects. These regulations include the creation of institutional review boards, which are responsible for reviewing research proposals and ensuring that researchers adequately protect research participants.

The establishment of these regulations can be traced to past ethical controversies, such as the one raised in the following selection by Diana Baumrind regarding Stanley Milgram's famous 1963 study of obedience. Baumrind's primary concern is that the psychological welfare of the study's participants was compromised not only through the course of the study but also through the course of their lives. She contends that participants were prone to obey the experimenter because of the atmosphere of the study and the participants' trust in the experimenter. As a result, participants behaved in ways that disturbed them considerably. Baumrind maintains that these disturbances could not be resolved through an after-study debriefing but rather remained with the participants.

In response to these accusations, Milgram argues that the atmosphere of a laboratory generalizes to other contexts in which obedience is prevalent and is thus appropriate to a study of obedience. Furthermore, he and a number of other professionals never anticipated the results of the study; they were genuinely surprised by its outcome. Milgram also asserts that the psychological distress experienced by some participants was temporary, not dangerous, and that it dissipated after the true nature of the study was revealed.

POINT

- Milgram's indifference toward distressed participants reveals his lack of concern for their well-being.
- A study of obedience should not be conducted in the laboratory because subjects are particularly prone to behave obediently and to put trust in the researcher.
- The psychological distress experienced by participants exceeded appropriate limits.
- Participants experienced long-term, negative psychological consequences as a result of their participation in Milgram's experiment.
- In planning and designing the study, Milgram ignored issues regarding the extreme psychological distress that was experienced by some participants.

COUNTERPOINT

- Milgram made special efforts to assure participants that their behavior was normal.
- The laboratory setting is well suited to a study of obedience because it is similar to other contexts in which obedience is prevalent.
- The psychological distress was brief and not injurious.
- Participants spoke positively about the experiment, indicating that it was psychologically beneficial.
- The extreme psychological tension experienced by some participants was unanticipated by Milgram and many other professionals.

Diana Baumrind  **YES**

Some Thoughts on Ethics
of Research

Certain problems in psychological research require the experimenter to balance his career and scientific interests against the interests of his prospective subjects. When such occasions arise the experimenter's stated objective frequently is to do the best possible job with the least possible harm to his subjects. The experimenter seldom perceives in more positive terms an indebtedness to the subject for his services, perhaps because the detachment which his functions require prevents appreciation of the subject as an individual.

Yet a debt does exist, even when the subject's reason for volunteering includes course credit or monetary gain. Often a subject participates unwillingly in order to satisfy a course requirement. These requirements are of questionable merit ethically, and do not alter the experimenter's responsibility to the subject.

Most experimental conditions do not cause the subjects pain or indignity, and are sufficiently interesting or challenging to present no problem of an ethical nature to the experimenter. But where the experimental conditions expose the subject to loss of dignity, or offer him nothing of value, then the experimenter is obliged to consider the reasons why the subject volunteered and to reward him accordingly.

The subject's public motives for volunteering include having an enjoyable or stimulating experience, acquiring knowledge, doing the experimenter a favor which may some day be reciprocated, and making a contribution to science. These motives can be taken into account rather easily by the experimenter who is willing to spend a few minutes with the subject afterwards to thank him for his participation, answer his questions, reassure him that he did well, and chat with him a bit. Most volunteers also have less manifest, but equally legitimate, motives. A subject may be seeking an opportunity to have contact with, be noticed by, and perhaps confide in a person with psychological training. The dependent attitude of most subjects toward the experimenter is an artifact of the experimental situation as well as an expression of some subjects' personal need systems at the time they volunteer.

From Diana Baumrind, "Some Thoughts on Ethics of Research: After Reading Milgram's 'Behavioral Study of Obedience,'" *American Psychologist,* vol. 19 (1964). Copyright © 1964 by The American Psychological Association. Reprinted by permission.

The dependent, obedient attitude assumed by most subjects in the experimental setting is appropriate to that situation. The "game" is defined by the experimenter and he makes the rules. By volunteering, the subject agrees implicitly to assume a posture of trust and obedience. While the experimental conditions leave him exposed, the subject has the right to assume that his security and self-esteem will be protected.

There are other professional situations in which one member—the patient or client—expects help and protection from the other—the physician or psychologist. But the interpersonal relationship between experimenter and subject additionally has unique features which are likely to provoke initial anxiety in the subject. The laboratory is unfamiliar as a setting and the rules of behavior ambiguous compared to a clinician's office. Because of the anxiety and passivity generated by the setting, the subject is more prone to behave in an obedient, suggestible manner in the laboratory than elsewhere. Therefore, the laboratory is not the place to study degree of obedience or suggestibility, as a function of a particular experimental condition, since the base line for these phenomena as found in the laboratory is probably much higher than in most other settings. Thus experiments in which the relationship to the experimenter as an authority is used as an independent condition are imperfectly designed for the same reason that they are prone to injure the subjects involved. They disregard the special quality of trust and obedience with which the subject appropriately regards the experimenter.

Other phenomena which present ethical decisions, unlike those mentioned above, *can* be reproduced successfully in the laboratory. Failure experience, conformity to peer judgment, and isolation are among such phenomena. In these cases we can expect the experimenter to take whatever measures are necessary to prevent the subject from leaving the laboratory more humiliated, insecure, alienated, or hostile than when he arrived. To guarantee that an especially sensitive subject leaves a stressful experimental experience in the proper state sometimes requires special clinical training. But usually an attitude of compassion, respect, gratitude, and common sense will suffice, and no amount of clinical training will substitute. The subject has the right to expect that the psychologist with whom he is interacting has some concern for his welfare, and the personal attributes and professional skill to express his good will effectively.

Unfortunately, the subject is not always treated with the respect he deserves. It has become more commonplace in sociopsychological laboratory studies to manipulate, embarrass, and discomfort subjects. At times the insult to the subject's sensibilities extends to the journal reader when the results are reported. Milgram's (1963) study is a case in point. The following is Milgram's abstract of his experiment:

> This article describes a procedure for the study of destructive obedience in the laboratory. It consists of ordering a naive S to administer increasingly more severe punishment to a victim in the context of a learning experiment. Punishment is administered by means of a shock generator with 30 graded switches ranging from Slight Shock to Danger: Severe

Shock. The victim is a confederate of E. The primary dependent variable is the maximum shock the S is willing to administer before he refuses to continue further. 26 Ss obeyed the experimental commands fully, and administered the highest shock on the generator. 14 Ss broke off the experiment at some point after the victim protested and refused to provide further answers. The procedure created extreme levels of nervous tension in some Ss. Profuse sweating, trembling, and stuttering were typical expressions of this emotional disturbance. One unexpected sign of tension—yet to be explained—was the regular occurrence of nervous laughter, which in some Ss developed into uncontrollable seizures. The variety of interesting behavioral dynamics observed in the experiment, the reality of the situation for the S, and the possibility of parametric variation within the framework of the procedure, point to the fruitfulness of further study [p. 371].

The detached, objective manner in which Milgram reports the emotional disturbance suffered by his subject contrasts sharply with his graphic account of that disturbance. Following are two other quotes describing the effects on his subjects of the experimental conditions:

I observed a mature and initially poised businessman enter the laboratory smiling and confident. Within 20 minutes he was reduced to a twitching, stuttering wreck, who was rapidly approaching a point of nervous collapse. He constantly pulled on his earlobe, and twisted his hands. At one point he pushed his fist into his forehead and muttered: "Oh, God, let's stop it." And yet he continued to respond to every word of the experimenter, and obeyed to the end [p. 377].

In a large number of cases the degree of tension reached extremes that are rarely seen in sociopsychological laboratory studies. Subjects were observed to sweat, tremble, stutter, bite their lips, groan, and dig their fingernails into their flesh. These were characteristic rather than exceptional responses to the experiment.

One sign of tension was the regular occurrence of nervous laughing fits. Fourteen of the 40 subjects showed definite signs of nervous laughter and smiling. The laughter seemed entirely out of place, even bizarre. Full-blown, uncontrollable seizures were observed for 3 subjects. On one occasion we observed a seizure so violently convulsive that it was necessary to call a halt to the experiment . . . [p. 375].

Milgram does state that,

After the interview, procedures were undertaken to assure that the subject would leave the laboratory in a state of well being. A friendly reconciliation was arranged between the subject and the victim, and an effort was made to reduce any tensions that arose as a result of the experiment [p. 374].

It would be interesting to know what sort of procedures could dissipate the type of emotional disturbance just described. In view of the effects on subjects, traumatic to a degree which Milgram himself considers nearly unprecedented in sociopsychological experiments, his casual assurance that these tensions were dissipated before the subject left the laboratory is unconvincing.

What could be the rational basis for such a posture of indifference? Perhaps Milgram supplies the answer himself when he partially explains the subject's destructive obedience as follows, "Thus they assume that the discomfort caused the victim is momentary, while the scientific gains resulting from the experiment are enduring [p. 378]." Indeed such a rationale might suffice to justify the means used to achieve his end if that end were of inestimable value to humanity or were not itself transformed by the means by which it was attained.

The behavioral psychologist is not in as good a position to objectify his faith in the significance of his work as medical colleagues at points of breakthrough. His experimental situations are not sufficiently accurate models of real-life experience; his sampling techniques are seldom of a scope which would justify the meaning with which he would like to endow his results; and these results are hard to reproduce by colleagues with opposing theoretical views. . . . [T]he concrete benefit to humanity of his particular piece of work, no matter how competently handled, cannot justify the risk that real harm will be done to the subject. I am not speaking of physical discomfort, inconvenience, or experimental deception per se, but of permanent harm, however slight. I do regard the emotional disturbance described by Milgram as potentially harmful because it could easily effect an alteration in the subject's self-image or ability to trust adult authorities in the future. It is potentially harmful to a subject to commit, in the course of an experiment, acts which he himself considers unworthy, particularly when he has been entrapped into committing such acts by an individual he has reason to trust. The subject's personal responsibility for his actions is not erased because the experimenter reveals to him the means which he used to stimulate these actions. The subject realizes that he would have hurt the victim if the current were on. The realization that he also made a fool of himself by accepting the experimental set results in additional loss of self-esteem. Moreover, the subject finds it difficult to express his anger outwardly after the experimenter in a self-acceptant but friendly manner reveals the hoax.

A fairly intense corrective interpersonal experience is indicated wherein the subject admits and accepts his responsibility for his own actions, and at the same time gives vent to his hurt and anger at being fooled. Perhaps an experience as distressing as the one described by Milgram can be integrated by the subject, provided that careful thought is given to the matter. The propriety of such experimentation is still in question even if such a reparational experience were forthcoming. Without it I would expect a naive, sensitive subject to remain deeply hurt and anxious for some time, and a sophisticated, cynical subject to become even more alienated and distrustful.

In addition the experimental procedure used by Milgram does not appear suited to the objectives of the study because it does not take into account the special quality of the set which the subject has in the experimental situation. Milgram is concerned with a very important problem, namely, the social consequences of destructive obedience. He says,

> Gas chambers were built, death camps were guarded, daily quotas of corpses were produced with the same efficiency as a manufacture of appliances. These inhumane policies may have originated in the mind of a single person, but they could only be carried out on a massive scale if a very large number of persons obeyed orders [p. 371].

But the parallel between authority-subordinate relationships in Hitler's Germany and in Milgram's laboratory is unclear. In the former situation the SS man or member of the German Officer Corps, when obeying orders to slaughter, had no reason to think of his superior officer as benignly disposed towards himself or their victims. The victims were perceived as subhuman and not worthy of consideration. The subordinate officer was an agent in a great cause. He did not need to feel guilt or conflict because within his frame of reference he was acting rightly.

It is obvious from Milgram's own descriptions that most of his subjects were concerned about their victims and did trust the experimenter, and that their stressful conflict was generated in part by the consequences of these two disparate but appropriate attitudes. Their distress may have resulted from shock at what the experimenter was doing to them as well as from what they thought they were doing to their victims. In any case there is not a convincing parallel between the phenomena studied by Milgram and destructive obedience as that concept would apply to the subordinate-authority relationship demonstrated in Hitler Germany. If the experiments were conducted "outside of New Haven [Connecticut] and without any visible ties to [Yale University]," I would still question their validity on similar although not identical grounds. In addition, I would question the representativeness of a sample of subjects who would voluntarily participate within a noninstitutional setting.

In summary, the experimental objectives of the psychologist are seldom incompatible with the subject's ongoing state of well being, provided that the experimenter is willing to take the subject's motives and interests into consideration when planning his methods and correctives. Section 4b in *Ethical Standards of Psychologists* (APA, undated) reads in part:

> Only when a problem is significant and can be investigated in no other way, is the psychologist justified in exposing human subjects to emotional stress or other possible harm. In conducting such research, the psychologist must seriously consider the possibility of harmful aftereffects, and should be prepared to remove them as soon as permitted by the design of the experiment. Where the danger of serious aftereffects exists, research should be conducted only when the subjects or their responsible agents are fully informed of this possibility and volunteer nevertheless [p. 12].

From the subject's point of view procedures which involve loss of dignity, self-esteem, and trust in rational authority are probably most harmful in the long run and require the most thoughtfully planned reparations, if engaged in at all. The public image of psychology as a profession is highly related to our own actions, and some of these actions are changeworthy. It is important that as research psychologists we protect our ethical sensibilities rather than adapt our personal standards to include as appropriate the kind of indignities to which Milgram's subjects were exposed. I would not like to see experiments such as Milgram's proceed unless the subjects were fully informed of the dangers of serious aftereffects and his correctives were clearly shown to be effective in restoring their state of well being.

References

American Psychological Association. Ethical Standards of Psychologists: A summary of ethical principles. Washington, D.C.: APA, undated.

Milgram, S. Behavioral study of obedience. *J. Abnorm. Soc. Psychol.,* 1963, 67, 371–378.

Stanley Milgram

 **NO**

Issues in the Study of Obedience:
A Reply to Baumrind

Obedience serves numerous productive functions in society. It may be ennobling and educative and entail acts of charity and kindness. Yet the problem of destructive obedience, because it is the most disturbing expression of obedience in our time, and because it is the most perplexing, merits intensive study.

In its most general terms, the problem of destructive obedience may be defined thus: If X tells Y to hurt Z, under what conditions will Y carry out the command of X, and under what conditions will he refuse? In the concrete setting of a laboratory, the question may assume this form: If an experimenter tells a subject to act against another person, under what conditions will the subject go along with the instruction, and under what conditions will he refuse to obey?

A simple procedure was devised for studying obedience (Milgram, 1963). A person comes to the laboratory, and in the context of a learning experiment, he is told to give increasingly severe electric shocks to another person. (The other person is an actor, who does not really receive any shocks.) The experimenter tells the subject to continue stepping up the shock level, even to the point of reaching the level marked "Danger: Severe Shock." The purpose of the experiment is to see how far the naive subject will proceed before he refuses to comply with the experimenter's instructions. Behavior prior to this rupture is considered "obedience" in that the subject does what the experimenter tells him to do. The point of rupture is the act of disobedience. Once the basic procedure is established, it becomes possible to vary conditions of the experiment, to learn under what circumstances obedience to authority is most probable, and under what conditions defiance is brought to the fore (Milgram, in press).

The results of the experiment (Milgram, 1963) showed, first, that it is more difficult for many people to defy the experimenter's authority than was generally supposed. A substantial number of subjects go through to the end of the shock board. The second finding is that the situation often places a person in considerable conflict. In the course of the experiment, subjects fidget, sweat, and sometimes break out into nervous fits of laughter. On the one hand, subjects want to aid the experimenter; and on the other hand, they do not want to shock the learner. The conflict is expressed in nervous reactions.

In a recent issue of *American Psychologist,* Diana Baumrind (1964) raised a number of questions concerning the obedience report. Baumrind expressed concern for the welfare of subjects who served in the experiment, and wondered whether adequate measures were taken to protect the participants. She also questioned the adequacy of the experimental design.

Patently, "Behavioral Study of Obedience" did not contain all the information needed for an assessment of the experiment. But . . . this was only one of a series of reports on the experimental program, and Baumrind's article was deficient in information that could have been obtained easily. . . .

At the outset, Baumrind confuses the unanticipated outcome of an experiment with its basic procedure. She writes, for example, as if the production of stress in our subjects was an intended and deliberate effect of the experimental manipulation. There are many laboratory procedures specifically designed to create stress (Lazarus, 1964), but the obedience paradigm was not one of them. The extreme tension induced in some subjects was unexpected. Before conducting the experiment, the procedures were discussed with many colleagues, and none anticipated the reactions that subsequently took place. Foreknowledge of results can never be the invariable accompaniment of an experimental probe. Understanding grows because we examine situations in which the end is unknown. An investigator unwilling to accept this degree of risk must give up the idea of scientific inquiry.

Moreover, there was every reason to expect, prior to actual experimentation, that subjects would refuse to follow the experimenter's instructions beyond the point where the victim protested; many colleagues and psychiatrists were questioned on this point, and they virtually all felt this would be the case. Indeed, to initiate an experiment in which the critical measure hangs on disobedience, one must start with a belief in certain spontaneous resources in men that enable them to overcome pressure from authority.

It is true that after a reasonable number of subjects had been exposed to the procedures, it became evident that some would go to the end of the shock board, and some would experience stress. That point, it seems to me, is the first legitimate juncture at which one could even start to wonder whether or not to abandon the study. But momentary excitement is not the same as harm. As the experiment progressed there was no indication of injurious effects in the subjects; and as the subjects themselves strongly endorsed the experiment, the judgment I made was to continue the investigation.

Is not Baumrind's criticism based as much on the unanticipated findings as on the method? The findings were that some subjects performed in what appeared to be a shockingly immoral way. If, instead, every one of the subjects had broken off at "slight shock," or at the first sign of the learner's discomfort, the results would have been pleasant, and reassuring, and who would protest?

Procedures and Benefits

A most important aspect of the procedure occurred at the end of the experimental session. A careful post-experimental treatment was administered to all subjects. The exact content of the dehoax varied from condition to condition and with increasing experience on our part. At the very least all subjects were told that the victim had not received dangerous electric shocks. Each subject had a friendly reconciliation with the unharmed victim, and an extended discussion with the experimenter. The experiment was explained to the defiant subjects in a way that supported their decision to disobey the experimenter. Obedient subjects were assured of the fact that their behavior was entirely normal and that their feelings of conflict or tension were shared by other participants. Subjects were told that they would receive a comprehensive report at the conclusion of the experimental series. In some instances, additional detailed and lengthy discussions of the experiments were also carried out with individual subjects.

When the experimental series was complete, subjects received a written report which presented details of the experimental procedure and results. Again their own part in the experiments was treated in a dignified way and their behavior in the experiment respected. All subjects received a follow-up questionnaire regarding their participation in the research, which again allowed expression of thoughts and feelings about their behavior.

The replies to the questionnaire confirmed my impression that participants felt positively toward the experiment. In its quantitative aspect (see Table 1), 84% of the subjects stated they were glad to have been in the experiment; 15% indicated neutral feelings, and 1.3% indicated negative feelings. To be sure, such findings are to be interpreted cautiously, but they cannot be disregarded.

Further, four-fifths of the subjects felt that more experiments of this sort should be carried out, and 74% indicated that they had learned something of personal importance as a result of being in the study. . . .

The debriefing and assessment procedures were carried out as a matter of course, and were not stimulated by any observation of special risk in the experimental procedure. In my judgment, at no point were subjects exposed to danger and at no point did they run the risk of injurious effects resulting from participation. If it had been otherwise, the experiment would have been terminated at once.

Table 1

Excerpt From Questionnaire Used in a Follow-up Study of the Obedience Research

Now that I have read the report and all things considered . . .	Defiant	Obedient	All
1. I am very glad to have been in the experiment	40.0%	47.8%	43.5%
2. I am glad to have been in the experiment	43.8%	35.7%	40.2%
3. I am neither sorry nor glad to have been in the experiment	15.3%	14.8%	15.1%
4. I am sorry to have been in the experiment	0.8%	0.7%	0.8%
5. I am very sorry to have been in the experiment	0.0%	1.0%	0.5%

Note: Ninety-two percent of the subjects returned the questionnaire. The characteristics of the nonrespondents were checked against the respondents. They differed from the respondents only with regard to age; younger people were overrepresented in the nonresponding group.

Baumrind states that, after he has performed in the experiment, the subject cannot justify his behavior and must bear the full brunt of his actions. By and large it does not work this way. The same mechanisms that allow the subject to perform the act, to obey rather than to defy the experimenter, transcend the moment of performance and continue to justify his behavior for him. The same viewpoint the subject takes while performing the actions is the viewpoint from which he later sees his behavior, that is, the perspective of "carrying out the task assigned by the person in authority."

Because the idea of shocking the victim is repugnant, there is a tendency among those who hear of the design to say "people will not do it." When the results are made known, this attitude is expressed as "if they do it they will not be able to live with themselves afterward." These two forms of denying the experimental findings are equally inappropriate misreadings of the facts of human social behavior. Many subjects do, indeed, obey to the end, and there is no indication of injurious effects.

The absence of injury is a minimal condition of experimentation; there can be, however, an important positive side to participation. Baumrind suggests that subjects derived no benefit from being in the obedience study, but this is false. By their statements and actions, subjects indicated that they had learned a good deal, and many felt gratified to have taken part in scientific research they considered to be of significance. A year after his participation one subject wrote:

> This experiment has strengthened my belief that man should avoid harm to his fellow man even at the risk of violating authority.

Another stated:

> To me, the experiment pointed up . . . the extent to which each individual should have or discover firm ground on which to base his decisions, no matter how trivial they appear to be. I think people should think more deeply about themselves and their relation to their world and to other people. If this experiment serves to jar people out of complacency, it will have served its end.

These statements are illustrative of a broad array of appreciative and insightful comments by those who participated.

The 5-page report sent to each subject on the completion of the experimental series was specifically designed to enhance the value of his experience. It laid out the broad conception of the experimental program as well as the logic of its design. It described the results of a dozen of the experiments, discussed the causes of tension, and attempted to indicate the possible significance of the experiment. Subjects responded enthusiastically; many indicated a desire to be in further experimental research. This report was sent to all subjects several years ago. The care with which it was prepared does not support Baumrind's assertion that the experimenter was indifferent to the value subjects derived from their participation.

Baumrind's fear is that participants will be alienated from psychological experiments because of the intensity of experience associated with laboratory procedures. My own observation is that subjects more commonly respond with distaste to the "empty" laboratory hour, in which cardboard procedures are employed, and the only possible feeling upon emerging from the laboratory is that one has wasted time in a patently trivial and useless exercise.

The subjects in the obedience experiment, on the whole, felt quite differently about their participation. They viewed the experience as an opportunity to learn something of importance about themselves, and more generally, about the conditions of human action.

A year after the experimental program was completed, I initiated an additional follow-up study. In this connection an impartial medical examiner, experienced in outpatient treatment, interviewed 40 experimental subjects. The examining psychiatrist focused on those subjects he felt would be most likely to have suffered consequences from participation. His aim was to identify possible injurious effects resulting from the experiment. He concluded that, although extreme stress had been experienced by several subjects,

> none was found by this interviewer to show signs of having been harmed by his experience. . . . Each subject seemed to handle his task [in the experiment] in a manner consistent with well established patterns of behavior. No evidence was found of any traumatic reactions.

Such evidence ought to be weighed before judging the experiment.

Other Issues

Baumrind's discussion is not limited to the treatment of subjects, but diffuses to a generalized rejection of the work.

Baumrind feels that obedience cannot be meaningfully studied in a laboratory setting: The reason she offers is that "The dependent, obedient attitude assumed by most subjects in the experimental setting is appropriate to that situation [p. 421]." Here, Baumrind has cited the very best reason for examining obedience in this setting, namely that it possesses "ecological validity." Here is one social context in which compliance occurs regularly. Military and job situations are also particularly meaningful settings for the study of obedience precisely because obedience is natural and appropriate to these contexts. I reject Baumrind's argument that the observed obedience does not count because it occurred where it is appropriate. That is precisely why it *does* count. A soldier's obedience is no less meaningful because it occurs in a pertinent military context. A subject's obedience is no less problematical because it occurs within a social institution called the psychological experiment.

Baumrind writes: "The game is defined by the experimenter and he makes the rules [p. 421]." It is true that for disobedience to occur the framework of the experiment must be shattered. That, indeed, is the point of the design. That is why obedience and disobedience are genuine issues for the subject. *He must really assert himself as a person against a legitimate authority.*

Further, Baumrind wants us to believe that outside the laboratory we could not find a comparably high expression of obedience. Yet, the fact that ordinary citizens are recruited to military service and, on command, perform far harsher acts against people is beyond dispute. Few of them know or are concerned with the complex policy issues underlying martial action; fewer still become conscientious objectors. Good soldiers do as they are told, and on both sides of the battle line. However, a debate on whether a higher level of obedience is represented by *(a)* killing men in the service of one's country, or *(b)* merely shocking them in the service of Yale science, is largely unprofitable. The real question is: What are the forces underlying obedient action?

Another question raised by Baumrind concerns the degree of parallel between obedience in the laboratory and in Nazi Germany. Obviously, there are enormous differences: Consider the disparity in time scale. The laboratory experiment takes an hour; the Nazi calamity unfolded in the space of a decade. There is a great deal that needs to be said on this issue, and only a few points can be touched on here.

1. In arguing this matter, Baumrind mistakes the background metaphor for the precise subject matter of investigation. The German event was cited to point up a serious problem in the human situation: the potentially destructive effect of obedience. But the best way to tackle the problem of obedience, from a scientific standpoint, is in no way restricted by "what happened exactly" in Germany. What happened exactly can *never* be duplicated in the laboratory or anywhere else. The real task is to learn more about the general problem of destructive obedience using a workable approach. Hopefully, such inquiry will stimulate insights and yield general propositions that can be applied to a wide variety of situations.
2. One may ask in a general way: How does a man behave when he is told by a legitimate authority to act against a third individual? In trying to find an answer to this question, the laboratory situation is one useful starting point—and for the very reason stated by Baumrind— namely, the experimenter does constitute a genuine authority for the subject. The fact that trust and dependence on the experimenter are maintained, despite the extraordinary harshness he displays toward the victim, is itself a remarkable phenomenon.
3. In the laboratory, through a set of rather simple manipulations, ordinary persons no longer perceived themselves as a responsible part of the causal chain leading to action against a person. The means through which responsibility is cast off, and individuals become thoughtless agents of action, is of general import. Other processes were revealed that indicate that the experiments will help us to understand why men obey. That understanding will come, of course, by examining the full account of experimental work and not alone the brief report in which the procedure and demonstrational results were exposed.

At root, Baumrind senses that it is not proper to test obedience in this situation, because she construes it as one in which there is no reasonable alternative to obedience. In adopting this view, she has lost sight of this fact: A substantial proportion of subjects do disobey. By their example, disobedience is shown to be a genuine possibility, one that is in no sense ruled out by the general structure of the experimental situation.

Baumrind is uncomfortable with the high level of obedience obtained in the first experiment. In the condition she focused on, 65% of the subjects obeyed to the end. However, her sentiment does not take into account that within the general framework of the psychological experiment obedience varied enormously from one condition to the next. In some variations, 90% of the subjects *dis*obeyed. It seems to be *not* only the fact of an experiment, but the particular structure of elements within the experimental situation that accounts for rates of obedience and disobedience. And these elements were varied systematically in the program of research.

A concern with human dignity is based on a respect for a man's potential to act morally. Baumrind feels that the experimenter *made* the subject shock the victim. This conception is alien to my view. The experimenter tells the subject to do something. But between the command and the outcome there is a paramount force, the acting person who may obey or disobey. I started with the belief that every person who came to the laboratory was free to accept or to reject the dictates of authority. This view sustains a conception of human dignity insofar as it sees in each man a capacity for *choosing* his own behavior. And as it turned out, many subjects did, indeed, choose to reject the experimenter's commands, providing a powerful affirmation of human ideals.

Baumrind also criticizes the experiment on the grounds that "it could easily effect an alteration in the subject's . . . ability to trust adult authorities in the future [p. 422]." But I do not think she can have it both ways. On the one hand, she argues the experimental situation is so special that it has no generality; on the other hand, she states it has such generalizing potential that it will cause subjects to distrust all authority. But the experimenter is not just any authority: He is an authority who tells the subject to act harshly and inhumanely against another man. I would consider it of the highest value if participation in the experiment could, indeed, inculcate a skepticism of this kind of authority. Here, perhaps, a difference in philosophy emerges most clearly. Baumrind sees the subject as a passive creature, completely controlled by the experimenter. I started from a different viewpoint. A person who comes to the laboratory is an active, choosing adult, capable of accepting or rejecting the prescriptions for action addressed to him. Baumrind sees the effect of the experiment as undermining the subject's trust of authority. I see it as a potentially valuable experience insofar as it makes people aware of the problem of indiscriminate submission to authority.

Conclusion

My feeling is that viewed in the total context of values served by the experiment, approximately the right course was followed. In review, the facts are these: (*a*) At the outset, there was the problem of studying obedience by means of a simple experimental procedure. The results could not be foreseen before the experiment was carried out. (*b*) Although the experiment generated momentary stress in some subjects, this stress dissipated quickly and was not injurious. *(c)* Dehoax and follow-up procedures were carried out to insure the subjects' well-being. *(d)* These procedures were assessed through questionnaire and psychiatric studies and were found to be effective. *(e)* Additional steps were taken to enhance the value of the laboratory experience for participants, for example, submitting to each subject a careful report on the experimental program. *(f)* The subjects themselves strongly endorse the experiment, and indicate satisfaction at having participated.

If there is a moral to be learned from the obedience study, it is that every man must be responsible for his own actions. This author accepts full responsibility for the design and execution of the study. Some people may feel it should not have been done. I disagree and accept the burden of their judgment.

Baumrind's judgment, someone has said, not only represents a personal conviction, but also reflects a cleavage in American psychology between those whose primary concern is with *helping* people and those who are interested mainly in *learning* about people. I see little value in perpetuating divisive forces in psychology when there is so much to learn from every side. A schism may exist, but it does not correspond to the true ideals of the discipline. The psychologist intent on healing knows that his power to help rests on knowledge; he is aware that a scientific grasp of all aspects of life is essential for his work, and is in itself a worthy human aspiration. At the same time, the laboratory psychologist senses his work will lead to human betterment, not only because enlightenment is more dignified than ignorance, but because new knowledge is pregnant with humane consequences.

References

Baumrind, D. Some thoughts on ethics of research: After reading Milgram's "Behavioral study of obedience." *Amer. Psychologist,* 1964, **19**, 421–423.

Lazarus, R. A laboratory approach to the dynamics of psychological stress. *Amer. Psychologist,* 1964, **19**, 400–411.

Milgram, S. Behavioral study of obedience. *J. Abnorm. Soc. Psychol.,* 1963, **67**, 371–378.

Milgram, S. Some conditions of obedience and disobedience to authority. *Hum. Relat.,* in press.

CHALLENGE QUESTIONS

Classic Dialogue:
Was Stanley Milgram's
Study of Obedience Unethical?

1. Investigate the role that your college's institutional review board (see the introduction to this issue) plays in protecting subjects from undue harm.
2. Sometimes people make the wrong decisions and end up hurting other people. Apart from utilizing institutional review boards, what can researchers do to avoid making wrong decisions regarding potentially harmful studies?
3. Imagine that you have just participated in Milgram's study. How would you feel about the deception that occurred? Is it ever appropriate to deceive participants in research studies? If so, when? If not, why not?
4. Both Baumrind and Milgram might agree that there are cases in which some low-level tension for research participants is allowable. Under what conditions might it be acceptable to allow participants to experience some distress? Under what conditions is it inappropriate to subject participants to any distress?
5. Baumrind raises the issue of trust. Do you think the participants in the Milgram study lost trust in psychological researchers or authority figures in general? Why, or why not?
6. If you were on an ethics review board and the Milgram study was brought before you, would you allow Milgram to run the study? Support your answer.

On the Internet . . .

APA Online

Information on psychology may be obtained at this Web site through the site map or by using the search engine. You can access the American Psychological Association's newspaper, the *APA Monitor,* APA books on a wide range of topics; PsychINFO, an electronic database of abstracts on over 1,350 scholarly journals; and the Help Center for information on dealing with modern life problems.

http://www.apa.org/topics/homepage.html

Research Methods & Statistics Links

This site of the Social Psychology Network features links related to research methodology, human and animal research ethics, statistics, data analysis, and more.

http://www.socialpsychology.org/methods.htm

National Health and Medical Research Council: Animal Ethical Issues

This site discusses the role of the National Health and Medical Research Council's Animal Welfare Committee and offers several links to further information about animal ethical issues.

http://www.health.gov.au/nhmrc/
issues/animalethics.htm

PsychotherapistResources.com

PsychotherapistResources.com provides interviews with leading contemporary therapists, high-quality therapy videos, book reviews, humor, and other resources for therapists. It also offers a selection of articles from leading and obscure practitioners, within and on the fringes of traditional psychotherapy, as well as reviews of books with topics that are relevant to psychotherapy.

http://www.psychotherapistresources.com/
current/index.html

PART 2

Biological Issues

*N*o behavioral or mental activity can occur without one's body. Many psychologists view our bodies and our biological processes as fundamental to all human activities, including emotion, perception, attention, and mental health. However, does this fundamental role of the body mean that it is the sole cause of our behaviors and our minds? Does the development of our bodies through evolution influence our most important emotions and behaviors such as love, hate, and the committing of violence? Are differing biological processes responsible for the learning and behavior problems of many young children?

- Are Humans Naturally Violent?

- Are Genetic Explanations of ADHD Faulty?

ISSUE 4

Are Humans Naturally Violent?

YES: Michael L. Wilson and Richard W. Wrangham, from "Intergroup Relations in Chimpanzees," *Annual Review of Anthropology* (2003)

NO: Robert W. Sussman, from "Exploring Our Basic Human Nature," *Anthro Notes* (Fall 1997)

ISSUE SUMMARY

YES: Field researcher Michael L. Wilson and biological anthropologist Richard Wrangham argue that humans are innately violent because their closest nonhuman relatives—chimpanzees—are themselves naturally violent and aggressive.

NO: Biological anthropologist Robert W. Sussman asserts that neither humans nor chimpanzees are inherently violent. Instead, he contends, culture and upbringing are significantly involved in the violence evident in both species.

Is there any length of recorded human history in which violence does not play a substantial role? Even ancient texts and religious scriptures often describe heinous acts of violence. Where does such violence come from? How can it be so seemingly universal from era to era and culture to culture?

One answer is that this violence is natural—that it is in our very nature to be violent. Such an answer is appealing because it accounts for so much of what we seem to know about violence. First, it appears to account for our long history of violence. Second, it seems to explain the apparent universality of violence across varied time periods and varied people. Third, it appears to account for the continuing violence in today's presumably more civil times. Increasing levels of civilization and organization seem to matter little.

If it is true that civilization and culture matter little, then are we doomed to commit violence? Can our own will help us to prevent our own violence? Is there nothing we can do to stop senseless violence? Psychologists are especially interested in these questions because they are interested in interventions, both individual and societal, that might be effective in curbing violence. Psychologists know that if we can answer the question of the ultimate origin of human violence, we can help solve the many problems related to violence today. Why is there so much violence in our high schools? Why do spouses batter each other and abuse their own children? Does media violence cause actual violence? All these very modern and very psychological issues depend ultimately on the answer to the question, Are humans inherently or naturally violent?

Michael Wilson and Richard Wrangham, the authors of the first selection, clearly answer this question affirmatively. They argue that new descriptions of intergroup aggression among chimpanzees provide a stronger case for the theory that human violence is a result of our evolutionary past. The authors note the many parallels between humans and our nearest evolutionary relatives—chimpanzees. One such parallel is that chimpanzees and hunter gatherers share a tendency to respond aggressively in encounters with members of other social groups. Although there are many aspects of human intergroup aggression that differ from chimpanzees, Wilson and Wrangham assert that common principles of evolved psychological tendencies are suggested by their anthropological data.

In the second selection, Robert W. Sussman reviews many of these so-called universal principles of sociobiology and considers them to be weak. For example, most modern gatherer-hunters and apes are remarkably nonaggressive. Indeed, some were more often the hunted than the hunters. As another example, female pygmy chimpanzees typically choose peace, form alliances, and mate with less aggressive males. According to Sussman, a good look at the killing among chimpanzees shows how rarely this occurs, not how often. Sussman also points to the wide variations in the quantities and qualities of violence in different human cultures and individuals. He concludes that if we have the plasticity to change through learning and culture, then socialization practices and cultural histories must determine our violence, not our nature.

POINT

- Violence and war are defining marks of humanity.
- Chimpanzees generally form male-bonded communities and defend their territories with aggression and violence.
- Humans were considered the only violent species until chimpanzees were observed killing chimpanzees.
- A behavioral biological approach provides more focused predictions for when aggression is likely to occur and how aggression can be reduced.

COUNTERPOINT

- The evidence for this universal is weak.
- In the communities monitored by ethologist Jane Goodall, only 10 percent were classified as violent, and many attacks resulted in no discernible injury.
- Looking carefully at the data reveals that there are many explanations for these killings other than natural violence.
- If we have the capacity to change by learning from example, then our behavior is determined by socialization practices and not by our nature.

**Michael L. Wilson and
Richard W. Wrangham**

 **YES**

Intergroup Relations in Chimpanzees

Introduction

A widespread assumption in the 1960s and 1970s was that warfare resulted from features unique to the human lineage, such as weapons or the dense populations created by agriculture. The observation of lethal intergroup attacks in wild chimpanzees challenged this view. Numerous comparisons between chimpanzee aggression and human warfare followed these first observations. Shared traits, such as the cooperation of males to defend group resources and the occurrence of lethal intergroup attacks, suggested that key features of human warfare evolved either in the common ancestor of humans and chimpanzees or independently in the two lineages for similar reasons.

Until recently, however, these comparisons rested on a narrow foundation. Most of the detailed information on intergroup aggression came from two sites in Tanzania, Gombe and Mahale, raising the possibility that patterns of intergroup aggression observed there resulted from some unusual feature of those sites, such as artificial feeding by observers.

In recent years, however, a new generation of studies has advanced our understanding of intergroup relations. New descriptions of intergroup aggression are emerging from unprovisioned sites, including Taï National Park, Côte d'Ivoire, Kibale National Park, Uganda, and Budongo Forest Reserve, Uganda. New technologies and methods have enabled researchers to ask new questions and answer previously unanswerable old questions. Entry of data into increasingly powerful computer systems is enabling researchers to examine long-term ranging and grouping data in unprecedented detail. Genetic analysis has enabled researchers to test the proportion of infants born from intergroup mating. Field experiments have made possible controlled tests of hypotheses that are difficult to test using only observational data.

In this chapter we review the current information on chimpanzee intergroup relations and discuss how results from recent studies affect prior generalizations. First, we describe the emerging consensus regarding chimpanzee social structure, territory characteristics, and intergroup interactions. Then we examine how recent studies have clarified questions about the

From *Annual Review of Anthropology*, vol. 32, 2003, pp. 363–365, 382–387. Copyright © 2003 by Annual Reviews, Inc. Reprinted by permission. References omitted.

functional goals and proximate mechanisms underlying intergroup aggression. Finally, we discuss the relevance of these findings to intergroup aggression in humans.

The comparisons of chimpanzee and human intergroup aggression have attracted three main objections. First, critics claim that the data on intergroup aggression are too few to support claims that chimpanzees are inherently violent. Second, some argue that intergroup aggression results from human influence, especially provisioning chimpanzees with artificial food. Third, it has been suggested that chimpanzee violence is irrelevant to understanding human behavior. According to this view, we already know that humans can be violent and that humans can be peaceful as well; what matters for humans are environmental factors such as culture rather than biology.

As we discuss below, recent studies provide strong evidence against these criticisms. First, evidence from classic and more recent studies shows that intergroup aggression, including lethal attacks, is a pervasive feature of chimpanzee societies. Second, the occurrence of intergroup aggression at unprovisioned sites allows us to reject the hypothesis that intergroup aggression and other patterns of social behavior were the result of provisioning. Instead, chimpanzee intergroup aggression is best explained by principles of behavioral biology that apply to other species such as lions, wolves, and hyenas. Third, the argument that, because humans can be both warlike and peaceful, war is not the result of biology or instinct is aimed at an outdated view of biology. Animals, especially large-brained animals such as primates, are no longer viewed as response-stimulus robots but rather as strategic actors who make decisions based on assessments of costs and benefits. Recent studies have improved our understanding of the costs and benefits underlying intergroup aggression for chimpanzees. These studies illustrate the promise for obtaining a better understanding of human intergroup aggression using principles generated by behavioral biology. . . .

Relevance to Humans

The first four decades of research on wild chimpanzees have produced evidence of important similarities between aspects of chimpanzee and human intergroup aggression. Comparisons between the two species are made difficult, admittedly, by many factors. In chimpanzees, the description of intergroup aggression is still in an early phase. In humans, quantitative data from the most relevant groups (hunter gatherers) are so rare that different authors reach widely differing conclusions about the frequency of aggression.

Yet despite these problems, it is clear that intergroup aggression has occurred among many, possibly all, hunter-gatherer populations and follows a rather uniform pattern. From the most northern to the most southern latitudes, the most common pattern of intergroup aggression was for a party of men from one group to launch a surprise attack in circumstances in which the attackers were unlikely to be harmed. Attacks were sometimes unsuccessful but were, at other times, responsible for the deaths of one or many victims. Women and girls were sometimes captured.

One factor that complicates efforts to compare patterns of intergroup aggression in humans and chimpanzees is that in chimpanzees the only large social group is the community, whereas no precise equivalent of the chimpanzee community exists for humans. Instead, human group membership always exists on several levels: residential group, clan, tribe, nation, and so on. The existence of these multiple types of group complicates the comparison of aggressive patterns between chimpanzees and humans because it means that aggression between groups can occur at many more levels among humans than among chimpanzees. At one extreme, aggression can be found between residential groups that both belong to the same linguistic, cultural, and tribal unit, within which individuals can move and intermarry [internal warfare]. At the other extreme, it can occur between culturally distinct groups having different languages (or dialects) and little or no tendency for intermarriage or friendly contact (external warfare).

Despite this variation, a useful comparison can be made between chimpanzees and humans by identifying the level at which relations are essentially anarchic, i.e., characterized by the lack of any central or cultural authority. Human societies normally feature such a level. The Ache, for example, lived in bands of 10 to 70 individuals who, in turn, formed groups of up to 550. Within these regional groups, the only form of culturally sanctioned violence among men was the club fight. By contrast, "anyone not in the group, including other Ache, could be shot on sight."

Among foraging societies, such regional groups frequently included around 500 individuals. Both the size and internal structure of such groups varied extensively, however, in relation to ecological and cultural factors, as indicated by the wide variety of terms used to describe them (e.g., dialect group, maximum band, tribe).

Whatever the name used, this level of grouping suggests a similarity to the chimpanzee community because aggressive interactions at this level are not regulated by the predictable intervention of allies. This essential similarity suggests that shared principles may help explain the occasionally intense escalation of interactions between such groups. But of course the similarity gives way to major differences in scale and organization, given that humans can expand their regional groupings all the way to nation-states containing hundreds of millions of individuals living in complex networks.

Chimpanzees and hunter gatherers, we conclude, share a tendency to respond aggressively in encounters with members of other social groups; to avoid intensely aggressive confrontations in battle line (typically, by retreating); and to seek, or take advantage of, opportunities to use imbalances of power for males to kill members of neighboring groups.

These similarities have been explained in parallel ways in the two species, using concepts from evolutionary ecology. The essential notion is that natural selection has favored specific types of motivational systems. In particular, motivations have been favored that have tended, over evolutionary time, to give individuals access to the resources needed for reproduction.

The motivations that drive intergroup killing among chimpanzees and humans, by this logic, were selected in the context of territorial competition because reproduction is limited by resources, and resources are limited by territory size. Therefore, it pays for groups to achieve dominance over neighboring groups so that they can enlarge their territories. To achieve dominance, it is necessary to have greater fighting power than the neighbors. This means that whenever the costs are sufficiently low it pays to kill or damage individuals from neighboring groups. Thus, intergroup killing is viewed as derived from a tendency to strive for status. According to this view, these several aspects of human intergroup aggression do not appear exceptional compared to other animals.

Many other aspects of human intergroup aggression, however, differ extensively from chimpanzees, such as the ability of residential groups to form alliances, the possibilities for expressing formal peace relations, the capacity for symbolic domination [through cannibalism, for example, the ability to kill large numbers at a time, and the integration of intergroup relations with ideology. Such differences suggest to some critics that human warfare cannot usefully be compared to chimpanzee aggression. No ultimate explanation has yet been offered, however, as an alternative to the hypothesis that territorial competition for resources for reproduction favors a drive for intergroup dominance.

Finally, it is important not to confuse levels of explanation. The comparison of chimpanzees and humans is useful in suggesting common principles generating evolved psychological tendencies. But it is not useful in directly accounting for intraspecific variation, which is the central concern of the anthropology of war. As with chimpanzees and other species, however, models based on evolutionary principles (such as behavioral ecology) provide powerful tools for understanding intraspecific variation.

Lethal Raiding in *Pan* and *Homo:* Homology Or Homoplasy?

It is currently unclear whether the patterns of intergroup aggression seen in humans and chimpanzees result from homology (shared evolutionary history) or homoplasy (convergent evolution). Various lines of evidence suggest that our common ancestor with chimpanzees was very much like a chimpanzee. In the five to seven million years that followed the divergence of the lines leading to *Pan* and *Homo*, however, the human lineage developed into a bushy tree. A variety of woodland apes evolved, including *Ardipithecus, Australopithecus,* and *Paranthropus.* These creatures do not closely resemble any living species, and we can make only educated guesses about their feeding ecology and social structure. Considerable behavioral diversity exists among extant apes; woodland apes probably varied as well, with societies that evolved to meet different ecological challenges. We know that social behavior can change quickly over evolutionary time. The two extant species of *Pan,* chimpanzees and bonobos, differ considerably in their intergroup relations despite generally similar feeding ecology, morphology, and recent date of divergence. Fossils can provide only a limited amount of information about social behavior. For example, lions and tigers differ strikingly in their social behavior, despite being closely related enough to interbreed. If we had only fossils of lions and tigers, it is hard to imagine that we would be able to infer cooperative territory defense for the one and solitary seclusion for the other.

The relevance of chimpanzee violence to the evolution of human warfare does not depend on the possibility that both species inherited this trait from a common ancestor. Instead, chimpanzees provide a valuable referential model. Before observers reported accounts of chimpanzee intergroup aggression, anthropologists assumed that human warfare resulted from some factor unique to the human lineage, such as social stratification, horticulture, high population density, or the use of tools as weapons. The observation of warlike behavior in chimpanzees demonstrated that none of these factors was required. A similar lesson could be drawn from the warlike behavior of social carnivores, such as lions, wolves, and spotted hyenas. The relevance of carnivore behavior to human evolution might be discounted, however, given that carnivores possess many specialized traits; intergroup killing in carnivores could be a byproduct of morphological and behavioral evolution for cooperative hunting. The benefit of using chimpanzees as a referential model is that, as our evolutionary cousins, they give us a more realistic picture of traits our ancestors may have possessed.

The benefits and limitations of using chimpanzee data to understand the evolution of human warfare are similar to those presented by data on another trait shared by chimpanzees and humans: hunting. In both species, hunting is conducted mainly by males, who often hunt in groups. As Mitani & Watts point out, chimpanzee hunting differs in various ways from human hunting. For example, chimpanzees pursue prey through the trees and kill with their hands and teeth, whereas humans pursue prey on the ground and kill with weapons. Chimpanzees hunt opportunistically, and the degree of cooperation involved remains the subject of debate, whereas human hunting clearly involves planning and cooperation. We don't know if *"Pan prior"* hunted, and the extent to which the various early woodland apes hunted or scavenged continues to be debated. Nevertheless, much like the case with intergroup aggression, data from chimpanzees (and other primates, such as baboons) challenged previous views that humans were the only hunting primate, and ongoing studies continue to provide valuable insight for guiding our thinking about human evolution.

Conclusion

Recent studies have shown that the patterns of intergroup aggression reported from Gombe and Mahale in the 1970s are, in many ways, typical of chimpanzees. Chimpanzees at all long-term study sites defend group territories, and chimpanzees at four out of five sites have conducted lethal attacks on members of neighboring groups. Studies of unprovisioned communities demonstrate that these patterns of intergroup aggression are not the result of provisioning. Indeed, the Ngogo community, which Power considered a prime example of peaceful intergroup relations, turns out to have an exceptionally high rate of intergroup violence.

Instead of being a maladaptive aberration, chimpanzee intergroup aggression appears to be typical of aggression in other wild animals in that it tends to provide fitness benefits for the aggressors. Two sets of genetic paternity tests demonstrate that males successfully kept outside males from mating with females in their community, a result supported by consistent behavioral observations. Females reproduced more quickly when territories were larger, indicating that both females and males benefit from defense and acquisition of feeding territory.

The chimpanzee studies suggest that our understanding of human intergroup aggression, particularly small-scale non-state violence, would benefit from more extensive testing of hypotheses generated by behavioral biology. The few studies that have focused on testing evolutionary principles have provoked hostile critiques. The hostility apparent in such critiques reflects a widespread concern that "biological" is equivalent to "fixed" or "unchangeable." Contemporary behavioral biology, however, views primate aggression as a strategic response to appropriate environmental conditions. Rather than viewing human aggression as inevitable, an approach rooted in behavioral biology would provide more focused predictions for when aggression is likely to occur and how aggression can be reduced.

Even among chimpanzees, rates of intergroup aggression vary considerably among sites and over time within sites. Understanding the factors responsible for that variation constitutes the next frontier in studies of chimpanzee intergroup relations. The range of variation may well prove greater than so far observed. For example, under appropriate conditions, captive chimpanzees can be induced to accept new adult males into their group, something not yet observed in the wild. Newly introduced males are predictably aggressive to one another, but appropriated management can lead to eventual acceptance.

Such observations indicate both that biology provides chimpanzees with clear dispositions (e.g., hostility toward stranger males) but also that even chimpanzees, under the right conditions, can learn to overcome such hostility. A fully developed behavioral biology of human intergroup aggression offers similar hope for understanding—and addressing—the roots of violence in our own species.

Robert W. Sussman  **NO**

Exploring Our Basic Human Nature

Are human beings forever doomed to be violent? Is aggression fixed within our genetic code, an inborn action pattern that threatens to destroy us? Or, as asked by Richard Wrangham and Dale Peterson in their recent book, *Demonic Males: Apes and the Origins of Human Violence,* can we get beyond our genes, beyond our essential "human nature"?

Wrangham and Peterson's belief in the importance of violence in the evolution and nature of humans is based on new primate research that they assert demonstrates the continuity of aggression from our great ape ancestors. The authors argue that 20–25 years ago most scholars believed human aggression was unique. Research at that time had shown great apes to be basically nonaggressive gentle creatures. Furthermore, the separation of humans from our ape ancestors was thought to have occurred 15–20 million years ago (Mya). Although Raymond Dart, Sherwood Washburn, Robert Ardrey, E.O. Wilson and others had argued through much of the 20th century that hunting, killing, and extreme aggressive behaviors were biological traits inherited from our earliest hominid hunting ancestors, many anthropologists still believed that patterns of aggression were environmentally determined and culturally learned behaviors, not inherited characteristics.

Demonic Males discusses new evidence that killer instincts are not unique to humans, but rather shared with our nearest relative, the common chimpanzee. The authors argue that it is this inherited propensity for killing that allows hominids and chimps to be such good hunters.

According to Wrangham and Peterson, the split between humans and the common chimpanzee was only 6–8 Mya. Furthermore, humans may have split from the chimpanzee-bonobo line after gorillas, with bonobos *(pygmy chimps)* separating from chimps only 2.5 Mya. Because chimpanzees may be the modern ancestor of all these forms, and because the earliest australopithecines were quite chimpanzee-like, Wrangham speculates (in a separate article) that "chimpanzees are a conservative species and an amazingly good model for the ancestor of hominids" (1995, reprinted in Sussman 1997:106). If modern chimpanzees and modern humans share certain behavioral traits, these traits have "long evolutionary roots" and are likely to be fixed, biologically inherited parts of our basic human nature and not culturally determined.

From *Anthro Notes,* Fall 1997, pp. 1–6, 17–19. Copyright © 1997 by Anthro Notes, NMNH Bulletin for Teachers. Reprinted by permission.

Wrangham argues that chimpanzees are almost on the brink of humanness:

> Nut-smashing, root-eating, savannah-using chimpanzees, resembling our ancestors, and capable by the way of extensive bipedalism. Using ant-wands, and sandals, and bowls, meat-sharing, hunting cooperatively. Strange paradox . . . a species trembling on the verge of hominization, but so conservative that it has stayed on that edge. . . . (1997:107).

Wrangham and Peterson (1996:24) claim that only two animal species, chimpanzees and humans, live in patrilineal, male-bonded communities "with intense, male initiated territorial aggression, including lethal raiding into neighboring communities in search of vulnerable enemies to attack and kill." Wrangham asks:

> Does this mean chimpanzees are naturally violent? Ten years ago it wasn't clear. . . . In this cultural species, it may turn out that one of the least variable of all chimpanzee behaviors is the intense competition between males, the violent aggression they use against strangers, and their willingness to maim and kill those that frustrate their goals. . . . As the picture of chimpanzee society settles into focus, it now includes infanticide, rape and regular battering of females by males (1997:108).

Since humans and chimpanzees share these violent urges, the implication is that human violence has long evolutionary roots. "We are apes of nature, cursed over six million years or more with a rare inheritance, a Dostoyevskyan demon . . . The coincidence of demonic aggression in ourselves and our closest kin bespeaks its antiquity" (1997: 108–109).

Intellectual Antecedents

From the beginning of Western thought, the theme of human depravity runs deep, related to the idea of humankind's fall from grace and the emergence of original sin. This view continues to pervade modern "scientific" interpretations of the evolution of human behavior. Recognition of the close evolutionary relationship between humans and apes, from the time of Darwin's *Descent of Man* (1874) on, has encouraged theories that look to modern apes for evidence of parallel behaviors reflecting this relationship.

By the early 1950s, large numbers of australopithecine fossils and the discovery that the large-brained "fossil" ancestor from Piltdown, in England, was a fraud, led to the realization that our earliest ancestors were more like apes than like modern humans. Accordingly, our earliest ancestors must have behaved much like other non-human primates. This, in turn, led to a great interest in using primate behavior to understand human evolution and the evolutionary basis of human nature. The subdiscipline of primatology was born.

Raymond Dart, discoverer of the first australopithecine fossil some thirty years earlier, was also developing a different view of our earliest ancestors. At first Dart believed that australopithecines were scavengers barely eking out an existence in the harsh savanna environment. But from the fragmented and damaged bones found with the australopithecines, together with dents and holes in these early hominid skulls, Dart eventually concluded that this species had used bone, tooth and antler tools to kill, butcher and eat their prey, as well as to kill one another. This hunting hypothesis (Cartmill 1997:511) "was linked from the beginning with a bleak, pessimistic view of human beings and their ancestors as instinctively bloodthirsty and savage." To Dart, the australopithecines were:

> confirmed killers: carnivorous creatures that seized living quarries by violence, battered them to death, tore apart their broken bodies, dismembered them limb from limb, slaking their ravenous thirst with the hot blood of victims and greedily devouring livid writhing flesh (1953:209).

Cartmill, in a recent book (1993), shows that this interpretation of early human morality is reminiscent of earlier Greek and Christian views. Dart's (1953) own treatise begins with a 17th century quote from the Calvinist R. Baxter: "of all the beasts, the man-beast is the worst/ to others and himself the cruellest foe."

Between 1961–1976, Dart's view was picked up and extensively popularized by the playwright Robert Ardrey (*The Territorial Imperative, African Genesis*). Ardrey believed it was the human competitive and killer instinct, acted out in warfare, that made humans what they are today. "It is war and the instinct for territory that has led to the great accomplishments of Western Man. Dreams may have inspired our love of freedom, but only war and weapons have made it ours" (1961: 324).

Man the Hunter

In the 1968 volume *Man the Hunter,* Sherwood Washburn and Chet Lancaster presented a theory of "The evolution of hunting," emphasizing that it is this behavior that shaped human nature and separated early humans from their primate relatives.

> To assert the biological unity of mankind is to affirm the importance of the hunting way of life. . . . However much conditions and customs may have varied locally, the main selection pressures that forged the species were the same. The biology, psychology and customs that separate us from the apes . . . we owe to the hunters of time past . . . for those who would understand the origins and nature of human behavior there is no choice but to try to understand "Man the Hunter" (1968:303).

Rather than amassing evidence from modern hunters and gatherers to prove their theory, Washburn and Lancaster (1968:299) use the 19th-century concept of cultural "survivals": behaviors that persist as evidence of an earlier time but are no longer useful in society.

> Men enjoy hunting and killing, and these activities are continued in sports even when they are no longer economically necessary. If a behavior is important to the survival of a species . . . then it must be both easily learned and pleasurable (Washburn & Lancaster, p. 299).

Man the Dancer

Using a similar logic for the survival of ancient "learned and pleasurable" behaviors, perhaps it could easily have been our propensity for dancing rather than our desire to hunt that can explain much of human behavior. After all, men and women love to dance; it is a behavior found in all cultures but has even less obvious function today than hunting. Our love of movement and dance might explain, for example, our propensity for face-to-face sex, and even the evolution of bipedalism and the movement of humans out of trees and onto the ground.

Could the first tool have been a stick to beat a dance drum, and the ancient Laetoli footprints evidence of two individuals going out to dance the "Afarensis shuffle"? Although it takes only two to tango, a variety of social interactions and systems might have been encouraged by the complex social dances known in human societies around the globe.

Sociobiology and E.O. Wilson

In the mid-1970s, E.O. Wilson and others described a number of traits as genetically based and therefore human universals, including territoriality, male–female bonds, male dominance over females, and extended maternal care leading to matrilineality. Wilson argued that the genetic basis of these traits was indicated by their relative constancy among our primate relatives and by their persistence throughout human evolution and in human societies. Elsewhere, I have shown that these characteristics are neither general primate traits nor human universals (Sussman 1995). Wilson, however, argued that these were a product of our evolutionary hunting past.

For at least a million years—probably more—Man engaged in a hunting way of life, giving up the practice a mere 10,000 years ago. . . . Our innate social responses have been fashioned through this life style. With caution, we can compare the most widespread hunter-gatherer qualities with similar behavior displayed by some of the non-human primates that are closely related to Man. Where the same pattern of traits occurs in . . . most or all of those primates—we can conclude that it has been subject to little evolution. (Wilson 1976, in Sussman 1997: 65–66).

Wilson's theory of sociobiology, the evolution of social behavior, argued that:

1. the goal of living organisms is to pass on one's genes at the expense of all others;
2. an organism should only cooperate with others if:
   (a) they carry some of his/her own genes (kin selection) or
   (b) if at some later date the others might aid you (reciprocal altruism).

To sociobiologists, evolutionary morality is based on an unconscious need to multiply our own genes, to build group cohesion in order to win wars. We

should not look down on our warlike, cruel nature but rather understand its success when coupled with "making nice" with *some* other individuals or groups.
The genetically driven "making nice" is the basis of human ethics and morality.

> Throughout recorded history the conduct of war has been common . . .
> some of the noblest traits of mankind, including team play, altruism, patri-
> otism, bravery . . . and so forth are the genetic product of warfare (Wilson
> 1975:572–3).

The evidence for any of these universals or for the tenets of sociobiology
is as weak as was the evidence for Dart's, Ardrey's and Washburn and Lancaster's theories of innate aggression. Not only are modern gatherer-hunters
and most apes remarkably non-aggressive, but in the 1970s and 1980s studies
of fossil bones and artifacts have shown that early humans were not hunters,
and that weapons were a later addition to the human repertoire. In fact, C.K.
Brain (1981) showed that the holes and dents in Dart's australopithecine
skulls matched perfectly with fangs of leopards or with impressions of rocks
pressing against the buried fossils. Australopithecines apparently were the
hunted, not the hunters (Cartmill, 1993, 1997).

Beyond Our Genes

Wrangham and Peterson's book goes beyond the assertion of human inborn
aggression and propensity towards violence. The authors ask the critical question: Are we doomed to be violent forever because this pattern is fixed within
our genetic code or can we go beyond our past?—get out of our genes, so to
speak.

The authors believe that we can look to the bonobo or pygmy chimpanzee as one potential savior, metaphorically speaking.

Bonobos, although even more closely related to the common chimpanzee
than humans, have become a peace-loving, love-making alternative to chim-
panzee-human violence. How did this happen? In chimpanzees and humans,
females of the species select partners that are violent . . . "while men have
evolved to be demonic males, it seems likely that women have evolved to prefer
demonic males . . . as long as demonic males are the most successful reproducers, any female who mates with them is provided with sons who themselves
will likely be good reproducers" (Wrangham and Peterson 1996:239). However,
among pygmy chimpanzees females form alliances and have chosen to mate
with less aggressive males. So, after all, it is not violent males that have caused
humans and chimpanzees to be their inborn, immoral, dehumanized selves, it
is rather, poor choices by human and chimpanzee females.

Like Dart, Washburn, and Wilson before them, Wrangham and Peterson
believe that killing and violence is inherited from our ancient relatives of the
past. However, unlike these earlier theorists, Wrangham and Peterson argue
this is not a trait unique to hominids, nor is it a by-product of hunting. In fact,
it is just this violent nature and a natural "blood lust" that makes both
humans and chimpanzees such good hunters. It is the bonobos that help the

authors come to this conclusion. Because bonobos have lost the desire to kill, they also have lost the desire to hunt.

> . . . do bonobos tell us that the suppression of personal violence carried with it the suppression of predatory aggression? The strongest hypothesis at the moment is that bonobos came from a chimpanzee-like ancestor that hunted monkeys and hunted one another. As they evolved into bonobos, males lost their demonism, becoming less aggressive to each other. In so doing they lost their lust for hunting monkeys, too . . . Murder and hunting may be more closely tied together than we are used to thinking (Wrangham and Peterson 1996:219).

The Selfish Gene Theory

Like Ardrey, Wrangham and Peterson believe that blood lust ties killing and hunting tightly together but it is the killing that drives hunting in the latter's argument. This lust to kill is based upon the sociobiological tenet of the selfish gene. "The general principle that behavior evolves to serve selfish ends has been widely accepted; and the idea that humans might have been favored by natural selection to hate and to kill their enemies has become entirely, if tragically, reasonable" (Wrangham and Peterson 1996:23).

As with many of the new sociobiological or evolutionary anthropology theories, I find problems with both the theory itself and with the evidence used to support it. Two arguments that humans and chimpanzees share biologically fixed behaviors are: (1) they are more closely related to each other than chimpanzees are to gorillas; (2) chimpanzees are a good model for our earliest ancestor and retain conservative traits that should be shared by both.

The first of these statements is still hotly debated and, using various genetic evidence, the chimp-gorilla-human triage is so close that it is difficult to tell exact divergence time or pattern among the three. The second statement is just not true. Chimpanzees have been evolving for as long as humans and gorillas, and there is no reason to believe ancestral chimps were similar to present-day chimps. The fossil evidence for the last 5–8 million years is extremely sparse, and it is likely that many forms of apes have become extinct just as have many hominids.

Furthermore, even if the chimpanzee were a good model for the ancestral hominid, and was a conservative representative of this phylogenetic group, this would not mean that humans would necessarily share specific behavioral traits. As even Wrangham and Peterson emphasize, chimps, gorillas, and bonobos all behave very differently from one another in their social behavior and in their willingness to kill conspecifics.

Evidence Against "Demonic Males"

The proof of the "Demonic Male" theory does not rest on any theoretical grounds but must rest solely on the evidence that violence and killing in chimpanzees and in humans are behaviors that are similar in pattern; have ancient, shared evolutionary roots; and are inherited. Besides killing of conspecifics, Wrangham "includes infanticide, rape, and regular battering of females by males" as a part of this inherited legacy of violent behaviors shared by humans and chimpanzees (1997:108).

Wrangham and Peterson state: "That chimpanzees and humans kill members of neighboring groups of their own species is . . . a startling exception to the normal rule for animals" (1996:63). "Fighting adults of almost all species normally stop at winning: They don't go on to kill" (1996:155). However, as Wrangham points out there are exceptions, such as lions, wolves, spotted hyenas, and I would add a number of other predators. In fact, most species do not have the weapons to kill one another as adults.

Just how common is conspecific killing in chimpanzees? This is where the real controversy may lie. Jane Goodall described the chimpanzee as a peaceful, non-aggressive species during the first 24 years of study at Gombe (1950–1974). During one year of concentrated study, Goodall observed 284 agonistic encounters: of these 66% were due to competition for introduced bananas, and only 34% "could be regarded as attacks occurring in 'normal' aggressive contexts" (1968:278). Only 10 percent of the 284 attacks were classified as 'violent', and "even attacks that appeared punishing to me often resulted in no discernable injury. . . . Other attacks consisted merely of brief pounding, hitting or rolling of the individual, after which the aggressor often touched or embraced the other immediately (1968:277).

Chimpanzee aggression before 1974 was considered no different from patterns of aggression seen in many other primate species. In fact, Goodall explains in her 1986 monograph, *The Chimpanzees of Gombe,* that she uses data mainly from after 1975 because the earlier years present a "very different picture of the Gombe chimpanzees" as being "far more peaceable than humans" (1986:3). Other early naturalists' descriptions of chimpanzee behavior were consistent with those of Goodall and confirmed her observations. Even different communities were observed to come together with peaceful, ritualized displays of greeting (Reynolds and Reynolds 1965; Suguyama 1972; Goodall 1968).

Then, between 1974 and 1977, five adult males from one subgroup were attacked and disappeared from the area, presumably dead. Why after 24 years did the patterns of aggression change? Was it because the stronger group saw the weakness of the other and decided to improve their genetic fitness? But surely there were stronger and weaker animals and subgroups before this time. Perhaps we can look to Goodall's own perturbations for an answer. In 1965, Goodall began to provide "restrictive human-controlled feeding." A few years later she realized that

> the constant feeding was having a marked effect on the behavior of the chimps. They were beginning to move about in large groups more often than they had ever done in the old days. Worst of all, the adult males were becoming increasingly aggressive. When we first offered the chimps bananas the males seldom fought over their food; . . . now . . . there was a great deal more fighting than ever before. . . . (Goodall 1971:143).

The possibility that human interference was a main cause of the unusual behavior of the Gombe chimps was the subject of an excellent, but generally ignored book by Margaret Power (1991). Wrangham and Peterson (1996:19) footnote this book, but as with many other controversies, they essentially ignore its findings, stating that yes, chimpanzee violence might have been unnatural behavior if it weren't for the evidence of similar behavior occurring since 1977 and "elsewhere in Africa" (1996:19).

Further Evidence

What is this evidence from elsewhere in Africa? Wrangham and Peterson provide only four brief examples, none of which is very convincing:

1. Between 1979–1982, the Gombe group extended its range to the south and conflict with a southern group, Kalande, was suspected. In 1982, a "raiding" party of males reached Goodall's camp. The authors state: "Some of these raids may have been lethal" (1996:19). However, Goodall describes this "raid" as follows: One female "was chased by a Kalande male and mildly attacked. . . . Her four-year-old son . . . encountered a second male—but was only sniffed" (1986:516). Although Wrangham and Peterson imply that these encounters were similar to those between 1974–77, no violence was actually witnessed. The authors also refer to the discovery of the dead body of Humphrey; what they do not mention is Humphrey's age of 35 and that wild chimps rarely live past 33 years!
2. From 1970 to 1982, six adult males from one community in the Japanese study site of Mahale disappeared, one by one over this 12 year period. None of the animals were observed being attacked or killed, and one was sighted later roaming as a solitary male (Nishida et al., 1985:287–289).
3. In another site in West Africa, Wrangham and Peterson report that Boesch and Boesch believe "that violent aggression among the chimpanzees is as important as it is in Gombe" (1986:20). However, in the paper referred to, the Boesches simply state that encounters by neighboring chimpanzee communities are more common in their site than in Gombe (one per month vs. 1 every 4 months). There is no mention of violence during these encounters.
4. At a site that Wrangham began studying in 1984, an adult male was found dead in 1991. Wrangham states: "In the second week of August, Ruizoni was killed. No human saw the big fight" (Wrangham & Peterson 1996:20). Wrangham gives us no indication of what has occurred at this site over the last 6 years.

In fact, this is the total amount of evidence of warfare and male-male killing among chimpanzees after 37 years of research!! The data for infanticide and rape among chimpanzees is even less impressive. In fact, data are so sparse for these behaviors among chimps that Wrangham and Peterson are forced to use examples from the other great apes, gorillas and orangutans. However, just as for killing among chimpanzees, both the evidence and the interpretations are suspect and controversial.

Can We Escape Our Genes?

What if Wrangham and Peterson are correct and we and our chimp cousins are inherently sinners? Are we doomed to be violent forever because this pattern is fixed within our genetic code?

After 5 million years of human evolution and 120,000 or so years of *Homo sapiens* existence, is there a way to rid ourselves of our inborn evils?

> What does it do for us, then, to know the behavior of our closest relatives? Chimpanzees and bonobos are an extraordinary pair. One, I suggest shows us some of the worst aspects of our past and our present; the other shows an escape from it. . . . Denial of our demons won't make them go away. But even if we're driven to accepting the evidence of a grisly past, we're not forced into thinking it condemns us to an unchanged future (Wrangham 1997:110).

In other words, we can learn how to behave by watching bonobos. But, if we can change our inherited behavior so simply, why haven't we been able to do this before *Demonic Males* enlightened us? Surely, there are variations in the amounts of violence in different human cultures and individuals. If we have the capacity and plasticity to change by learning from example, then our behavior is determined by socialization practices and by our cultural histories and not by our nature! This is true whether the examples come from benevolent bonobos or conscientious objectors.

Conclusion

The theory presented by Wrangham and Peterson, although it also includes chimpanzees as our murdering cousins, is very similar to "man the hunter" theories proposed in the past. It also does not differ greatly from early European and Christian beliefs about human ethics and morality. We are forced to ask:

Are these theories generated by good scientific fact, or are they just "good to think" because they reflect, reinforce, and reiterate our traditional cultural beliefs, our morality and our ethics? Is the theory generated by the data, or are the data manipulated to fit preconceived notions of human morality and ethics?

Since the data in support of these theories have been weak, and yet the stories created have been extremely similar, I am forced to believe that "Man the Hunter" is a myth, that humans are not necessarily prone to violence and aggression, but that this belief will continue to reappear in future writings on human nature. Meanwhile, primatologists must continue their field research, marshaling the actual evidence needed to answer many of the questions raised in Wrangham and Peterson's volume.

References

Ardrey, Robert. 1961. *African Genesis: A Personal Investigation into Animal Origins and Nature of Man.* Atheneum.
———. *The Territorial Imperative.* Atheneum, 1966.

Brain, C.K. 1981. *The Hunted or the Hunter? An Introduction to African Cave Taphonomy.* Univ. of Chicago.

Dart, Raymond. 1953. "The Predatory Transition from Ape to Man." *International Anthropological and Linguistic Review* 1:201–217.

Darwin, Charles. 1874. *The Descent of Man and Selection in Relation to Sex.* 2nd ed. The Henneberry Co.

Cartmill, Matt 1997. "Hunting Hypothesis of Human Origins." In *History of Physical Anthropology: An Encyclopedia,* ed. F. Spencer, pp. 508–512. Garland.

——. 1993. *A View to a Death in the Morning: Hunting and Nature Through History.* Harvard Univ.

Goodall, Jane. 1986. *The Chimpanzees of Gombe: Patterns of Behavior.* Belknap.

——. 1971. *In the Shadow of Man.* Houghton Mifflin.

Goodall, Jane. 1968. "The Behavior of Free-Living Chimpanzees in the Gombe Stream Reserve." *Animal Behavior Monographs* 1:165–311.

Nishida, T., Hiraiwa-Hasegawa, M., and Takahtat, Y. "Group Extinction and Female Transfer in Wild Chimpanzees in the Mahali Nation Park, Tanzania." *Zeitschrift für Tierpsychologie* 67:281–301.

Power, Margaret. 1991. *The Egalitarian Human and Chimpanzee: An Anthropological View of Social Organization.* Cambridge University.

Reynolds, V. and Reynolds, F. 1965. "Chimpanzees of Budongo Forest." In *Primate Behavior: Field Studies of Monkeys and Apes,* ed. I. DeVore, pp. 368–424. Holt, Rinehart, and Winston.

Suguyama, Y. 1972. "Social Characteristics and Socialization of Wild Chimpanzees." In *Primate Socialization,* ed. F.E. Poirier, pp. 145–163. Random House.

Sussman, R.W., ed. 1997. *The Biological Basis of Human Behavior.* Simon and Schuster.

Sussman, R.W. 1995. "The Nature of Human Universals." *Reviews in Anthropology* 24:1–11.

Washburn, S.L. and Lancaster, C. K. 1968. "The Evolution of Hunting." In *Man the Hunter,* eds. R. B. Lee and I. DeVore, pp. 293–303. Aldine.

Wilson, E. O. 1997. "Sociobiology: A New Approach to Understanding the Basis of Human Nature." *New Scientist* 70(1976):342–345. (Reprinted in R.W. Sussman, 1997.)

——. 1975. Sociobiology: *The New Synthesis.* Cambridge: Harvard University.

Wrangham, R.W. 1995. "Ape, Culture, and Missing Links." *Symbols* (Spring):2–9, 20. (Reprinted in R. W. Sussman, 1997.)

Wrangham, Richard and Peterson, Dale. 1996. *Demonic Males: Apes and the Origins of Human Violence.* Houghton Mifflin.

CHALLENGE QUESTIONS

Are Humans Naturally Violent?

1. What might Wilson and Wrangham's position about our violent nature mean for psychology, especially clinical psychology's therapy and social psychology's helping behaviors?
2. Sussman attributes the popularity of Wilson and Wrangham's position to our Western cultural tradition, not to scientifically demonstrate fact. Describe how you think this is possible with scientists. (Hint: Consider the work of the philosopher of science Thomas Kuhn.)
3. Why is the selfish-gene theory so important to the arguments of each of these authors? How does it help the arguments of Wilson and Wrangham and hurt the arguments of Sussman?
4. One what issues to these authors agree?
5. There are important disagreements between these authors on the interpretations of the same sets of data. Find the original publication of one such set and provide your own informed opinion about whose interpretation is the more correct, and discuss why you think so.

ISSUE 5

Are Genetic Explanations of Attention Deficit Hyperactivity Disorder Faulty?

YES: Jay Joseph, from "Not in Their Genes: A Critical View of the Genetics of Attention-Deficit Hyperactivity Disorder," *Developmental Review* (December 2000)

NO: Stephen V. Faraone and Joseph Biederman, from "Nature, Nurture, and Attention Deficit Hyperactivity Disorder," *Developmental Review* (December 2000)

ISSUE SUMMARY

YES: After reviewing the literature on the genetic causes of attention deficit hyperactivity disorder (ADHD), clinical psychologist Jay Joseph concludes that such claims are unsupported and that psychosocial causes need further exploration.

NO: Clinical psychologists Stephen V. Faraone and Joseph Biederman reject Joseph's conclusions on the grounds that he makes errors in scientific logic and ignores much of the relevant research.

For many years, children who were hyper and who experienced learning problems were viewed as needing special education. According to this perspective, if they could just be educated differently, these children would probably be all right. Today, however, many psychologists are considering the possibility that these children—now called ADHD (for attention deficit hyperactivity disorder) children—have biological, or, more specifically, neurochemical, problems; that is, problems of "nature" rather than just problems of "nurture."

Many psychologists today believe not only that the mind and body are intricately connected but also that the body causes the problems of the mind. If medical illnesses such as Down's syndrome and cancer are biological in nature, then why not mental illness? If genes that cause cancer and other illnesses can be found, then why not try to find the genes that cause mental illness? If one's heart and other organs can become diseased and ill, perhaps mental illness is a sickness of the brain.

As plausible as this biological explanation of psychology might sound, a causal connection between the mind and the body has not been discovered. Indeed, some critics suggest that there is such a desire for this connection that its existence is assumed without any proof or taken on faith. Consequently, many of these critics contend that psychologists should avoid pie-in-the-sky mind/body connections and search instead for nonbiological causes for mental illness, such as poverty, neglect, abuse, and socioeconomic injustice.

It is in this spirit that Jay Joseph, in the first of the following selections, examines the evidence supporting a genetic link between the mind and body for ADHD. Specifically, he examines the three main buttresses that supposedly support a genetic cause of ADHD: family studies, twin studies, and adoption studies. Joseph argues against these three kinds of studies and offers a twofold conclusion: that there is no substantive research to support a genetic cause for ADHD and that psychosocial causes need to be explored further.

Replying to Joseph in the second selection are Stephen V. Faraone and Joseph Biederman. They reject Joseph's conclusions on the grounds that he makes serious errors of scientific logic and ignores much of the relevant research. They admit that the environment plays a major role in ADHD. However, they argue that ADHD is ultimately caused by a complex interaction between genes and environment—both of which are equally important.

POINT

- Family studies cannot distinguish between genetic and environmental components.
- The assumption in twin studies that both identical and fraternal twins share equal environments is false.

- Adoption studies have major flaws and are inconclusive.

- The role of genetic factors in ADHD is not supported, and future research should focus on psychosocial causes.

COUNTERPOINT

- Family studies show that ADHD runs in families.

- Unequal environments does not mean that identical twins are exposed to more "trait-relevant" environmental factors than fraternal twins are.

- Minor methodological flaws only limit the strength with which conclusions can be drawn.
- Genetic theories are the most parsimonious explanations for ADHD.

YES

Jay Joseph

Not in Their Genes: A Critical View of the Genetics of Attention-Deficit Hyperactivity Disorder

This article examines evidence cited in favor of the operation of genetic factors in attention-deficit hyperactivity disorder (ADHD). Like other psychiatric conditions, a belief in the genetic basis of ADHD is derived from the results of family, twin, and adoption studies. Because family studies are widely believed to be confounded by environmental factors, primary emphasis is placed on twin and adoption studies. ADHD twin studies depend on the validity of the equal environment assumption (EEA), which holds that the environments of identical (MZ) and fraternal (DZ) twins are the same. Here it is argued that however the EEA is defined, it cannot be accepted. Therefore, the greater similarity or concordance of MZ twins when compared to DZ twins is plausibly explained by environmental factors. Adoption studies constitute a third method of investigating the role of genetic factors in ADHD. It is argued that these studies are greatly flawed by factors including non blinded diagnoses and the failure to study the biological relatives of adoptees. After an examination of the total weight of evidence in favor of a genetic basis or predisposition for ADHD, it is concluded that a role for genetic factors is not supported and that future research should be directed toward psychosocial causes

The current period is marked by the widespread acceptance of an important genetic influence on most psychological traits. This view is based on three pillars of support: (1) family studies, (2) twin studies, and (3) adoption studies. In psychiatry, schizophrenia has served as the model for the use of these methods. For the most part, the authors of over 2 dozen schizophrenia family studies, 14 schizophrenia twin studies, and 6 schizophrenia adoption studies concluded that their findings supported the existence of a genetic predisposition for the condition.

Here, we are interested in assessing the evidence in support of a genetic component for "attention-deficit hyperactivity disorder" (ADHD) which, like schizophrenia, is a psychiatric diagnosis made on the basis of a person's behavior and whose supposed genetic component is based on the evidence from family, twin, and adoption studies. For reasons of consistency, the term

From Jay Joseph, "Not in Their Genes: A Critical View of the Genetics of Attention-Deficit Hyperactivity Disorder," *Developmental Review,* vol. 20, no. 4 (December 2000). Copyright © 2000 by Academic Press. Reprinted by permission of Elsevier and the author.

"ADHD" is used throughout this article in place of diagnoses which include "hyperactive child syndrome," "minimal brain dysfunction," "hyperactivity," "attention deficit disorder," and so on. As is shown, the way the condition has been defined is of secondary importance to an examination of the methods used to determine its possible genetic component.

According to Russell Barkley (1998a), ADHD is a "developmental failure in the brain circuitry that underlies inhibition and self-control" (p. 67). Barkley cites studies whose authors claimed to have found that a portion of ADHD children's brains are smaller than in normal children, which he links to genetic factors. Tannock (1998) also concluded that ADHD is caused by a brain dysfunction of probable genetic origin. Some have taken a more interactionist approach (e.g., Diller, 1998), while others have stressed environmental factors and have questioned the validity of the ADHD concept (e.g., Breggin, 1998; DeGrandpre, 1999). What follows is a review of the ADHD genetic study literature. In the concluding section, I will discuss possible future directions for research into the causes of the condition.

ADHD Family Studies

Background

The family (or consanguinity) method of study constitutes the first systematic attempt to determine whether a condition clusters in families, thereby laying the basis for the possibility of finding a genetic component. Family studies locate persons affected with a particular trait or condition and attempt to determine whether their biological relatives are similarly affected more often than members of the general population or a control group. If a condition is found to cluster or "run" in families, it is said to be familial. Note that "familial" is not the same as "genetic." Unfortunately, many people view these terms as being synonymous, when in fact they are not. As most genetic researchers now acknowledge, the aggregation of a particular condition in families is consistent with a genetic or an environmental etiology. Psychiatric geneticists Faraone and Tsuang (1995), for example, noted that a family study can provide "the initial hint that a disorder might have a genetic component," while cautioning that "Disorders can 'run in families' for nongenetic reasons such as shared environmental adversity, viral transmission, and social learning. . . . Although family studies are indispensable for establishing the familiality of disorders, they cannot, by themselves, establish what type of transmission" (pp. 88–89). However, this has not always been the prevailing view.

The first schizophrenia family study (Rüdin, 1916) was published over 80 years ago, and the most influential study of this type was performed by Kallmann (1938). Most of the early family studies were authored by strong proponents of the genetic position, and most did not perform blind diagnoses. Kallmann believed that the familiality of schizophrenia *proved* that the condition was genetic in origin: "The principal aim of our investigations was to offer *conclusive proof* [italics added] of the inheritance of schizophrenia and to help, in this way, to establish a dependable basis for the clinical and eugenic activities of psychiatry" (Kallmann, 1938, p. xiv). Pam (1995) noted Kallmann's faulty logic and commented further on the family study method:

> The most serious breach in inductive logic committed by Kallmann was his use of kinship concordance rates to determine genetic transmission of psychopathology. We have already noted that no family inheritance study can control for environment in human research; such data, therefore, are nowhere near "suggestive"—they are at best inconclusive and at worst mis-leading. . . . This inferential limitation holds with respect to any consan-guinity finding, even if the design and technique employed in the investigation were scientifically impeccable. (p. 19)

Today, most behavior genetic and psychiatric genetic researchers (e.g., Faraone & Tsuang, 1995; Gottesman, 1991; Plomin, DeFries, & McClearn, 1990; Rosenthal, 1970; Wender, 1995) acknowledge that family studies by themselves cannot establish the existence of genetic factors and have cited twin and adoption studies as the primary evidence in favor of the genetic basis of schizophrenia and other conditions.

The authors of the ADHD family studies (Biederman et al., 1986, 1995; Biederman, Faraone, Keenan, Knee, & Tsuang, 1990; Cantwell, 1972; Faraone, Biederman, Keenan, & Tsuang, 1991a; Morrison & Stewart, 1971; Nichols & Chen, 1981; Welner, Welner, Stewart, Palkes, & Wish, 1977) have found con-sistent evidence for the familiality of the condition. Although several of these studies suffer from serious methodological problems (such as nonblind diag-noses), partisans of the genetic *or environmental* positions would be surprised if they *did not* find a familial clustering of ADHD.

In spite of the formal pronouncement that family studies by themselves cannot be used as evidence of genetic transmission, several important ADHD researchers have written that the evidence from these studies suggests a genetic basis for the condition. For example, in Barkley's authoritative hand-book for the diagnosis and treatment of ADHD, the author writes, "Family aggregation studies find that ADHD clusters among biological relatives of chil-dren or adults with the disorder, strongly implying a hereditary basis to this condition" (Barkley, 1998b, p. 36). While Faraone and Tsuang (1995) viewed the results from family studies as providing only the "initial hint" of genetic factors, Barkley believes that these findings "strongly imply" such an etiology.

Several ADHD family researchers have implied that their results support the genetic position. For example, Nichols and Chen (1981) concluded that the "greater risks to relatives of the severely affected children and to relatives of girls, the less frequently affected sex, provided some evidence that the familial association was determined partly by polygenic inheritance" (p. 276), and Biederman et al. (1995) have written, "Additional lines of evidence from second-degree relative, twin . . . adoption, and segregation analysis studies suggest that the familial aggregation of ADHD has a substantial genetic com-ponent" (p. 432). However, a method which by itself cannot be regarded as evidence in favor of the genetic hypothesis does not become evidence when combined with the supposed findings of another type of study. As noted by Diller, Tanner, and Weil (1995), "Familial clustering, as noted in the [Biederman et al. 1995 family study] article, cannot distinguish between potential genetic and environmental etiologies. While the authors are careful to describe the new data as familial, they nevertheless discuss them only in the context of a genetic etiology" (p. 451).

There is little reason to engage in a detailed discussion of the ADHD family studies, since their results are in accordance with the expectations of environmentalists and hereditarians alike. Therefore, this article focuses on the two methods most often cited in support of the genetic basis of ADHD: twin and adoption studies.

ADHD Twin Studies

Overview

As we have seen, the finding that a trait or condition runs in families is consistent with both genetic and environmental etiologies. For this reason, the results from twin studies have been promoted as evidence in favor of the genetic position. According to Barkley (1998a), twin studies have provided "the most conclusive evidence that genetics can contribute to ADHD" (p. 68). Several ADHD twin studies have been published since 1965 (Eaves et al., 1993; Edelbrock, Rende, Plomin, & Thompson, 1995; Gilger, Pennington, & DeFries, 1992; Gillis, Gilger, Pennington, & DeFries, 1992; Gjone, Stevenson, & Sundet, 1996; Goodman & Stevenson, 1989a, 1989b; Levy, Hay, McStephen, Wood, & Waldman, 1997; Lopez, 1965; Nadder, Silberg, Eaves, Maes, & Meyer, 1998; Sherman, Iacono, & McGue, 1997; Silberg et al., 1996; Steffensson et al., 1999; Stevenson, 1992; Thapar, Hervas, & McGuffin, 1995; van den Oord, Verhulst, & Boomsma, 1996; Willerman, 1973). All of these studies utilized the so-called "classical twin method" (also known as the "twin method"), which compares the concordance rates or correlations of reared-together identical twins (also known as monozygotic or MZ) to the same measures of reared-together fraternal twins (also known as dizygotic or DZ). A significantly greater similarity or concordance of MZ twins when compared with DZs is usually cited as evidence in favor of the genetic basis for the trait or condition under study. All ADHD twin studies have investigated pairs who were reared *together;* there have been no studies of reared-apart pairs. Separated twin studies typically look at similarities in personality and cognitive ability, but have been plagued by methodological problems and questionable theoretical assumptions (see Farber, 1981; Joseph, in press-d; Kamin, 1974; Taylor, 1980).

The authors of ADHD twin studies have found consistently that identical twins are more concordant for ADHD or correlate higher for ADHD-related behaviors than fraternals, and there is little doubt that in spite of these studies' methodological problems, MZ twins are significantly more similar than DZ twins. The question which concerns us here is whether the greater phenotypic similarity of MZ twins is caused by their greater genetic similarity, as the proponents of the twin method maintain. In order to answer this question, it is necessary to examine the theoretical underpinnings of the twin method itself.

So before returning to the ADHD twin studies, we must assess the validity of the most important assumption of the twin method.

The "Equal Environment Assumption" in Twin Studies

Because MZs rate more similarly on ADHD-related measures than DZs, twin studies would be considered solid evidence in favor of a genetic predisposition for ADHD were it not for one important detail: Since its inception in the mid-1920s, the twin method has been based on the theoretical assumption that identical and fraternal twins share equal environments. The equal environment assumption (EEA) must be valid in order to claim that the MZ/DZ concordance rate difference, found in most types of human behavior, can be attributed to genetic factors. According to Kendler, the most prominent contemporary defender of the equal environment assumption, "The EEA is crucial because, if the EEA is incorrect, excess resemblance of MZ twins compared with DZ twins ascribed to genetic factors could be partly or entirely due to environmental effects" (1993, p. 906). Kendler is quite right: If the EEA is false, the twin method could be measuring nothing else than the more similar environment and greater emotional bond experienced by MZ twins.

Although the validity of the EEA is crucial to the viability of the twin method, it is not often discussed in detail by its defenders. The EEA has been the subject of at least two critical reviews (Joseph, 1998b; Pam, Kemker, Ross, & Golden, 1996), whose authors concluded that the assumption is untenable.

Until the late 1950s, the assumption of equal environments between MZ and DZ pairs was taken for granted by most twin researchers, although little theoretical or empirical justification for this clearly counterintuitive assumption was offered. In 1960, Don Jackson published a critique of the five schizophrenia twin studies which had been published up to that time. Jackson pointed out that female twins were consistently more concordant than male twins, that same-sex DZs were more concordant than opposite-sex DZs, and that fraternal twins were more concordant than ordinary siblings, though they each share the same genetic relationship to each other. Jackson noted that common environment, "ego fusion," and association could explain these differences, and he implied that the MZ/DZ concordance rate difference could also be explained on this basis. As a "plausible hypothesis," Jackson (1960, p. 67) predicted that "according to the degree of likeness in siblings, we will find an increased concordance for schizophrenia, without concern for genetic similarity." (Slightly modifying Jackson's position, we might say that according to the degree of *environmental similarity* among siblings, we would expect greater behavioral similarity, without concern for genetic relationship.) The reaction of the schizophrenia twin studying world followed, for the most part, two different paths. The first was an attempt to discredit Jackson's theory by claiming that its validity rested on Jackson's hypothesis that the identical twinship itself might create conditions more conducive to schizophrenia and that we would therefore expect to find a higher rate of schizophrenia among individual MZ twins than among the single-born population. Although Rosenthal (1960)

and others claimed to have provided evidence that twins are no more susceptible than nontwins, the evidence is in fact equivocal (Joseph, 1998a; Kläning,
Mortensen, & Kyvik, 1996). More importantly, Jackson's "theory of identity
confusion" does not require twins to be more susceptible than singletons for
the trait in question. The thrust of Jackson's theory dealt with the reasons
why the *second* member of a twin pair fell to schizophrenia, not the first
(Joseph, in press-c).

The second way that the proponents of the twin method responded to
Jackson's ideas was to concede some of his most important points while continuing to uphold the twin method as a valid instrument for the detection of
genetic influences. As demonstrated elsewhere (Joseph, 1998b), the most
important twin researchers of the 1960s and 1970s were in agreement that
environmental similarity and association were *partly* responsible for the MZ/
DZ concordance rate difference. But I ask the reader: How did they know that
environmental influences were not *entirely* responsible for the difference? In
fact, they didn't know—they only *hoped* that their studies had measured
genetic influences. In one of the early collaborations of Gottesman and
Shields (1966), we find that the authors were willing to acknowledge that the
greater psychological identification of MZ twins could affect concordance
rates "provided that the same proportion of potential schizophrenics are held
back from overt illness by identifying with a normal twin as those who
become ill by identifying with an abnormal one" (p. 55). Gottesman and
Shields provided no evidence in support of their attempt to balance the led-
gers of the twin method. On what grounds, one might ask, did Gottesman
and Shields insist on a one-to-one correspondence between those twins who
became concordant for reasons of association and those who stayed "well" for
the same reason? Could we not just as easily surmise that, for reasons of identification, there are *five* twins who become concordant for every *one* who
remains well? The reasoning of Gottesman and Shields constituted little more
than wishful thinking in the service of keeping a theory intact.

. . . ADHD twin studies are based on an unsupported theoretical assumption and therefore offer, like family studies, only a "hint" about the possible
genetic basis of ADHD. It is quite possible, and even likely, that these studies
have recorded nothing more than the greater psychological bond and environmental similarity experienced by identical twins.

ADHD Adoption Studies

Overview

The third method used to establish the genetic basis of a condition is the
study of individuals who have been adopted. In theory, the adoption method
is able to disentangle a person's genetic heritage from his or her rearing environment. Of course, if the twin method could satisfactorily accomplish this
task, adoption studies would hardly be necessary, since they are more difficult
to perform than twin studies. The well-known Danish/American schizophrenia
adoption studies were performed by Kety, Rosenthal, Wender, and others.

These researchers came together on the basis of a common belief that the twin method was unable to satisfactorily separate genetic and environmental influences. For example, Kety wrote,

> Twin studies are a more compelling form of genetic data [than family studies], but even twin studies depend on the assumption that the only thing that differentiates monozygotic from dizygotic twins is their genetic relatedness, and that environmental factors are somehow canceled out or randomized. But that is not the case. Monozygotic twins share much of their environment as well as their genetic endowment. They live together; they sleep together; they are dressed alike by parents; they are paraded in a double parambulator as infants; their friends cannot distinguish one from the other. In short, they develop a certain ego identification with each other that is very hard to dissociate from the purely genetic identity with which they were born. (Kety, 1978, p. 48)

And Rosenthal (1979) concluded, "in both family and twin studies, the possible genetic and environmental factors are confounded, and one can draw conclusions about them only at considerable risk" (p. 25). Wender, of course, is well known in the ADHD field in addition to being a schizophrenia researcher. He too has doubts about genetic inferences from twin studies: "The roles of 'heredity' (nature) and 'environment' (nurture) in the etiology of ADHD (as with other psychiatric disorders) cannot be determined by adding data from twin studies to the data from family studies" (Wender, 1995, p. 93). As an important advocate of adoption studies, Wender concluded that the roles of heredity and environment in ADHD "can, however, be more conclusively separated by adoption studies, in which the parents providing the genetic constitution (the biological parents) and those who provide the psychological environment (the adoptive parents) are different people" (p. 93).

While the method of studying adoptees as a way of definitively separating genetic and environmental influences may appear straightforward, the most important psychiatric adoption studies (e.g., Heston, 1966; Kety, Rosenthal, Wender, & Schulsinger, 1968; Kety, Rosenthal, Wender, Schulsinger, & Jacobsen, 1975; Kety et al., 1994; Rosenthal, Wender, Kety, Welner, & Schulsinger, 1971; Tienari et al., 1994) were likely confounded by the selective placement of adoptees on the basis of the socioeconomic and psychiatric status of index adoptees' biological families (Joseph, 1999a, 1999b, in press-b; Lewontin, Rose, & Kamin, 1984). Like family and twin studies, adoption studies are susceptible to the confounding influence of environmental factors.

As of this writing, there have been five ADHD adoption studies (Alberts-Corush, Firestone, & Goodman, 1986; Cantwell, 1975; Morrison & Stewart, 1973; Safer, 1973; van den Oord, Boomsma, & Verhulst, 1994). In spite of the numerous flaws of the schizophrenia adoption studies, they possessed two important virtues not found in ADHD adoption studies: (1) most diagnoses were made blindly and (2) their authors studied or had information on the biological families of their adoptees. . . .

Summary and Discussion of the Findings of ADHD Adoption Studies

. . . The fact that ADHD adoption studies typically fail to perform blind evaluations of their participants is reason enough to question their conclusions. As a leading schizophrenia adoption researcher has noted, "With respect to all such research, in which the dependent variable is the diagnosis of relatives, it is essential that the diagnostician not know whether the individual examined is related to an index or control proband . . . because it is easy to be swayed by knowledge regarding index or control status" (Rosenthal, 1975, p. 20). For Rosenthal, who had intimate knowledge of how these studies were performed, blind diagnoses are "essential" because it is "easy" to be influenced by knowledge of the group status of the participant under study. The authors of the ADHD adoption studies noted the difficulty of remaining blind to the status of their participants because details of the adoption process are usually disclosed in the interview process. Nevertheless, our understanding of the difficulties faced by these researchers does not mean that we must accept their conclusions. Summarizing the evidence in favor of the genetic basis of ADHD, Wender (1995) wrote, "What have these adoption studies added to the data on ADHD from the family and twin studies? First, they have provided more solid data showing that 'hyperactivity' (broadly defined) has genetic contributions" (p. 99). Because, as we have seen, Wender considered family and twin studies to be confounded by environmental factors, one might ask what "solid data" he was referring to. Like other genetically oriented commentators, Wender implied that the alleged findings from one research method can legitimize—or "unconfound"—the results from another. However, if family and twin studies are contaminated by environmental factors, the results from an adoption study cannot alter this finding. According to Wender, another important finding of the ADHD adoption studies was that "they have shown that some psychiatric disorders associated with conduct disorder—'alcoholism,' Antisocial Personality Disorder ('psychopathy,' 'sociopathy'), somatization disorder ('Briquet's Syndrome,' 'hysteria')—are associated with hyperactivity and are also genetically transmitted" (1995, p. 99). The authors of the original ADHD adoption studies (Cantwell, 1975; Morrison & Stewart, 1973) believed that there was a genetic link between ADHD and alcoholism, sociopathy, and hysteria on the basis of the (extremely weak) evidence in support of the genetic foundation of these diagnoses. That Wender continues to see a genetic linkage is based on two unlikely assumptions: (1) that the evidence in favor of the genetic basis of alcoholism, sociopathy, and hysteria is solid; and (2) that the mere association of psychiatric conditions is evidence for their *genetic* association. The most outstanding example of Wender's embrace of assumption 2 was his support of the questionable Danish/American "schizophrenia spectrum" concept (see Joseph, 1998a).

Psychiatric genetics has a long history of the mistaken belief that the mere association of conditions implies their genetic relationship. Kallmann's (1938) consanguinity study looked at the families of 1087 people diagnosed with schizophrenia who had been admitted to Herzberge Hospital in Berlin.

In addition to finding that the relatives of his "probands" were diagnosed with schizophrenia at rates significantly higher than population expectations, he also found that patients and their relatives had died of tuberculosis at rates several times greater than in the general population. This finding led Kallmann to conclude, with certainty, that tuberculosis and schizophrenia were genetically related diseases:

> Because in our estimate of the causes of death we naturally counted only the absolutely assured deaths from tuberculosis, the assumption will have to be made for the probands that at least one third of them, and possibly even more, died of tuberculosis. Thus no doubt can remain that *within our own proband material the death rate from tuberculosis was also much higher than in the general population, and that, on the whole, a very particular significance must be assigned to tuberculosis in the entire heredity-circle of schizophrenia* [emphasis in original]. (Kallmann, 1938, p. 86)

Today it is apparent that Kallmann's "finding" was actually a textbook example of what is known as a spurious correlation, which has been defined as a "correlation that results not from any direct relationship between the variables under assessment, but because of their relationships to a third variable (or fourth, or more) that has no connecting relationship between them" (Reber, 1985, p. 161). Kallmann failed to recognize that the high rate of tuberculosis among schizophrenia patients and their relatives was the result of environmental conditions common to both schizophrenics and tuberculosis sufferers: namely that the socioeconomic and hygienic conditions of mental patients and their family members were inferior to the conditions of a typical German family. Similarly, the conclusion that alcoholism, sociopathy, and hysteria are genetically related to ADHD could be the result of a correlation as spurious as Kallmann's.

To summarize, the ADHD adoption literature reveals a handful of greatly flawed studies which, even when combined, provide (at best) inconclusive evidence in favor of either a genetic basis for ADHD or its genetic relationship to any other condition.

Summary and Conclusions

We have seen that the genetic basis of ADHD has been supported with the same types of studies cited in favor of the genetic basis of schizophrenia and other psychiatric diagnoses. There are three main ways that psychiatric geneticists and behavior geneticists have made the case for the genetic basis of ADHD: family, twin, and adoption studies. We have seen that although family studies might be able to demonstrate the familiality of ADHD, the fact that families share a common environment as well as common genes does not permit any conclusion about a genetic component for the diagnosis.

It was argued that the classical twin method is no less confounded by environmental factors than family studies because identical twins clearly share a more similar environment than fraternals. Twin researchers have attempted to defend the assumption of equal environments but have failed to provide convincing evidence that the EEA, whether using the traditional or trait-relevant definition, is valid. It is therefore likely that the greater similarity of MZ vs DZ twins on measures related to ADHD symptoms records nothing more than the greater environmental similarity and identification of MZ twins. Typically, ADHD twin study articles discuss the EEA briefly or not at all, and in no study do the authors come out in favor of the trait-relevant EEA. The conclusions of these studies, therefore, are based on the simple assumption that MZ and DZ environments are equal when it is clear that these environments are not equal.

ADHD adoption studies are greatly inferior to the already flawed schizophrenia adoption studies which preceded them and therefore offer no important evidence in favor of the genetic position. Apart from the other methodological problems with these studies, the fact that most made non-blind diagnoses and did not assess adoptees' biological relatives invalidates any inferences of the operation of genetic factors. After an examination of the total weight of evidence in favor of a genetic basis or predisposition for ADHD, it is concluded that a role for genetic factors is not supported and that future research should be directed toward psychosocial causes.

A reevaluation of the genetic evidence is important in the context of how ADHD is viewed and what directions will be taken in future research. Proponents of the brain dysfunction model of ADHD (and other psychiatric conditions) often point to the evidence from genetic studies in support of their position, since defective genes are seen as creating associated biological defects. The belief in the biological/genetic basis of ADHD has hindered investigation into possible environmental factors (McCubbin & Cohen, 1999), but it is just this area that demands greater attention. While there is little solid evidence in support of specific environmental factors, there are theories requiring further investigation. DeGrandpre (1999) sees the condition as the result of some children's problems with impulse control in our increasingly "rapid-fire culture," leading to children's "rapid-fire consciousness":

> At the heart of the developmental problem lies the emergence of a phenomenological experience of unsettledness, characterized by feelings of restlessness, anxiety, and impulsivity. Hyperactivity and the inability to attend to mundane activities exemplify the type of escape behavior that the "sensory addicted" child or adult uses in order to maintain his or her needed stream of stimulation. (p. 32)

It is reasonable to propose that future research be directed toward psychosocial theories such as DeGrandpre's. If future studies are also able to detect genetic factors, this information could be used to identify children in need of special intervention. Unfortunately, history has shown that the results of genetic studies have often been used to stigmatize individuals and groups, to discourage the search for other relevant and necessary factors, and to support the use of psychotropic drugs to treat problems caused by social and psychological factors. This article, therefore, is a necessary counterweight to the prevailing biopsychiatric/pharmacological view of ADHD.

References

Alberts-Corush, J., Firestone, P., & Goodman, J. (1986). Attention and impulsivity characteristics of the biological and adoptive parents of hyperactive and normal control children. *American Journal of Orthopsychiatry, 56*, 413–423.

Barkley, R. (1998a, September). Attention-deficit hyperactivity disorder. *Scientific American, 66*–71.

Barkley, R. (1998b). *Attention-deficit hyperactivity disorder: A handbook for diagnosis and treatment* (2nd ed.). New York: The Guilford Press.

Biederman, J., Faraone, S., Mick, E., Spencer, T., Wilens, T., Kiely, K., Guite, J., Ablon, S., Reed, E., & Warburton, R. (1995). High risk for attention deficit hyperactivity disorder among children of parents with childhood onset of the disorder: A pilot study. *American Journal of Psychiatry, 152*, 431–435.

Biederman, J., Munir, K., Knee, D., Habelow, M., Autor, S., Hoge, S., & Waternaux, C. (1986). A family study of patients with attention deficit disorder and normal controls. *Journal of Psychiatric Research, 20*, 263–274.

Breggin, P. (1998). *Talking back to Ritalin*. Monroe, ME: Common Courage Press.

Cantwell, D. (1972). Psychiatric illness in the families of hyperactive children. *Archives of General Psychiatry, 27*, 414–417.

Cantwell, D. (1975). Genetic studies of hyperactive children: Psychiatric illness in biologic and adopting parents. In R. Fieve, D. Rosenthal, & H. Brill (Eds.), *Genetic research in psychiatry* (pp. 273–280). Baltimore: The Johns Hopkins Press.

DeGrandpre, R. (1999). *Ritalin nation*. New York: Norton.

Diller, L., Tanner, J., & Weil, J. (1995). Etiology of ADHD: Nature or Nurture? [Letter to the editor]. *American Journal of Psychiatry, 153*, 451–452.

Diller, L. (1998). *Running on Ritalin*. New York: Bantam Books.

Eaves, L., Silberg, J., Hewitt, J., Meyer, J., Rutter, M., Simonoff, E., Neale, M., & Pickles, A. (1993). Genes, personality, and psychopathology: A latent class analysis of liability to symptoms of attention-deficit hyperactivity disorder in twins. In R. Plomin & G. McClearn (Eds.), *Nature, nurture, & psychology* (pp. 285–303). Washington, DC: American Psychological Association Press.

Edelbrock, C., Rende, R., Plomin, R., & Thompson, L. (1995). A twin study of competence and problem behavior in childhood and early adolescence. *Journal of Child Psychology and Psychiatry, 36*, 775–785.

Faraone, S., Biederman, J., Keenan, K., & Tsuang, M. (1991a). A family-genetic study of girls with DSM-III attention deficit disorder. *American Journal of Psychiatry, 148*, 112–117.

Faraone, S., & Tsuang, M. (1995). Methods in psychiatric genetics. In M. Tsuang, M. Tohen, & G. Zahner (Eds.), *Textbook in psychiatric epidemiology* (pp. 81–134). New York: Wiley–Liss.

Farber, S. (1981). *Identical twins reared apart: A reanalysis*. New York: Basic Books.

Gilger, J., Pennington, B., & DeFries, J. (1992). A twin study of the etiology of comorbidity: Attention-deficit hyperactivity disorder and dyslexia. *Journal of the American Academy of Child and Adolescent Psychiatry, 31*, 343–348.

Gillis, J., Gilger, J., Pennington, B., & DeFries, J. (1992). Attention deficit disorder in reading-disabled twins: Evidence for a genetic etiology. *Journal of Abnormal Child Psychology, 20*, 303–315.

Gjone, H., Stevenson, J., & Sundet, J. (1996). Genetic influence on parent-reported attention-related problems in a Norwegian general population twin study. *Journal of the American Academy of Child and Adolescent Psychiatry, 35*, 588–596.

Goodman, R., & Stevenson, J. (1989a). A twin study of hyperactivity: I. An examination of hyperactivity scores and categories derived from the Rutter Teacher and Parent Questionnaires. *Journal of Child Psychology and Psychiatry, 30*, 671–689.

Goodman, R., & Stevenson, J. (1989b). A twin study of hyperactivity: II. The aetiological role of genes, family relationships and perinatal adversity. *Journal of Child Psychology and Psychiatry, 30*, 691–709.

Gottesman, I. (1991). *Schizophrenia genesis*. New York: W. H. Freeman.

Gottesman, I., & Shields, J. (1966). Contributions of twin studies to perspectives on schizophrenia. In B. Maher (Ed.), *Progress in experimental personality research* (Vol. 3, pp. 1–84). New York: Academic Press.

Heston, L. (1966). Psychiatric disorders in foster home reared children of schizophrenic mothers. *British Journal of Psychiatry, 112,* 819–825.

Jackson, D. (1960). A critique of the literature on the genetics of schizophrenia. In D. Jackson (Ed.), *The etiology of schizophrenia* (pp. 37–87). New York: Basic Books.

Joseph, J. (1998a). *A critical analysis of the genetic theory of schizophrenia*. Unpublished doctoral dissertation, California School of Professional Psychology, Alameda.

Joseph, J. (1998b). The equal environment assumption of the classical twin method: A critical analysis. *Journal of Mind and Behavior, 19,* 325–358.

Joseph, J. (1999a). A critique of the Finnish Adoptive Family Study of Schizophrenia. *Journal of Mind and Behavior, 20,* 133–154.

Joseph, J. (1999b). The genetic theory of schizophrenia: A critical overview. *Ethical Human Sciences and Services, 1,* 119–145.

Joseph, J. (in press-c). Don Jackson's "A critique of the literature on the genetics of schizophrenia"—A reappraisal after 40 years. *Genetic, Social, and General Psychology Monographs.*

Joseph, J. (in press-d). Separated twins and the genetics of personality differences: A critique. *American Journal of Psychology.*

Kallmann, F. (1938). *The genetics of schizophrenia: A study of heredity and reproduction in the families of 1,087 schizophrenics.* New York: J. J. Augustin.

Kamin, L. (1974). *The science and politics of I.Q.* Potomac, MD: Erlbaum.

Kendler, K. (1993). Twin studies of psychiatric illness: Current status and future directions. *Archives of General Psychiatry, 50,* 905–915.

Kety, S. (1978). Heredity and environment. In J. Shershow (Ed.), *Schizophrenia: Science and practice* (pp. 47–68). Cambridge, MA: Harvard Univ. Press.

Kety, S., Rosenthal, D., Wender, P., & Schulsinger, F. (1968). The types and prevalence of mental illness in the biological and adoptive families of adopted schizophrenics. In D. Rosenthal & S. Kety (Eds.), *The transmission of schizophrenia* (pp. 345–362). New York: Pergamon Press.

Kety, S., Rosenthal, D., Wender, P., Schulsinger, F., & Jacobsen, B. (1975). Mental illness in the biological and adoptive families of adopted individuals who have become schizophrenic: A preliminary report based on psychiatric interviews. In R. Fieve, D. Rosenthal, & H. Brill (Eds.), *Genetic research in psychiatry* (pp. 147–165). Baltimore: The Johns Hopkins Press.

Kety, S., Wender, P., Jacobsen, B., Ingraham, L., Jansson, L., Faber, B., & Kinney, D. (1994). Mental illness in the biological and adoptive relatives of schizophrenic adoptees: Replication of the Copenhagen study to the rest of Denmark. *Archives of General Psychiatry, 51,* 442–455.

Kläning, U., Mortensen, P., & Kyvik, K. (1996). Increased occurrence of schizophrenia and other psychiatric illnesses among twins. *British Journal of Psychiatry, 168,* 688–692.

Lewontin, R., Rose, S., & Kamin, L. (1984). *Not in our genes.* New York: Pantheon.

Levy, F., Hay, D., McStephen, M., Wood, C., & Waldman, I. (1997). Attention-deficit hyperactivity disorder: A category or a continuum? Genetic analysis of a large-scale twin study. *Journal of the American Academy of Child and Adolescent Psychiatry, 36,* 737–744.

Lopez, R. (1965). Hyperactivity in twins. *Canadian Psychiatric Association Journal, 10,* 421–426.

McCubbin, M., & Cohen, D. (1999). Empirical, ethical, and political perspectives on the use of methylphenidate. *Ethical Human Sciences and Services, 1,* 81–101.

Morrison, J., & Stewart, M. (1971). A family study of the hyperactive child syndrome. *Biological Psychiatry, 3,* 189–195.

Morrison, J., & Stewart, M. (1973). The psychiatric status of the legal families of adopted hyperactive children. *Archives of General Psychiatry, 28,* 888–891.

Nadder, T., Silberg, J., Eaves, L., Maes, H., & Meyer, J. (1998). Genetic effects on ADHD symptomatology in 7–13-year-old twins: Results from a telephone survey. *Behavior Genetics, 28*, 83–99.

Nichols, P., & Chen, T. (1981). *Minimal brain dysfunction.* Hillsdale, NJ: Erlbaum.

Pam, A. (1995). Biological psychiatry: Science or pseudoscience? In C. Ross & A. Pam (Eds.), *Pseudoscience in biological psychiatry: Blaming the body* (pp. 7–84). New York: Wiley.

Pam, A., Kemker, S., Ross, C., & Golden, R. (1996). The "equal environment assumption" in MZ–DZ comparisons: An untenable premise of psychiatric genetics? *Acta Geneticae Medicae et Gemellologiae, 45*, 349–360.

Plomin, R., DeFries, J., & McClearn, G. (1990). *Behavioral genetics: A primer* (2nd ed.). New York: W. H. Freeman.

Reber, A. (1985). *The Penguin dictionary of psychology.* London: Penguin Books.

Rosenthal, D. (1960). Confusion of identity and the frequency of schizophrenia in twins. *Archives of General Psychiatry, 3*, 101–108.

Rosenthal, D. (1970). *Genetic theory and abnormal behavior.* New York: McGraw-Hill.

Rosenthal, D. (1975). The spectrum concept in schizophrenic and manic-depressive disorders. In D. Freedman (Ed.), *Biology of the major psychoses* (pp. 19–25). New York: Raven.

Rosenthal, D. (1979). Genetic factors in behavioural disorders. In M. Roth & V. Cowie (Eds.), *Psychiatry, genetics and pathography: A tribute to Eliot Slater* (pp. 22–33). London: Oxford Univ. Press.

Rosenthal, D., Wender, P., Kety, S., Welner, J., & Schulsinger, F. (1971). The adopted-away offspring of schizophrenics. *American Journal of Psychiatry, 128*, 307–311.

Rüdin, E. (1916). *Zur Vererbung und Neuentstehung der Dementia praecox.* Berlin: Springer-Verlag OHG.

Safer, D. (1973). A familial factor in minimal brain dysfunction. *Behavior Genetics, 3*, 175–186.

Sherman, D., Iacono, W., & McGue, M. (1997). Attention-deficit hyperactivity disorder dimensions: A twin study of inattention and impulsivity-hyperactivity. *Journal of the American Academy of Child and Adolescent Psychiatry, 36*, 745–753.

Silberg, J., Rutter, M., Meyer, J., Maes, H., Hewitt, J., Simonoff, E., Pickles, A., & Loeber, R. (1996). Genetic and environmental influences on the covariation between hyperactivity and conduct disturbance in juvenile twins. *Journal of Psychology and Psychiatry, 37*, 803–816.

Steffensson, B., Larsson, J., Fried, I., El-Sayed, E., Rydelius, P., & Lichtenstein, P. (1999). Genetic disposition for global maturity: An explanation for genetic effects on parental report of ADHD. *International Journal of Behavioral Development, 23*, 357–374.

Stevenson, J. (1992). Evidence for a genetic etiology in hyperactivity in children. *Behavior Genetics, 22*, 337–344.

Tannock, R. (1998). Attention deficit hyperactivity disorder: Advances in cognitive, neurobiological, and genetic research. *Journal of Child Psychology and Psychiatry, 39*, 65–99.

Taylor, H. (1980). *The IQ game: A methodological inquiry into the heredity–environment controversy.* New Brunswick, NJ: Rutgers Univ. Press.

Tienari, P., Wynne, L., Moring, J., Lahti, I., Naarala, M., Sorri, A., Wahlberg, K., Saarento, O., Seitamaa, M., Kaleva, M., & L‰osky, K. (1994). The Finnish adoptive family study of schizophrenia. *British Journal of Psychiatry, 164*(Suppl. 23), 20–26.

van den Oord, E., Boomsma, D., & Verhulst, F. (1994). A study of problem behaviors in 10- to 15-year-old biologically related and unrelated international adoptees. *Behavior Genetics, 24*, 193–205.

van den Oord, E., Verhulst, F., & Boomsma, D. (1996). A genetic study of maternal and paternal ratings of problem behaviors in 3-year-old twins. *Journal of Abnormal Psychology, 105*, 349–357.

Welner, Z., Welner, A., Stewart, M., Palkes, H., & Wish, E. (1977). A controlled study of siblings of hyperactive children. *Journal of Nervous and Mental Disease,* **165**, 110–117.

Wender, P. (1995). *Attention-deficit hyperactivity disorder in adults.* New York: Oxford Univ. Press.

Willerman, L. (1973). Activity level and hyperactivity in twins. *Child Development,* **44**, 288–293.

NO

Stephen V. Faraone and
Joseph Biederman

Nature, Nurture, and Attention Deficit Hyperactivity Disorder

This commentary shows that [Jay] Joseph's . . . review of the genetics of attention deficit hyperactivity disorder (ADHD) contains errors of scientific logic and ignores much relevant research. Thus, we reject his conclusions. We also reject Joseph's approach of pitting nature against nurture as if these two facets of human life are at odds with one another. Instead, most scientists who study the genetics of psychiatric disorders embrace the idea that these disorders are influenced by both genes and environmental factors. In fact, the twin studies criticized by Joseph provide the strongest evidence that environmental risk factors play a substantial role in the etiology of ADHD. They do so by showing that when one identical twin has ADHD the risk to the co-twin is much less than 100%, a fact which can only be explained by environmental risk factors. We also reject the idea that genetic studies have hindered psychosocial research, stigmatized patients, or promoted psychopharmacologic treatments. Genetic studies have aimed at solving one part of the puzzle of ADHD. By testing a parsimonious theory, they have set the stage for gene discovery and the delineation of how genes and environment combine to cause this impairing disorder.

Attention deficit hyperactivity disorder (ADHD) is a childhood-onset, clinically heterogeneous disorder of inattention, hyperactivity, and impulsivity. Its impact on society is enormous in terms of its financial cost, stress to families, adverse academic and vocational outcomes, and negative effects on self-esteem (Barkley, 1998). For these reasons, discussions of the etiology of ADHD have serious implications. Because conclusions from such discussions are likely to drive future research and treatment development, how we address these issues will ultimately affect the lives of the many children, adolescents, and adults who suffer from this disorder.

For these reasons it is essential that readers carefully evaluate the controversial conclusion drawn by Joseph (2000): "After an examination of the total weight of evidence in favor of a genetic basis or predisposition for ADHD, it is concluded that a role for genetic factors is not supported and that future research should be directed toward psychosocial causes." In this commentary we show this conclusion to be wrong, not only because it runs counter to

From Stephen V. Faraone and Joseph Biederman, "Nature, Nurture, and Attention Deficit Hyperactivity Disorder," *Developmental Review*, vol. 20, no. 4 (December 2000). Copyright © 2000 by Academic Press. Reprinted by permission of Elsevier and Stephen V. Faraone.

the prevailing view in the scientific community (Barkley, 1998; Faraone & Biederman, 1998; Faraone & Doyle, in press; Swanson, Castellanos, Murias, LaHoste, & Kennedy, 1998; Thapar, Holmes, Poulton, & Harrington, 1999), but also because it is based on errors in scientific logic compromised by an incomplete review of relevant data.

Joseph's Errors of Inference

Joseph's main logical error is his lack of attention to the nature of scientific theory building and hypothesis testing. The theory that genes influence ADHD is a viable theory because it makes several predictions which, *if proven wrong,* would disprove the theory. The first is that ADHD should run in families. It does (Faraone & Doyle, in press). The second is that identical twins should show a greater concordance for ADHD than fraternal twins. They do (Faraone & Doyle, in press). The third is that ADHD should be transmitted through biological, not adoptive family relationships. It is (Faraone & Doyle, in press). The fourth is that the familial transmission of ADHD should conform to genetic, not cultural transmission, models. It does (Faraone & Doyle, in press). The fifth is that molecular genetic studies should find evidence that specific genes cause ADHD. They have (Faraone & Doyle, in press).

Joseph does not claim that any of these predictions have been proven wrong. In fact, he does not even address predictions four and five. Thus, his article cannot be viewed as disproving the hypothesis that genes influence the etiology of ADHD. Instead, his argument can be boiled down to three key claims. His first claim is that studies showing ADHD runs in families are irrelevant to the question of genetic transmission because familial transmission can be caused by environmental factors. It is true that disorders can run in families due to either environmental or genetic reasons (Faraone, Tsuang, & Tsuang, 1999). But it is wrong to state that family studies are irrelevant to testing the theory that genes influence ADHD. The theory provides the testable prediction that ADHD should run in families, which has yet to be proven wrong.

The second claim made by Joseph is that twin studies of ADHD are flawed by the equal environment assumption, which holds that the trait-relevant environments of identical and fraternal twins are the same. He finds this assumption untenable for two reasons. First, several studies have shown that, compared with fraternal twins, identical twins are treated more alike, spend more time together, have more common friends, and experience greater levels of identity confusion. Second, he *infers* from these data that identical twins are more likely to be similarly exposed to "trait-relevant" environmental factors. Notably, Joseph presents no data to support his inference. Thus, readers should view it as a hypothesis to be tested rather than a conclusion to be accepted. In fact, although not mentioned by Joseph, this hypothesis was tested by Thapar et al. (1995). They found that the equal environment assumption was violated because identical twins scored significantly higher on an index of environmental sharing than did fraternal twins. But, contrary to Joseph's inference, this index of environmental sharing did not predict twin similarity for ADHD scores, i.e., it was not trait relevant.

Joseph's third claim is that adoption studies of ADHD are flawed in several ways. We agree with Joseph that no ADHD adoption study has directly compared the biological and adoptive families of the same child. These, along with the other relatively minor methodological problems detailed by Joseph, limit the strength of any inferences we can draw from these studies.

What should readers conclude about the three areas of genetic research discussed by Joseph? The standard interpretation of these data would be that the theory of genes influencing ADHD has not been disproven. We have chosen our language carefully here to correspond to the logic of scientific inference. Experiments subject theories to falsification. They can fail to falsify a theory but cannot prove that it is correct. Of course, consistent failures to falsify a theory will strengthen our belief that the theory (or parts of it) are true. Thus, most scientists find value in the theory that genes influence ADHD because it has consistently made predictions which turn out to be correct.

Joseph rejects the standard interpretation yet provides no theory of his own beyond vague assertions that psychosocial events could account for the pattern of data observed in family, twin, and adoption studies. But scientists need more than vague assertions, we need theories which make testable predictions. A testable psychosocial theory of the apparent genetic transmission of ADHD would need to specify a psychosocial causal factor that (a) is transmitted from parents to children, (b) is more likely to be shared by identical than fraternal twins, and (c) explains the elevated rates of ADHD and associated traits among the biological relatives of adopted away ADHD children. Unfortunately, Joseph does not present a testable theory that can be assessed as a potential alternative to the theory that genes influence ADHD.

Another lacuna in Joseph's argument is his failure to address the principle of parsimony when considering the value of alternative theories. This principle states that, other things being equal, a theory which makes fewer assumptions is better than one requiring more assumptions. Any genetic theory of ADHD explains the family, twin, and adoption data with a single idea, the idea that genes influence the etiology of the disorder. In contrast, Joseph must appeal to several different mechanisms to explain these findings. One mechanism must explain transmission from parent to child (perhaps modeling or cultural transmission; he does not say). Another mechanism (the idea that identical twins share a more trait-relevant environment than fraternal twins) must be invoked to account for twin data. And a third mechanism (faulty study design) must be conjured up to explain the results of adoption studies. It is, of course, *possible* that three different mechanisms have converged to produce a pattern of results that simulates genetic transmission. But such a three-factor theory is not parsimonious, especially when compared with the idea that genes account for the observed data.

Joseph's Incomplete Literature Review

Joseph's literature review ignores two domains of research into the genetics of ADHD: segregation analyses and molecular genetic studies. Segregation analysis is a mathematical method which examines evidence for genetic transmission by determining if the pattern of illness in families follows known genetic mechanisms. Morrison and Stewart (1974) concluded that polygenic inheritance was a likely mode of transmission for ADHD. Recent studies have, however, been more consistent with the idea that one gene may have a more robust effect than others (e.g., Deutsch, Matthysse, Swanson, & Farkas, 1990). Faraone et al. (1992) showed that the familial transmission of ADHD was consistent with single-gene effects but not with cultural transmission. Consistent findings have also emerged in a study of a South American sample (Lopera et al., 1999) in which the only models of inheritance that could not be rejected were those of dominant and codominant gene effects. In addition, Maher et al. (1999) found that a Mendelian model was the best explanation for the pattern of transmission of ADHD.

Because, in some of these studies (i.e., Deutsch et al., 1990; Faraone et al., 1992) the differences in fit between genetic models involving multifactorial and single gene inheritance was modest, several interpretations are possible. If ADHD had more than one genetic cause, then the evidence for any single mode of transmission might be relatively weak. Alternatively, ADHD may be caused by several interacting genes of modest effect, which is consistent with ADHD's high population prevalence (2 to 7% for ADHD) and high concordance in MZ [identical] twins but modest recurrence risks to first-degree relatives. In summary, segregation analyses have not resolved ADHD's mode of transmission, but they do implicate genetics as opposed to environmental mechanisms.

Although still in their infancy, molecular genetic studies have already implicated several genes as mediating the susceptibility to ADHD. Researchers have examined genes in catecholaminergic pathways because animal models, theoretical considerations, and the effectiveness of stimulant treatment implicate catecholaminergic dysfunction in the pathophysiology of this disorder (Faraone & Biederman, 1998).

Seven groups have reported an association between ADHD and the 7-repeat allele of the DRD4 gene (Barr et al., 2000; Comings et al., 1999; Faraone et al., 1999; LaHoste et al., 1996; Rowe et al., 1998; Smalley et al., 1998; Swanson et al., 1998). Six groups, however, could not replicate this association (Asherson et al., 1998; Castellanos et al., 1998; Comings et al., 1999; Daly, Hawi, Fitzgerald, & Gill, 1998; Eisenberg et al., 2000; Hawi, McCarron, Kirley, Fitzgerald, & Gill, 2000). Despite the negative findings, a meta-analysis of these data concluded that the DRD4 7-repeat allele was significantly associated with ADHD (Faraone, 1999).

Notably, the DRD4 7-fold repeat allele mediates a blunted response to dopamine (Asghari et al., 1995) and has been implicated in novelty seeking (Benjamin, Patterson, Greenberg, Murphy, & Hamer, 1996; Ebstein et al., 1996), a personality trait related to ADHD. When the D4 gene is disabled in a knockout mouse model, dopamine synthesis increases in the dorsal striatum and the mice show locomotor supersensitivity to ethanol, cocaine, and methamphetamine (Rubinstein et al., 1997). D4 knockout mice also show reduced novelty-related exploration (Dulawa, Grandy, Low, Paulus, & Geyer, 1999), which is consistent with human data suggesting a role for D4 in novelty-seeking behaviors.

Cook (1995) reported an association between ADHD and the 480-bp allele of the dopamine transporter (DAT) gene using a family-based association study. This finding was replicated in family-based studies of ADHD by Gill et al. (1997), Daly et al. (1998), and Waldman et al. (1998) but not in two other studies (Asherson et al., 1998; Poulton et al., 1998). The link between the DAT gene and ADHD is further supported by a study that relates this gene to poor methylphenidate response in ADHD children (Winsberg & Comings, 1999), a knockout mouse study showing that its elimination leads to hyperactivity in mice (Majzoub & Muglia, 1996), and a neuroimaging study showing DAT activity in the striatum is elevated by 70% in ADHD adults (Dougherty et al., 1999).

Four studies examined the Catechol-O-Methyltransferase (COMT) gene, the product of which is involved in the breakdown of dopamine and norepinephrine. One study (Eisenberg et al., 1999) found that ADHD was associated with the high enzyme activity COMT Val allele; three others (Barr et al., 1999; Hawi, Millar, Daly, Fitzgerald, & Gill, 2000; Tahir et al., 2000) did not. One study implicated the A1 allele of the dopamine D2 receptor gene (Comings et al., 1991) and found additive effects of DRD2, DBH, and DAT with regard to ADHD symptoms. Another study (Jiang et al., 2000) found an association with the DXS7 locus of the X chromosome, a marker for MAO which encodes enzymes that metabolize dopamine and other neurotransmitters. Finally, Comings et al. (1999) found associations and additive effects of polymorphisms at three noradrenergic genes [the adrenergic alpha 2A (ADRA2A), adrenergic alpha 2C (ADRA2C), and DBH] on an ADHD symptom score in a sample of individuals with Tourette's syndrome.

Like family, twin, and adoption studies, segregation analysis and molecular genetic studies have not disproven the theory that genes influence ADHD. Segregation studies are consistent with the idea that familial transmission follows genetic mechanisms. In contrast, they reject the idea that familial transmission can be accounted for by environmental risk factors. In addition, molecular genetic studies have implicated two genes, DRD4 and DAT, in the etiology of ADHD.

Further Considerations

Joseph's confrontational approach to psychiatric genetics misleads readers in several ways. He states that "The belief in the biological/genetic basis of ADHD has hindered investigation into possible environmental factors." This statement errs by conflating biological with genetic thus denying the potential biological nature of environmental risk factors. Moreover, even a cursory review of the literature shows that the investigation of environmental factors has not been hindered.

With regard to the biological environment, the idea that food additives cause ADHD has been studied and rejected (Conners, 1980) as has the theory that excessive sugar intake leads to ADHD (Wolraich, Wilson, & White, 1995). Some toxins have been implicated in the etiology of ADHD. Lead contamination leads to distractibility, hyperactivity, restlessness, and lower intellectual functioning (Needleman, 1982). But many ADHD children do not show lead contamination and many children with high lead exposure do not develop ADHD. Thus, lead exposure cannot account for the bulk of ADHD cases.

The literature examining the association of ADHD with pregnancy and delivery complications [PDCs] supports the idea that PDCs predispose children to ADHD (e.g., Chandola, Robling, Peters, Melville-Thomas, & McGuffin, 1992; Conners, 1975; Hartsough & Lambert, 1985; Milberger, Biederman, Faraone, Guite, & Tsuang, 1997; Nichols & Chen, 1981; Sprich-Buckminster, Biederman, Milberger, Faraone, & Krifcher Lehman, 1993). The PDCs implicated in ADHD frequently lead to hypoxia and tend to involve *chronic* exposures to the fetus, such as toxemia, rather than *acute,* traumatic events, such as delivery complications (Faraone & Biederman, 1998). Notably, maternal smoking during pregnancy predicts behavioral and cognitive impairment in children and ADHD (e.g., Denson, Nanson, & McWatters, 1975; Milberger, Biederman, Faraone, Chen, & Jones, 1996).

Researchers have also implicated the psychosocial environment in the etiology of ADHD. Rutter's (1975) classic studies of the Isle of Wight and the inner borough of London provide a compelling example of how psychosocial risk factors influence child psychopathology. This research revealed six risk factors within the family environment that correlated significantly with childhood mental disturbances: (a) severe marital discord; (b) low social class; (c) large family size; (d) paternal criminality; (e) maternal mental disorder; and (f) foster placement. Rutter found that it was the aggregate of adversity factors, rather than the presence of any single one, that impaired development. Other studies also find that as the number of adverse conditions accumulates, the risk of impaired outcome in the child increases proportionally (Blanz, Schmidt, & Esser, 1991). Biederman et al. (1995) found a positive association between Rutter's index of adversity and ADHD, measures of ADHD-associated psychopathology, impaired cognition, and psychosocial dysfunction.

Other cross-sectional and longitudinal studies have identified variables such as marital distress, family dysfunction, and low social class as risk factors for psychopathology and dysfunction in children. For example, the Ontario Child Health Study showed that family dysfunction and low income predicted persistence and onset of one or more psychiatric disorders over a 4-year follow-up period (Offord et al., 1992). Other work implicates low maternal education, low social class, and single parenthood as important adversity factors for ADHD (e.g., Nichols & Chen, 1981; Palfrey, Levine, Walker, & Sullivan, 1985). These studies suggest that the mothers of ADHD children have more negative communication patterns, more conflict with their child, and a greater intensity of anger than do control mothers.

Biederman et al. (1995) showed that chronic conflict, decreased family cohesion, and exposure to parental psychopathology, particularly maternal psychopathology, were more common in ADHD families compared with control families. The differences between ADHD and control children could not be accounted for by either SES or parental history of major psychopathology. Moreover, increased levels of family–environment adversity predicted impaired psychosocial functioning. Measures indexing chronic family conflict had a more pernicious impact on the exposed child than those indexing exposure to parental psychopathology. Indeed, marital discord in families has consistently predicted disruptive behaviors in boys (Institute of Medicine, 1989). This research shows that it is the extent of discord and overt conflict, regardless of whether the parents are separated, that predicts the child's risks for psychopathology and dysfunction (Hetherington, Cox, & Cox, 1982).

Low maternal warmth and high maternal malaise and criticism have been previously associated with ADHD in children (Barkley, Fischer, Edlebrock, & Smallish, 1991). An epidemiologic study examining family attributes in children who had undergone stressful experiences, found that children's perceptions of mothers, but not fathers, differentiated stress-resilient and stress-affected children (Wyman et al., 1992).

Another misleading conclusion from Joseph's article is his statement "Unfortunately, history has shown that the results of genetic studies have often been used to stigmatize individuals and groups, to discourage the search for other relevant and necessary factors. . . ." Joseph presents no data to show that the results of genetic studies stigmatize individuals and groups. We realize that psychiatric genetic data had been used by the Nazis to justify eugenic sterilization and murder (Gottesman & Bertelsen, 1996), but that would not be a fair assessment of contemporary psychiatric genetics. Today, people with mental illness are stigmatized, but we know of no data showing that genetic studies lead to stigma. In fact, in the 19th century and earlier, long before the advent of psychiatric genetics, patients with psychiatric disorders were stigmatized much more than they are today (e.g., as being witches and/or possessed by the devil).

Moreover, Joseph fails to mention that psychosocial theories can stigmatize families. We recall the now-discredited theory of the schizophrenogenic mother which burdened an entire generation of mothers of schizophrenic patients. In fact, data supporting a genetic and biological etiology of ADHD can be used to reduce stigma by teaching patients, relatives, and the public that ADHD is an illness which can be treated not an inadequacy to be ashamed of.

Another misleading conclusion made by Joseph is his statement that the results of genetic studies have often been used "to support the use of psychotropic drugs to treat problems caused by social and psychological factors." This statement confuses the etiology of a disorder with its treatment. Although this error in logic was corrected by Meehl (1973), it periodically recurs in the literature. Meehl used the term "therapeutic nihilism" to refer to the belief that a genetic cause for a disorder means that psychosocial therapies will be useless. He showed that therapeutic nihilism was wrong because the idea that genes cause a disorder does not rule out the possibility that environmental factors also influence its etiology or modulate its course.

In practice, most psychiatric and psychological treatment programs reject therapeutic nihilism. For example, schizophrenia is influenced by genes and has a strong biological basis. Yet, its medication treatment is often supplemented with psychosocial therapies (Tsuang, Faraone, & Green, 1999). Similarly, despite knowing of the genetic basis of ADHD for many years, the National Institute of Mental Health (NIMH) launched a multisite study to evaluate the efficacy of stimulant medication, psychosocial treatment, and their combination in the treatment of ADHD (Arnold et al., 1997).

Another form of therapeutic nihilism occurs with the belief that problems caused by psychological or social factors can only be treated with psychosocial therapies. Should traumatized people with severe, recurrent anxiety be denied antianxiety medication because the cause of their disorder was a psychosocial event? Should those who become depressed and suicidal in the wake of a family tragedy be denied antidepressants? Should patients with a reactive psychosis be denied antipsychotic medication?

Clearly, choosing treatment options based on the presumed psychosocial or genetic origin of a disorder can lead to serous clinical errors. Instead, we suggest that clinicians use controlled clinical trials to determine which treatments are most appropriate for their patients. For example, the recent NIMH multisite study of ADHD treatment showed that stimulant treatment was more effective than psychosocial treatment and that the combination of stimulant and psychosocial treatment did not improve outcome beyond what was found with stimulant treatment alone (Arnold et al., 1997).

Conclusions

We have shown that Joseph's review contains errors of scientific logic and ignores a substantial body of research relevant to the theory that genes influence ADHD. For these reasons, we reject his conclusions, especially since he does not provide an alternative theory that better describes the relevant data. We also encourage readers to reject Joseph's approach of pitting nature against nurture as if these two facets of human life are somehow at odds with one another. Instead, readers should recognize that most scientists who study the genetics of psychiatric disorders embrace the idea that these disorders are influenced by both genes and environmental factors. In fact, the twin studies so severely criticized by Joseph provided the strongest evidence that environmental risk factors play a substantial role in the etiology of ADHD. They do so by showing that when one identical twin has ADHD the risk to the co-twin is much less than 100%, a fact which can only be explained by environmental risk factors.

We also reject the idea that genetic studies of ADHD have hindered psychosocial research, stigmatized patients, or promoted psychopharmacologic treatments. Genetic studies have simply aimed at solving one part of the puzzle that is ADHD. By repeatedly testing a parsimonious theory, genetic studies have begun to clarify the genetic component to ADHD. By doing so they have set the stage for gene discovery and the delineation of how genes and environment combine to cause this impairing disorder.

References

Arnold, L. E., Abikoff, H. B., Cantwell, D. P., Conners, C. K., Elliot, G., Greenhill, L. L., Hechtman, L., Hinshaw, S. P., Hoza, B., Jensen, P. S., Kraemer, H. C., March, J. S., Newcorn, J. H., Pelham, W. E., Richters, J. E., Schiller, E., Severe, J. B., Swanson, J. M., Vereen, D., & Wells, K. C. (1997). National Institute of Mental Health Collaborative Multimodal Treatment Study of Children with ADHD (the MTA). Design challenges and choices. *Archives of General Psychiatry, 54*, 865–870.

Asghari, V., Sanyal, S., Buchwaldt, S., Paterson, A., Jovanovic, V., & Van Tol, H. H. (1995). Modulation of intracellular cyclic AMP levels by different human dopamine D4 receptor variants. *Journal of Neurochemistry, 65*, 1157–1165.

Asherson, P., Virdee, V., Curran, S., Ebersole, S., Freeman, B., Craig, I., Simonoff, E., Eley, T., Plomin, R., & Taylor, E. (1998). Association of DSM-IV attention deficit hyperactivity disorder and monoamine pathway genes. *American Journal of Medical Genetics, Neuropsychiatric Genetics, 81*, 548.

Barkley, R. A. (1998). *Attention Deficit Hyperactivity Disorder: A handbook for diagnosis and treatment*. New York: Guilford.

Barkley, R. A., Fischer, M., Edlebrock, C., & Smallish, L. (1991). The adolescent outcome of hyperactive children diagnosed by research criteria: III. Mother-child interactions, family conflicts and maternal psychopathology. *Journal of Child Psychology and Psychiatry, 32*, 233–255.

Barr, C. L., Wigg, K., Malone, M., Schachar, R., Tannock, R., Roberts, W., & Kennedy, J. L. (1999). Linkage study of catechol-O-methyltransferase and attention-deficit hyperactivity disorder. *American Journal of Medical Genetics, 88*, 710–713.

Barr, C. L., Wigg, K. G., Bloom, S., Schachar, R., Tannock, R., Roberts, W., Malone, M., & Kennedy, J. L. (2000). Further evidence from haplotype analysis for linkage of the dopamine D4 receptor gene and attention-deficit hyperactivity disorder. *American Journal of Medical Genetics (Neuropsychiatric Genetics), 96*(3), 244–250.

Benjamin, J., Patterson, C., Greenberg, B. D., Murphy, D. L., & Hamer, D. H. (1996). Population and familial association between the D4 dopamine receptor gene and measures of novelty seeking. *Nature Genetics, 12*, 81–84.

Biederman, J., Milberger, S., Faraone, S. V., Kiely, K., Guite, J., Mick, E., Ablon, S., Warburton, R., & Reed, E. (1995). Family-environment risk factors for attention deficit hyperactivity disorder: A test of Rutter's indicators of adversity. *Archives of General Psychiatry, 52*, 464–470.

Biederman, J., Milberger, S. V., Faraone, S., Kiely, K., Guide, J., Mick, E., Ablon, S., Warburton, R., Reed, E., & Davis, S. (1995). Impact of adversity on functioning and comorbidity in children with attention-deficit hyperactivity disorder. *Journal of the American Academy of Child and Adolescent Psychiatry, 34*, 1495–1503.

Blanz, B., Schmidt, M. H., & Esser, G. (1991). Familial adversities and child psychiatric disorders. *Journal of Child Psychology and Psychiatric Disorders, 32*, 939–950.

Castellanos, F. X., Lau, E., Tayebi, N., Lee, P., Long, R. E., Giedd, J. N., Sharp, W., Marsh, W. L., Walter, J. M., Hamburger, S. D., Ginns, E. I., Rapoport, J. L., & Sidransky, E. (1998). Lack of an association between a dopamine-4 receptor polymorphism and attention-deficit/hyperactivity disorder: Genetic and brain morphometric analyses. *Molecular Psychiatry, 3*, 431–434.

Chandola, C., Robling, M., Peters, T., Melville-Thomas, G., & McGuffin, P. (1992). Pre- and perinatal factors and the risk of subsequent referral for hyperactivity. *Child Psychology and Psychiatry, 33*, 1077–1090.

Comings, D., Gade-Andavolu, R., Gonzalez, N., Blake, H., & MacMurray, J. (1999). Additive effect of three naradenergic genes (ADRA2A, ADRA2C, DBH) on attention-deficit hyperactivity disorder and learning disabilities on Tourette syndrome subjects. *Clinical Genetics, 55*, 160–172.

Comings, D. E., Comings, B. G., Muhleman, D., Dietz, G., Shahbahrami, B., Tast, D., Knell, E., Kocsis, P., Baumgarten, R., Kovacs, B. W., Levy, D. L., Smith, M., Borison, R. L., Evans, D. D., Klein, D. N., MacMurray, J., Tosk, J. M., Sverd, J., Gysin, R., & Flanagan, S. D. (1991). The dopamine D2 receptor locus as a modifying gene in neuropsychiatric disorders. *Journal of the American Medical Association, 266,* 1793–1800.

Comings, D. E., Gonzalez, N., Wu, S., Gade, R., Muhleman, D., Saucier, G., Johnson, P., Verde, R., Rosenthal, R. J., Lesieur, H. R., Rugle, L. J., Miller, W. R., & MacMurray, J. P. (1999). Studies of the 48 bp repeat polymorphism of the DRD4 gene in impulsive, compulsive, addictive behaviors: Tourette syndrome, ADHD, pathological gambling, and substance abuse. *American Journal of Medical Genetics (Neuropsychiatric Genetics),* **88,** 358–368.

Conners, C. K. (1975). Controlled trial of methylphenidate in preschool children with minimal brain dysfunction. *International Journal of Mental Health,* 4, 61–74.

Conners, C. K. (1980). *Food additives and hyperactive children.* New York: Plenum.

Cook, E. H., Stein M. A., Krasowski, M. D., Cox, N. J., Olkon, D. M., Kieffer, J. E., & Leventhal, B. L. (1995). Association of attention deficit disorder and the dopamine transporter gene. *American Journal of Human Genetics,* **56,** 993–998.

Daly, G., Hawi, Z., Fitzgerald, M., & Gill, M. (1998). Attention deficit hyperactivity disorder: Association with the dopamine transporter (DATI) but not with the dopamine D4 receptor (DRD4). *American Journal of Medical Genetics, Neuropsychiatric Genetics,* **81,** 501.

Denson, R., Nanson, J., & McWatters, J. (1975). Hyperkinesis and maternal smoking. *Canadian Psychiatric Association Journal,* **20,** 183–187.

Deutsch, C. K., Matthysse, S., Swanson, J. M., & Farkas, L. G. (1990). Genetic latent structure analysis of dysmorphology in attention deficit disorder. *Journal of the American Academy of Child and Adolescent Psychiatry,* **29,** 189–194.

Dougherty, D. D., Bonab, A. A., Spencer, T. J., Rauch, S. L., Madras, B. K., & Fischman, A. J. (1999). Dopamine transporter density is elevated in patients with ADHD. *Lancet,* **354,** 2132–2133.

Dulawa, S. C., Grandy, D. K., Low, M. J., Paulus, M. P., & Geyer, M. A. (1999). Dopamine D4 receptor-knock-out mice exhibit reduced exploration of novel stimuli. *Journal of Neuroscience,* **19,** 9550–9556.

Ebstein, R. P., Novick, O., Umansky, R., Priel, B., Osher, Y., Blaine, D., Bennett, E. R., Nemanov, L., Katz, M., & Belmaker, R. H. (1996). Dopamine D4 receptor (D4DR) exon III polymorphism associated with the human personality trait of novelty seeking. *Nature Genetics,* **12,** 78–80.

Eisenberg, J., Mei-Tal, G., Steinberg, A., Tartakovsky, E., Zohar, A., Gritsenko, I., Nemanov, L., & Ebstein, R. P. (1999). Haplotype relative risk study of catechol-*O*-methyltransferase (COMT) and attention deficit hyperactivity disorder (ADHD): Association of the high-enzyme activity Val allele with ADHD impulsive-hyperactive phenotype. *American Journal of Medical Genetics,* **88,** 497–502.

Eisenberg, J., Zohar, A., Mei-Tal, G., Steinberg, A., Tartakovsky, E., Gritsenko, I., Nemanov, L., & Ebstein, R. P. (2000). A haplotype relative risk study of the dopamine D4 receptor (DRD4) exon III repeat polymorphism and attention deficit hyperactivity disorder (ADHD). *American Journal of Medical Genetics (Neuropsychiatric Genetics),* **96**(3), 258–261.

Faraone, S., Biederman, J., Chen, W. J., Krifcher, B., Keenan, K., Moore, C., Sprich, S., & Tsuang, M. (1992). Segregation analysis of attention deficit hyperactivity disorder: Evidence for single gene transmission. *Psychiatric Genetics,* 2, 257–275.

Faraone, S. V. (1999). A family based association study of the DAT and DRD4 genes in ADHD. Presented at the World Congress of Psychiatric Genetics. Monterey, CA.

Faraone, S. V., & Biederman, J. (1998). Neurobiology of attention-deficit hyperactivity disorder. *Biological Psychiatry,* **44,** 951–958.

Faraone, S. B., Biederman, J., Weiffenbach, B., Keith, T., Chu, M. P., Weaver, A., Spencer, T. J., Wilens, T. E., Frazier, J., Cleves, M., & Sakai, J. (1999). Dopamine

D4 gene 7-repeat allele and attention deficit hyperactivity disorder. *American Journal of Psychiatry,* **156,** 768–770.

Faraone, S. V., & Doyle, A. (in press). The nature and heritability of attention deficit hyperactivity disorder. In R. Todd (Ed.), *Genetic contributions to early onset psychopathology.* Philadelphia, PA: W. B. Saunders.

Faraone, S. V., Tsuang, D., & Tsuang, M. T. (1999). *Genetics and mental disorders: A guide for students, clinicians, and researchers.* New York: Guilford.

Gill, M., Daly, G., Heron, S., Hawi, Z., & Fitzgerald, M. (1997). Confirmation of association between attention deficit hyperactivity disorder and a dopamine transporter polymorphism. *Molecular Psychiatry,* **2,** 311–313.

Gottesman, I. I., & Bertelsen, A. (1996). Legacy of German psychiatric genetics: Hindsight is always 20/20. *American Journal of Medical Genetics,* **67,** 317–322.

Hartsough, C. S., & Lambert, N. M. (1985). Medical factors in hyperactive and normal children: Prenatal, developmental, and health history findings. *American Journal of Orthopsychiatry,* **55,** 191–201.

Hawi, Z., McCarron, M., Kirley, A., Fitzgerald, M., & Gill, M. (2000). No association of dopamine DRD4 receptor gene polymorphism in Attention Deficit Hyperactivity disorder in the Irish population. *American Journal of Medical Genetics (Neuropsychiatric Genetics).*

Hawi, Z., Millar, N., Daly, G., Fitzgerald, M., & Gill, M. (2000). No association between Catechol-O-methyltransferase (COMT) gene polymorphism and ADHD in an Irish sample. *American Journal of Medical Genetics (Neuropsychiatric Genetics),* **96**(3), 241–243.

Hetherington, E. M., Cox, M., & Cox, R. (1982). Effects of divorce on parents and children. In M. Lamb (Ed.), *Non-traditional families* (pp. 223–285). Hillsdale, NJ: Erlbaum.

Institute of Medicine. (1989). *Research on children and adolescents with mental, behavioral and developmental disorders.* Washington, DC: National Academy Press.

Jiang, S., Xin, R., Wu, X., Lin, S., Qian, Y., Ren, D., Tang, G., & Wang, D. (2000). Association between attention deficit disorder and the DXS7 locus. *Neuropsychiatric Genetics.*

Joseph, J. (2000). Not in their genes: A critical view of the genetics of attention deficit hyperactivity disorder. *Developmental Review,* **20,** 539–567.

LaHoste, G. J., Swanson, J. M., Wigal, S. B., Glabe, C., Wigal, T., King, N., & Kennedy, J. L. (1996). Dopamine D4 receptor gene polymorphism is associated with attention deficit hyperactivity disorder. *Molecular Psychiatry,* **1,** 121–124.

Lopera, F., Palacio, L. G., Jimenez, I., Villegas, P., Puerta, I. C., Pineda, D., Jimenez, M., & Arcos-Burgos, M. (1999). [Discrimination between genetic factors in attention deficit] *Revista de Neurologia,* **28,** 660–664.

Majzoub, J., & Muglia, L. (1996). Knockout mice. *The New England Journal of Medicine,* **334,** 904–907.

Manji, H. K., Moore, G. J., & Chen, G. (1999). Lithium at 50: Have the neuroprotective effects of this unique cation been overlooked? *Biological Psychiatry,* **46,** 929–940.

Meehl, P. E. (1973). Specific genetic etiology, psychodynamics, and therapeutic nihilism. In *Psychodiagnosis: Selected papers* (pp. 182–199). New York: Norton.

Milberger, S., Biederman, J., Faraone, S., Chen, L., & Jones, J. (1996). Is maternal smoking during pregnancy a risk factor for attention deficit hyperactivity disorder in children? *American Journal of Psychiatry,* **153,** 1138–1142.

Milberger, S., Biederman, J., Faraone, S., Guite, J., & Tsuang, M. (1997). Pregnancy delivery and infancy complications and ADHD: Issues of gene-environment interactions. *Biological Psychiatry,* **41,** 65–75.

Morrison, J. R., & Stewart, M. A. (1974). Bilateral inheritance as evidence for polygenicity in the hyperactive child syndrome. *Journal of Nervous and Mental Disease,* **158,** 226–228.

Needleman, H. L. (1982). The neuropsychiatric implications of low level exposure to lead. *Psychological Medicine, 12*, 461–463.

Nichols, P. L., & Chen, T. C. (1981). *Minimal brain dysfunction: A prospective study.* Hillsdale, NJ: Erlbaum.

Offord, D. R., Boyle, M. H., Racine, Y. A., Fleming, J. E., Cadman, D. T., Blum, H. M., Byrne, C., Links, P. S., Lipman, E. L., & Macmillan, H. L. (1992). Outcome, prognosis and risk in a longitudinal follow-up study. *Journal of the American Academy of Child and Adolescent Psychiatry, 31*, 916–923.

Palfrey, J. S., Levine, M. D., Walker, D. K., & Sullivan, M. (1985). The emergence of attention deficits in early childhood: A prospective study. *Developmental and Behavioral Pediatrics, 6*, 339–348.

Poulton, K., Holmes, J., Hever, T., Trumper, A., Fitzpatrick, H., McGuffin, P., Owen, M., Worthington, J., Ollier, W., Harrington, R., & Thapar, A. (1998). A molecular genetic study of hyperkinetic disorder/attention deficit hyperactivity disorder. *American Journal of Medical Genetics, Neuropsychiatric Genetics, 81*, 458.

Rowe, D. C., Stever, C., Giedinghagen, L. N., Gard, J. M., Cleveland, H. H., Terris, S. T., Mohr, J. H., Sherman, S., Abramowitz, A., & Waldman, I. D. (1998). Dopamine DRD4 receptor polymorphism and attention deficit hyperactivity disorder. *Molecular Psychiatry, 3*, 419–426.

Rubinstein, M., Phillips, T. J., Bunzow, J. R., Falzone, T. L., Dziewczapolski, G., Zhang, G., Fang, Y., Larson, J. L., McDougall, J. A., Chester, J. A., Saez, C., Pugsley, T. A., Gershanik, O., Low, M. J., & Grandy, D. K. (1997). Mice lacking dopamine D4 receptors are supersensitive to ethanol, cocaine, and methamphetamine. *Cell, 90*, 991–1001.

Rutter, M., Cox, A., Tupling, C., Berger, M., & Yule, W., (1975). Attainment and adjustment in two geographical areas: Vol. 1. The prevalence of psychiatric disorders. *British Journal of Psychiatry, 126*, 493–509.

Smalley, S. L., Bailey, J. N., Palmer, C. G., Cantwell, D. P., McGough, J. J., Del'Homme, M. A., Asarnow, J. R., Woodward, J. A., Ramsey, C., & Nelson, S. F. (1998). Evidence that the dopamine D4 receptor is a susceptibility gene in attention deficit hyperactivity disorder. *Molecular Psychiatry, 3*, 427–430.

Sprich-Buckminster, S., Biederman, J., Milberger, S., Faraone, S., & Krifcher Lehman, B. (1993). Are perinatal complications relevant to the manifestation of ADD? Issues of comorbidity and familiality. *Journal of the American Academy of Child and Adolescent Psychiatry, 32*, 1032–1037.

Swanson, J., Castellanos, F., Murias, M., LaHoste, G., & Kennedy, J. (1998). Cognitive neuroscience of attention deficit hyperactivity disorder and hyperkinetic disorder. *Current Opinion in Neurobiology, 8*, 263–271.

Swanson, J. M., Sunohara, G. A., Kennedy, J. L., Regino, R., Fineberg, E., Wigal, T., Lerner, M., Williams, L., LaHoste, G. J., & Wigal, S. (1998). Association of the dopamine receptor D4 (DRD4) gene with a refined phenotype of attention deficit hyperactivity disorder (ADHD): A family-based approach. *Molecular Psychiatry, 3*, 38–41.

Tahir, E., Curran, S., Yazgan, Y., Ozbay, F., Cirakoglu, B., & Asherson, P. J. (2000). No association between low and high activity catecholamine-methl-transferase (COMT) and Attention deficit hyperactivity disorder (ADHD) in a sample of Turkish children. *American Journal of Medical Genetics (Neuropsychiatric Genetics), 96*(3), 285–288.

Thapar, A., Hervas, A., & McGuffin, P. (1995). Childhood hyperactivity scores are highly heritable and show sibling competition effects: Twin study evidence. *Behavior Genetics, 25*, 537–544.

Thapar, A., Holmes, J., Poulton, K., & Harrington, R. (1999). Genetic basis of attention deficit and hyperactivity. *British Journal of Psychiatry, 174*, 105–111.

Tsuang, M. T., Faraone, S. V., & Green, A. L. (1999). Schizophrenia and other psychotic disorders. In M. Amand & J. Nicholi (Eds.), *The Harvard guide to psychiatry.* Cambridge, MA: Harvard Univ. Press.

Waldman, I. D., Rowe, D. C., Abramowitz, A., Kozel, S. T., Mohr, J. H., Sherman, S. L., Cleveland, H. H., Sanders, M. L., Gard, J. M., & Stever, C. (1998). Association and linkage of the dopamine transporter gene and attention-deficit hyperactivity disorder in children: Heterogeneity owing to diagnostic subtype and severity. *American Journal of Human Genetics, 63*, 1767–1776.

Winsberg, B. G., & Comings, D. E. (1999). Association of the dopamine transporter gene (DAT1) with poor methylphenidate response [see comments]. *Journal of the American Academy of Child and Adolescent Psychiatry, 38*, 1474–1477.

Wolraich, M., Wilson, D., & White, W. (1995). The effect of sugar on behavior or cognition in children. *Journal of the American Medical Association, 274*, 1617–1621.

Wyman, P. A., Cowen, E. L., Work, W. C., Raoof, A., Gribble, P. A., Parker, G. R., & Wannon, M. (1992). Interviews with children who experienced major life stress: Family and child attributes that predict resilient outcomes. *Journal of the American Academy of Child and Adolescent Psychiatry, 31*, 904–911.

CHALLENGE QUESTIONS

Are Genetic Explanations of Attention Deficit Hyperactivity Disorder Faulty?

1. What do you think is the best way for parents to view their ADHD children, from Joseph's perspective or from Faraone and Biederman's perspective? What are the advantages and disadvantages of each perspective from the viewpoint of a parent?
2. A pivotal point in this issue is the presence (or absence) of a mind/body connection. What is the current thinking on this connection in medicine? In philosophy? In psychology?
3. What do you think about the movement toward biological explanations in psychology? What are the advantages and disadvantages of this trend in psychology?
4. What implications does this issue have for the free will and determinism of ADHD children? That is, would a perspective that says ADHD is genetically caused (even if it is also caused by the environment) mean that the actions of ADHD children are determined (not within their control)? If so, what implications would a lack of control have?

Families and Work Institute

This Web site provides resources from the Families and Work Institute, which conducts policy research on issues related to the changing workforce and operates a national clearinghouse on work and family life.

http://www.familiesandwork.org/index.html

Childcare Resource and Research Unit

The Childcare Resource and Research Unit, which is part of the Centre for Urban and Community Studies at the University of Toronto, focuses on early childhood care and education research and policy. The research section contains information about new research findings and news about ongoing research.

http://www.childcarecanada.org

Children of Divorce: All Kinds of Problems

This Americans for Divorce Reform page offers links to studies of problems experienced by children of divorce.

http://www.divorcereform.org/all.html

Tufts University Child & Family Web Guide

This page links to a handful of quality sites on divorce.

http://cfw.tufts.edu/viewtopics.asp?
categoryid=2&topicid=32

The Psi Cafe: A Psychology Resource Site

This site discusses different aspects of psychological research and provides helpful links to other sites that focus on becoming a more effective parent.

http://www.psy.pdx.edu/PsiCafe/Areas/
Developmental/Parenting/

PART 3

Human Development

*T*he objective of most developmental psychologists is to document the course of our physical, social, and intellectual changes over the entire span of our lives. Childhood has probably received the most attention because it is often thought to set the stage for rest of human development. For instance, in an effort to ensure healthy childhood development many parents and educators shower their children with praise. But is it possible this kind of constant positive reinforcement does more harm than good? In addition to parenting methods, researchers are also investigating how mothers working and divorce affects children and their development. More mothers than ever are choosing careers over homemaking and are doing so earlier than ever before. Does their absence harm their children? Divorce, too, has changed the traditional nuclear family dynamic. Is it possible that the affects of divorce on a child's life could remain into adulthood?

- Does Giving Praise Harm Children?

- Does a Mother's Employment Harm Her Children?

- Does the Divorce of Parents Harm Their Children?

ISSUE 6

Does Giving Praise Harm Children?

YES: Alfie Kohn, from "Five Reasons to Stop Saying 'Good Job!'" *Young Children* (September 2001)

NO: Phillip S. Strain and Gail E. Joseph, from "A Not So Good Job With 'Good Job': A Response to Kohn 2001," *Journal of Positive Behavior Interventions* (Winter 2004)

ISSUE SUMMARY

YES: Popular author and lecturer Alfie Kohn lists five reasons why parents and educators should discontinue using praise to motivate children and offers several suggestions about how to more appropriately help children appreciate their own accomplishments.

NO: Professor of educational psychology Phillip S. Strain and assistant research professor Gail E. Joseph contend positive reinforcement is a time-tested and scientifically sound way to teach children the difference between good and bad behavior and to help them develop a healthy sense of self-worth.

You have been entrusted with the care of your best friend's daughter. If she cleans up her toys without being asked, what do you do to ensure this kind of behavior will continue? Most people attempt to encourage a child's positive behavior with what behaviorists call "positive reinforcement" (i.e., praise), but is this effective? There are those who feel that children depend too much on praise and reinforcement and have difficulty functioning when it is not available.

Some psychological research tends to support these problems with positive reinforcement. This research seems to indicate that the more people are externally rewarded for performing a task, the more they will lose motivation and interest in that task. Moreover, these problems are not just motivational; positive reinforcement also affects behavior. Unless a person is somehow intrinsically or internally rewarded for performing a certain task, his or her behavioral performance of that task will also decrease when external rewards are absent. Consequently, many scholars favor helping children to develop their own (intrinsic) desire to behave, rather than rewarding good behavior extrinsically by providing praise.

Alfie Kohn, in the first article, proves that he is one of those scholars. He claims that praising children can be detrimental to their healthy development. Kohn insists that giving praise is a manipulative tool used to tailor a child's behavior to what is most convenient for the praise-giver. In addition, Kohn feels consistent praise turns kids into praise junkies who consistently under-perform, unless praised, and lose interest in the behavior for which they are being praised. As an alternative to praising, Kohn suggests parents and educators simply state what they see, ask questions, or say nothing at all in order to help children develop genuine personal interests and become intrinsically motivated to behave and achieve.

In opposition to Kohn, Phillip S. Strain and Gail E. Joseph claim positive reinforcement can be a valuable tool for teaching children the difference between good and bad behavior. They feel abandoning it would only rob children of the emotional support they need to properly develop. They also object to Kohn's critique of praise "manipulation." They argue that this critique is not scientifically based, especially in comparison to the time- and scientifically tested success of positive reinforcement. Additionally, Strain and Joseph balk at Kohn's suggestion that parents, childcare providers, and teachers have self-serving motives for giving praise. In these authors' eyes, this suggestion is as an unwarranted slap in the face for those most concerned with the welfare of children.

POINT

- Praise is manipulative and more for a parent's convenience than for a child's education.
- Praise makes children dependent on an external reward structure.
- Praise is a value judgment that steals the pleasure found in success.
- Children lose interest in a task they are consistently praised for performing.
- Praise can reduce achievement.

COUNTERPOINT

- Praise is both convenient for the parent and an effective way to encourage proper childhood development.
- Scientific data support the proper use of praise to help children gain independence.
- It is unreasonable to expect young children to develop social and emotional skills without some external support and validation.
- Praise increases the likelihood a child will repeat a desired action.
- Praise strengthens behavior.

Alfie Kohn  **YES**

Five Reasons to Stop Saying "Good Job!"

Hang out at a playground, visit a school, or show up at a child's birthday party, and there's one phrase you can count on hearing repeatedly: "Good job!" Even tiny infants are praised for smacking their hands together ("Good clapping!"). Many of us blurt out these judgments of children to the point that it has become almost a verbal tic.

Plenty of books and articles advise us against relying on punishment, from spanking to forcible isolation (time-out). Occasionally someone will even ask us to rethink the practice of bribing children with stickers or food. But it's much harder to find a discouraging word about what is euphemistically called positive reinforcement.

Lest there be any misunderstanding, the point here is not to call into question the importance of supporting and encouraging children, the need to love them and hug them and help them feel good about themselves. Praise, however, is a different story entirely. Here's why.

1. Manipulating Children

Suppose you offer a verbal reward to reinforce the behavior of a child who cleans up her art supplies. Who benefits from this? Is it possible that telling kids they've done a good job may have less to do with their emotional needs than with our convenience?

Rheta DeVries, a professor of education at the University of Northern Iowa, refers to this as "sugar-coated control." Very much like tangible rewards—or, for that matter, punishments—it's a way of doing something *to* children to get them to comply with our wishes. It may be effective at producing this result (at least for a while), but it's very different from working *with* kids—for example, by engaging them in conversation about what makes a classroom function smoothly or how other people are affected by what we have done (or failed to do). The latter approach is not only more respectful but more likely to help kids become thoughtful people.

The reason praise can work in the short run is that young children are hungry for our approval. But we have a responsibility not to exploit that dependence for our own convenience. A "Good job!" to reinforce something that makes our lives a little easier can be an example of taking advantage of children's dependence. Kids may also come to feel manipulated by this, even if they can't quite explain why.

2. Creating Praise Junkies

To be sure, not every use of praise is a calculated tactic to control children's behavior. Sometimes we compliment kids just because we're genuinely pleased by what they've done. Even then, however, it's worth looking more closely. Rather than bolstering children's self-esteem, praise may increase kids' dependence on us. The more we say, "I like the way you . . ." or "Good . . . ing," the more kids come to rely on *our* evaluations, *our* decisions about what's good and bad, rather than learning to form their own judgments. It leads them to measure their worth in terms of what will lead *us* to smile and dole out some more approval.

Mary Budd Rowe, a researcher at the University of Florida, discovered that students who were praised lavishly by their teachers were more tentative in their responses, more apt to answer in a questioning tone of voice ("Um, seven?"). They tended to back off from an idea they had proposed as soon as an adult disagreed with them. And they were less likely to persist with difficult tasks or share their ideas with other students.

In short, "Good job!" doesn't reassure children; ultimately, it makes them feel less secure. It may even create a vicious circle such that the more we slather on the praise, the more kids seem to need it, so we praise them some more. Sadly, some of these kids will grow into adults who continue to need someone else to pat them on the head and tell them that what they did was OK. Surely this is not what we want for our daughters and sons.

3. Stealing a Child's Pleasure

Apart from the issue of dependence, a child deserves to take delight in her accomplishments, to feel pride in what she's learned how to do. She also deserves to decide when to feel that way. Every time we say, "Good job!" though, we're telling a child how to feel.

To be sure, there are times when our evaluations are appropriate and our guidance is necessary—especially with toddlers and preschoolers. But a constant stream of value judgments is neither necessary nor useful for children's development. Unfortunately, we may not have realized that "Good job!" is just as much an evaluation as "Bad job!" The most notable feature of a positive judgment isn't that it's positive, but that it's a judgment. And people, including kids, don't like being judged.

I cherish the occasions when my daughter manages to do something for the first time or does something better than she's ever done it before. But I try to resist the knee-jerk tendency to say, "Good job!" because I don't want to dilute her joy. I want her to share her pleasure with me, not look to me for a verdict. I want her to exclaim, "I did it!" (which she often does) instead of asking me uncertainly, "Was that good?"

4. Losing Interest

"Good painting!" may get children to keep painting for as long as we keep watching and praising. But, warns Lilian Katz, "once attention is withdrawn, many kids won't touch the activity again." Indeed, an impressive body of scientific research has shown that the more we reward people for doing something, the more they tend to lose interest in whatever they had to do to get the reward. Now the point isn't to draw, to read, to think, to create—the point is to get the goody, whether it's an ice cream, a sticker, or a "Good job!"

In a troubling study conducted by Joan Grusec at the University of Toronto, young children who were frequently praised for displays of generosity tended to be slightly *less* generous on an everyday basis than other children were. Every time they had heard "Good sharing!" or "I'm so proud of you for helping," they became a little less interested in sharing or helping. Those actions came to be seen not as something valuable in their own right but as something they had to do to get that reaction again from an adult. Generosity became a means to an end.

Does praise motivate kids? Sure. It motivates kids to get praise. Alas, that's often at the expense of commitment to whatever they were doing that prompted the praise.

5. Reducing Achievement

As if it weren't bad enough that "Good job!" can undermine independence, pleasure, and interest, it can also interfere with how good a job children actually do. Researchers keep finding that kids who are praised for doing well at a creative task tend to stumble at the next task—and they don't do as well as children who weren't praised to begin with.

Why does this happen? Partly because the praise creates pressure to "keep up the good work" that gets in the way of doing so. Partly because their *interest* in what they're doing may have declined. Partly because they become less likely to take risks—a prerequisite for creativity—once they start thinking about how to keep those positive comments coming.

More generally, "Good job!" is a remnant of an approach to psychology that reduces all of human life to behaviors that can be seen and measured. Unfortunately, this ignores the thoughts, feelings, and values that lie behind behaviors. For example, a child may share a snack with a friend as a way of attracting praise or as a way of making sure the other child has enough to eat. Praise for sharing ignores these different motives. Worse, it actually promotes the less desirable motive by making children more likely to fish for praise in the future.

❧❦❧

Once you start to see praise for what it is—and what it does—these constant little evaluative eruptions from adults start to produce the same effect as fingernails being dragged down a blackboard. You begin to root for a child to give his teacher a taste of her own treacle by turning around and saying (in the same saccharine tone of voice), "Good praising!"

Still, it's not an easy habit to break. It can seem strange, at least at first, to stop praising; it can feel as though you're being chilly or withholding something. But that, it soon becomes clear, suggests that *we praise more because we need to say it than because children need to hear it.* Whenever that's true, it's time to rethink what we're doing.

What kids do need is unconditional support—love with no strings attached. That's not just different from praise, it's the *opposite* of praise. "Good job!" is conditional. It means we're offering attention and acknowledgment and approval for jumping through our hoops, for doing things that please us.

This point, you'll notice, is very different from a criticism that some people offer to the effect that we give kids too much approval or give it too easily. They recommend that we become more miserly with our praise and demand that kids "earn" it. But the real problem isn't that children expect to be praised for everything they do these days. It's that *we're* tempted to take shortcuts, to manipulate kids with rewards instead of explaining and helping them to develop needed skills and good values.

So, what's the alternative? That depends on the situation. But whatever we decide to say instead has to be offered in the context of genuine affection and love for who kids are rather than for what they've done. When unconditional support is present, "Good job!" isn't necessary; when it's absent, "Good job!" won't help.

If we're praising positive actions as a way of discouraging misbehavior, this strategy is unlikely to be effective for long. Even when it works, we can't really say the child is now "behaving himself"; it would be more accurate to say the praise is behaving him. The alternative is to work *with* the child, to figure out the reasons he's acting that way. We may have to reconsider our own requests rather than just looking for a way to get kids to obey. (Instead of using "Good job!" to get a four-year-old to sit quietly through a long class meeting, perhaps we should ask whether it's reasonable to expect a child to do so.)

We also need to bring kids in on the process of making decisions. If a child is doing something that disturbs others, then sitting down with her later and asking, "What do you think we can do to solve this problem?" will likely be more effective than bribes or threats. It also helps a child learn how to solve problems and teaches her that her ideas and feelings are important. Of course, this process takes time and talent, care and courage. Tossing off a "Good job!" when the child acts in the way we deem appropriate takes none of those things, which helps to explain why "doing to" strategies are a lot more popular than "working with" strategies.

And what can we say when kids just do something impressive? Consider three possible responses:

- **Say nothing.** Some people insist a helpful act must be reinforced because, secretly or unconsciously, they believe it was a fluke. If children are basically evil, then they have to be given an artificial reason for being nice (namely, to get a verbal reward). But if that cynicism is unfounded—and a lot of research suggests that it is—then praise may not be necessary.

- **Say what you saw.** A simple, evaluation-free statement ("You put your shoes on by yourself" or even just "You did it") tells a child that you noticed. It also lets her take pride in what she did. In other cases, a more elaborate description may make sense. If a child draws a picture, you might provide feedback—not judgment—about what you notice: "This mountain is huge!" "Boy, you sure used a lot of purple today!"

    If a child does something caring or generous, you might gently draw his attention to the effect of his action *on the other person:* "Look at Abigail's face! She seems pretty happy now that you gave her some of your snack." This is completely different from praise, where the emphasis is on how *you* feel about her sharing.

- **Talk less, ask more.** Even better than descriptions are questions. Why tell a child what part of his drawing most impressed *you* when you can ask him what *he* likes best about it? Asking "What was the hardest part to draw?" or "How did you figure out how to make the feet the right size?" is likely to nourish his interest in drawing. Saying "Good job!" as we've seen, may have exactly the opposite effect.

This doesn't mean that all compliments, all thank-you's, all expressions of delight are harmful. We need to consider our *motives* for what we say (a genuine expression of enthusiasm is better than a desire to manipulate the child's future behavior) as well as the actual *effects* of doing so. Are our reactions helping the child to feel a sense of control over her life—or to constantly look to us for approval? Are they helping her to become more excited about what she's doing in its own right—or turning it into something she just wants to get through in order to receive a pat on the head?

It's not a matter of memorizing a new script, but of keeping in mind our long-term goals for our children and watching for the effects of what we say. The bad news is that the use of positive reinforcement really isn't so positive. The good news is that you don't have to evaluate in order to encourage.

NO

**Phillip S. Strain and
Gail E. Joseph**

A Not So Good Job with "Good Job": A Response to Kohn 2001

The field of early intervention has long been involved in a heated debate between proponents of behavioral teaching strategies and professionals against it. This debate has become more focused and clearly more relevant to the quality of services afforded to young children with special needs because more of these youngsters are being served in typical early-care and education settings. Not only are more children with special needs being served in these settings, but recent national survey data have suggested that the number of children who engage in challenging behaviors is increasing also.

Given the increasing number of typical early-care and general education providers who are intimately involved in the education and care of young children with special needs, it is particularly disturbing to note that a major professional journal serving this group (*Young Children*) recently published an article that blatantly misrepresented behavioral teaching strategies and was openly hostile to adults who use praise. The case-in-point is the article by Kohn, "Five Reasons to Stop Saying, 'Good Job.'"

In September of 2001, more than 100,000 early childhood professionals received a copy of *Young Children* with the following banner header: "What really happens when children hear 'good job.'" Since then, we have had numerous experiences in which educators in inclusive settings have asserted that they no longer use "manipulative, demeaning" behavioral practices since being enlightened by Kohn's article. Briefly, Kohn suggested that there are five reasons not to say, "Good job," that is, not to use praise. These are as follows:

1. It represents manipulation of children in order to maximize adult convenience.
2. It creates "praise junkies."
3. It steals the child's pleasure by telling him or her how to feel.
4. It results in less interest, not more.
5. It reduces achievement.

Moreover, Kohn took the opportunity to question the ethics and motivation of persons who use praise.

From *Journal of Positive Behavior Interventions*, vol. 1, no. 1, Winter 2004, pp. 55–59. Copyright © 2004 by Pro-Ed, Inc. Reprinted by permission. References omitted.

First, let us state from the outset that we are not universal apologists for behavioral interventions in general, for those persons who practice them, or for positive reinforcement strategies per se. Certainly, there are examples to which most of us can point where positive reinforcement has been used haphazardly and inappropriately. Also, there certainly are examples of so-called child-focused interventions being misused. What is most disturbing about Kohn's article is that the author misrepresents behavioral interventions, depreciates professionals who use them (a strange choice, given the overall humanistic tone of the article), and specifically distorts positive reinforcement. Moreover, it has been our experience that Kohn's article has been widely circulated and used as "evidence" for ending use of social praise. We argue here that Kohn's article is misleading, does not accurately depict the available evidence on positive reinforcement, demeans children and practitioners, and—worst of all—may serve to limit the use of a powerful, evidence-based practice for facilitating children's development. In organizing our response, we critique his five reasons to stop saying, "Good job." Finally, we suggest that Kohn's position is harmful to children, families, and the professionals who serve them.

Response to Kohn's Five Reasons

In the following, we address each of the reasons Kohn provides for not saying, "Good job."

Manipulating Children

Kohn's first reason for stopping the use of praise is that it is manipulative and serves the purposes of adults only. No one would disagree that willfully setting out to manipulate children so that they engage in behaviors that are developmentally inappropriate and nonfunctional is wrong. Kohn offered two examples of such potential manipulation. First, he took issue with adults reinforcing a 2-year-old for eating without spilling. He then took issue with adults reinforcing a 5-year-old for cleaning up art supplies. Who are these people who willfully and purposefully set out to manipulate children for their convenience? Given the examples, perhaps it is parents who wish to encourage some social graces or fine-motor skills in their toddler, or perhaps it is all care providers who have a "clean-up" activity after choice time in preschool. Kohn asked if this adult behavior has less to do with the emotional needs of children than with adult convenience. We ask, is it not possible that the children in both examples would acquire valuable skills and that adults and other children in these settings would benefit as well? Beyond these examples, is it not true that children, family members, peers, and caregivers all benefit when intentional teaching results in more independence, more communication skills, more social skills, and an increased ability to self-manage behavior?

Kohn proposed that instead of using praise, one should have a conversation with children about what makes a classroom or family function smoothly or how other people are affected by what we have done or failed to do. This conversational alternative is not incompatible with the use of praise;

however, having such a conversation immediately after the problem behavior occurs could serve to reinforce the behavior. In addition, this conversational alternative is developmentally inappropriate for very young children, for many children with special needs, and for any child who does not have the language and cognitive capacity to (a) understand what a smoothly running classroom or family might look like, (b) understand retrospectively how his or her behavior might have affected someone, and (c) independently generate behavior alternatives. In short, Kohn seems to have offered an intervention alternative of minimal applicability.

Finally, we agree here with Kohn that the use of "Good job" or any other form of positive reinforcement used to exploit children is totally unacceptable. But, what if reinforcement is used successfully to teach creativity in toy play, to make choices, or to solve interpersonal conflicts? An impressive body of literature has demonstrated that these outcomes have been achieved through the use of positive reinforcement strategies.

Creating Praise Junkies

Kohn asserted that positive reinforcement may even create a vicious circle such that "the more we slather on praise, the more kids seem to need it, so we praise them some more." This assertion, should it be true, would indeed be troublesome. We could only find evidence that pointed to its inaccuracy, however. For example, there is a well-developed set of strategies for systematically reducing reinforcement over time and some three decades of research on its efficacy with children's behavior. Persistent, continuous positive reinforcement is not and should not be the norm. If Kohn has seen such, he has witnessed bad practice with an otherwise empirically validated technique. To banish the strategy because of its supposed misuse makes no more sense than to ban all surgery because some operations go awry.

Kohn also suggested that children who are frequently praised will have poor self-esteem and poor adult outcomes. We do not know the longitudinal data that suggest a spiral of emotional decay in children who are praised. To the contrary, one might consider the longitudinal data on children from abusive and neglectful circumstances as depicting the consequences of too little positive reinforcement. Or, we might consider the observational data on the advanced academic achievement and social competence of children in elementary school who receive the most praise. Relatedly, if Kohn were correct in his assertion, surely we would all know a troubled adolescent who got that way from too much praise early on in life. We have yet to run across such a person.

Stealing a Child's Pleasure

We agree with Kohn that children should take pleasure in their accomplishments. The real question is how to help children learn to take pleasure in accomplishments that are developmentally enhancing, prosocial, and supportive of others. From what is known about socialization, we contend that feedback from adults, some of which might include positive reinforcement, is the primary means by which children learn to take pride in those acts that reflect prosocial values. This adult-mediated process is also how the traditions of culture, language, community, and religion are transmitted from one generation to the next.

Kohn also expressed concern about the judgmental nature of "Good job." As the literature suggests, this phrase is but one example of adult behavior that could operate as positive reinforcement. Other nonevaluative statements, such as, "You helped your friend with her coat" or "You are using so many colors," have equal or greater potential because they are more descriptive and thus more likely to function as positive reinforcement. Not all phrases that function as positive reinforcement need to have an evaluative element, as Kohn implied.

We are also a bit puzzled as to why Kohn seemed so deeply concerned that children would come to care about what significant others see as important as a result of being given positive reinforcement. We couldn't disagree more. In fact, we think that an essential ingredient to positive parenting and effective teaching is communicating one's deeply held principles. Clearly, using positive reinforcement is one way to do just that.

We find a number of Kohn's other arguments in this section to be illogical. He suggested, for example, that there is equivalence in being told "Good job" and "Bad job." He then suggested that children do not like being told that they have done a good job. Presumably, this rejection of praise stems from the equivalence Kohn sees between being told one has done well and being told one has done poorly. The evidence, on the other hand, has suggested that children's immediate and long-term responses to positive feedback versus negative feedback are fundamentally different. Perhaps the best test for the validity of Kohn's assertion is simply to ask yourself how you react to positive feedback versus negative feedback on your job performance.

Finally, we are totally baffled by the seeming 180-degree turn of opinion regarding the use of positive reinforcement with young children. Kohn stated, "To be sure, there are times when our evaluations are appropriate and our guidance is necessary—especially with toddlers and preschoolers." We could not agree more.

Although it is somewhat lost in Kohn's mordant diatribe about stealing children's pleasure with praise, we think he is promoting the importance of children engaging in self-evaluation. We agree that being able to pass judgment on one's own behavior and feel pride in one's accomplishments without relying on external feedback is an important long-term goal. Perhaps children who come from family environments in which they have received large amounts of positive feedback and support will have the self-confidence and skills to begin to evaluate their own efforts early in life. Even in these cases, it is not developmentally appropriate to expect young children who are still developing social and emotional skills to be able to do this without some external support and validation. Furthermore, consider the child who comes from a family environment or childcare setting where he or she has experienced a great deal of negative feedback, rejection, or situations where adults, overwhelmed with other problems, were unable or unavailable to build positive relationships to foster self-confidence. In these situations, the child most likely has a negative self-evaluation and low self-esteem. If this child were left to his or her own devices to evaluate his or her work and behavior, the child probably would pronounce it to be worthless. Just as we teach preacademic skills to young children, we need to provide scaffolding for children to learn how to self-evaluate and self-praise. This is done by adults' providing children with positive feedback—modeling praise. This planned behavior by warm and responsive caregivers is necessary for young children until they begin to internalize the positive feedback and grow capable of realistic and constructive self-evaluation.

Losing Interest

Kohn was troubled by the possibility that praise would result in children working for the "goody" only. For us, the "goody" is positive child outcomes, and positive reinforcement has effectively been employed to meet these ends.

Kohn also suggested that praise motivates children to get more praise. What is true, based on hundreds of empirical demonstrations, is that praise (when it in fact operates as positive reinforcement) increases the likelihood that the prosocial behavior will increase in the future, not decrease, as Kohn suggested.

Perhaps a real teaching example is appropriate here. Suppose that a child comes to school not knowing how to share (an important skill for present and later life success). One strategy used to teach this skill might be positive reinforcement. That is, when the child is first learning to share toys and materials, the adults in the class are vigilant and try to provide positive comments when they see this behavior occurring. As is commonplace when children begin to use this friendship skill, sharing becomes reinforcing in and of itself, calling for adults to use less and less support to encourage this behavior.

Reducing Achievement

In a continuation of his confusion, Kohn suggested that "Good job" functions to diminish the behaviors it is intended to increase. Theoretically, saying "Good job" might serve to decrease the future likelihood of some behavior that it is contingent upon. However, the data suggest, without equivocation, that positive reinforcement only serves to strengthen behavior. Moreover, children who have received a lot of positive reinforcement are popular with other children because they utilize positive feedback in their interactions with others.

In this section, Kohn also argued that "Good job" is a remnant of an approach to psychology that reduces all of human life to behaviors that can be seen and measured. Unfortunately, this ignores the thoughts, feelings, and values that lie behind behaviors. We presume that Kohn refers to behaviorism, and he is wrong once again. It is not true that behaviorism rejects the existence of thoughts, feelings, and emotions. Moreover, behavioral intervention strategies involving teaching self-regulation of emotion and cognitive behavior modification rely greatly on the existence of these internal events. Rather than adopting Kohn's pejorative view, perhaps it is necessary to first consider that the environmental view promoted by behaviorism is essentially optimistic; it suggests that (except for gross genetic factors) all individuals possess roughly equal potential. Our society includes individuals who do not acquire essential developmental competencies, fail to make adequate adjustment to school, succeed at lower levels in vocational settings, and experience little happiness as adults; unfortunately, these poor outcomes are often associated with factors such as disability, race, and socioeconomic status. Rather than assuming that these individuals lack some essential internal characteristics, behaviorists assume that the poor outcomes originate in the ways the environment and experience shaped the individual's current behavior. Once these environmental and experiential factors are identified, we can design prevention and intervention programs to improve the outcomes for individuals who should, on every other basis, have opportunities for good development, success, and adjustment. Thus, the emphasis on external control in the behavioral approach is not dehumanizing; rather, it offers a conceptual model that celebrates the possibilities for each individual.

Conclusion

Parents, childcare providers, and teachers are undervalued and underpaid, and they have the heavy burden of doing the right thing for children. In our view, they don't hear "Good job" nearly enough. Rather than providing emotional and instrumental support, Kohn has made their task more difficult. He has done so by suggesting self-serving motives on their part, misrepresenting a powerful evidence-based practice, and suggesting his own nonvalidated alternatives. Kohn's piece is particularly detrimental to individuals who work to close the achievement gap for children from impoverished school settings and for children with special needs.

At first blush, Kohn's treatise on "Good job" may hold some liberal appeal; however, promoting nonvalidated strategies and therefore potentially precluding children from reaching their optimum development only serves to continue the status quo. In our opinion, children ought to have many rights in the education process, first of which is the right to receive those effective teaching strategies best suited to their individual needs.

Contrary to Kohn's rhetoric, the planned use of positive reinforcement is antithetical to blurted-out judgments, slathered-on praise, knee-jerk tendencies, and evaluative eruptions. Kohn's use of excessive language once again reveals his apparent disdain for individuals who would use positive reinforcement. Moreover, Kohn's transparent language serves only to construct a fictitious "straw man" that Kohn conveniently burns in effigy. It is a pedantic tactic more aligned with high school debate than with reflective practice, critical inquiry, and the advancement of meaningful discourse about facilitating children's development.

CHALLENGE QUESTIONS

Does Giving Praise Harm Children?

1. Consider the major disagreements between the authors of the two selections. Would you use praise to motivate your own child? Why or why not?
2. Give examples from your own experience where praising children made them less interested in what they were doing or reduced how well they performed.
3. Give examples from your own experience where praising children made them more interested in what they were doing or improved how well they performed.
4. How do you account for the apparent contradiction between your answers to the previous two questions? Does Kohn or Strain and Joseph account for it? If so, how?
5. At the end of his article, Kohn discusses some alternatives to using positive reinforcement. Are these alternatives really that different from traditional positive reinforcement? Why or why not?

ISSUE 7

Does a Mother's Employment Harm Her Children?

YES: Jeanne Brooks-Gunn, Wen-Jui Han, and Jane Waldfogel, from "Maternal Employment and Child Cognitive Outcomes in the First Three Years of Life: The NICHD Study of Early Child Care," *Child Development* (July/August 2002)

NO: Thomas M. Vander Ven et al., from "Home Alone: The Impact of Maternal Employment on Delinquency," *Social Problems* (May 2001)

ISSUE SUMMARY

YES: Child developmentalists Jeanne Brooks-Gunn, Wen-Jui Han, and Jane Waldfogel assert that their findings show many types of negative effects from maternal employment on the later cognitive and educational outcomes of children.

NO: Professor of sociology and anthropology Thomas M. Vander Ven and his colleagues argue that their studies show that the qualities or quantities of a mother working have relatively little or no influence on the social, emotional, and behavioral functioning of her children.

Dramatic changes have taken place in the United States over the last two decades. One of the most significant changes in the eyes of many people is the number and timing of mothers working outside the home. Certainly, many more mothers now work outside the home than ever before, but perhaps more striking is the number of mothers who *return* to work before their child's first birthday. That number has nearly doubled since the mid-1970s.

Some people have focused on the causes of this striking trend, pointing, for example, to the feminist movement or economic forces. However, this debate is concerned less about the possible causes and more about the potential effects. What effect does a mother's return to work have on the life and development of the children involved? How does a mother's working outside the home affect the family in general?

These questions are hot topics on radio talk shows. Many commentators assert that there is scientific proof that the kids of working mothers are less well behaved and more involved in criminal activities than the kids of non-working mothers. Is this true? Another view is that the income of a mother allows her to feel less economic stress, more financial stability, and greater access to adult interpersonal relations. If so, could these benefits for the mother translate into a better relationship with her children?

The authors of the following selections attempt to answer many of these questions with real empirical research, not with radio talk show speculation. Interestingly, however, the authors disagree about the general tenor of this empirical research: Jeanne Brooks-Gunn, Wen-Jui Han, and Jane Waldfogel confirm the general belief that most of the effects of working mothers are negative, particularly those who return to work early, while Thomas M. Vander Ven and his colleagues question this general belief.

How can these researchers disagree if they are both working scientifically? Some people assume that science means no disagreement because the methods of science reveal the reality of the issues being debated. However, this assumption is rarely true. The process of empirical investigation is fraught with twists and turns, and the answers to important questions are generally more complicated than initially thought. Could this be the case with the issue of maternal employment?

POINT

- Earlier studies tended to find negative effects of first-year maternal employment.
- Recent research shows the negative effects of maternal employment on children's later cognitive outcomes.
- The children of mothers who worked longer hours had more negative effects.
- The earlier in the life of the child that a mother works, the more negative the outcome.
- One clear implication is the need to improve child care for children with working mothers.

COUNTERPOINT

- Supporting evidence is scarce for the notion that maternal employment causes negative child outcomes.
- Recent research shows that children of working mothers evidence no deficits in social, emotional, or behavioral functioning.
- Delinquency is less about the characteristics of maternal employment and more about family resources.
- The effects do not last because the children of working mothers are not any more likely to become delinquent.
- If children of working mothers experience no more problems than other children, then such improvement may not be required.

Jeanne Brooks-Gunn, Wen-Jui Han, and Jane Waldfogel

 **YES**

Maternal Employment and Child Cognitive Outcomes in the First Three Years of Life

The past few decades have seen an unprecedented increase in early maternal employment. The share of mothers who return to work before their child's first birthday doubled from 1976 to 1998, rising from 31% to 59% (Bachu & O'Connell, 1998). Women are now nearly as likely to be working when they have an infant as they are when they have an older preschooler (U.S. Department of Labor, Bureau of Labor Statistics, 2000). Yet, questions remain as to what the impact of this rapid shift toward early maternal employment might be. With increased attention being paid on the part of parents and policy makers to the importance of early experiences for children, establishing what links might exist between early maternal employment and child cognitive outcomes is more important than ever.

The potential impacts of early maternal employment and early child care on child development have been extensively studied (for reviews, see Belsky, 2001; Bornstein, Gist, Hahn, Haynes, & Voigt, 2001; Lamb, 1998; Shonkoff & Phillips, 2000; Weinraub & Jaeger, 1990). Most relevant to the present study are the results from (1) studies using the National Longitudinal Survey of Youth–Child Supplement (NLSY-CS) to examine the effects of early maternal employment on child outcomes, and (2) studies using the National Institute of Child Health and Human Development Study of Early Child Care (NICHD-SECC) to examine the effects of early child care on child development.

A large literature has studied the effects of early maternal employment on children's cognitive outcomes using data on children born to respondents of the NLSY-CS (for a helpful overview of this dataset, see Chase-Lansdale, Mott, Brooks-Gunn, & Phillips, 1991). Because these NLSY-CS studies are reviewed elsewhere (see, e.g., Han, Waldfogel, & Brooks-Gunn, 2001), only a brief overview is provided here. The studies that have examined the effects of first-year maternal employment separately from the effects of employment later in the preschool years have tended to find negative effects of first-year maternal employment on children's later cognitive outcomes (see, e.g., Baydar & Brooks-Gunn, 1991; Belsky & Eggebeen, 1991; Blau & Grossberg, 1992; Han et al., 2001; Hill, Waldfogel, Brooks-Gunn, & Han, 2001; Ruhm, 2000; Waldfogel, Han, & Brooks-Gunn, 2002; but see also Harvey, 1999). An important limitation of these studies is that none have been able to control for the quality of the child-care settings in which the children of the working mothers are placed. Although the NLSY-CS contains retrospective data on the type of child care in which children are placed, it does not contain any assessment of the quality of that care. A further limitation is that none of the NLSY-CS studies have been able to control for the quality of the mothers' interactions with their children. The NLSY-CS contains no direct assessment of the sensitivity of the mother's care for the child. The NLSY-CS does contain data on one measure of the quality of the home environment, the Home Observation of the Measurement of the Environment (HOME) Scale, but it did not start administering the HOME until 1986, so for many children in the sample (children born in 1983 or earlier) this measure was not administered until they were age 3 or older and therefore no data on the earlier home environment are available.

Thus, when studies using the NLSY-CS have found that early maternal employment has negative effects on children's later cognitive outcomes, the extent to which these effects might be due to the poor quality of child care experienced by these children and/or the poor quality of their home environments has not been clear. Establishing the mechanism by which early maternal employment is linked to poorer cognitive outcomes, and the role played by child care or home environments, is critical to understanding the source of the links and also potential policy remedies.

For this reason, the present study turned to newly available data from the NICHD-SECC. This dataset is extremely well suited to address the limitations of the prior NLSY-CS studies and the questions they could not answer, because it contains data on child-care quality and the quality of children's home environment, as well as detailed data on maternal employment and child outcomes (for an excellent overview of this dataset, see NICHD Early Child Care Research Network, in press). It also contains a rich set of data on child and mother characteristics, including a measure of maternal depression, which is not available in the NLSY-CS. The NICHD-SECC dataset has not been used to study the effects of early maternal employment. It was designed as a study of the effects of early child care on child development and has been used extensively to study that topic (for results on the effects of early child care on children's development at age 54 months, see, e.g., NICHD Early Child Care Research Network, in press). . . .

Methods

Data for the present study were obtained from the NICHD-SECC, a unique longitudinal dataset that has followed 1,364 children from 10 sites around the nation since the time of their birth in 1991. (For a detailed description of the dataset, including how the sample was selected and interviewed, see

NICHD Early Child Care Research Network, 2000, in press). It is important to note that some groups were excluded from the sample (e.g., mothers under 18, families who anticipated moving, infants who were multiple births or had health problems or disabilities, mothers who did not speak English, mothers with medical problems or substance-abuse problems, or families living in a dangerous neighborhood). A total of 1,525 families were deemed eligible for inclusion in the study and agreed to be interviewed; of these, 1,364 completed an interview and became participants in the study.

The NICHD-SECC conducted home visits to the children in the sample at 1, 6, 15, 24, and 36 months, supplemented by phone interviews every 3 months to track maternal employment and child-care use. The study also conducted visits to the children's child-care settings at 6, 15, 24, and 36 months (if children were in care more than 10 hr per week). In addition, the children were assessed at home and in the laboratory at ages 15, 24, and 36 months (later visits and assessments were also conducted, but those data have not yet been released for public use). . . .

Discussion

The present study took advantage of a newly available dataset, the NICHD-SECC, to examine the effects of early maternal employment on children's cognitive outcomes at ages 15, 24, and 36 months, controlling for child care (quality and type) and home environment (assessed with the HOME Scale and a rating of maternal sensitivity). The study analyzed three related sets of questions: (1) Is maternal employment in the first year of life associated with negative child cognitive outcomes in the first 3 years of life and, if so, are these effects more pronounced when mothers work full-time? (2) Are there subgroups for whom these effects are more likely to be found? and (3) To what extent are these effects mediated by quality of child care and home environment in the first 3 years of life? These analyses took as their point of departure the literature on the timing of early maternal employment, which has relied mainly on analyses of the NLSY-CS. Because this literature (with important input from developmentalists, economists, and sociologists) has been increasingly concerned with issues of selection bias and model specification, the present study included a large array of covariates that were not available in the NLSY-CS, such as measures of child care and the early home environment. It also drew extensively on the literature on the effects of early child care, in particular the recent work by the NICHD Early Child Care Research Network on the timing and intensity of early child care. The work of the NICHD Early Child Care Research Network was followed closely in terms of how the rich child-care and child-assessment data available in the NICHD-SECC dataset were utilized and also in how the factors that might mediate the effects of early maternal employment on later child outcomes were conceptualized. However, unlike the NICHD Early Child Care Research Network, the focus in the present research was on early maternal employment rather than early child care, reflecting our interest in extending and updating the prior work from the NLSY-CS as well as contributing to the literature regarding women and employment. Thus, we believe the results of the present study complement those of the NICHD Early Child Care Research Network, because it tackled essentially different questions than those addressed in that group's work.

To review the main findings, with regard to the first research question, this study found that children whose mothers worked at all by the ninth month of their life had lower scores on the Bracken [School Readiness Scale] at 36 months than did children whose mothers did not work by that time. The effects of any maternal employment by 1, 3, 6, or 12 months were also negative, although only the effect of maternal employment by 9 months was statistically significant (the effect of employment by 6 months was marginally significant at $p < .10$). This pattern of results suggests that there may be something particularly problematic about having a mother who went to work between 6 and 9 months and/or something unusual about the children whose mothers began employment at this time (which about 5% of the sample did), and the few prior studies that had examined timing effects of maternal employment within the first year (Baydar & Brooks-Gunn, 1991; Han et al., 2001) provided some support for this idea. However, it is also important to note that these results provided some evidence of negative effects of earlier employment as well. Moreover, once the intensity of employment was taken into account, larger negative effects were found, which were statistically significant for employment beginning by 6 months as well as 9 months. Specifically, the negative effect of having a mother who began employment by the ninth month was most pronounced for children whose mothers worked longer hours (30 hr or more per week) in the first year; the same was true for children whose mothers began employment by the sixth month.

The significant negative effects found on the Bracken at 36 months for any employment by the ninth month, and for employment of 30 hr or more per week by the sixth month or ninth month, were consistent with previous findings from the NLSY indicating that early maternal employment had significant negative effects on children's PPVT-R [Peabody Picture Vocabulary Test-Revised] at 36 months (see, e.g., Han et al., 2001; Waldfogel et al., 2002). The fact that these effects were strongest for European American non-Hispanic children was also consistent with prior findings from the NLSY-CS. No effects were found for early maternal employment on children's Bayley MDI [Mental Development Index] scores at 15 or 24 months. The fact that there were negative effects of early maternal employment on the Bracken at 36 months but not on the Bayley MDI in the first 2 years of life is most likely due to the different cognitive competencies tapped in the first 2 years compared with the later preschool years. The cognitive competencies tapped at 15 and 24 months may be less likely to be influenced by environmental events than those tapped later on. Studies that looked at the effects of poverty, for example, found few effects on cognition in the first 18 months of life using the Bayley MDI, but found effects when language and reasoning were assessed in the third year of life (see, e.g., Klebanov et al., 1998). In addition, competencies tapped in the first 2 years of life may not be as predictive of later functioning (McCall, 1983; McCall, Hogarty, & Hurlbut, 1972).

With regard to the second research question, the present results showed that some subgroups of children were more likely to be affected than were others. The effects of early and full-time maternal employment were larger for children whose mothers were rated as insensitive at 6 months (compared with those whose mothers were rated as sensitive), for boys (compared with girls), and for children with married parents (compared with single mothers). The finding on sensitivity was consistent with prior results from the NICHD-SECC (i.e., investigators found that children whose mothers were rated as not sensitive and were in early child care more than 10 hr per week were more vulnerable to attachment problems than were other children in care more than 10 hr per week; NICHD Early Child Care Research Network, 1997). The findings on differences by gender and by parents' marital status were consistent with prior results from the NLSY-CS (see Desai et al., 1989, on gender; Han et al., 2001, on marital status). With regard to the more negative impacts for boys, some analysts have observed that boys are more vulnerable to early stressors in general (see, e.g., Rutter, 1979; Zaslow & Hayes, 1986) and that boys may be more affected by nonmaternal child care as well (for an excellent discussion on this topic, see Bornstein et al., 2001). With regard to the more negative impacts for children of married parents, one possible explanation is that the extra income generated by the mothers' employment may be more valuable, on average, to families headed by unmarried mothers than it is to married-couple families. If so, to the extent that positive income effects offset otherwise negative effects of early maternal employment, this would explain why the observed effects of early maternal employment seemed to be more negative in married-couple families. These differences by subgroup are intriguing and warrant further research, which might shed more light on the mechanisms that underlie the effects of early maternal employment on child cognitive outcomes. In this regard, it would also be useful to conduct research on individual differences in children's vulnerability to early and full-time maternal employment.

With regard to the third research question, it was found that both child care (quality and type) and home environment (as measured by both maternal sensitivity and the HOME Scale) mattered for children's Bracken scores at 36 months. Also found was some evidence that early and full-time maternal employment was negatively associated with the quality of subsequent child care and home environments. Children whose mothers worked more than 30 hr per week by 9 months were in lower quality child-care settings at 36 months than children whose mothers worked fewer hours per week in the first year. Moreover, children whose mothers worked more than 30 hr per week by 9 months had mothers who were rated as providing less sensitive care at 36 months than children whose mothers did not work in the first year (this result is consistent with the finding of the NICHD Early Child Care Research Network, 1999, that children who spent more hours in early child care had mothers who provided less sensitive care at 36 months), although their home environments (as assessed by the HOME Scale) were not significantly different (this latter result may indicate that early and full-time maternal employment may have offsetting effects, reducing some resources due to the limitations on mothers' time available for activities with their children but increasing other resources due to the increased income available to the family through the mothers' employment). However, even after controlling for child care and home environment, a negative association was still found between full-time employment begun in the first 9 months of children's lives and the children's Bracken scores at 36 months.

Because the NICHD-SECC is an observational (rather than experimental) study, it is important to be cautious in interpreting these results. It is possible that mothers' entry into full-time work in the first 9 months did adversely affect their children's cognitive performance at age 3. If this is correct, then one could conclude that encouraging mothers who would otherwise be employed full-time to stay home or work part-time during the first year would produce children with higher Bracken School Readiness scores. However, the NICHD-SECC did not experimentally assign mothers to employment or non-employment, so it is not known from these estimates whether full-time maternal employment by 9 months was causing the lower Bracken School Readiness scores. It is possible that there were pre-existing differences between mothers who did and did not work full-time in the first 9 months of their children's lives that were not observed in the data and that mattered for children's cognitive outcomes. These differences may have had to do with characteristics of the mothers, or with the reasons that they were working. Although selection bias in the present study was controlled for to the extent possible by including a large set of covariates (several of which were not available in prior work with the NLSY-CS), clearly, further work on this topic is needed.

The results of the present study do have some implications for policy. One clear implication is the need to improve the quality of child care that children experience in the first 3 years of life. The results confirm that quality of care matters and also document that, all else equal, children whose mothers work full-time in the first year of life go on to experience poorer quality care in their first 3 years. This lower quality of care in part explains why cognitive outcomes are worse at 36 months for children whose mothers worked full-time rather than part-time in the first year of life. This suggests that improving the quality of child care used by the children of full-time working mothers might help to mitigate the observed negative effects of mothers' early and full-time employment on children's cognitive development. It is important to keep in mind that the present study examined a specific group of children who were infants and toddlers in the early 1990s, and was, therefore, situated in the context of the quality of child care available in the United States during those years. If the quality of that care was, on average, lower than the quality of care that the children's mothers would have offered had they not been working, then that "mismatch" could help to explain the negative relation between early and full-time maternal employment and cognitive development at age 36 months reported in this article. (It was not possible to control for this directly because we did not observe the care that the mother would have provided had she not been working; we only observed the care that she did provide, which may have been affected by the fact that she was employed.) Studies in other countries in which the quality of care is higher have reported different results (see, e.g., Andersson, 1989, 1992, who found that Swedish children who entered child care earlier in the first year of life had better cognitive outcomes than those who entered care later).

A second implication has to do with family leave policy. The United States currently has family leave provisions that guarantee less than 3 months of leave for new mothers as compared with an average of 10 months in the advanced industrialized nations who are members of the Organization for Economic and Community Development (OECD); the United States also differs from peer industrialized nations by not providing paid leave and by having a national law that covers less than half the private sector workforce (Kamerman, 2000; Waldfogel, 2001a). If any maternal employment by the ninth month (and maternal employment of 30 hr or more per week by the sixth or ninth month) has adverse effects on children's cognitive develop-ment, this is relevant to consideration of proposals to extend U.S. leave provi-sions to the 10-month OECD average, provide paid leave, and provide coverage for a larger portion of the U.S. workforce (see, e.g., Kamerman, 2000; Waldfogel, 2001a).

A third implication has to do with family-friendly policies that make it easier for mothers (and fathers) to combine work and family responsibili-ties. In addition to child care and family leave, such policies include flexible hours, part-time or job-sharing arrangements, and other workplace policies that might reduce the stress or fatigue experienced by working parents with young children. Although, as noted above, the United States lags behind other countries in its provision of family leave, it has at least made some progress in this area with the passage of the Family and Medical Leave Act (FMLA) in 1993. The same is not true of other family-friendly benefits for families with young children. The share of employers who provide such benefits is quite low and has not increased in recent years (Waldfogel, 2001b).

Taken together, the results of the present study illustrate the extent to which the effects of early maternal employment on children's cognitive out-comes depend crucially on both the quality of care that children receive at home and the quality of care that children receive in child care. Good-quality care at home, and good-quality child care, can go a long way toward buffering the negative links between early maternal employment and later child out-comes. Nevertheless, it is concerning that even after controlling for home-environment quality and child-care quality, full-time maternal employment by the ninth month was found to be associated with lower Bracken scores at 36 months. Until there is better understanding with regard to what causes this association and how to buffer it, it would be prudent for policy makers to go slow on measures (such as the recent Temporary Assistance to Needy Families reforms) that would require mothers to enter the labor force (full-time) early in the first year of life and to consider measures (such as proposed FMLA extensions) that would allow more mothers to choose to delay their return to the labor force and/or to work part-time until later in the first year of life. More generally, we concur with the conclusions of the recent National Academy of Sciences expert panel on the science of early development (Shonkoff & Phillips, 2000), that call for policies to improve the quality of child care, extend family leave provisions, and expand other family-friendly policies, to give parents more and better choices about how to balance their work and family responsibilities in the first year of their children's lives.

Thomas M. Vander Ven et al.

 **NO**

Home Alone: The Impact of Maternal Employment on Delinquency

In recent decades, American family life has been transformed dramatically. Family scholars debate the causes and consequences of these major changes, routinely dashing over whether family forms are changing for the better (Stacey 1993) or whether our most important social institution is experiencing a moral and functional freefall (Gill 1993; Poponoe 1993).

One of the most profound changes is the unprecedented number of women who have entered the paid workforce since the 1950s. Census data show that female labor force participation rose from approximately 23 percent in 1940 to close to 60 percent in 1992 (U.S. Bureau of Census 1993). This wave of women entering the labor force was accompanied by a large increase in maternal employment. While only 16 percent of all children had working mothers in 1950, close to 70 percent of all mothers with dependent children work today (Coontz 1997). Recent estimates show that over half of those with children less than one year old are employed outside the home and over 60 percent of those with children younger than six are employed (Gerson 1996).

While the mass entrance of women and mothers into the labor market might be regarded as a sign of social progress, many Americans are worried about the trend and have been for some time (Greenberger, Goldberg, Crawford, and Granger 1988). And in what may be seen as part of the "backlash" to feminist political victories (Faludi 1991), politicians, social critics, and parenting "experts" have frequently pointed to the working mother as the cause of many of our social problems.

While supporting empirical evidence is scarce, the political Right charges that feminist philosophies damage the American family by encouraging women to choose work and self-fulfillment over family obligations (Cohen and Katzenstein 1988). Additionally, noted psychologists argue that the neglected child of the working mother may suffer from an attachment disorder, which is widely believed to be a major causal factor in the production of extreme child behavior problems. One pediatrician and TV personality warns that mothers should stay home to raise their infants or risk the disruption of

From Thomas M. Vander Ven, Francis T. Cullen, Mark A. Carrozza, and John Paul Wright, "Home Alone: The Impact of Maternal Employment on Delinquency," *Social Problems,* vol. 48, no. 2 (May 2001). Copyright © 2001 by The Society for the Study of Social Problems, Inc. Reprinted by permission of The University of California Press and Thomas M. Vander Ven. Notes and some references omitted.

the critical mother-child bonding period: "if he doesn't have that through infancy, it's hard to put it in later . . . and these kids that never get it . . . will become difficult in school, they'll never succeed in school, they'll make every-body angry, they'll become delinquents later and eventually they'll become terrorists" (see Eyer 1996:6).

Although there is no shortage of claims that maternal employment causes negative child outcomes, there is little evidence that this is the case. Recent research shows that the children of working mothers are no less attached than other children (Chira 1998) and that they experience no defi-cits in social, emotional, or behavioral functioning (Harvey 1999; Hoffman 1989; Parcel and Menaghan 1994). While no work and family issue attracts more scholarly attention than the potential effects of maternal employment on children's development (Barling 1990), few researchers have investigated the possible link between working mothers and delinquency.

In this context, we analyze the impact of maternal employment—of kids being left "home alone"—on delinquency using models that include different characteristics of maternal employment (e.g., hours, workplace controls), vari-ations in maternal non-employment (e.g., welfare reliance), and child care arrangements. Our analysis is influenced by the research program of Parcel and Meneghan (1994, 1994a), who investigated the impact of various dimen-sions of parental work on a range of social, cognitive, and behavioral out-comes. Similarly, we test models that consider the number of hours usually employed, working conditions, and the timing of work. This more compre-hensive measurement of maternal work improves upon past research on maternal employment and delinquency, where mother's work was simply divided into "working mother" and "non-working mother" categories (e.g., Glueck and Glueck 1950; Hirschi 1969; Sampson and Laub 1993).

Furthermore, in an attempt to isolate the independent effects of mater-nal work, we simultaneously consider the impact of maternal resources (i.e., maternal cognitive skills, maternal education, family income), child care arrangements, and marital status. By controlling for maternal resources, we are better able to isolate the independent effects of maternal employment. . . .

Although there is a tremendous body of literature on the effects of maternal employment on child outcomes, studies on the link between maternal work and delinquency are relatively scarce. Early researchers tended to find a small positive effect of maternal employment on delinquency, which they usually assumed was the consequence of low maternal supervision (Glueck and Glueck 1950; Hirschi 1969; Nye 1963; Roy 1963; see also, Sampson and Laub 1993). Most contemporary researchers found little or no connection between maternal work status and delinquency (Broidy 1995; Hillman and Sawilowsky 1991; Riege 1972; Wadsworth 1979). Other studies suggest that delinquency is less common among the children of regularly employed mothers (Farnworth 1984; West 1982; Zhao, Cao, and Cao 1997). In some cases, maternal work actually served as insulation against delinquent risks because working mothers effectively raised the family income, thus improving the living conditions of their children. Maternal employment, then, should be considered as an economic dimension of family life and may be most beneficial for children when the alternative is poverty or welfare dependency (Baca-Zinn 1989).

When examined closely, the extant literature on maternal employment and delinquency suggests that working conditions are an important factor that must be included in analytical models. Glueck and Glueck (1950), for example, found that delinquency was highest among the children of occasionally employed mothers. This finding is provocative because occasional or sporadic work may be indicative of secondary labor market employment. Employment in the secondary labor market is often erratic and coercive due to the vulnerability of the low-skilled, uneducated workers at this level (Edwards 1979). Such employment may be criminogenic if coercive workplace experiences negatively shape parenting techniques (Colvin and Pauly 1983).

In a related vein, Roy (1963) found that maternal work was related to delinquency in urban settings, but not in rural areas. This effect, also, may reflect important differences between working conditions in urban vs. rural communities. It may be that maternal work in urban centers and among minority populations is, on average, more likely to be coercive, secondary labor market work (see Haurin 1992). In light of these findings, better measures of maternal employment—including measures for workplace controls and regularity of employment (part-time vs. full-time) are needed. . . .

Methodology

Sample

In the 1960s, the United States Department of Labor hired the Center for Human Resource Research at the Ohio State University to gather longitudinal data on the labor market experiences of four representative target groups among the U.S. population (Fahey 1995). A fifth cohort of men and women between the ages of 14 and 22 was identified in 1979. Known as the National Longitudinal Survey of Youth (NLSY), this project involved a multistaged stratified random sampling that produced 12,686 subjects, 11,404 of whom were interviewed annually about their occupational, educational, familial, and childbearing experiences (see Chase-Lansdale, Mott, Brooks-Gunn, and Phillips 1991; Parcel and Menaghan 1994).

By 1994, 10,042 children of sample mothers were identified to report on their home environment, family relations, and school experiences in addition to taking a number of inventories designed to measure cognitive and socioemotional development. To investigate the relationship between maternal work and delinquency, we conduct our analysis on a sample of 707 adolescents who were between the ages of 12 and 14 in 1994. These children are the offspring of female respondents originally interviewed in 1979. Each of these respondents completed the Child Self-Administered Supplement (CSAS) in 1992 and in 1994. This self-report booklet collects information on a wide range of variables including child-parent interaction, peer relationships, and involvement in various delinquent activities. . . .

Dependent Variable: Delinquency

The 1994 CSAS includes nine highly correlated items that assess involvement in deviant and delinquent acts. Five of the items measure relatively minor to moderate acts of youth deviance: breaking parents' curfew, dishonesty (i.e., lying to a parent), school problems (i.e., parent came to school because of child behavior), truancy, and staying out all night. The other four items involve more serious acts of lawbreaking: alcohol abuse, vandalism (i.e., damaged school property on purpose), store theft, and violence (i.e., hurt someone badly enough to need bandages or a doctor). These nine items are summed to create our scale measuring youth deviance and delinquency (alpha = .78). . . .

Independent Variables

Maternal employment status. A continuous measure of hours usually worked is used in this analysis. In past studies (e.g., Parcel and Menaghan 1994, 1994a), investigators assigned missing values to work-hour variables for non-employed mothers, who were then excluded from the analysis. Thus, these studies focused on the effects of paid maternal employment among a sub-group of working mothers only. Other studies include non-employed mothers but as a dummy category that is used in equations with other dummy variables capturing increasing levels of time commitment to paid employment (e.g., part-time, full-time, over-time) (Baydar and Brooks-Gunn 1991; Muller 1995; Parcel, Nickoll, and Dufur 1996). Measuring maternal work hours via a series of dummy variables is arguably a good strategy for organizing information and for detecting non-linear effects (see Harvey 1999). As Harvey points out, however, this method is problematic because the dummy categories are formed from continuous variables so there are infinite ways one could create categories and arbitrary boundaries between categories are often created. Moreover, using continuous variables does not prevent the detection of non-linear effects (Harvey 1999). Based on this rationale, we use a continuous measure of hours worked in our primary analysis. . . .

Occupational class. We measure occupational class in two ways. First, following Parcel and Menaghan (1994), we construct a 19-item-based occupational complexity scale by matching occupational titles reported by NLSY respondents to job descriptions reported in the Dictionary of Occupational Titles. . . .

Our primary measure of workplace conditions is developed based on the work of Mark Colvin (Colvin 2000; Colvin and Pauly 1983). Drawing from Kohn (1977) and Edwards (1979), Colvin links the workplace controls experienced by parents to the patterns and styles of control parents exert upon children. Unskilled, non-unionized employees (Fraction I workers) are subjected to "simple control" in the workplace, which is coercive and alienating. . . .

Skilled laborers and craftspersons (Fraction II workers), who often belong to labor unions, experience greater job security and are controlled via "technical control"—the machine-paced atmosphere of manufacturing and industrial workplaces where workers are motivated to produce by wage increases and job security. . . .

Fraction III workers are those skilled workers, technicians, salaried professionals, and supervisory staff who experience greater self-direction, job complexity, and job security in the workplace. . . .

Family income.   Total family income is included in all models. By employing a family income measure, we are able to assess the impact of mother's employment experiences while controlling for the total standard of living of each family included in the analysis. Controlling for family income helps to isolate the independent effects of occupational variables in the analysis.

Child care.   Following Parcel and Menaghan (1994), we measure child care with a series of dummy variables. Dummy variables representing professional daycare settings, childcare provided by a relative (including fathers), and childcare provided by a non-relative are included. . . .

Discussion

Are the children of working mothers more likely to be delinquent than other children? According to past studies and to the results of our analysis, the answer is a qualified "No." The present study demonstrates that regardless of how this issue is examined, having a working mother has only a small and indirect effect on delinquency. This general pattern holds whether we considered maternal employment in a child's pre-school years or maternal work in adolescence. Furthermore, with the lone exception of maternal supervision, maternal employment has little influence on several known pathways to delinquency.

Like Parcel and Menaghan (1994, 1994a) and more recent findings by Harvey (1999), our research suggests that the widespread concern over the fates of working women and their children is largely unsupported. Rather than being a social problem whose untoward effects can be demonstrated empirically, the maternal employment-delinquency connection is better understood as a socially constructed problem. As a perceived social problem, the dark side of maternal employment has a long history in America. Fueled by scientific data on the link between early family processes and delinquency and by cherished popular beliefs in the sanctity of the "first relationship"—the coupling of mother and child—for decades politicians and social commentators have pointed to modern trends in female labor participation to explain social problems such as crime. But if the unprecedented entrance of mothers into the paid workforce is related to delinquency, it must be because working mothers fail their children by depriving them of the support and discipline they need. The current study adds to the growing literature that casts doubt on these assumptions.

Our findings suggest other notable conclusions. First, it is maternal and family resources, rather than the characteristics of maternal work, that most influence some well-known pathways to delinquency in our study. Maternal AFQT [Armed Forces Qualifications Test] score, a measure of intellectual resources, affects both parental support and mother-child bonds in early childhood and in adolescence: mothers who draw from greater cognitive resources are more supportive in parenting and raise more securely attached children.

Although the AFQT measures an individual's intellectual capacity, it reflects the subject's developed abilities rather than a biologically assigned aptitude (Menaghan and Parcel 1991). The AFQT score varies with family of origin, geographic region, and years of schooling, which implies that, like maternal education, an AFQT score reflects relative social advantage or disadvantage (Maume, Cancio, and Evans 1996; Menaghan and Parcel 1991). Our findings should be interpreted as further evidence that social disadvantage is reproduced partly through its effect on parent-child relations. Consistent with this theme, our analysis found that an important family resource, family income, exerts a positive influence on warm and responsive parenting in adolescence, while welfare reliance has the opposite effect. This relationship is consistent with past research that identified economic hardship as a strain on family functioning (McLoyd 1990; Siegal 1984).

The most powerful predictors of delinquency in our analysis are maternal supervision, delinquent peer association, and school attachment. Adolescents who are supervised more closely, those who have fewer delinquent peers, and those who are more attached to school show less involvement in delinquency. This result supports a large body of research that identifies these factors as important to the production of antisocial behavioral patterns. We reiterate, here, our discovery that maternal employment had relatively little negative impact on these important pathways to delinquency.

In one instance, however, workplace controls had a small indirect effect on delinquency. Specifically, bureaucratic work controls were negatively related to maternal supervision and, thus, had a slightly positive effect on delinquency. One interpretation of this result is that professional mothers may invest more time in their careers than the average mother does which may diminish their ability to monitor children. On the other hand, the negative effect of bureaucratic controls on supervision may not reflect a difference in time spent with children so much as a difference in parenting style. The freedom and autonomy experienced by the professional parent may translate into a parenting style characterized by less overt supervision and greater attempts to equip children with internal normative controls.

Conversely, we found that maternal work hours were indirectly related to lower involvement in delinquency, through their positive effect on supervision. Again, although the effect is small, maternal work hours is actually related to greater supervision in our sample. This may be due to the stabilizing influence of steady employment on family life. As Wilson (1996:73) has argued, a job "constitutes a framework for daily behavior and patterns of interaction because it imposes disciplines and regularities" upon a parent.

Furthermore, while no maternal employment variable is related to delinquent peer association, neighborhood disorder is. This finding is consistent with social disorganization theory (Shaw and McKay 1942): the breakdown of informal neighborhood controls leaves children at a greater risk for being socialized in intimate delinquent peer groups. It is instructive that our analysis points to community breakdown, as it operates through delinquent peer influence, as a cause of delinquency rather than family breakdown related to the absence of a working mother.

Finally, if improving family life is a goal of crime control policy, it would make good sense to aim at addressing the structural factors that limit maternal and family resources and that contribute to community disorder. Our study suggests that policy debates should avoid ideological attacks on working mothers, which portray them as leaving their children "home alone," and concentrate instead on the economic and educational inequalities that weaken families and neighborhoods.

Note

1. Contrary to past work by Parcel and Menaghan (e.g., 1994), we did not find that mother's working conditions had a substantial impact on parenting or home environment. In their research, higher quality work was related to higher quality home environments. Whether we measured mother's working conditions with the occupational complexity scale favored by Parcel and Menaghan or our series of dummy variables representing the three fractions of the working class, we found no such effect. Our contradictory findings may be explained, in part, by the measurement of our pathway variables. As discussed earlier, many of our delinquency pathway variables are one-item measures that lack the sensitivity of the multi-item family and home variables used by Parcel and Menaghan.

CHALLENGE QUESTIONS

Does a Mother's Employment Harm Her Children?

1. Are there ways to reconcile the findings found in the two selections? Much of the authors' conclusions seem incompatible, but are their data and findings necessarily in conflict?
2. On what issues do the two sets of authors agree?
3. Imagine that you were a political leader attempting to make public policy decisions. What would be your policies regarding the regulation of day-care centers, family leave, and labor laws if you took the views of Brooks-Gunn, Han, and Waldfogel? What would be your policies if you sided with Vander Ven et al.?
4. Vander Ven et al. suggest that issues of political liberalism and conservativism have infiltrated the discussion of maternal employment. Do you agree? How might valid empirical data aid this discussion?

ISSUE 8

Does the Divorce of Parents Harm Their Children?

YES: Judith S. Wallerstein and Julia M. Lewis, from "The Unexpected Legacy of Divorce: Report of a 25-Year Study," *Psychoanalytic Psychology* (Summer 2004)

NO: E. Mavis Hetherington and John Kelly, from *For Better or For Worse: Divorce Reconsidered* (W. W. Norton, 2002)

ISSUE SUMMARY

YES: Clinical psychologist Judith S. Wallerstein and professor of psychology Julia Lewis argue their research indicates that the vast majority of children from divorced families are harmed in many subtle and obvious ways at various times and stages of their lives.

NO: Developmental psychologist E. Mavis Hetherington and writer John Kelly do not deny that divorce can have some harmful effects, especially in the short term, but they maintain that most of these children eventually become well adjusted.

One of the unfortunate facts of modern life is that all first marriages stand a 45 percent chance of breaking up and all second marriages stand a 60 percent chance of breaking up. Since these percentages have remained fairly constant for nearly two generations, some researchers have estimated that nearly a quarter of all the people living today between the ages of 18 and 44 have parents who divorced. What effect, if any, does the divorce of parents have on their children? Does this event have a lasting influence, or is it eventually overcome by other life events?

Answering these questions is one of the many interests of two subdisciplines of psychology—clinical and developmental. Clinical psychologists are often concerned with influences that would hinder a person from well-being and a good life. They might wonder if divorce contributes to the problems that lead people to psychotherapy and counseling. Developmental psychologists can have similar interests. Their emphasis, however, is often on how events of childhood and adolescence, such as parental divorce, impact successful aging and development.

As it happens, the senior authors of the following selections represent these two subdisciplines of psychology. They are also two of the leading researchers on the effects of divorce. Intriguingly, they come to dramatically differing conclusions about these effects, with Judith S. Wallerstein emphasizing the short- and long-term harms of divorce and E. Mavis Hetherington stressing people's flexibility and adaptability in responding to their parents' divorce.

Wallerstein, for instance, finds not only that divorce is primarily harmful to children but also that other authorities researching divorce are beginning to agree with her. In fact, she contends that there is now a twofold convergence among family scholars: children raised in divorced families are less well adjusted than those raised in intact families, and these effects are long-term. As Wallerstein et al. argue in the first selection, divorce appears to affect people at virtually every stage of development, from childhood to adolescence to adulthood. Instead of these children overcoming the effects of divorce in adulthood, Wallerstein et al. contend that adulthood is when the children suffer most. They lack inner images of stable relationships and, thus, are less likely to attain love, sexual intimacy, and lasting commitment.

In the second selection, Hetherington and Kelly draw a more positive outlook on the effects of divorce from three major longitudinal studies (investigations that study the same people across their life spans), the most prominent of which is the Virginia Longitudinal Study of Divorce (VLS). Unlike Wallerstein et al.'s sense of later adjustment, the VLS leads Hetherington and Kelly to conclude that fully 80 percent of the children from divorced homes become reasonably well adjusted. But how can this be, given the obvious trauma of divorce? Hetherington and Kelly insist that, contrary to some people's opinions, this event is not a form of "developmental predestination." Although the effects of divorce still echo in some families, they contend, the vast majority of young people from these families cope well in relationships of all types.

POINT

- Divorce is a scar with many and varied long-term negative consequences.

- Most family scholars agree that children of divorced homes are less well adjusted as adults than children of intact homes.

- Divorce is a cumulative experience, increasing its harm over time.

- Many children of divorced parents have difficulties establishing relationships of lasting commitment.

- Wide differences are seen between children of divorced and nondivorced families.

COUNTERPOINT

- Divorce carries no inevitable long-term effects because people have and do overcome this event.

- Three rigorous, longitudinal studies show that the legacy of divorce is largely overcome by adulthood.

- Parent, child, and sibling relationships seldom deteriorate in adulthood.

- Children of divorce may have more problems, but many are caring spouses and parents.

- Coming from a nondivorced family does not always protect a person against becoming a troubled young adult.

Judith S. Wallerstein and
Julia M. Lewis

 **YES**

The Unexpected Legacy of Divorce: Report of a 25-Year Study

. . . The study we report here begins with the first no-fault divorce legislation in the nation and tracks a group of 131 California children whose parents divorced in the early 1970s. They were seen at regular intervals over the 25-year span that followed. When we first met our young participants, they were between ages 3 and 18; by the mid- to late 1990s, when our study ended, they were 28–43 years old. They were the vanguard of an army of adults raised in divorced families who made up one quarter of the American population between the ages of 18 and 44, as reported in 1991 in the National Survey of Families and Households.

Whereas it is well known that in the closing three decades of the last century the incidence of divorce hovered at nearly half of all first marriages, it is less known that half of the one million children whose parents make up the annual divorce rate are age 6 or under at the breakup. Like our subjects, these children will spend the bulk of their growing-up years in postdivorce families, often within a range of new relationships of one or both parents that include cohabitations and remarriages, and they will experience new losses due to their parents' broken love affairs or second, and even third, divorces. This is the first and only such report that tells the story of growing up in the postdivorce family through the eyes of children.

The divorced family is a new kind of family and not a truncated version of the familiar intact family that has been studied within and across many disciplines. Relationships with stepparents, visiting parents, stepsiblings, and lifestyles that include joint custody have no counterpart in the intact family. Moreover, as we report, when the marital bond is severed, parent–child relationships are likely to change radically in ways that are not predictable from their course during the marriage. Both childhood and parenthood are challenged and often heavily burdened within the divorced family, at the same time that many adults are set free from unhappy and sometimes tragic situations. If we recall what Erikson taught us about the close connection between childhood and society, then we are, as a society, in the midst of profound changes in our relationships with each other and in relationships between the generations. The impact of these far-reaching changes on the society as a

From *Psychoanalytic Psychology*, vol. 21, no. 3, Summer 2004, pp. 353–354, 359–360, 366–370.
Copyright © 2001 by Lawrence Erlbaum Associates. Reprinted by permission of the author.
References omitted.

whole, as well as on the many individuals whose lives have been profoundly affected, has been hardly addressed or even appreciated.

The Study

The aim of our study was to illuminate the social and psychological experiences of children and parents at the marital breakup and during the postdivorce years. We were especially interested in the impact of the divorce experience on the child's developmental course, self-concept, and feelings, and on critical passages of growing up to adulthood. Early on, we were concerned with the bewildered and frightened responses of children to their parents' breakup. Several years later, when most of the initial crisis-engendered responses had faded, we focused on the many issues associated with adolescence in this group. We were especially concerned with the vulnerability of young adolescent girls in divorced families, the anger and widespread acting out of both the girls and the boys, and their profound need for both committed parents at this often turbulent developmental stage. In the final years of the study, as the youngsters entered adulthood and moved into their 20s and 30s, we were interested in their relationships and overall adjustment within adult society, including their self-concept and values. Our findings at each point have been reported in many publications and are well known to professional and lay audiences both here and abroad. Here we review our earlier findings briefly and then turn to some of our major findings at the 25-year mark, when the participants in the study were well into adulthood. We also construct a beginning agenda for clinical and educational interventions designed to alleviate the widespread anxiety and suffering that we found at that later time. . . .

Findings

Early Changes

We present here only a few of the major findings from our work. To summarize some early findings: Growing up was harder for most of the children during the postdivorce years. The lives of parents and children changed radically almost overnight, as parents struggled to reestablish economic, social, and parental functioning, while trying to rebuild the tattered social network of their lives. Children of every age struggled with bewildering, demanding adjustments in their contact with both parents. Often they faced relocation to a new neighborhood and a new school, along with consequent disruptions and losses in their friendships and activities. At home, they confronted seriously diminished parenting just at the time when they needed their parents' help to make sense of what was happening and to support their efforts to adjust to the major changes within and outside the family. Typically, the parents themselves became the source of the child's worry. "Who is taking care of my dad?" was a frequent question. The consequences of the family's disruption were especially serious for the younger children. "I need a new mommy," an anxious 5-year-old insisted. To her young mind, her loving, devoted mother had disappeared and been replaced by a tense, cranky, unavailable stranger. The major changes in both parent–child relationships, along with the high anxiety of the children, almost all of whom were taken by surprise by the breakup, have been well documented in our earlier work and by others.

Out of their experience of the parental breakup, children of all ages reached a conclusion that terrified them: Personal relationships are unreliable, and even the closest family relationships cannot be expected to hold firm. As we discovered later, this was an enduring theme that rose to new prominence as the youngsters reached adulthood. Their conviction that relationships are unlikely to endure was reinforced by their experiences over the postdivorce years and were entirely unaffected by the amount of time they spent with each parent. Two thirds of the children experienced the multiple marriages and divorces, plus the unrecorded broken love affairs and temporary cohabitations, of one or both parents. Less than 10% of the children had parents who established stable, lasting second marriages in which the children felt fully welcome and included. The frequent discrepancy in the postdivorce adjustment of their parents was also a source of deep distress to the children well into adulthood.

Loneliness and Fear of Abandonment Recalled

Specific events, including the conflicts surrounding the separation and divorce of their parents, had faded but were not forgotten by these children of divorce 25 years later. Early conflict from before the breakup did not dominate their memories, unless the conflict continued to plague the family over several years. In the main, children recalled their own feelings of shock and unhappiness at the time of the separation and its aftermath. Almost all remembered feelings of loneliness, bewilderment, and anger at the parents. Many cried as they recounted their history and their childhood fears that they would be forgotten by their preoccupied parents. These feelings were especially powerful, decades later, among those who had been 6 years old or younger at that time. For them, the loss of the parents' availability was most distressing, because they had so little capacity to comfort themselves. "I remember feeling so alone. I would go for days with no one to talk to or play with." "I remember being angry at everyone." . . .

Discussion

The call to liberalize divorce in the early 1970s promised happier and better marriages. Ironically, findings from this study show that although divorce sets many adults free, and many second marriages are happier, these benefits do not extend to their children. Divorce begets fewer marriages, poorer marriages, and more divorces. This should not encourage us to retreat from regarding divorce as an adult right. However, it does call attention to enduring problems in the lives of the children involved. Where did we go wrong, and what can we do?

The findings from this study call for a shift in our dominant paradigm of understanding the impact of divorce on children and in the interventions that have been developed to mitigate its effects. The widely accepted premise has been that divorce represents an acute crisis from which resilient children recover, typically within a 2-year period, and then resume their normal developmental progress, if three conditions obtain: (a) the parents are able to settle their differences without fighting; (b) the financial arrangements are fair; and (c) the child has continued contact with both parents over the years that follow. Implicit in this model is the notion that after the turmoil of the divorce, the parent–child relationships return to the status quo ante; parenting resumes much as it was before the split, and the child continues to do well, or even better, minus the marital conflict of the predivorce years. A parallel paradigm places loss at the center of the divorce: The hazard to the child is primarily the loss of one parent, usually the father. In this view, it is held that the child will be protected against long-term problems if continued contact with both parents is ensured.

The first model has led to a range of interventions centering on reducing conflict between the parents, including mediation, collaborative divorce, programs provided under the aegis of the courts to educate parents in ways to eschew conflict and litigation, and a range of other educational programs to help high-conflict parents bring their anger under control. The second model has found its expression in joint custody, in legal efforts to block the mother's move away from the community where the father resides, and in encouraging fathers to value their continuing role of active participation in their child's upbringing after the breakup.

However, most of the children in this study were in ongoing contact with their fathers throughout their childhood. One third visited weekly or more frequently. None of the parents engaged in conflict through the courts over visitation or custody. When parents got along and both maintained caring relationships with their children of the first marriage, undiminished by their postdivorce relationships, and when both parents were doing reasonably well in their personal lives, the childhood and adolescence of the children were protected. However, even a protected childhood did not shield the children, at late adolescence and young adulthood, from the fear that their love relationships would fail.

This 25-year study points to divorce not as an acute stress from which the child recovers but as a *life-transforming experience* for the child. The divorced family is not simply an intact family from which the troubled marital bond has been removed. There are many stresses in the postdivorce family, and a great many daunting adjustments are required of the children. Hence, though the divorce was designed to relieve stress and may well have done so for the adult, for the child the stresses of the divorced family may be more burdensome, and he may feel correctly that he has lost more than he has gained. This is especially the case if, like most children in this study, the child was relatively content before the breakup and had no expectation of the upheaval ahead. Our findings suggest that whereas children in intact homes often seek continuity with their parents, those from divorced homes seek discontinuity. They fear identification with their parents. Those in our study who were close to stable grandparents felt reassured and comforted by the models that the grandparents provided, but only a minority had extended family members who remained, in the words of the children, "faithful" to them. Contrary to the loss model, remaining in frequent contact with both parents did not alleviate their suffering in adulthood, especially if the condition of the parents was discrepant and one parent remained lonely and unhappy.

It appears that when the child of divorce arrives on the stage of adulthood, the setting is lacking in good images of how an adult man and woman can live together in a stable relationship—and this becomes the central impediment that blocks the child's developmental journey. The need for a good internal image of the parents, as a couple, is important to every child during his growing-up years. The significance of this internal template increases in adolescence. Sad memories from the past and observations from the present build to a dramatic crescendo as young people from divorced homes confront the issues of love, sex, and lasting commitment, and as they address the practical workaday problems of choosing a life partner, of forming a realistic image of what they are looking for, of distinguishing love from dependency, and of creating an intimate relationship that holds.

How is the inner template of the child of divorce different from that of the young adult in the intact family, especially if the child has access to both parents and the parents refrain from fighting? As every "child of divorce" in our sample told us, no matter how often they see their parents through the years, the image of them together as a couple is forever lost; and a father in one home and a mother in another does not represent a marriage. Joint custody does not teach children how to create adult intimacy and mutual affection, how to resolve marital conflicts, or how to deal, as a couple, with a family crisis. As they grew up, these children lacked this central reassuring image. By strong contrast, the children from intact families told many stories about their home life and how their parents met and married. They had spent their growing-up years observing their parents' interactions and learning about marriage, and they were well aware of the expectable ups and downs. For the children of divorce, the parents' interactions—including the courtship, the marriage, and the divorce—collapsed into a black hole, as if the parents as a unified *couple* had vanished from the world and from the child's inner life.

Implications for Interventions

This study, along with others, has spawned educational and clinical programs throughout the country that address parents and children at the time of the breakup. There are no studies as yet of the long-term effectiveness of these or other interventions.

There are several policy issues that emerge from this study. They include: (a) equalizing access to higher education by extending child support nationwide beyond age 18 for youngsters in college, in families where the youngster would expectably have received substantial financial support had the parents remained together; (b) greater recognition by courts, mediators, and parents of the importance of considering the interests and concerns of adolescents in setting custody schedules; and (c) treatment at the time of the breakup for children and parents in families where the children have witnessed parental violence, in order to prevent posttraumatic symptoms from consolidating. We believe that these measures would ease the suffering and reduce the lasting anger of many children toward their parents.

The major challenges of engendering hope, creating good images of man–woman relationships, and teaching young people to choose appropriate partners and create a relationship that will hold are staggering in their complexity and go far beyond any interventions yet attempted. What follows are some initial suggestions based largely on reports from clinicians and reports of treatment from the subjects of this study.

There are indications from university counseling services that many adults who grew up in divorced families seek out therapy, especially during their first two college years. Counseling centers have successfully initiated groups and individual therapy for these students, who come with urgent pleas for help with their failed relationships or grave concerns about their parents— including those parents who waited to divorce until the youngest child went to college. This population would provide a splendid opportunity for a range of pilot projects.

Findings from this study have provided a detailed agenda for groups in several locales, including groups run by private practitioners. One such program, run by Dr. S. Demby in New York City, entitled "Leftover Business From My Folks' Divorce," has drawn a lively response. Also, our experience at the Judith Wallerstein Center for the Family in Transition in Corte Madera, California, showed similar strong interest among young professionals who were suffering from failures in relationships, sexual inhibitions, and difficulty in separating emotionally from their parents. Our experience has been that daughters feel especially guilty about enjoying a happier relationship with a man than their mothers were able to achieve.

Organized groups or courses in high school and, especially, in college might prove effective in eliciting attitudes of doubt and cynicism as well as stereotypes about men's and women's behavior in close relationships. The challenge would be to find counselors, therapists, or teachers who could hold the students' interest, raise provocative questions rather than preaching at these young people, and deal candidly with issues of trust, love, and sex, while conveying honesty, integrity, and hope.

One third of the subjects in this study sought individual therapy in adulthood. It is encouraging that those who benefited were able to terminate exploitative relationships quickly and went on to find appropriate partners. Clinicians reported that these people were excellent candidates for expressive therapy because of their youth, their pain, and their high motivation to work hard to change their lives. The problems they presented are in keeping with this study. Therapists need training in understanding and developing appropriate strategies geared specifically to the special challenges these young people bring. They make very quick contact with the therapist, but as they begin to value the therapy, their fears of being abandoned emerge powerfully in the transference, and their impulse is to flee before the therapist leaves them. If the therapist addresses these fears early in the treatment, it will enable the therapy to continue. These young adults are also in danger of feeling overwhelmed by sorrows and angers that lie close to the surface, as if their parents' divorce happened only yesterday. The therapist can help by acknowledging how long and how bravely these individuals have kept their suffering to themselves, perhaps in order to protect a needy parent, but that it is now safe to close the door on the past. This, then, defines their task.

Finally, a major theme in family life education might be to help parents discuss the reasons for the divorce with their children, as they become older adolescents. Silence or vague explanations offered by most parents only contribute to the young person's sense that divorce strikes suddenly, without warning. The family-life educator could also help the parents review with the child the mistakes that were made by both parties. Most important, the parents should assure the adolescent of their hope that their youngster will succeed in creating lasting relationships of his or her own. Such explicit assurances might alleviate the "fear of success" that haunts so many children of divorce. The goal should be to help the young person view divorce not as inevitable but as a result of avoidable human error.

It remains to be seen how much these and other, yet to be developed interventions can reduce anxieties and change attitudes that are continually reinforced by the surrounding culture. We are in new territory as clinicians and educators, and as members of a society in flux.

**E. Mavis Hetherington
and John Kelly**

For Better or For Worse

My interest in divorce grew out of my work in another area of family life. I think I have always had a special interest in the role fathers play in girls' lives because I had the good fortune to have a father who promoted female achievement and independence at a time when fathers rarely encouraged either.

In the late 1960s, my interest in fathers and daughters led to a startling research finding. At the time, informed opinion held that a mother shaped a daughter's gender identity, a father a son's. But a series of studies I did in the 1960s showed that fathers play the more important role in the gender identity of both boys and girls. The finding raised an interesting and important question: What happens to a girl when a father is absent due to death or divorce?

In my first study of families without fathers, I found that peers and especially mothers step in and assume the gender-shaping role men play in two-parent families. But the new study also raised a new question. Why did girls from divorced families have more social and psychological problems than girls from widowed families? Was there a unique developmental dynamic—perhaps even a uniquely harmful dynamic—in divorced families?

The Virginia Longitudinal Study (VLS), the most comprehensive study of divorce ever conducted, was intended to answer this question.

Most earlier research had relied only on the report of a single family member, usually a mother, to study the effects of divorce. The VLS expanded the study base to include not only the mother, father, and one focal child and a sibling in the family, but also people around the family. I also used a vast array of study tools, including interviews, questionnaires, standardized tests, and observations. Some of these instruments had never been used before, though they are now common in family studies. For example, I devised detailed methods of observing family interactions and activities; I and my team of investigators studied families in the home as they solved problems, as they chatted over dinner, and in the hours between the child's arrival at home and bedtime. We had a very personal look at how our families behaved when they disagreed, fought, relaxed, played, and soothed each other.

The VLS also was the first study to employ a structured diary in studying divorce. In order to assess each adult's mood fluctuations and activities, I had them keep diaries. Three days a week at half-hour intervals, parents had to note where they were, who they were with, what they were doing, and how they were feeling. If a person was having sex, she had to note that in the diary; the same was true if she were out on a date, having a fight at work, sitting in a singles bar, arguing with her mother, or trying to soothe an upset child.

The diaries yielded a great deal of unique and very fine-grained detail. For example, I found that a woman's feelings of anger and helplessness usually lasted longer after a fight with a son than a daughter. I also found that casual sex produced extreme depression and feelings of being unloved in many women and sent a few to the edge. Though suicide attempts were rare in the VLS, the seven that did occur were all attempts by women, and all were triggered by casual sex.

The children in the study—who were age four at the start of the VLS—received even more intense scrutiny. They were observed alone and with parents, peers, and siblings. We observed them at home, in school, on the playground, and also at the Hetherington Laboratory at the University of Virginia. Parents, teachers, and study observers were asked to assess each "target child." As the child grew older, the list of assessors grew to include peers, brothers and sisters, and the child himself, who was periodically asked to make self-assessments.

One of the most important aspects of the VLS was the use of a non-divorced comparison group. With its help, we were able to distinguish between the normal changes all families and family members undergo and changes that were linked directly to the impact of divorce and remarriage.

Initially, the Virginia Longitudinal Study of Divorce, which was launched in 1972, was intended to study how seventy-two preschool children and their families adapted to divorce at two months, one year, and two years. To provide a yardstick of comparison, seventy-two non-divorced families were also included in the study. The study's two-year time limit reflected then current thinking that most families had restabilized by two years after divorce.

But then something unexpected happened. The seventy-two men and women in my divorced group began to remarry and form stepfamilies, and the seventy-two couples in my married comparison group began to divorce. I seemed to be studying a moving target!

At first, I was frustrated. Didn't these folks have any respect for science? But then I realized I had been given a golden opportunity. Women's liberation and employment, no-fault divorce, the sexual revolution, self-actualization, the movements of the sixties and seventies, all were dramatically changing American mating habits. In the blink of an eye, the entire country seemed to jump from the paternal certainties of *Father Knows Best* to the postmodern chaos of *The Brady Bunch*.

Politicians, religious leaders, newspapers, magazines, and television documentaries decried the "breakdown of the nuclear family"; my fellow academics hailed the "emergence of the non-traditional family." But whatever phrase people chose, everyone agreed: America was in the midst of an unprecedented social change—one that would be played out for decades to come in the nation's living rooms, bedrooms, courtrooms, and legislatures.

But was the change positive or negative or a little bit of both? . . .

Mostly Happy: Children of Divorce as Young Adults

David Coleman has his father's imposing height and muscularity, but whereas on Richard, size added to his air of menace, making him look explosive even at rest, the son's six-foot-three frame has the opposite effect. It underscores his gentleness, makes you notice it in a way you wouldn't if he were a smaller, more delicate-looking man.

At a time when genetic theories threatened to reduce human development to a branch of biology, the difference between gentle David and violent Richard reminds us of the powerful role nurture plays in development. Genes are important, yes, certainly, but life experiences—especially with those closest to us—can take a given set of genes and make them add up in many different ways.

Much of the credit for the way David and his older sister, Leah, have ended up goes to Janet. Both benefited immensely from her ability to maintain a stable, loving, emotionally safe environment through Richard's stalking, through the family's sojourn on welfare, and through [stepfather] Nick and Leah's fights. When the VLS ended, David had taken over much of the responsibility for running "Janet's Garden," and Leah was a happily married mother, with a young daughter.

In the 1970s, a fierce debate broke out about the future of children like David and Leah. Critics of the divorce revolution believed that as the generation of children from divorced families matured, American society would descend into disorder and chaos. The collapse of the two-parent family, the traditional engine of socialization, critics argued, would lead to a *Clockwork Orange* generation of unstable, reckless, indulgent young adults, who would overrun the nation's prisons, substance abuse centers, and divorce courts.

"Nonsense," declared supporters of the divorce revolution, who saw divorce as a kind of cleansing agent. At last, the dark gloomy oppressive Victorian house that was the nuclear family would get a long-overdue spring cleaning, one that would produce a new and more egalitarian, tolerant, and fulfilled generation of men and women.

While I found evidence to support both views, the big headline in my data is that *80 percent of children from divorced homes eventually are able to adapt to their new life and become reasonably well adjusted.* A subgroup of girls even become exceptionally competent as a result of dealing with the challenges of divorce, enjoy a normal development, and grow into truly outstanding young adults. The 20 percent who continue to bear the scars of divorce fall into a troubled group, who display impulsive, irresponsible, antisocial behavior or are depressed. At the end of the VLS, troubled youths were having difficulty at work, in romantic relationships, and in gaining a toehold in adult life. They had the highest academic dropout rate and the highest divorce rate in the study, and were more likely to be faring poorly economically. In addition, being troubled and a girl made a young woman more likely to have left home early and to have experienced at least one out-of-wedlock pregnancy, birth, or abortion.

However, coming from a non-divorced family did not always protect against growing into a troubled young adult. Ten percent of youths in non-divorced families, compared to 20 percent in divorced and remarried families, were troubled. Most of our troubled young men and women came from families where conflict was frequent and authoritative parenting rare. In adulthood, as was found in childhood and adolescence, those who had moved from a highly contentious intact home situation to a more harmonious divorced family situation, with a caring, competent parent, benefited from the divorce and had fewer problems. But the legacy of the stresses and inept parenting associated with divorce and remarriage, and especially with living in a complex stepfamily, are still seen in the psychological, emotional, and social problems in 20 percent of young people from these families.

A piece of good news about our youths was that their antisocial behavior declined as they matured. Much of the adolescent exploration, experimentation, and sense of invulnerability had abated. Although excessive use of alcohol remained a problem for one quarter, drug abuse and lawbreaking had declined in all of our groups; but the decrease had been most marked in those who married.

What about the other 80 percent of young people from divorced and remarried families?

While most were not exactly the New Man or New Woman that the divorce revolution's supporters had predicted, they were behaving the way young adults were supposed to behave. They were choosing careers, developing permanent relationships, ably going about the central tasks of young adulthood, and establishing a grown-up life.

They ranged from those who were remarkably well adjusted to Good Enoughs and competent-at-a-costs, who were having a few problems but coping reasonably well to very well.

Finally, it should be a reassuring finding for divorced and remarried parents, and their children, that for every young man or woman who emerged from postnuclear family life with problems, four others were functioning reasonably or exceptionally well.

I think our findings ultimately contain two bottom-line messages about the long-term effects of divorce on children. The first is about parents, especially mothers. If someone creates a Nobel Prize for Unsung Hero, my nominee will be the divorced mother. Even when the world was collapsing round them, many divorced mothers found the courage and resiliency to do what had to be done. Such maternal tenacity and courage paid off. Despite all the emotional and financial pressures imposed by marital failure, most of our divorced women managed to provide the support, sensitivity, and engagement their children needed for normal development. And while divorce creates developmental risks, except in cases of extraordinary stress, children can be protected by vigorous, involved, competent parenting.

The second bottom line is about flexibility and diversity. Divorce is not a form of developmental predestination. Children, like adults, take many different routes out of divorce; some lead to unhappiness, others to a rewarding and fulfilling life. And since over the course of life, new experiences are being encountered and new relationships formed, protective and risk factors alter, and the door to positive change always remains open. . . .

Twenty Years Later

The adverse effects of divorce and remarriage are still echoing in some divorced families and their offspring twenty years after divorce, but they are in the minority. The vast majority of young people from these families are reasonably well adjusted and are coping reasonably well in relationships with their families, friends, and intimate partners. Most are moving toward establishing careers, economic independence, and satisfying social and intimate relationships. Some are caring spouses and parents. Although the divorce may resonate more in the memories of these children, most parents and children see the divorce as having been for the best, and have moved forward with their lives.

Points to Remember

- Parent, child, and sibling relationships that have been close in childhood seldom deteriorate in adulthood.
- Even if absence doesn't make the heart grow fonder, conflict usually diminishes once the protagonists are apart and contact becomes optional. Disengagement often replaces conflict in stepparent-stepchild and sibling relationships in divorced and remarried families in young adulthood.
- Biologically related siblings, whether in divorced, non-divorced, or remarried families, tend to have both more attached and more rivalrous relationships than those found in stepsiblings.
- Men remain reluctant to do their fair share. In most first- and second-generation VLS homes, the burden of household labor continued to fall predominantly on female shoulders. After a demanding eight- or ten-hour day at the office, many of our women would come home to cope with unmade beds, unwashed laundry, unfed children, and the morning's unwashed breakfast dishes in the sink.
- A family history of divorce does leave children of divorce relationship- and marriage-challenged. Children of divorce are often reluctant to commit wholeheartedly to a marriage, have fewer relationship skills, and in some cases show a genetic predisposition to destabilizing behaviors like antisocial behavior, impulsivity, and depression.
- Gender affects a person's divorce risk more than the kind of family the person was brought up in. In divorced, remarried, and non-divorced families alike, male belligerence, withdrawal, and lack of affection often produce thoughts of divorce in a woman; female contempt, nagging, or reciprocated aggression, thoughts of divorce in a man.
- Although marital instability is higher in offspring from divorced families, marriage to a stable, supportive spouse from a non-divorced family eliminates the intergenerational transmission of divorce. A caring, mature spouse can teach their partner from a divorced family skills they never learned at home.

- Young adults from complex stepfamilies continue to have more adjustment and family problems than young adults in other kinds of stepfamilies.
- For most youths, the legacy of divorce is largely overcome. Twenty years after divorce, most men and women who had grown up in divorced families and stepfamilies are functioning reasonably well. Only a minority still exhibited emotional and social problems, and had difficulties with intimate relationships and achievement.

CHALLENGE QUESTIONS

Does the Divorce of Parents Harm Their Children?

1. Too much emphasis can be placed on the differences between these two selections. What are some of their many points of agreement?
2. How is it that two top researchers in the field can differ at all in their conclusions? Does this necessarily mean problems with their investigations?
3. Interview a student whose parents are divorced. Make sense of their experiences from one or the other of these authors' perspectives.
4. How might the implications of the conclusions of Wallerstein et al. and Hetherington/Kelly differ for parenting and psychotherapy?
5. If you and your spouse were faced with the possibility of divorce, what would you do with the information obtained from one or both of these selections?

Families and Work Institute

This Web site provides resources from the Families and Work Institute, which conducts policy research on issues related to the changing workforce and operates a national clearinghouse on work and family life.

    http://www.familiesandwork.org/index.html

Childcare Resource and Research Unit

The Childcare Resource and Research Unit, which is part of the Centre for Urban and Community Studies at the University of Toronto, focuses on early childhood care and education research and policy. The research section contains information about new research findings and news about ongoing research.

    http://www.childcarecanada.org

Children of Divorce: All Kinds of Problems

This Americans for Divorce Reform page offers links to studies of problems experienced by children of divorce.

    http://www.divorcereform.org/all.html

Tufts University Child & Family Web Guide

This page links to a handful of quality sites on divorce.

    http://cfw.tufts.edu/viewtopics.asp?
        categoryid=2&topicid=32

The Psi Cafe: A Psychology Resource Site

This site discusses different aspects of psychological research and provides helpful links to other sites that focus on becoming a more effective parent.

    http://www.psy.pdx.edu/PsiCafe/Areas/
        Developmental/Parenting/

PART 4

Cognitive Processes

*T*he nature and limits of our mental (or cognitive) processes pose fundamental questions for psychologists. For example, how much control do we truly have over our actions? Some psychologists contend that we do not have any real choices and that we are ultimately the products of an unchangeable past, such as our memories. How would society change if this theory were adopted? Also, are cognitive capacities, such as intelligence, determined at birth? Is it even valid to speak of intelligence as one entity, cutting across all activities and skills, or is it better to think of multiple intelligences?

- Are Human Cognitive and Behavioral Activities Determined?

- Should Psychology Adopt a Theory of Multiple Intelligences?

ISSUE 9

Are Human Cognitive and Behavioral Activities Determined?

YES: John A. Bargh and Tanya L. Chartrand, from "The Unbearable Automaticity of Being," *American Psychologist* (July 1999)

NO: Amy Fisher Smith, from "Automaticity: The Free Will Determinism Debate Continued" (An Original Article Written for This Volume)

ISSUE SUMMARY

YES: Psychologists John A. Bargh and Tanya L. Chartrand assert that people are controlled not by their purposeful choices and intentions but by the environment through automatic cognitive processes.

NO: In response, psychologist Amy Fisher Smith agrees that people do, in fact, have automatic behaviors but she believes these behaviors can be explained by mental processes akin to a free will.

Imagine yourself as a juror with an accused rapist standing in front of you. The rapist explains to you that his behavior is the product of a history of child abuse and that he had no control over his violent actions toward the victim. In other words, he presents himself as having been ultimately determined by his environment. Would you believe this rapist's explanation? Or, would you tend to assume that he could have acted otherwise than his tragic history—that he has something like a free will?

Many people do not realize there are many psychological theories that ultimately assume we do not have any choices and that we are the product of an unchangeable past. One such theory, radical behaviorism, states that we are mere products of our environment, implying that the accused rapist is not personally responsible for his crime. His past experiences with the environment (e.g., reinforcement history) are responsible. Contrast these implications with the theory of Carl Jung, a noted psychoanalyst. Although he believes in many unconscious and, thus, automatic behaviors, Jung views the person as the free agent of all of them. From this perspective, the rapist would be ultimately responsible for his actions, despite his unfavorable childhood.

In the first selection, psychological researchers John A. Bargh and Tanya L. Chartrand would seem to disagree with this view. They contend that most of a person's everyday life is determined not by his or her conscious intentions and purposeful choices but by mental processes that are determined by the environment. Bargh and Chartrand explain that perceiving an action increases a person's likelihood of performing that action. For example, if a man sees a movie that depicts violence against another, he is more likely to become violent because he has witnessed this action. Since perceptual activity is primarily involuntary, Bargh and Chartrand conclude that the environment controls our mental activity and, hence, our actions. Because goals are also considered to be mental activity, Bargh and Chartrand suggest that goals are automatically activated by the environment as well.

Theoretical psychologist, Amy Fisher Smith, responds to Bargh and Chartrand's arguments by agreeing with their data on automatic behaviors but rejecting their interpretation of that data. Specifically, she questions whether their findings have to be interpreted within a deterministic framework. She contends that this framework is contrary to many of the assumptions that society needs for people's behaviors. For example, Smith believes that people are rightly viewed as responsible agents, both personally and culturally. She then offers an alternative way of understanding automatic thoughts and behaviors in which people are not determined by environmental stimuli, but are actively interpreting what they perceive in the environment. Finally, Smith argues that the activation of goals is ultimately directed by the person and not by the environment, even though we might not have an immediate awareness of our guiding beliefs and assumptions.

POINT

- Our environment determines the way we think and behave.
- Individuals are more likely to repeat an action they see.
- The environment automatically activates both conscious and unconscious goals.
- We are ultimately not responsible for our actions.
- Data on automatic behaviors prove that we are determined by forces beyond our control.

COUNTERPOINT

- It is possible to understand automatic behaviors in a nondeterministic way.
- We are not passively shaped by stimuli from the environment.
- Individuals ultimately direct their own goals by actively bestowing meaning upon experiences.
- The legal system generally views people as agentic beings.
- The automaticity data do not objectively reveal that the environment determines our thoughts and behaviors.

John A. Bargh and
Tanya L. Chartrand

 **YES**

The Unbearable Automaticity of Being

> The strongest knowledge—that of the total unfreedom of the human will—is nonetheless the poorest in successes, for it always has the strongest opponent: human vanity.
>
> —Nietzsche, *Human, All Too Human*

Imagine for a moment that you are a psychology professor who does experiments on conscious awareness. You keep finding that your subtle manipulations of people's judgments and even behavior are successful—causing your experimental participants to like someone or to dislike that same person, to feel happy or sad, to behave rudely or with infinite patience. However, none of your participants have a clue as to what caused them to feel or behave in these ways. In fact, they don't believe you, and sometimes even argue with you, when you try to explain your experiment to them and how they were caused to feel or behave.

Now, let's say you are home with your family for the holidays or on vacation. Your aunt or brother-in-law asks politely what your job is like. You attempt to explain your research and even some of your more interesting findings. Once again you are met with incredulity. "This can't be so," says your brother-in-law. "I can't remember this ever happening to me, even once."

Our thesis here—that most of a person's everyday life is determined not by their conscious intentions and deliberate choices but by mental processes that are put into motion by features of the environment and that operate outside of conscious awareness and guidance—is a difficult one for people to accept. One cannot have any experiences or memories of being nonconsciously influenced, of course, almost by definition. But let us move from the layperson to the experts (namely, psychological researchers) and see what they have to say about the relative roles played by conscious versus nonconscious causes of daily experience.

The major historical perspectives of 20th-century psychology can be distinguished from one another based on their positions on this question: Do

From *American Psychologist*, vol. 54, no. 7, July 1999, pp. 462–466, 468–469, 476. Copyright © 1999 by American Psychological Association. Reprinted by permission of the author. References omitted.

people consciously and actively choose and control (by acts of will) these various experiences and behaviors, or are those experiences and behaviors instead determined directly by other factors, such as external stimuli or internal, unconscious forces?

Freud, for example, considered human behavior to be determined mainly by biological impulses and the unconscious interplay of the psychic forces those impulses put into motion. The individual was described as usually unaware of these intrapsychic struggles and of their causal effect on his or her behavior, although it was possible to become aware of them (usually on Freud's couch) and then change one's patterns of behavior.

Early behaviorist theory similarly proposed that behavior was outside of conscious control, but placed the source of the control not in the psyche but in external stimulus conditions and events. Environmental events directed all behavior in combination with the person's reinforcement history.

A third major perspective emerged in midcentury with Rogers's self theory and the humanist movement. In what was a reaction to the then-dominant Freudian and behavioristic perspectives, in which "people were thought to be either pushed by their inner drives or pulled by external events," the "causal self" was placed as a mediator between the environment and one's responses to it. In these self-theories, behavior was adapted to the current environment, but it was determined by an act of conscious choice. Fifty years later, this perspective remains dominant among theories of motivation and self-regulation.

Finally, the contemporary cognitive perspective, in spirit as well as in practice, seeks to account for psychological phenomena in terms of deterministic mechanisms. Although there exist models that acknowledge the role played by higher-order choice or "executive" processes, the authors of these models generally acknowledge that the lack of specification of how these choices are made is an inadequacy of the model. Neisser's seminal book *Cognitive Psychology*, for example, describes the "problem of the executive," in which the flexible choice and selection processes are described as a homunculus or "little person in the head" that does not constitute a scientific explanation. This position is echoed in Barsalou's text, in which he too calls free will a homunculus, noting that "most cognitive psychologists believe that the fundamental laws of the physical world determine human behavior completely."

Fortunately, contemporary psychology for the most part has moved away from doctrinaire either—or positions concerning the locus of control of psychological phenomena, to an acknowledgment that they are determined jointly by processes set into motion directly by one's environment and by processes instigated by acts of conscious choice and will. Such dual-process models, in which the phenomenon in question is said to be influenced simultaneously by conscious (control) and nonconscious (automatic) processes, are now the norm in the study of attention and encoding, memory, emotional appraisal, emotional disorders, attitudes and persuasion, and social perception and judgment. Thus, the mainstream of psychology accepts both the fact of conscious or willed causation of mental and behavioral processes and the fact of automatic or environmentally triggered processes. The debate has shifted from the existence (or not) of these different causal forces to the circumstances under which one versus the other controls the mind. Is everyday life mainly comprised of consciously or of nonconsciously caused evaluations, judgments, emotions, motivations, and behavior?

As Posner and Snyder noted a quarter century ago, this question of how much conscious control we have over our judgments, decisions, and behavior is one of the most basic and important questions of human existence. The title of the present article makes our position on this question a matter of little suspense, but to make the reasons for that position clear and hopefully compelling, we must start by defining what we mean by a conscious mental process and an automatic mental process. The defining features of what we are referring to as a *conscious* process have remained consistent and stable for over 100 years: These are mental acts of which we are aware, that we intend (i.e., that we start by an act of will), that require effort, and that we can control (i.e., we can stop them and go on to something else if we choose). In contrast, there has been no consensus on the features of a single form of *automatic* process; instead two major strains have been identified and studied over the past century, similar only in that they do not possess all of the defining features of a conscious process.

First, research on skill acquisition focused on intentional, goal-directed processes that became more efficient over time and practice until they could operate without conscious guidance. These were intentional but effortless mental processes. Second, research on the initial perceptual analysis or encoding of environmental events (called "preattentive" or "preconscious" processing) showed that much of this analysis takes place not only effortlessly, but without any intention or often awareness that it was taking place. The "new look" in perception of the 1940s and 1950s, in which threatening or emotion-laden words or symbols were purportedly shown to be "defended against" through having higher perceptual thresholds than more neutral stimuli, is a prototypic example of this line of research. These are the two classic forms of "not-conscious" mental processes; both forms operate effortlessly and without need for conscious guidance, but one (mental skills) requires an act of will to start operation, and the other (preconscious) does not.

So much for how the field of psychology has historically thought about automatic processes; let's return to our aunts and in-laws. What does the concept mean to them? The popular meaning of "automatic" is something that happens, no matter what, as long as certain conditions are met. An automatic answering machine clicks into operation after a specified number of phone rings and then records whatever the caller wants to say. No one has to be at home to turn it on to record whenever the phone happens to ring. Automatic piloting systems on airplanes now perform many sophisticated and complex functions to keep the plane on course and to land it under poor visibility and weather conditions, actually making air travel safer than when such functions were handled entirely by the human pilots.

In modern technological societies one encounters many such automatic devices and systems in the course of daily life. They are all devised and intended to free us from tasks that don't really require our vigilance and intervention, so that our time and energy can be directed toward those that do. And these systems also perform their tasks with a greater degree or reliability, as they are not prone to sources of human error, such as fatigue, distraction, and boredom.

Just as automatic mechanical devices free us from having to attend to and intervene in order for the desired effect to occur, automatic mental processes free one's limited conscious attentional capacity from tasks in which they are no longer needed. Many writers have pointed out how impossible it would be to function effectively if conscious, controlled, and aware mental processing had to deal with every aspect of life, from perceptual comprehension of the environment (both physical and social) to choosing and guiding every action and response to the environment. But none put it so vividly as the philosopher A. N. Whitehead:

> It is a profoundly erroneous truism, repeated by all copy-books and by eminent people making speeches, that we should cultivate the habit of thinking of what we are doing. The precise opposite is the case. Civilization adva.nces by extending the number of operations which we can perform without thinking about them. Operations of thought are like cavalry charges in a battle—they are strictly limited in number, they require fresh horses, and must only be made at decisive moments.

Whitehead presaged what psychological research would discover 86 years later. Baumeister, Tice, and their colleagues recently demonstrated just how limited conscious self-regulatory capacities are in a series of studies on what they called "ego depletion." In their experiments, an act of self-control in one domain (being told not to eat any of the chocolate chip cookies sitting in front of you) seriously depletes a person's ability to engage in self-control in a subsequent, entirely unrelated domain (persistence on a verbal task), which was presented to participants as being a separate experiment. . . .

Tice and Baumeister concluded after their series of eight such experiments that because even minor acts of self-control, such as making a simple choice, use up this limited self-regulatory resource, such conscious acts of self-regulation can occur only rarely in the course of one's day. Even as they were defending the importance of the conscious self for guiding behavior, Baumeister et al. concluded it plays a causal role only 5% or so of the time.

Given one's understandable desire to believe in free will and self-determination, it may be hard to bear that most of daily life is driven by automatic, nonconscious mental processes—but it appears impossible, from these findings, that conscious control could be up to the job. As Sherlock Holmes was fond of telling Dr. Watson, when one eliminates the impossible, whatever remains—however improbable—must be the truth.

It follows, as Lord Whitehead argued, that most of our day-to-day actions, motivations, judgments, and emotions are not the products of conscious choice and guidance, but must be driven instead by mental processes put into operation directly by environmental features and events. Is this the case? The logical and empirical limits on conscious self-regulation tell us where to look for automatic phenomena—not only in perceptual activity and crude, simple processes (to which cognitive psychologists originally believed they were limited, but everywhere. We and other researchers have been looking, and here is what we have found.

Perceiving Is for Doing

Humans and other primates have an innate capacity for imitative behavior and vicarious learning. This has led many theorists over many years to argue that there must be a strong associative connection between representations used in perceiving the behavior of others and those used to behave in the same way oneself. Some have even argued that the same representation is used both in perceiving others' behavior and to behave that way oneself. William James, following the ideas of the physiologist William Carpenter, popularized the principle of "ideo-motor action" to account for how merely thinking about an action increases its likelihood of occurring. For Carpenter as well as James, the important feature of ideomotor action was that mere ideation about the behavior was sufficient to cause one to act—no separate act of volition was necessary. Although James argued that "thinking is for doing," we sought to extend the source of ideation from inside the head to out in the world—specifically, by considering whether merely perceiving an action increases the person's likelihood of performing the same act.

Automatic Perception Induces the Ideas

Of course, one's own thinking is more or less under one's own conscious control, so the principle of ideomotor action by itself does not mean the resultant behavior is caused by nonconscious, external environmental events. But because perceptual activity is largely automatic and not under conscious or intentional control (the orange on the desk cannot be perceived as purple through an act of will), perception is the route by which the environment directly causes mental activity—specifically, the activation of internal representations of the outside world. The activated contents of the mind are not only those in the stream of consciousness but also include representations of currently present objects, events, behavior of others, and so on. In short, the "ideo" in ideomotor effects could just as well come from outside the head as within it.

When one considers that this automatic perception of another person's behavior introduces the idea of action—but from the outside environment instead of from internal, intentionally directed thought—a direct and automatic route is provided from the external environment to action tendencies, via perception. The idea that social perception is a largely automated psychological phenomenon is now widely accepted. Many years of research have demonstrated the variety of ways in which behaviors are encoded spontaneously and without intention in terms of relevant trait concepts, how contextual priming of trait concepts changes the perceiver's interpretation of an identical behavior (through temporarily increasing their accessibility or readiness to be used), and how stereotypes of social groups become activated automatically on the mere perception of the distinguishing features of a group member. Perceptual interpretations of behavior, as well as assumptions about an individual's behavior based on identified group membership, become automated like any other representation if they are frequently and consistently made in the presence of the behavioral or group membership features.

The Perception–Behavior Link

Thus, the external environment can direct behavior non-consciously through a two-stage process: automatic perceptual activity that then automatically creates behavioral tendencies through the perception–behavior link. That is, the entire environment–perception–behavior sequence is automatic, with no role played by conscious choice in producing the behavior. Berkowitz posited that such a mechanism underlies media effects on behavior and modeling effects more generally. In his account, perceiving the aggressiveness (for example) of an actor in a movie or television show activated, in an unintentional and nonconscious manner, the perceiver's own behavioral representation of aggressiveness, thereby increasing the likelihood of aggressive behavior. Carver et al. experimentally tested this hypothesis by first exposing some participants (and not others) to hostility-related words in a first "language experiment," and then—in what was believed to be a separate experiment—putting the participants in the role of a "teacher" who was to give shocks to a "learner" participant. Those who had been "primed" with hostile-related stimuli subsequently gave longer shocks to the learner than did control participants.

Carver et al. had explicitly told their participants to give the shocks, however, and so the question remained whether external events could induce the idea of the behavior itself. Bargh, Chen, and Burrows found that it indeed could. When trait constructs or stereotypes were nonconsciously activated during an unrelated task (i.e., "primed"), participants were subsequently more likely to act in line with the content of the primed trait construct or stereotype. In one experiment, participants were first exposed to words related to either rudeness (e.g., rude, impolite, obnoxious), politeness (e.g., respect, considerate, polite) or neither (in the control condition) in an initial "language experiment." They were then given a chance to interrupt an ongoing conversation (in order to ask for the promised next experimental task). Significantly more participants in the "rude" priming condition interrupted (67%) than did those in the control condition (38%), whereas only 16% of those primed with "polite" interrupted the conversation.

Experiment 2 extended these findings to the case of stereotype activation. In a first task, participants were primed (in the course of an ostensible language test) either with words related to the stereotype of the elderly (e.g., Florida, sentimental, wrinkle) or with words unrelated to the stereotype. As predicted, participants primed with the elderly-related material subsequently behaved in line with the stereotype—specifically, they walked more slowly down the hallway after leaving the experiment. Dijksterhuis, Bargh, and Miedema have shown that these effects also hold for another central feature of the elderly stereotype—forgetfulness. Those participants whose stereotype for the elderly had been unobtrusively activated in the "first experiment" subsequently could not remember as many features of the room in which that experiment was conducted as could control participants. (For similar findings of behavioral consequences of automatic stereotype activation with different stereotypes, including those for professors and for soccer hooligans, see Dijksterhuis & van Knippenberg. . . .

Goals and Motivations

Although the effect of perception on behavior occurs passively, without the need for a conscious choice or intention to behave in the suggested manner, this does not mean that people do not have goals and purposes and are merely passive experiencers of events. People are active participants in the world with purposes and goals they want to attain. Much, if not most, of our responses to the environment in the form of judgments, decisions, and behavior are determined not solely by the information available in that environment but rather by how it relates to whatever goal we are currently pursuing.

For example, when we are trying to get a new acquaintance to like us and perhaps be our friend, the things about that person to which we pay attention and later best remember are quite different than if we meet the same person in a different context, such as if they are a person to whom we are considering subletting our apartment or someone sitting across from us late at night on the subway. And as for behavioral responses to one's environment, the idea that behavior is largely purposive and determined by one's current goals has long had broad support within psychology—not only among those with a humanistic orientation but among cognitive psychologists and neobehaviorists as well.

But if the currently-held goal largely determines whether judgments are made (and the quality of those judgments) and how one behaves, this would seem to rule out much of a role for automatic, environmentally driven influences. How can the environment directly control much of anything if goals play such a mediational role?

The answer is as follows: if (and perhaps only if) the environment itself activates and puts the goal into motion. To entertain this possibility, one must assume that goals are represented mentally and like any other mental representation are capable of becoming automatically activated by environmental features. There is no reason, a priori, to assume that goal representations cannot become automated in the same way that stereotypes and other perceptual structures do, as long as the same conditions for development of automatic activation occur.

The Acquisition of Automaticity

What are those conditions? As discussed above, the development of most acquired forms of automaticity (i.e., skill acquisition) depends on the frequent and consistent pairing of internal responses with external events. Initially, conscious choice and guidance are needed to perform the desired behavior or to generate what one hopes are accurate and useful expectations about what is going to happen next in the situation. But to the extent the same expectations are generated, or the same behavior is enacted, or the same goal and plan are chosen in that situation, conscious choice drops out as it is not needed—it has become a superfluous step in the process. According to James,

> It is a general principle in Psychology that consciousness deserts all processes where it can no longer be of use . . . We grow unconscious of every feeling which is useless as a sign to lead us to our ends, and where one sign will suffice others drop out, and that one remains, to work alone.

Intentional Acquisition of Automaticity

At some level, people are aware of this phenomenon by which conscious choice-points drop out of mental sequences to the extent they are no longer needed (because the same choice is made frequently and consistently at a given point). This is shown by the fact that we often use it in a strategic fashion in order to develop a desired skill, such as driving a car or playing the violin. We purposefully engage in the considerable practice (frequent and consistent performances) required to sublimate many of the components of the skill. In this way, the conscious capacity that is freed up from not having to direct and coordinate the lower level components of the skill can be used instead to plot and direct higher-level strategy during the game or performance. And so, one sees the teenager go from being an overwhelmed tangle of nerves at the first attempts to drive a car to soon being able to do so while conversing, tuning the radio, and getting nervous instead over that evening's date.

Unintentional Acquisition of Automaticity

But what we find most intriguing, in considering how mental processes recede from consciousness over time with repeated use, is that the process of automation itself is automatic. The necessary and sufficient ingredients for automation are frequency and consistency of use of the same set of component mental processes under the same circumstances—regardless of whether the frequency and consistency occur because of a desire to attain a skill, or whether they occur just because we have tended in the past to make the same choices or to do the same thing or to react emotionally or evaluatively in the same way each time. These processes also become automated, but because we did not start out intending to make them that way, we are not aware that they have been and so, when that process operates automatically in that situation, we aren't aware of it.

This is how goals and motives can eventually become automatically activated by situations. For a given individual, his or her motivations (e.g., to gain the love and respect of one's parents) are represented in memory at the most abstract level of an organized hierarchy, followed by the various goals one can pursue to satisfy those motivations (e.g., to be a success, to become a lawyer, to have a family). Each of these motivations is associated with goals that will fulfill it, and these goals in turn have associated with them the various plans and strategies that can be used to attain the goals (e.g., study hard). These plans are in turn linked to specific behaviors by which the plan is carried out. However, an individual's motivations are chronic and enduring over time. And thus, because of the stability over time of one's motivations, in many situations a given individual will frequently and consistently pursue the same goal. If the same goal is pursued within the same situation, then conscious choice eventually drops out of the selection of what goal to pursue—the situational features themselves directly put the goal into operation. . . .

Conclusions

The heavier the burden, the closer our lives come to the earth, the more real and truthful they become. Conversely, the absolute absence of a burden causes man to be lighter than air, to soar into the heights, take leave of the earth and his earthly being, and become only half real, his movements free as they are insignificant. What then shall we choose? Weight or lightness?

For many years now, researchers have studied two main types of mental processes, both in isolation and in interaction with each other. The two types are known by a variety of names—conscious–nonconscious, controlled–automatic, explicit–implicit, systematic–heuristic—but it is clear which one is "heavy" and which one is "light." To consciously and willfully regulate one's own behavior, evaluations, decisions, and emotional states requires considerable effort and is relatively slow. Moreover, it appears to require a limited resource that is quickly used up, so conscious self-regulatory acts can only occur sparingly and for a short time. On the other hand, the nonconscious or automatic processes we've described here are unintended, effortless, very fast, and many of them can operate at any given time. Most important, they are effortless, continually in gear guiding the individual safely through the day. Automatic self-regulation is, if you will, thought lite—"one third less effort than regular thinking." The individual is free, in Kundera's sense, of the burden of their operation.

Some of the automatic guidance systems we've outlined are "natural" and don't require experience to develop. These are the fraternization of perceptual and behavioral representations and the connection between automatic evaluation processes on the one hand and mood and behavior on the other. Other forms of automatic self-regulation develop out of repeated and consistent experience; they map onto the regularities of one's experience and take tasks over from conscious choice and guidance when that choice is not really being exercised. This is how goals and motives can come to operate nonconsciously in given situations, how stereotypes can become chronically associated with the perceptual features of social groups, and how evaluations can become integrated with the perceptual representation of the person, object, or event so that they become active immediately and unintentionally in the course of perception.

To produce the empirical evidence on which these claims rest, we and others have conducted a variety of experiments in which goals, evaluations, and perceptual constructs (traits, stereotypes) were primed in an unobtrusive manner. Through use of these priming manipulations, the mental representations were made active to later exert their influence without an act of will and without the participants' awareness of the influence. Yet in all of these studies, the effect was the same as when people are aware of and intend to engage in that process. Thus it is no coincidence that goals, evaluations, and perceptual constructs have the same essential structure, because the underlying principle is the same in all three: Mental representations designed to perform a certain function will perform that function once activated, regardless of where the activation comes from. The representation does not "care" about the source of the activation; it is blind to it and has no "memory" about it that might cause it to behave differently depending on the particular source. The activated mental representation is like a button being pushed; it can be pushed by one's finger intentionally (e.g., turning on the electric coffeemaker) or accidentally (e.g., by the cat on the countertop) or by a decision made in the past (e.g., by setting the automatic turn-on mechanism the night before). In whatever way the start button is pushed, the mechanism subsequently behaves in the same way.

And so, the evaluations we've made in the past are now made for us and predispose us to behave in consistent ways; the goals we have pursued in the past now become active and guide our behavior in pursuit of the goal in relevant situations; and our perceptions of the emotional and behavioral reactions of others makes us tend to respond in the same way, establishing bonds of rapport and liking in a natural and effortless way. Thus "the automaticity of being" is far from the negative and maladaptive caricature drawn by humanistically oriented writers; rather, these processes are in our service and best interests—and in an intimate, knowing way at that. They are, if anything, "mental butlers" who know our tendencies and preferences so well that they anticipate and take care of them for us, without having to be asked.

The Dangers of Automatically Interpreting "Automaticity": The New Face of Determinism

> Joe is a regular guy who is driving in fairly heavy traffic, when suddenly, another driver cuts in front of Joe, causing him to slam on the brakes to avoid a near collision. Joe's heart is racing; his knuckles are white from gripping the steering wheel; and his breathing is short and fast. Joe finds himself enraged at the other driver. He begins to honk at the other driver, screaming obscenities and threats—possibly even attempting to follow the other driver to demand an apology or to exact some sort of revenge.

Joe represents a classic example of road rage—people who fly off the handle in inappropriate ways when confronted with offensive or dangerous driving in other drivers. How are behaviors such as Joe's road rage to be explained? Many psychologists are currently puzzling over such phenomena, especially since the anger of someone like Joe seems so automatic and non-conscious. In other words, Joe's rage seems to be an involuntary reaction—his rage does not seem to be something that he necessarily "chooses." Does this mean that Joe is determined—or forced—by his environment to become enraged? Would this mean that Joe is not responsible for his rage? Where does Joe's free will and choice enter in as a factor, if at all?

Answers to these questions are vital to psychologists. What is at stake is whether we are determined by environmental stimuli or whether we have some degree of freedom from such stimuli. If we are determined, it means that we can never really be responsible for our behaviors, because our behaviors are always caused by some other factor, stimulus, or situation outside of us. Alternatively, if we have agency or free will, it means that we can choose courses of behavior—we can act otherwise than the environmental stimuli might suggest. The ability to choose also means that we can be held accountable for our behaviors, because we are the initiating agents of our action—not some outside source.

A Deterministic Interpretation

One recently proposed theory (Bargh & Chartrand, 1999) attempts to explain our emotional responses (like Joe's road rage) as being caused and determined by environmental triggers (like the dangerous driver mentioned above). Bargh and Chartrand (1999), the proponents of this "automaticity" theory, argue that not only our emotional responses, but our thoughts and behaviors, are initiated and determined by environmental stimuli. If we consider Joe's road rage from this perspective, Joe does not consciously and willfully decide to become angry or enraged when the other driver cuts him off. Rather, Joe seems to be involuntarily responding to a specific environmental trigger—namely, the other bad driver. From Bargh and Chartrand's (1999) perspective, we automatically respond to external "features of the environment" (p. 462) in an "environment–perception–behavior sequence" with "no role played by conscious choice in producing the behavior" (p. 466). In other words, Joe perceives a "feature" or stimulus in the environment (i.e., the other driver), and then he automatically responds to this threatening stimulus in an unthinking way with a defensive emotion—anger or rage.

This means that Joe could not help but become enraged by the other driver. Indeed, Joe was determined to become so enraged. This determinism means that Joe is not responsible for his actions—the other driver is—and thus we cannot really hold Joe accountable for his rage, because his emotional response and subsequent behaviors are viewed as an involuntary and uncontrollable reaction to a specific trigger in the environment. What if exposure to the dangerous driver leads Joe to physically assault the other driver, or worse, what if Joe harms or kills the other driver? From the perspective of Bargh and Chartrand's (1999) determinism, the harmed or killed driver is to blame—not Joe.

Bargh and Chartrand's (1999) determinism is not limited to an understanding of emotional responses and behaviors like Joe's road rage (p. 473). Rather, Joe's road rage is a model for understanding *all* thoughts, emotions, and behaviors, whether conscious or non-conscious, voluntary or involuntary. When the authors discuss consciously chosen goals, for instance, they state that the "environment itself activates and puts the goal into motion" (Bargh & Chartrand, 1999, p. 468). This means that even when we think that we are consciously and willfully choosing our actions, we are actually engaged in a self-deception, because the environment has unwittingly set "the goal into motion" (p. 468). In other words, we do not really choose goals—ever. Rather, exposure to a particular kind of stimulus automatically activates both conscious and non-conscious goals, in which case, the goals themselves are never freely chosen.

A Free Will-ist Possibility

Interestingly, this deterministic view runs counter to many of the assumptions that we naturally make about our behaviors, both personally and culturally. For instance, we generally view ourselves as agents of our own actions, and this agentic view is embedded in our culture's legal system. From most judicial perspectives, Joe would be held accountable if he harmed the other driver in the road rage incident, because our legal system often presumes that people have a choice about their thoughts and actions. There are exceptions to the general rule (e.g., insanity defense), but for the most part, people are viewed as responsible agents. Hence, an age-old question is implicitly raised in Bargh and Chartrand's (1999) thesis—are we determined or are we free?

This article has two purposes. First, I critically examine Bargh and Chartrand's (1999) explanation of "automaticity"—the non-conscious and involuntary thoughts, behaviors, and emotions that they describe as being determined by the environment. Second, I offer a different way of understanding these non-conscious thoughts and behaviors that explains all the "data" like Joe's experiences and yet does not result in us losing our free will. Let us begin by noting how often people seem to act in ways that are automatic and non-conscious. Once we have mastered certain skills like driving, for instance, most of us can drive automatically without consciously choosing or intending the behavioral skills that are required (Bargh & Chartrand, 1999, p. 468). For instance, we commonly say that we drive on "auto-pilot," meaning that we coordinate the steering with the acceleration and breaking without consciously intending to do so.

Hence, the question is not whether automatic and non-conscious behaviors exist—they do. The question is whether automatic behaviors have to be explained as determined by environmental triggers as Bargh and Chartrand (1999) argue. Consider Joe again. Do we have to explain Joe's automatic rage as determined by environmental cues? Are there other equally plausible explanations or interpretations of Joe's automatic behavior that avoid such deterministic outcomes? Such alternative interpretations *are* possible.

The Relationship Between Interpretation and Data

The issue of interpretation is an important one—not only for the case of Joe's automatic road rage—but to scientific inquiry in general. As philosophers of science and many researchers have long noted, empirical findings (i.e., data) that emerge from scientific experiments are not immutable facts (Kuhn, 1962/1996; Popper, 1963). Rather, the data or brute "facts" that emerge in experiments must be meaningfully organized and interpreted in terms of the researcher's pre-existing theoretical frame of reference. The data themselves cannot tell us the facts of the matter, because the data themselves are not completely organized. What is needed is the organizing and meaning-making properties of the researcher's theory to make sense of the data. As Slife and Williams (1995) argue, "the experimental data are not experimental *findings* without the organization imposed on them by the scientist" (p. 75).

Data, then, are always interpreted, and this interpretation arises from the researchers' pre-existing philosophical and theoretical commitments as well as the history, traditions, expectations, and values of the researcher (Slife & Williams, 1995). The empirical findings or "data" about automaticity that Bargh and Chartrand (1999) report are equally interpreted. The automaticity data themselves do not objectively reveal that automatic thoughts and behaviors are determined by environmental triggers. Rather, Bargh and Chartrand (1999) bring their deterministic theory to the automaticity data as an organizing framework, and therefore they *interpret* the data in light of their deterministic assumptions.

Because data are not inherently meaningful or organized in themselves, there are multiple interpretations of data possible at any given time. Another way to say this is that our theories are underdetermined by the empirical data (Curd & Cover, 1998; Duhem, 1982). As much as we might like to access the brute facts of the matter through scientific experimentation, there are always multiple theories available to us to make sense of the data. Of course, there are limitations to the number of applicable theories given the configuration of the data, but there is more than one theory-contender at play. The question is which theory or interpretation seems to fit or explain the data the best. Hence, scientists and researchers are often concerned with competing explanations or interpretations of the *same* data rather than with the data themselves.

Bargh and Chartrand (1999) either fail to recognize that they have a particular interpretation of the data, or they refuse to recognize an alternative theory that might make equally good sense of the data. They seem to presume that their deterministic interpretation of the automaticity data is the fact of the matter, when, in principle, there are multiple interpretations of the automaticity data, some of which might not lead to deterministic outcomes. Paradoxically, Bargh and Chartrand (1999) automatically bring their pre-investigatory theoretical assumptions to the automaticity data without either telling the reader or consciously realizing that they are doing so. In other words, they are non-consciously and automatically interpreting the automaticity data according to their deterministic assumptions. Before considering how other kinds of theories and assumptions might help us to *re*-interpret the automaticity data, we will examine the philosophical and theoretical assumptions made by Bargh and Chartrand (1999), which led them to view non-conscious and automatic behavior as determined.

Empiricistic Interpretations of Automaticity

When Bargh and Chartrand (1999) state that the environment initiates behavior, they seem to be tacitly assuming that there are triggering events that begin in the environment, cross space, and enter our minds through our senses. Whether or not they know it, the authors subscribe to a particular philosophical or theoretical position—that of empiricism. Empiricism posits the environment as the originator of cognitive representations (Robinson, 1995; Slife & Williams, 1995). Environmental stimuli, as experienced through our senses, take precedence in the empiricistic model, because such stimuli are thought to initiate and incrementally build-up the contents of the mind over time. From this perspective, Joe can only know what he has been exposed to in the environment via his senses, because his mind is the result of an accumulation of past sensory experiences. Perception itself is thought to be a relatively transparent vehicle for this building-up or accumulation process. In other words, empiricists assume that what we perceive is an accurate representation of what exists in the environment. Perception is not thought to add or subtract anything from the objects of experience. Joe's perception of the other driver is thought to be relatively transparent. That is, Joe simply takes into his mind an objective representation of the other driver, and then responds automatically with road rage.

Bargh and Chartrand (1999) make these empiricistic assumptions when they explain that "perception is the route by which the environment directly causes mental activity—specifically, the activation of internal representations of the outside world" (p. 465). Consistent with their empiricistic bias, Bargh and Chartrand (1999) presume that environmental objects or stimuli "directly cause" cognitions and emotions (p. 465). Another way to say this is that environmental objects determine cognitions and emotions. Of course, the authors do not see this direct causation or determinism in their data; this presumption is "read in" to the data from their empiricistic framework. Nevertheless, given their interpretation of direct causation, the authors contend that environmental stimuli—rather than conscious choice or independent will—"introduce(s) the idea of action" or behavior (p. 465).

What initiates thought and action, then, is not us. Rather, what initiates thought and action are objects and events that we are exposed to in the environment. This means that Joe is like a captain-less and rudderless boat at sea, passively moving where the wind and waves take him. He is completely vulnerable to the active stimulus forces impinging upon him from the outside. In this view, Joe will never be the initiating center of his own action. Joe might think that he chooses behaviors and goals, but he is really automatically responding in a passive and non-thinking way to environmental cues. Bargh and Chartrand (1999) elaborate, ". . . a direct and automatic route is provided from the external environment to [behavioral] action tendencies, via perception" (p. 465).

In their defense, Bargh and Chartrand (1999) might claim that the "automaticity" theory is itself born out of the facts of empirical research. That is, they only view the environment as the initiator of thought and behavior, because previous scientific research has suggested that this is the case. The problem with this claim has to do with the relationship between interpretation and scientific "data" that was discussed previously. Recall that data are always interpreted. When Bargh and Chartrand (1999) argue that the "environment directly causes mental activity" (p. 465), they are making an *inference* or an interpretation of causation. They infer or presume that a causal relationship exists between the environmental stimuli and the cognition/behavior when such a relationship cannot be observed directly.

The philosopher David Hume showed us this problem of causation long ago, and much of what he argued is still considered relevant today (Jones,

1969; Slife & Williams, 1995). For Hume, the presumed causal connection between events is something that we attribute to events, rather than something that exists independently of us in nature. Hume argued that what we call causation is nothing more than the repeated occurrence of a pairing of events (Jones, 1969). That is, when we see one event follow another event (e.g., when we see Joe become enraged when exposed to a dangerous driver), we presume that the first event causes or produces the second event.

However, there is no empirical evidence for this presumed causal connection. In other words, Bargh and Chartrand (1999) cannot directly see or observe the causal force that they presume exists between the environmental stimulus and the cognition/behavior. The causal force itself does not fall upon the retina of the researcher to be observed. The only empirical evidence is the observation of two seemingly related events—two events that occur in temporal sequence—the environmental stimulus (e.g., the driver who cuts in front of Joe) and the emotional/behavioral response (e.g., Joe's road rage). Do Bargh and Chartrand (1999) "see" the cause (e.g., image of the driver) *produce* the emotional response? Or do they see merely the driver, and then the response? Correlation does not imply causation, as Hume has taught us.

Just as they read causation into the automaticity data, Bargh and Chartrand (1999) read determinism into the data, all in accordance with their pre-held empiricistic causal framework. In other words, because they have already decided (from the outset) that the environment is the source or originator of cognition, it logically follows that cognition and behaviors (automatic or otherwise) are caused and determined by the environment. Their already deciding and accepting these empiricistic assumptions as fact also means that they are not really attempting to test these assumptions. They are, rather, looking for *how* cognition/behavior are determined by the environment, instead of *whether* they are determined by the environment.

Alternative Interpretations of Automaticity

If Bargh and Chartrand (1999) have, in fact, brought their own philosophic bias (i.e., empiricism) to the automaticity data, resulting in a deterministic view, are there non-deterministic philosophies or theories available that fit the automaticity data equally well, or perhaps better? Recall that the data of scientific experiments are always underdetermined, meaning that there are multiple interpretations of data possible (Duhem, 1982). Why shouldn't we consider some of these alternatives? Why are we tied to one philosophical perspective (empiricism) in our interpretation of the automaticity data? At a minimum, we ought to consider other theories and their applicability to the automaticity data like Joe's road rage. The question, as it is for many scientists, is one of competing theoretical explanations. Which theory fits the automaticity data the best?

As just such an alternative to empiricism, there is an entire tradition of thought beginning with the philosophies of Continental Rationalism and moving through to Continental Hermeneutics that emphasize the active role of the mind rather than the passive role suggested by empiricism (Bernstein,

1983; Gadamer,1960/1995; Heidegger,1926/1962; Wood, 2001). These philosophies are complex, but for our purposes they can be boiled down to some basic points. Perhaps foremost, we are not thought to simply take in environmental stimuli via the "environment–perception–behavior" sequence that Bargh and Chartrand (1999) discuss (p. 466). Rather, the mind is given at least an equal priority, because the mind is assumed to extend order and structure to what it encounters in the environment, even as perception occurs. Another way to say this is that we actively interpret what we encounter in the environment, rather than passively taking in stimuli to be shaped by it.

Consider Joe again. The emphasis of these Continental philosophies on interpretation would imply that Joe is not passively and automatically responding in an unthinking way to the stimulus of the dangerous driver. Rather, Joe actively brings an entire interpretive world-view to his driving experience that tacitly affects how he understands driving, driving etiquette, and other drivers. Whether or not Joe becomes enraged has to do with the nature of the interpretive worldview, which he actively creates. What if Joe implicitly believes that his goals and progress should not be impeded— particularly his driving goals and progress. If Joe maintains this belief, he is more likely to become angered and enraged when other drivers cut him off (thereby impeding his driving progress).

Consider an alternative interpretation of belief system, to emphasize the mind's activity, and perhaps even "free will." What if Joe implicitly believes that people who are in a hurry *should* cut other people off? If Joe brings this interpretive framework to his driving situation, then he is probably less likely to become angry or enraged when he is cut-off by another driver. Indeed, he might even expect to be cut-off by other drivers given his appreciation of their being in a hurry. In this case, Joe automatically interprets drivers who cut people off as drivers with important things to do, and therefore, he does not become enraged when such drivers cut him off.

In this situation, when Joe is confronted with the stimulus of a bad driver, the stimulus itself is not objectively imprinted on a passive mind to ultimately direct behavior as the empiricists might claim. Rather, the stimulus is actively made meaningful within the interpretive framework that Joe brings with him to the driving experience. In this case, what empiricists like to call a "stimulus" is really not a stimulus at all, because whatever is stimulating to us has to do with what our mind's consider meaningful rather than any intrinsic, objective property of the "stimulus" itself. The point, from the Continental perspective, is that a stimulus is not a stimulus without a mind that actively bestows meaning upon it.

This emphasis on interpretation implies that perception is not as transparent as empiricism might suggest. Recall that in the empiricistic view, we are thought to take in stimuli as they exist in the environment. From the Continental perspective, this transparency contention is problematic, because different persons can be exposed to the same stimulus, but respond in very divergent ways given their propensity to interpret stimuli differently. When confronted with the stimulus of another driver, Joe may interpret the driver as "bad" (e.g., taking my space in line) and become enraged, whereas a different driver might interpret the same driver as "good" (e.g, helping his wife get to the hospital) and not become enraged. This emphasis on active interpretation means that the mind affects environmental stimuli as much as environmental stimuli affect the mind, and therefore, cognitions and behavior cannot be completely determined by environmental triggers.

The Nature of Interpretive Frameworks

One question that arises with respect to the Continental tradition and its emphasis on an active mind has to do with the nature of the interpretive frameworks themselves. How is it that we come to create such interpretive frameworks? How is it that Joe's interpretive framework constitutes the particular meanings that it does rather than other meanings?

The empiricist response to this question is "Joe's previous sensory experience!" Empiricists like Bargh and Chartrand (1999) might argue that Joe's "interpretive driving framework" is the result of being exposed over time to certain kinds of driving stimuli that have accumulated in mind and shaped the interpretive framework that Joe is currently using. Maybe Joe was exposed to a road-raging father when he was a child. In this case, Joe passively takes in the stimulus of a raging father, which imprints upon his mind, initiating and shaping Joe's beliefs and expectations for driving. Consistent with an empiricistic view, Joe's mind is like a sponge, passively absorbing objective stimulus events. Being exposed to a road-raging father means that Joe is determined to be a road-rager himself.

However, for rationalists and hermeneuticists, interpretive frameworks are not the result of accumulated past sensory experiences. Rather, our interpretive frameworks (and the mind itself) are not thought to be solely or exclusively dependent on environmental stimuli. This means that we come into the world with an intelligent, structuring and organizing mind that actively interprets stimuli that it encounters *from birth* (Rychlak, 1981)! Even from birth, then, we can view Joe as actively organizing and structuring his experience rather than being wholly shaped by the environment. Joe can extend meanings to "stimuli" or situations that are completely of his own making.

Hence, when Joe is exposed as a child to a road-raging father, what matters is how Joe actively interprets and understands his father's behavior—and these interpretations and meanings are not necessarily contingent on previous sensory inputs. Joe, then, has the capacity to think and reason to other courses of thought and behavioral action than those modeled by his father. This means that Joe has a *choice* about his thoughts, emotions, and behaviors. *Joe* is the originator of his interpretive frameworks. *Joe* is at least partially responsible for the meanings that he extends to his driving and other experiences, which means that Joe is accountable for his actions.

Because the Continental tradition allows for this kind of freedom and choice, people like Joe and everyone else are thought to have possibility. We are not determined by environmental triggers—this means that we are without possibility. Rather, we have the possibility to interpret and understand events in multiple ways. We have the possibility to change our interpretations and understandings, and thereby change ourselves, and therefore we are viewed as active agents with the capacity for free will and choice.

Non-Consciousness and Free Will

But how can our automatic and non-conscious thoughts, emotions, and behaviors be "chosen" or actively created by us? As we noted early on, Joe did not seem to "choose" to become enraged. Is it really possible to view Joe's automatic road rage as chosen by him and ultimately within his control? Hermeneutic philosophies are particularly helpful here, because they emphasize the often tacit, implicit, and unthematized nature of the mind's active interpreting process (Heidegger, 1926/1962). In other words, much of the mind's active extension of meanings through interpretive frameworks occurs outside of our conscious awareness. We still respond to stimuli automatically in the way that Bargh and Chartrand (1999) describe, but this automaticity is not automatically involuntary—it is *automatically voluntary.*

Consider Joe again. Recall from the rationalistic and hermeneutic perspective that Joe's road rage is dependent upon his pre-existing interpretive framework—his worldview of meanings surrounding driving, driving etiquette, and other drivers. From this perspective, Joe only becomes enraged when his interpretive framework is filled with meanings that lead to rage—for instance, Joe's belief that his goals and progress should not be impeded. Joe does not necessarily have an immediate, conscious awareness of his guiding beliefs and assumptions. On the contrary, these guiding beliefs and assumptions—the nexus of the interpretive framework—are mostly non-conscious. They recede into the background. Indeed, Joe probably takes these beliefs and assumptions for granted—they are the givens of his experience and are not immediately and consciously known.

Nevertheless, as was discussed earlier, the interpretations and understandings that Joe extends to experience—however conscious or non-conscious—are of his own making. In other words, he continues to be an active shaper of the interpretations and meanings that constitute his interpretive frameworks. He may simply lack an awareness of his active shaping. As Merleau-Ponty (1983/1942), a famous Continental philosopher argues, consciousness is "a network of significative intentions which are sometimes clear to themselves and sometimes, on the contrary, lived rather than known" (p. 173).

This alternative agentic or free-willist account of automaticity not only fits the experience of Joe, but fits all of the automaticity data that Bargh and Chartrand (1999) cite. Whatever it is that we do automatically—respond with road rage, socially interact with others, activate goals, form evaluations and judgments—we can view all of these thoughts, emotions, and behaviors as ultimately being directed by the person rather than by the environment. This is good news, because it means that we are not doomed to the determinism that accompanies Bargh and Chartrand's empiricistic theoretical framework. We do not have to view people as passive responders to environmental stimuli who are ultimately shaped by their environments.

On the contrary, we can view persons as actively shaping and interpreting what they encounter such that they can never be reduced to the environment alone. However, much of this active shaping and interpretation escapes our notice, because it occurs non-consciously and automatically. Despite the non-consciousness and automaticity, we are still willing complicated patterns of behavior. The test of agency is whether we can act otherwise—whether we can change the pattern of thought and behavior and act differently.

If Joe decides to see a professor about a course grade, he does not consciously *will* each literal, physical step along the way to the professor's office. Rather, he has automatically willed a whole pattern of behavior (e.g., going to see a professor), the parts of which (e.g., the literal steps) remain outside of his awareness. Was Joe's automatic walking the result of exposure to a stimulus in the environment? The test, again, is whether Joe can behave otherwise. If a friend calls out to Joe along the walk, he may nonconsciously choose to alter the pattern of his behavior. He may not visit the professor after all, opting instead to visit with his friend. The point is that Joe always has the possibility of changing the pattern of non-conscious behavior. Joe may continue toward the professor, or he may stop and visit with his friend. In either case, Joe is non-consciously willing his behavior— and therefore he is agentic and free.

Because the automaticity data are as easily subsumed by a free willist account as by a deterministic account, why not consider the free willist view? The question may now be which of these competing theories fits the data the best—and if our experience of ourselves is grounded in free will rather than determinism—then the free willist view ought to be taken under serious consideration.

References

Bargh, J. A., & Chartrand, T. L. (1999). The unbearable automaticity of being. *American Psychologist, 54* (7), 462–479.

Bernstein, R. J. (1983). *Beyond objectivism and relativism: Science, hermeneutics, and praxis.* Philadelphia: University of Pennsylvania Press.

Curd, M., & Cover, J. A. (1998). *Philosophy of science: The central issues.* New York: W. W. Norton & Co.

Duhem, P. (1982). *The aim and structure of physical theory.* Princeton, NJ: Princeton University Press.

Gadamer, H. G. (1995). *Truth and method* (2nd rev.ed.). (J. Weinsheimer & D. G. Marshall, Trans.). New York: Continuum. (Original work published 1960).

Heidegger, M. (1962). *Being and time.* (J. Macquarrie & E. Robinson, Trans.). San Francisco: Harper Collins. (Original work published 1926).

Kuhn, T. S. (1996). *The structure of scientific revolutions* (3rd ed.). Chicago, IL: University of Chicago Press. (Original work published 1962).

Jones, W. T. (1969). *Hobbes to Hume: A history of western philosophy* (2nd ed.). New York: Harcourt Brace Jovanovich.

Merleau-Ponty, M. (1983). *The structure of behavior.* (Trans. A. L. Fisher). Pittsburgh, PA: Duquesne University Press. (Original work published 1942)

Popper, K. (1963). *Conjectures and refutations: The growth of scientific knowledge.* London: Routledge & Kegan Paul.

Robinson, D. N. (1995). *An intellectual history of psychology* (3rd ed.). Madison, WI: University of Wisconsin Press.

Rychlak, J. F. (1981). *Introduction to personality and psychotherapy: A theory-construction approach*. Dallas, TX: Houghton Mifflin.

Slife, B. D., & Williams, R. N. (1995). *What's behind the research? Discovering hidden assumptions in the behavioral sciences*. Thousand Oaks, CA: Sage.

Wood, A. W. (2001). *Basic writings of Kant*. New York: Random House.

CHALLENGE QUESTIONS

Are Human Cognitive and Behavioral Activities Determined?

1. Bargh/Chartrand and Smith interpret the same sets of data in completely different ways. How can this be possible? (Hint: Read the Smith article carefully.)
2. On what issues do Bargh/Chartrand and Smith agree? How does this help the effectiveness of Smith's argument?
3. As Smith notes, Bargh/Chartrand do not tell their readers that other interpretations of their data are possible. Do you believe they should? Why or why not?
4. Consider the implications of both Bargh/Chartrand and Smith's theories. If your life were determined or free, how would it be different than how you currently understand it?
5. Do you agree with Smith that free will is our everyday experience of ourselves? Why or why not? How much confidence should we put in that type of experience?

ISSUE 10

Should Psychology Adopt a Theory of Multiple Intelligences?

YES: Howard Gardner, from "A Multiplicity of Intelligences," *Scientific American Presents* (Winter 1998)

NO: Linda S. Gottfredson, from "The General Intelligence Factor," *Scientific American Presents* (Winter 1998)

ISSUE SUMMARY

YES: Psychologist Howard Gardner argues that humans are better understood as having eight or nine different kinds of intelligence rather than as having one general intelligence.

NO: Psychologist Linda S. Gottfredson contends that despite some popular assertions, a single factor for intelligence can be measured with IQ tests and is predictive of success in life.

Most people who have seen Michael Jordan play professional basketball have been amazed by his grace and poise. Even when ill, he can outscore most other players. What is the source of his abilities? Does his being so good at playing basketball necessarily imply that he is good at other activities? In addition to being an outstanding basketball player, Jordan is generally acknowledged as being bright, articulate, and socially skilled. On the other hand, his attempt to play baseball at the major league level was less than successful. Can people only be really good at one thing and not any others, or is some general ability—some general intelligence—involved?

The traditional view of intelligence is that there is a single factor, often called g, that underlies most other abilities. Most tests of intelligence yield a single score, which emphasizes the idea that intelligence is a single, measurable entity. However, Howard Gardner is noted for having challenged this traditional view. Gardner has argued that intelligence is best understood as a number of distinct and relatively independent abilities, such as musical intelligence and bodily-kinesthetic intelligence.

In the following selection, Gardner argues that the single-factor theory of intelligence is outdated and should be replaced by a theory of multiple intelligences. He argues that individuals have profiles reflecting both strengths and weaknesses in different areas of intelligence. He also contends that when people have strokes, often only one ability (e.g., memory) is affected while others (e.g., musical abilities) are completely spared. This type of evidence leads Gardner to postulate the existence of multiple intelligences.

In the second selection, Linda S. Gottfredson contends that a general theory of intelligence explains most differences among individuals. She sees the *g* factor as the apex of a hierarchical model that reflects all the combined abilities. For example, Michael Jordan may indeed have a type of kinesthetic intelligence or ability, but the *g* factor reflects all his other abilities, including his logical and cognitive abilities. Gottfredson cites research that suggests that highly intelligent people have quicker reaction times and faster brain processing than less intelligent people. She also asserts that the *g* factor is useful in predicting job performance as well as academic ability.

POINT

- Humans are best understood as having a number of relatively independent intellectual faculties.
- Psychometric tests devalue capacities such as musical or bodily-kinesthetic intelligences as talents but not intelligence.
- Different factors are developed, prized, or ignored in different cultures.
- Recent neuroscience and evolutionary psychology support a multiple intelligence concept.

COUNTERPOINT

- The overlap among cognitive skills suggests that there is one global element of intelligence.
- Psychometric tests are the best way to measure human intelligence.
- The general factor (*g*) of intelligence exists in all cultures and is not a social artifact.
- Biological studies of brain waves support the general factor theory.

Howard Gardner  **YES**

A Multiplicity of Intelligences

As a psychologist, I was surprised by the huge public interest in *The Bell Curve*, the 1994 book on human intelligence by the late Harvard University psychologist Richard J. Herrnstein and policy analyst Charles Murray. Most of the ideas in the book were familiar not only to social scientists but also to the general public. Indeed, educational psychologist Arthur R. Jensen of the University of California at Berkeley as well as Herrnstein had written popularly about the very same ideas in the late 1960s and the early 1970s. Perhaps, I reasoned, every quarter-century a new generation of Americans desires to be acquainted with "the psychologist's orthodoxy" about intelligence—namely, that there is a single, general intelligence, often called *g*, which is reflected by an individual's intelligence quotient, or IQ.

This concept stands in contrast to my own view developed over the past decades: that human intelligence encompasses a far wider, more universal set of competencies. Currently I count eight intelligences, and there may be more. They include what are traditionally regarded as intelligences, such as linguistic and logical-mathematical abilities, but also some that are not conventionally thought of in that way, such as musical and spatial capacities. These intelligences, which do not always reveal themselves in paper-and-pencil tests, can serve as a basis for more effective educational methods.

Defining Brainpower

The orthodox view of a single intelligence, widely, if wrongly, accepted today in the minds of the general population, originated from the energies and convictions of a few researchers, who by the second decade of this century had put forth its major precepts. In addition to its basic assumption, the orthodoxy also states that individuals are born with a certain intelligence or potential intelligence, that this intelligence is difficult to change and that psychologists can assess one's IQ using short-answer tests and, perhaps, other "purer" measures, such as the time it takes to react to a sequence of flashing lights or the presence of a particular pattern of brain waves.

Soon after this idea had been proposed—I like to call it "hedgehog orthodoxy"—more "foxlike" critics arose. From outside psychology, commentators such as American newspaper columnist Walter Lippmann challenged the criteria used to assess intelligence, contending that it was more complex and less fixed than the psychometricians had proposed.

From within psychology, scientists questioned the notion of a single, overarching intelligence. According to their analyses, intelligence is better thought of as a set of several factors. In the 1930s Louis L. Thurstone of the University of Chicago said it makes more sense to think of seven, largely independent "vectors of the mind." In the 1960s Joy P. Guilford of the University of Southern California enunciated 120 factors, later amended to 150. Scottish investigator Godfrey Thomson of the University of Edinburgh spoke around the 1940s of a large number of loosely coupled faculties. And in our own day, Robert J. Sternberg of Yale University has proposed a triarchic theory of intellect. These arches comprise a component that deals with standard computational skill, a component that is sensitive to contextual factors and a component that is involved with novelty.

Somewhat surprisingly, all these commentators—whether in favor of or opposed to the notion of single intelligence—share one conviction. They all believe that the nature of intelligence will be determined by testing and analyzing the data thus secured. Perhaps, reason orthodox defenders like Herrnstein and Murray, performance on a variety of tests will yield a strong general factor of intelligence. And indeed, there is evidence for such a "positive manifold," or high correlation, across tests. Perhaps, counter pluralists like Thurstone and Sternberg, the right set of tests will demonstrate that the mind consists of a number of relatively independent factors, with strength in one area failing to predict strength or weakness in other areas.

But where is it written that intelligence needs to be determined on the basis of tests? Were we incapable of making judgments about intellect before Sir Francis Galton and Alfred Binet cobbled together the first set of psychometric items a century ago? If the dozens of IQ tests in use around the world were suddenly to disappear, would we no longer be able to assess intellect?

Break From Orthodoxy

Nearly 20 years ago, posing these very questions, I embarked on quite a different path into the investigation of intellect. I had been conducting research primarily with two groups: children who were talented in one or more art form and adults who had suffered from strokes that comprised specific capacities while sparing others. Every day I saw individuals with scattered profiles of strengths and weaknesses, and I was impressed by the fact that a strength or a deficit could cohabit comfortably with distinctive profiles of abilities and disabilities across the variety of humankind.

On the basis of such data, I arrived at a firm intuition: human beings are better thought of as possessing a number of relatively independent faculties, rather than as having a certain amount of intellectual horsepower, or IQ, that can be simply channeled in one or another direction. I decided to search for a better formulation of human intelligence. I defined an intelligence as "a psychobiological potential to solve problems or to fashion products that are valued in at least one cultural context." In my focus on fashioning products and cultural values, I departed from orthodox psychometric approaches, such as those adopted by Herrnstein, Murray and their predecessors.

CRITERIA FOR AN INTELLIGENCE

1. *Potential isolation by brain damage.* For example, linguistic abilities can be compromised or spared by strokes.
2. *The existence of prodigies, savants and other exceptional individuals.* Such individuals permit the intelligence to be observed in relative isolation.
3. *An identifiable core operation or set of operations.* Musical intelligence, for instance, consists of a person's sensitivity to melody, harmony, rhythm, timbre and musical structure.
4. *A distinctive developmental history within an individual, along with a definable nature of expert performance.* One examines the skills of, say, an expert athlete, salesperson or naturalist, as well as the steps to attaining such expertise.
5. *An evolutionary history and evolutionary plausibility.* One can examine forms of spatial intelligence in mammals or musical intelligence in birds.
6. *Support from tests in experimental psychology.* Researchers have devised tasks that specifically indicate which skills are related to one another and which are discrete.
7. *Support from psychometric findings.* Batteries of tests reveal which tasks reflect the same underlying factor and which do not.
8. *Susceptibility to encoding in a symbol system.* Codes such as language, arithmetic, maps and logical expression, among others, capture important components of respective intelligences.

To proceed from an intuition to a definition of a set of human intelligences, I developed criteria that each of the candidate intelligences had to meet *[see box]*. These criteria were drawn from several sources:

- Psychology: The existence of a distinct developmental history for a capacity through which normal and gifted individuals pass as they grow to adulthood; the existence of correlations (or the lack of correlations) between certain capacities.
- Case studies of learners: Observations of unusual humans, including prodigies, savants or those suffering from learning disabilities.
- Anthropology: Records of how different abilities were developed, ignored or prized in different cultures.
- Cultural studies: The existence of symbol systems that encode certain kinds of meanings—language, arithmetic and maps, for instance.
- Biological sciences: Evidence that a capacity has a distinct evolutionary history and is represented in particular neural structures. For instance, various parts of the left hemisphere dominate when it comes to motor control of the body, calculation and linguistic ability; the right hemisphere houses spatial and musical capacities, including the discrimination of pitch.

The Eight Intelligences

Armed with the criteria, I considered many capacities, ranging from those based in the senses to those having to do with planning, humor and even sexuality. To the extent that a candidate ability met all or most of the criteria handily, it gained plausibility as an intelligence. In 1983 I concluded that seven abilities met the criteria sufficiently well: linguistic, logical-mathematical, musical, spatial, bodily-kinesthetic (as exemplified by athletes, dancers and other physical performers), interpersonal (the ability to read other people's moods, motivations and other mental states), and intrapersonal (the ability to access one's own feelings and to draw on them to guide behavior). The last two can generally be considered together as the basis for emotional intelligence (although in my version, they focus more on cognition and understanding than on feelings). Most standard measures of intelligence primarily probe linguistic and logical intelligence; some survey spatial intelligence. The other four are almost entirely ignored. In 1995, invoking new data that fit the criteria, I added an eighth intelligence—that of the naturalist, which permits the recognition and categorization of natural objects. Examples are Charles Darwin, John James Audubon and Rachel Carson. I am currently considering the possibility of a ninth: existential intelligence, which captures the human proclivity to raise and ponder fundamental questions about existence, life, death, finitude. Religious and philosophical thinkers such as the Dalai Lama and Søren A. Kierkegaard exemplify this kind of ability. Whether existential intelligence gets to join the inner sanctum depends on whether convincing evidence accrues about the neural basis for it.

The theory of multiple intelligences (or MI theory, as it has come to be called) makes two strong claims. The first is that all humans possess all these intelligences: indeed, they can collectively be considered a definition of *Homo sapiens,* cognitively speaking. The second claim is that just as we all look different and have unique personalities and temperaments, we also have different profiles of intelligences. No two individuals, not even identical twins or clones, have exactly the same amalgam of profiles, with the same strengths and weaknesses. Even in the case of identical genetic heritage, individuals undergo different experiences and seek to distinguish their profiles from one another.

Within psychology, the theory of multiple intelligences has generated controversy. Many researchers are nervous about the movement away from standardized tests and the adoption of a set of criteria that are unfamiliar and less open to quantification. Many also balk at the use of the word "intelligence" to describe some of the abilities, preferring to define musical or bodily-kinesthetic intelligences as talents. Such a narrow definition, however, devalues those capacities, so that orchestra conductors and dancers are talented but not smart. In my view, it would be all right to call those abilities talents, so long as logical reasoning and linguistic facility are then also termed talents.

Some have questioned whether MI theory is empirical. This criticism, however, misses the mark. MI theory is based completely on empirical evidence. The number of intelligences, their delineation, their subcomponents are all subject to alteration in the light of new findings. Indeed, the existence of the naturalist intelligence could be asserted only after evidence had accrued that parts of the temporal lobe are dedicated to the naming and recognition of natural things, whereas others are attuned to human-made objects. (Good evidence for a neural foundation comes from clinical literature, which reported instances in which brain-damaged individuals lost the capacity to identify living things but could still name inanimate objects. Experimental findings by Antonio R. Damasio of the University of Iowa, Elizabeth Warrington of the Dementia Research Group at National Hospital in London and others have confirmed the phenomenon.)

Much of the evidence for the personal intelligences has come from research in the past decade on emotional intelligence and on the development in children of a "theory of mind"—the realization that human beings have intentions and act on the basis of these intentions. And the intriguing finding by Frances H. Rauscher of the University of Wisconsin—Oshkosh and her colleagues of the "Mozart effect"—that early musical experiences may enhance spatial capacities—raises the possibility that musical and spatial intelligences draw on common abilities.

It is also worth noting that the movement toward multiple intelligences is quite consistent with trends in related sciences. Neuroscience recognizes the modular nature of the brain; evolutionary psychology is based on the notion that different capacities have evolved in specific environments for specific purposes; and artificial intelligence increasingly embraces expert systems rather than general problem-solving mechanisms. Within science, the believers in a single IQ or general intelligence are increasingly isolated, their positions more likely to be embraced by those, like Herrnstein and Murray, who have an ideological ax to grind.

If some psychologists expressed skepticism about the theory of multiple intelligences, educators around the world have embraced it. MI theory not only comports with their intuitions that children are smart in different ways; it also holds out hope that more students can be reached more effectively if their favored ways of knowing are taken into account in curriculum, instruction and assessment. A virtual cottage industry has arisen to create MI schools, classrooms, curricula, texts, computer systems and the like. Most of this work is well intentioned, and some of it has proved quite effective in motivating students and in giving them a sense of involvement in intellectual life.

Various misconceptions, however, have arisen: for example, that every topic should be taught in seven or eight ways or that the purpose of school is to identify (and broadcast) students' intelligences, possibly by administering an octet of new standardized tests. I have begun to speak out against some of these less advisable beliefs and practices.

My conclusion is that MI theory is best thought of as a tool rather than as an educational goal. Educators need to determine, in conjunction with their communities, the goals that they are seeking. Once these goals have been articulated, then MI theory can provide powerful support. I believe schools should strive to develop individuals of a certain sort—civic-minded, sensitive to the arts, deeply rooted in the disciplines. And schools should probe pivotal topics with sufficient depth so that students end up with a comprehensive understanding of them. Curricular and assessment approaches founded on MI theory, such as Project Spectrum at the Eliot-Pearson Pre-school at Tufts University, have demonstrated considerable promise in helping schools to achieve these goals.

The Future of MI

Experts have debated various topics in intelligence—including whether there is one or more—for nearly a century, and it would take a brave seer to predict that these debates will disappear. (In fact, if past cycles repeat themselves, a latter-day Herrnstein and Murray will author their own *Bell Curve* around 2020.) As the person most closely associated with the theory of multiple intelligences, I record three wishes for this line of work.

The first is a broader but not infinitely expanded view of intelligence. It is high time that intelligence be widened to incorporate a range of human computational capacities, including those that deal with music, other persons and skill in deciphering the natural world. But it is important that intelligence not be conflated with other virtues, such as creativity, wisdom or morality.

I also contend that intelligence should not be so broadened that it crosses the line from description to prescription. I endorse the notion of emotional intelligence when it denotes the capacity to compute information about one's own or others' emotional life. When the term comes to encompass the kinds of persons we hope to develop, however, then we have crossed the line into a value system—and that should not be part of our conception of intelligence. Thus, when psychologist and *New York Times* reporter Daniel Goleman emphasizes in his recent best-seller, *Emotional Intelligence,* the importance of empathy as part of emotional intelligence, I go along with him. But he also urges that individuals care for one another. The possession of the capacity to feel another's suffering is not the same as the decision to come to her aid. Indeed, a sadistic individual might use her knowledge of another's psyche to inflict pain.

My second wish is that society shift away from standardized, short-answer proxy instruments to real-life demonstrations or virtual simulations. During a particular historical period, it was perhaps necessary to assess individuals by administering items that were themselves of little interest (for example, repeating numbers backward) but that were thought to correlate with skills or habits of importance. Nowadays, however, given the advent of computers and virtual technologies, it is possible to look directly at individuals' performances—to see how they can argue, debate, look at data, critique experiments, execute works of art, and so on. As much as possible, we should train students directly in these valued activities, and we should assess how they carry out valued performances under realistic conditions. The need for ersatz instruments, whose relation to real-world performance is often tenuous at best, should wane.

My third wish is that the multiple-intelligences idea be used for more effective pedagogy and assessment. I have little sympathy with educational efforts that seek simply to "train" the intelligences or to use them in trivial ways (such as singing the math times tables or playing Bach in the background while one is doing geometry). For me, the educational power of multiple intelligences is exhibited when these faculties are drawn on to help students master consequential disciplinary materials.

I explain how such an approach might work in my book, *A Well-Disciplined Mind . . .* (1999). I focus on three rich topics: the theory of evolution (as an example of scientific truth), the music of Mozart (as an example of artistic beauty), and the Holocaust (as an example of immorality in recent history). In each case, I show how the topic can be introduced to students through a variety of entry points drawing on several intelligences, how the subject can be made more familiar through the use of analogies and metaphors drawn from diverse domains, and how the core ideas of the topic can be captured not merely through a single symbolic language but rather through a number of complementary model languages or representations.

Pursuing this approach, the individual who understands evolutionary theory, for instance, can think of it in different ways: in terms of a historical narrative, a logical syllogism, a quantitative examination of the size and dispersion of populations in different niches, a diagram of species delineation, a dramatic sense of the struggle among individuals (or genes or populations), and so on. The individual who can think of evolution in only one way—using only one model language—actually has only a tenuous command of the principal concepts of the theory.

The issue of who owns intelligence has been an important one in our society for some time—and it promises to be a crucial and controversial one for the foreseeable future. For too long, the rest of society has been content to leave intelligence in the hands of psychometricians. Often these test makers have a narrow, overly scholastic view of intellect. They rely on a set of instruments that are destined to valorize certain capacities while ignoring those that do not lend themselves to ready formulation and testing. And those with a political agenda often skirt close to the dangerous territory of eugenics.

MI theory represents at once an effort to base the conception of intelligence on a much broader scientific basis, one that offers a set of tools to educators that will allow more individuals to master substantive materials in an effective way. Applied appropriately, the theory can also help each individual achieve his or her human potential at the workplace, in avocations and in the service of the wider world.

NO

Linda S. Gottfredson

The General Intelligence Factor

No subject in psychology has provoked more intense public controversy than the study of human intelligence. From its beginning, research on how and why people differ in overall mental ability has fallen prey to political and social agendas that obscure or distort even the most well-established scientific findings. Journalists, too, often present a view of intelligence research that is exactly the opposite of what most intelligence experts believe. For these and other reasons, public understanding of intelligence falls far short of public concern about it. The IQ experts discussing their work in the public arena can feel as though they have fallen down the rabbit hole into Alice's Wonderland.

The debate over intelligence and intelligence testing focuses on the question of whether it is useful or meaningful to evaluate people according to a single major dimension of cognitive competence. Is there indeed a general mental ability we commonly call "intelligence," and is it important in the practical affairs of life? The answer, based on decades of intelligence research, is an unequivocal yes. No matter their form or content, tests of mental skills invariably point to the existence of a global factor that permeates all aspects of cognition. And this factor seems to have considerable influence on a person's practical quality of life. Intelligence as measured by IQ tests is the single most effective predictor known of individual performance at school and on the job. It also predicts many other aspects of well-being, including a person's chances of divorcing, dropping out of high school, being unemployed or having illegitimate children.

By now the vast majority of intelligence researchers take these findings for granted. Yet in the press and in public debate, the facts are typically dismissed, downplayed or ignored. This misrepresentation reflects a clash between a deeply felt ideal and a stubborn reality. The ideal, implicit in many popular critiques of intelligence research, is that all people are born equally able and that social inequality results only from the exercise of unjust privilege. The reality is that Mother Nature is no egalitarian. People are in fact unequal in intellectual potential—and they are born that way, just as they are born with different potentials for height, physical attractiveness, artistic flair, athletic prowess and other traits. Although subsequent experience shapes this potential, no amount of social engineering can make individuals with widely divergent mental aptitudes into intellectual equals.

Of course, there are many kinds of talent, many kinds of mental ability and many other aspects of personality and character that influence a person's chances of happiness and success. The functional importance of general mental ability in everyday life, however, means that without onerous restrictions on individual liberty, differences in mental competence are likely to result in social inequality. This gulf between equal opportunity and equal outcomes is perhaps what pains Americans most about the subject of intelligence. The public intuitively knows what is at stake: when asked to rank personal qualities in order of desirability, people put intelligence second only to good health. But with a more realistic approach to the intellectual differences between people, society could better accommodate these differences and minimize the inequalities they create.

Extracting *g*

Early in the century-old study of intelligence, researchers discovered that all tests of mental ability ranked individuals in about the same way. Although mental tests are often designed to measure specific domains of cognition— verbal fluency, say, or mathematical skill, spatial visualization or memory— people who do well on one kind of test tend to do well on the others, and people who do poorly generally do so across the board. This overlap, or intercorrelation, suggests that all such tests measure some global element of intellectual ability as well as specific cognitive skills. In recent decades, psychologists have devoted much effort to isolating that general factor, which is abbreviated *g*, from the other aspects of cognitive ability gauged in mental tests.

The statistical extraction of *g* is performed by a technique called factor analysis. Introduced at the turn of the century by British psychologist Charles Spearman, factor analysis determines the minimum number of underlying dimensions necessary to explain a pattern of correlations among measurements. A general factor suffusing all tests is not, as is sometimes argued, a necessary outcome of factor analysis. No general factor has been found in the analysis of personality tests, for example; instead the method usually yields at least five dimensions (neuroticism, extraversion, conscientiousness, agreeableness and openness to ideas), each relating to different subsets of tests. But, as Spearman observed, a general factor does emerge from analysis of mental ability tests, and leading psychologists, such as Arthur R. Jensen of the University of California at Berkeley and John B. Carroll of the University of North Carolina at Chapel Hill, have confirmed his findings in the decades since. Partly because of this research, most intelligence experts now use *g* as the working definition of intelligence.

The general factor explains most differences among individuals in performance on diverse mental tests. This is true regardless of what specific ability a test is meant to assess, regardless of the test's manifest content (whether words, numbers or figures) and regardless of the way the test is administered (in written or oral form, to an individual or to a group). Tests of specific mental abilities do measure those abilities, but they all reflect *g* to varying degrees as well. Hence, the *g* factor can be extracted form scores on any diverse battery of tests.

Conversely, because every mental test is "contaminated" by the effects of specific mental skills, no single test measures only g. Even the scores from IQ tests—which usually combine about a dozen subtests of specific cognitive skills—contain some "impurities" that reflect those narrower skills. For most purposes, these impurities make no practical difference, and g and IQ can be used interchangeably. But if they need to, intelligence researchers can statistically separate the g component of IQ. The ability to isolate g has revolutionized research on general intelligence, because it has allowed investigators to show that the predictive value of mental tests derives almost entirely from this global factor rather than from the more specific aptitudes measured by intelligence tests.

In addition to quantifying individual differences, tests of mental abilities have also offered insight into the meaning of intelligence in everyday life. Some tests and test items are known to correlate better with g than others do. In these items the "active ingredient" that demands the exercise of g seems to be complexity. More complex tasks require more mental manipulation, and this manipulation of information—discerning similarities and inconsistencies, drawing inferences, grasping new concepts and so on—constitutes intelligence in action. Indeed, intelligence can best be described as the ability to deal with cognitive complexity.

This description coincides well with lay perceptions of intelligence. The g factor is especially important in just the kind of behaviors that people usually associate with "smarts": reasoning, problem solving, abstract thinking, quick learning. And whereas g itself describes mental aptitude rather than accumulated knowledge, a person's store of knowledge tends to correspond with his or her g level, probably because that accumulation represents a previous adeptness in learning and in understanding new information. The g factor is also the one attribute that best distinguishes among persons considered gifted, average or retarded.

Several decades of factor-analytic research on mental tests have confirmed a hierarchical model of mental abilities. The evidence, summarized most effectively in Carroll's 1993 book, *Human Cognitive Abilities*, puts g at the apex in this model, with more specific aptitudes arrayed at successively lower levels: the so-called group factors, such as verbal ability, mathematical reasoning, spatial visualization and memory, are just below g, and below these are skills that are more dependent on knowledge or experience, such as the principles and practices of a particular job or profession.

Some researchers use the term "multiple intelligences" to label these sets of narrow capabilities and achievements. Psychologist Howard Gardner of Harvard University, for example, has postulated that eight relatively autonomous "intelligences" are exhibited in different domains of achievement. He does not dispute the existence of g but treats it as a specific factor relevant chiefly to academic achievement and to situations that resemble those of school. Gardner does not believe that tests can fruitfully measure his proposed intelligences; without tests, no one can at present determine whether the intelligences are indeed independent of g (or each other). Furthermore, it is

Figure 1

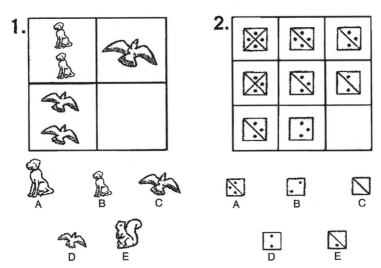

Matrix Reasoning

Number Series

3. 2, 4, 6, 8, __, __

4. 3, 6, 3, 6, __, __

5. 1, 5, 4, 2, 6, 5, __, __

6. 2, 4, 3, 9, 4, 16, __, __

Analogies

7. brother: sister ➝ father: _____
A. child   B. mother   C. cousin   D. friend

8. joke: humor ➝ law: _____
A. lawyer   B. mercy   C. courts   D. justice

Answers: 1. A; 2. D; 3. 10, 12; 4. 3, 6; 5. 3, 7; 6. 5, 25; 7. B; 8. D

Sample IQ Items resembling those on current tests require the test taker to fill in the empty spaces based on the pattern in the images, numbers or words. Because they can vary in complexity, such tasks are useful in assessing *g* level.

not clear to what extent Gardner's intelligences tap personality traits or motor skills rather than mental aptitudes.

Other forms of intelligence have been proposed; among them, emotional intelligence and practical intelligence are perhaps the best known. They are probably amalgams either of intellect and personality or of intellect and informal experience in specific job or life settings, respectively. Practical intelligence like "street smarts," for example, seems to consist of the localized knowledge and know-how developed with untutored experience in particular everyday settings and activities—the so-called school of hard knocks. In contrast, general intelligence is not a form of achievement, whether local or renowned. Instead the *g* factor regulates the rate of learning: it greatly affects the rate of return in knowledge to instruction and experience but cannot substitute for either.

The Biology of *g*

Some critics of intelligence research maintain that the notion of general intelligence is illusory: that no such global mental capacity exists and that apparent "intelligence" is really just a by-product of one's opportunities to learn skills and information valued in a particular cultural context. True, the concept of intelligence and the way in which individuals are ranked according to this criterion could be social artifacts. But the fact that *g* is not specific to any particular domain of knowledge or mental skill suggests that *g* is independent of cultural content, including beliefs about what intelligence is. And tests of different social groups reveal the same continuum of general intelligence. This observation suggests either that cultures do not construct *g* or that they construct the same *g*. Both conclusions undercut the social artifact theory of intelligence.

Moreover, research on the physiology and genetics of *g* has uncovered biological correlates of this psychological phenomenon. In the past decade, studies by teams of researchers in North America and Europe have linked several attributes of the brain to general intelligence. After taking into account gender and physical stature, brain size as determined by magnetic resonance imaging is moderately correlated with IQ (about 0.4 on a scale of 0 to 1). So is the speed of nerve conduction. The brains of bright people also use less energy during problem solving than do those of their less able peers. And various qualities of brain waves correlate strongly (about 0.5 to 0.7) with IQ: the brain waves of individuals with higher IQs, for example, respond more promptly and consistently to simple sensory stimuli such as audible clicks. These observations have led some investigators to posit that differences in *g* result from differences in the speed and efficiency of neural processing. If this theory is true, environmental conditions could influence *g* by modifying brain physiology in some manner.

Studies of so-called elementary cognitive tasks (ECTs), conducted by Jensen and others, are bridging the gap between the psychological and the physiological aspects of *g*. These mental tasks have no obvious intellectual content and are so simple that adults and most children can do them accurately in less than a second. In the most basic reaction-time tests, for example, the subject must react when a light goes on by lifting her index finger off a home button and immediately depressing a response button. Two measurements are taken: the number of milliseconds between the illumination of the light and the subject's release of the home button, which is called decision time, and the number of milliseconds between the subject's release of the home button and pressing of the response button, which is called movement time.

In this task, movement time seems independent of intelligence, but the decision times of higher-IQ subjects are slightly faster than those of people with lower IQs. As the tasks are made more complex, correlations between average decision times and IQ increase. These results further support the notion that intelligence equips individuals to deal with complexity and that its influence is greater in complex tasks than in simple ones.

The ECT-IQ correlations are comparable for all IQ levels, ages, genders and racial-ethnic groups tested. Moreover, studies by Philip A. Vernon of the University of Western Ontario and others have shown that the ECT-IQ overlap results almost entirely from the common g factor in both measures. Reaction times do not reflect differences in motivation or strategy or the tendency of some individuals to rush through tests and daily tasks—that penchant is a personality trait. They actually seem to measure the speed with which the brain apprehends, integrates and evaluates information. Research on ECTs and brain physiology has not yet identified the biological determinants of this processing speed. These studies do suggest, however, that g is as reliable and global a phenomenon at the neural level as it is at the level of the complex information processing required by IQ tests and everyday life.

The existence of biological correlates of intelligence does not necessarily mean that intelligence is dictated by genes. Decades of genetics research have shown, however, that people are born with different hereditary potentials for intelligence and that these genetic endowments are responsible for much of the variation in mental ability among individuals. [Recently] an international team of scientists headed by Robert Plomin of the Institute of Psychiatry in London announced the discovery of the first gene linked to intelligence. Of course, genes have their effects only in interaction with environments, partly by enhancing an individual's exposure or sensitivity to formative experiences. Differences in general intelligence, whether measured as IQ or, more accurately, as g are both genetic and environmental in origin—just as are all other psychological traits and attitudes studied so far, including personality, vocational interests and societal attitudes. This is old news among the experts. The experts have, however, been startled by more recent discoveries.

One is that the heritability of IQ rises with age—that is to say, the extent to which genetics accounts for differences in IQ among individuals increases as people get older. Studies comparing identical and fraternal twins, published in the past decade by a group led by Thomas J. Bouchard, Jr., of the University of Minnesota and other scholars, show that about 40 percent of IQ differences among preschoolers stems from genetic differences but that heritability rises to 60 percent by adolescence and to 80 percent by late adulthood. With age, differences among individuals in their developed intelligence come to mirror more closely their genetic differences. It appears that the effects of environment on intelligence fade rather than grow with time. In hindsight, perhaps this should have come as no surprise. Young children have the circumstances of their lives imposed on them by parents, schools and other agents of society, but as people get older they become more independent and tend to seek out the life niches that are most congenial to their genetic proclivities.

A second big surprise for intelligence experts was the discovery that environments shared by siblings have little to do with IQ. Many people still mistakenly believe that social, psychological and economic differences among families create lasting and marked differences in IQ. Behavioral geneticists refer to such environmental effects as "shared" because they are common to siblings who grow up together. Research has shown that although shared environments do have a modest influence on IQ in childhood, their effects dissipate by adolescence. The IQs of adopted children, for example, lose all resemblance to those of their adoptive family members and become more like the IQs of the biological parents they have never known. Such findings suggest that siblings either do not share influential aspects of the rearing environment or do not experience them in the same way. Much behavioral genetics research currently focuses on the still mysterious processes by which environments make members of a household less alike.

g on the Job

Although the evidence of genetic and physiological correlates of *g* argues powerfully for the existence of global intelligence, it has not quelled the critics of intelligence testing. These skeptics argue that even if such a global entity exists, it has no intrinsic functional value and becomes important only to the extent that people treat it as such: for example, by using IQ scores to sort, label and assign students and employees. Such concerns over the proper use of mental tests have prompted a great deal of research in recent decades. This research shows that although IQ tests can indeed be misused, they measure a capability that does in fact affect many kinds of performance and many life outcomes, independent of the tests' interpretations or applications. Moreover, the research shows that intelligence tests measure the capability equally well for all native-born English-speaking groups in the U.S.

If we consider that intelligence manifests itself in everyday life as the ability to deal with complexity, then it is easy to see why it has great functional or practical importance. Children, for example, are regularly exposed to complex tasks once they begin school. Schooling requires above all that students learn, solve problems and think abstractly. That IQ is quite a good predictor of differences in educational achievement is therefore not surprising. When scores on both IQ and standardized achievement tests in different subjects are averaged over several years, the two averages correlate as highly as different IQ tests from the same individual do. High-ability students also master material at many times the rate of their low-ability peers. Many investigations have helped quantify this discrepancy. For example, a 1969 study done for the U.S. Army by the Human Resources Research Office found that enlistees in the bottom fifth of the ability distribution required two to six times as many teaching trials and prompts as did their higher-ability peers to attain minimal proficiency in rifle assembly, monitoring signals, combat plotting and other basic military tasks. Similarly, in school settings the ratio of learning rates between "fast" and "slow" students is typically five to one.

The scholarly content of many IQ tests and their strong correlations with educational success can give the impression that *g* is only a narrow academic ability. But general mental ability also predicts job performance, and in more complex jobs it does so better than any other single personal trait, including education and experience. The army's Project A, a seven-year study conducted in the 1980s to improve the recruitment and training process, found that general mental ability correlated strongly with both technical proficiency and soldiering in the nine specialties studied, among them infantry, military police and medical specialist. Research in the civilian sector has revealed the same pattern. Furthermore, although the addition of personality traits such as conscientiousness can help hone the prediction of job performance, the inclusion of specific mental aptitudes such as verbal fluency or mathematical skill rarely does. The predictive value of mental tests in the work arena stems almost entirely from their measurement of g, and that value rises with the complexity and prestige level of the job.

Half a century of military and civilian research has converged to draw a portrait of occupational opportunity along the IQ continuum. Individuals in the top 5 percent of the adult IQ distribution (above IQ 125) can essentially train themselves, and few occupations are beyond their reach mentally. Persons of average IQ (between 90 and 110) are not competitive for most professional and executive-level work but are easily trained for the bulk of jobs in the American economy. In contrast, adults in the bottom 5 percent of the IQ distribution (below 75) are very difficult to train and are not competitive for any occupation on the basis of ability. Serious problems in training low-IQ military recruits during World War II led Congress to ban enlistment from the lowest 10 percent (below 80) of the population, and no civilian occupation in modern economies routinely recruits its workers from that range. Current military enlistment standards exclude any individual whose IQ is below about 85.

The importance of g in job performance, as in schooling, is related to complexity. Occupations differ considerably in the complexity of their demands, and as that complexity rises, higher g levels become a bigger asset and lower g levels a bigger handicap. Similarly, everyday tasks and environments also differ significantly in their cognitive complexity. The degree to which a person's g level will come to bear on daily life depends on how much novelty and ambiguity that person's everyday tasks and surroundings present and how much continual learning, judgment and decision making they require. As gamblers, employers and bankers know, even marginal differences in rates of return will yield big gains—or losses—over time. Hence, even small differences in g among people can exert large, cumulative influences across social and economic life.

In my own work, I have tried to synthesize the many lines of research that document the influence of IQ on life outcomes. As [Figure 2] shows, the odds of various kinds of achievement and social pathology change systematically across the IQ continuum, from borderline mentally retarded (below 70) to intellectually gifted (above 130). Even in comparisons of those of somewhat below average (between 76 and 90) and somewhat above average (between 111 and 125) IQs, the odds for outcomes having social consequence are stacked against the less able. Young men somewhat below average in general mental ability, for example, are more likely to be unemployed than men somewhat above average. The lower-IQ woman is four times more likely to bear illegitimate children than the higher-IQ woman; among mothers, she is eight times more likely to become a chronic welfare recipient. People somewhat below average are 88 times more likely to drop out of high school, seven times more likely to be jailed and five times more likely as adults to live in poverty than people of somewhat above-average IQ. Below-average individuals are 50 percent more likely to be divorced than those in the above-average category.

These odds diverge even more sharply for people with bigger gaps in IQ, and the mechanisms by which IQ creates this divergence are not yet clearly understood. But no other single trait or circumstance yet studied is so deeply

Figure 2

Life Chances	High Risk	Uphill Battle	Keeping Up	Out Ahead	Yours to Lose
Training Style	Slow, simple, supervised	Very explicit, hands-on	Written materials, plus experience / Mastery learning, hands-on	Gathers, infers own information / College format	
Career Potential		Assembler, food service, nurse's aide	Clerk, teller, police officer, machinist, sales	Manager, teacher, accountant	Attorney, chemist, executive
IQ	70	80	90 100 110	120	130

Population Percentages

	High Risk	Uphill Battle	Keeping Up	Out Ahead	Yours to Lose
Total population distribution	5	20	50	20	5
Out of labor force more than 1 month out of year (men)	22	19	15	14	10
Unemployed more than 1 month out of year (men)	12	10	7	7	2
Divorced in 5 years	21	22	23	15	9
Had illegitimate children (women)	32	17	8	4	2
Lives in poverty	30	16	6	3	2
Ever incarcerated (men)	7	7	3	1	0
Chronic welfare recipient (mothers)	31	17	8	2	0
High school dropout	55	35	6	0.4	0

Correlation of IQ scores with occupational achievement suggests that *g* reflects an ability to deal with cognitive complexity. Scores also correlate with some social outcomes (the percentages apply to young white adults in the U.S.).

Adapted from *Intelligence,* Vol. 24, No.1: January/February 1997. Reprinted by permission of John Mengel, Ponzi & Weill, Inc.

implicated in the nexus of bad social outcomes—poverty, welfare, illegitimacy and educational failure—that entraps many low-IQ individuals and families. Even the effects of family background pale in comparison with the influence of IQ. As shown most recently by Charles Murray of the American Enterprise Institute in Washington, D.C., the divergence in many outcomes associated with IQ level is almost as wide among siblings from the same household as it is for strangers of comparable IQ levels. And siblings differ a lot in IQ—on average, by 12 points, compared with 17 for random strangers.

An IQ of 75 is perhaps the most important threshold in modern life. At that level, a person's chances of mastering the elementary school curriculum are only 50–50, and he or she will have a hard time functioning independently without considerable social support. Individuals and families who are only somewhat below average in IQ face risks of social pathology that, while lower, are still significant enough to jeopardize their well-being. High-IQ individuals may lack the resolve, character or good fortune to capitalize on their intellectual capabilities, but socioeconomic success in the postindustrial information age is theirs to lose.

What Is Versus What Could Be

The foregoing findings on *g*'s effects have been drawn from studies conducted under a limited range of circumstances—namely, the social, economic and political conditions prevailing now and in recent decades in developed countries that allow considerable personal freedom. It is not clear whether these findings apply to populations around the world, to the extremely advantaged and disadvantaged in the developing world or, for that matter, to people living under restrictive political regimes. No one knows what research under different circumstances, in different eras or with different populations might reveal. But we do know that, wherever freedom and technology advance, life is an uphill battle for people who are below average in proficiency at learning, solving problems and mastering complexity. We also know that the trajectories of mental development are not easily deflected. Individual IQ levels tend to remain unchanged from adolescence onward, and despite strenuous efforts over the past half a century, attempts to raise *g* permanently through adoption or educational means have failed. If this is a reliable, ethical way to raise or equalize levels of *g*, no one has found it.

Some investigators have suggested that biological interventions, such as dietary supplements of vitamins, may be more effective than educational ones in raising *g* levels. This approach is based in part on the assumption that improved nutrition has caused the puzzling rise in average levels of both IQ and height in the developed world during this century. Scientists are still hotly debating whether the gains in IQ actually reflect a rise in *g* or are caused instead by changes in less critical, specific mental skills. Whatever the truth may be, the differences in mental ability among individuals remain, and the conflict between equal opportunity and equal outcome persists. Only by accepting these hard truths about intelligence will society find humane solutions to the problems posed by the variations in general mental ability.

CHALLENGE QUESTIONS

Should Psychology Adopt a Theory of Multiple Intelligences?

1. What do you think intelligence testing should be used for in society? Should IQ tests be used to place students in certain kinds of classes? How might the acceptance of a multiple theory of intelligence change how IQ tests are used in society and education?
2. Gardner asserts that some intelligences are not covered by IQ tests. How might a psychologist evaluate these intelligences? What kind of test or evaluation would you use to determine an individual's musical intelligence?
3. If culture is a factor in understanding and measuring intelligence, as Gardner argues, how should psychologists go about testing the IQ of individuals who are not part of Western culture? Do prominent IQ tests have a cultural or gender bias?
4. What is the difference between talent and intelligence? Should intelligence be considered primarily a measure of cognitive and academic abilities?

On the Internet . . .

National Council on Alcoholism and Drug Dependence

This site contains objective information and referrals for individuals, families, and others who seek intervention and treatment.

http://www.ncadd.org

The Vaults of Erowid: Addiction

Information on addiction, journal articles, personal experiences with various drugs, and more can be found at this site.

http://www.erowid.org/psychoactives/
addiction/addiction.shtml

Mental Health Infosource: Disorders

This no-nonsense page lists hotlinks to pages dealing with psychological disorders, including anxiety, panic, phobic disorders, schizophrenia, and violent/self-destructive behaviors.

http://www.mhsource.com/disorders/

Wikipedia: The Free Encyclopedia

An on-line encyclopedia, this site includes information on a variety of topics. This particular link contains information on ADHD and provides a forum for discussion.

http://en.wikipedia.org/wiki/Attention-
deficit_hyperactivity_disorder

A Guide to Psychology and its Practice

This Web site provides information about the practice of Clinical Psychology. This particular page discusses psychiatric medication issues and provides links to related issues on and off the site.

http://www.guidetopsychology.com/meds.htm

PART 5

Mental Health

A *mental disorder is often defined as a pattern of thinking or behavior that is either disruptive to others or harmful to the person with the disorder. This definition seems straightforward, yet there is considerable debate about whether or not some disorders truly exist. For example, does a child s acute disruptive behavior and short attention span unquestionably warrant he or she being diagnosed with Attention Deficit Hyperactive Disorder (ADHD)? Also, many psychological disorders, including ADHD, are treated with medications, most of which have side effects. Could some of these side effects make certain medications unsafe? Some psychologists claim that antidepressants can make patients suicidal, but is there any other option? Psychologists have found that it can be extremely difficult for patients to control their symptoms without the help of treatment. But do some patients, such as those who suffer from drug addiction, have no choice but to submit to the influence of their addiction?*

- Does ADHD Exist?

- Does Taking Antidepressants Lead to Suicide?

- Is Drug Addiction a Choice?

ISSUE 11

Does ADHD Exist?

YES: Russell A. Barkley, from "International Consensus Statement on ADHD," *Clinical Child and Family Psychology Review* (June 2002)

NO: Sami Timimi et al., from "A Critique of the International Consensus Statement on ADHD," *Clinical Child and Family Psychology Review* (March 2004)

ISSUE SUMMARY

YES: Russell A. Barkley, a professor in the department of psychiatry and neurology, leads a team of researchers who claim that current scientific evidence, particularly evidence provided by heritability and neuro-imaging studies, points unarguably toward ADHD's validity and existence.

NO: Another group of researchers, led by psychiatrist Sami Timimi, claims the current ADHD epidemic is the result of unrealistic expectations for today's children and the pharmaceutical companies' desire to sell more drugs.

Over the past several years, the acronym "ADHD" (attention deficit hyperactivity disorder) has almost become a household term. Just about everybody knows someone, usually a child, who has been diagnosed with ADHD. Still, the current popularity and prevalence of ADHD has brought with it a heated controversy over whether the disorder even exists. Because ADHD involves childlike behavior, some people have wondered if this diagnosis is a sign that childishness is no longer tolerated in our culture, even in children. Is ADHD a mental disease or are psychologists and scientists unwittingly trying to purge the childishness out of children?

If ADHD can be shown to have a biological basis, then it would follow that it is more than merely an intolerance of childlike behavior. Many psychologists attribute mental illness today to an irregularity in the physiological make-up of the brain, making the cause of psychological disorders just as biological as heart disease or cancer. This focus on "nature" or biology, rather than "nurture" or environment, has persuaded many psychologists to favor biological explanations for the inattentiveness and hyperactivity of ADHD children. However, these explanations normally mean that the mechanisms of ADHD are outside the control of the children or their parents. The emphasis in treatment then shifts from educating the children to medicating them.

In the *International Consensus Statement on ADHD*, a group of psychologists led by Russell A. Barkley asserts that ADHD does exist in this biological manner. In support of their claim, these psychologists cite studies of genetic heritability, particularly those involving twins, which they believe establishes the heritability of ADHD. They also point toward neuro-imaging studies that show a common structural and chemical irregularity in the brains of many children diagnosed with ADHD. By providing this type of empirical or scientific evidence, these psychologists hope to solidify ADHD's relation to other known biological disorders and thus prove the reality of its existence.

Other psychologists, however, question the biological reality of ADHD. In their critique of the International Consensus Statement on ADHD, Sami Timimi, along with another group of psychologists, claim current scientific evidence does not support ADHD as a neurobiological disorder. They accuse Barkley and his colleagues of trying to close an issue that has yet to be resolved. Timimi and his colleagues attribute the increasing number of ADHD diagnoses in the Western world to a new cultural demand for children to behave more like adults. They also accuse pharmaceutical companies of being too eager to help parents cover up poor childrearing by medicating their kids. In an effort to debunk some of the most popular evidence for the existence of ADHD, Timimi et al. claim that the psychotropic medications used to treat children diagnosed with ADHD have the same effect on "normal" children and might actually cause the apparent brain irregularities depicted in neuro-imaging.

POINT

- The vast majority of competent scholars agree that ADHD is a valid disorder.
- Neuro-imaging studies show brain irregularities are common among ADHD children.
- ADHD meets the rigorous scientific criteria for its recognition as a valid psychological disorder.
- Twin studies show that ADHD is extremely heritable.
- Not enough ADHD sufferers are receiving the available medications for treatment.

COUNTERPOINT

- There is no stable definition for ADHD and, therefore, it is impossible to diagnose correctly.
- Neuro-imaging studies have not adequately shown that ADHD is a biochemical brain disorder.
- The prevalence of ADHD is the result of unrealistic cultural expectations for children and drug companies' eagerness to push medications.
- The idea that ADHD is strongly heritable is open to interpretation.
- ADHD medications have similar effects on non-ADHD children and have dangerous, long-term side effects.

Russell A. Barkley

 **YES**

International Consensus Statement on ADHD January 2002

We, the undersigned consortium of international scientists, are deeply concerned about the periodic inaccurate portrayal of attention deficit hyperactivity disorder (ADHD) in media reports. This is a disorder with which we are all very familiar and toward which many of us have dedicated scientific studies if not entire careers. We fear that inaccurate stories rendering ADHD as myth, fraud, or benign condition may cause thousands of sufferers not to seek treatment for their disorder. It also leaves the public with a general sense that this disorder is not valid or real or consists of a rather trivial affliction.

We have created this consensus statement on ADHD as a reference on the status of the scientific findings concerning this disorder, its validity, and its adverse impact on the lives of those diagnosed with the disorder as of this writing (January 2002).

Occasional coverage of the disorder casts the story in the form of a sporting event with evenly matched competitors. The views of a handful of nonexpert doctors that ADHD does not exist are contrasted against mainstream scientific views that it does, as if both views had equal merit. Such attempts at balance give the public the impression that there is substantial scientific disagreement over whether ADHD is a real medical condition—In fact, there is no such disagreement—at least no more so than there is over whether smoking causes cancer, for example, or whether a virus causes HIV/AIDS.

The U.S. Surgeon General, the American Medical Association, the American Psychiatric Association, the American Academy of Child and Adolescent Psychiatry, the American Psychological Association, and the American Academy of Pediatrics, among others, all recognize ADHD as a valid disorder. Although some of these organizations have issued guidelines for evaluation and management of the disorder for their membership, this is the first consensus statement issued by an independent consortium of leading scientists concerning the status of the disorder. Among scientists who have devoted years, if not entire careers, to the study of this disorder there is no controversy regarding its existence.

ADHD and Science

We cannot overemphasize the point that, as a matter of science, the notion that ADHD does not exist is simply wrong. All of the major medical associations and government health agencies recognize ADHD as a genuine disorder because the scientific evidence indicating it is so overwhelming.

Various approaches have been used to establish whether a condition rises to the level of a valid medical or psychiatric disorder. A very useful one stipulates that there must be scientifically established evidence that those suffering the condition have a serious deficiency in or failure of a physical or psychological mechanism that is universal to humans. That is, all humans normally would be expected, regardless of culture, to have developed that mental ability.

And there must be equally incontrovertible scientific evidence that this serious deficiency leads to harm to the individual. Harm is established through evidence of increased mortality, morbidity, or impairment in the major life activities required of one's developmental stage in life. Major life activities are those domains of functioning such as education, social relationships, family functioning, independence and self-sufficiency, and occupational functioning that all humans of that developmental level are expected to perform.

As attested to by the numerous scientists signing this document, there is no question among the world's leading clinical researchers that ADHD involves a serious deficiency in a set of psychological abilities and that these deficiencies pose serious harm to most individuals possessing the disorder. Current evidence indicates that deficits in behavioral inhibition and sustained attention are central to this disorder—facts demonstrated through hundreds of scientific studies. And there is no doubt that ADHD leads to impairments in major life activities, including social relations, education, family functioning, occupational functioning, self-sufficiency, and adherence to social rules, norms, and laws. Evidence also indicates that those with ADHD are more prone to physical injury and accidental poisonings. This is why no professional medical, psychological, or scientific organization doubts the existence of ADHD as a legitimate disorder.

The central psychological deficits in those with ADHD have now been linked through numerous studies using various scientific methods to several specific brain regions (the frontal lobe, its connections to the basal ganglia, and their relationship to the central aspects of the cerebellum). Most neurological studies find that as a group those with ADHD have less brain electrical activity and show less reactivity to stimulation in one or more of these regions. And neuro-imaging studies of groups of those with ADHD also demonstrate relatively smaller areas of brain matter and less metabolic activity of this brain matter than is the case in control groups used in these studies.

These same psychological deficits in inhibition and attention have been found in numerous studies of identical and fraternal twins conducted across various countries (US, Great Britain, Norway, Australia, etc.) to be primarily inherited. The genetic contribution to these traits is routinely found to be among the highest for any psychiatric disorder (70–95% of trait variation in the population), nearly approaching the genetic contribution to human height. One gene has recently been reliably demonstrated to be associated with this disorder and the search for more is underway by more than 12 different scientific teams worldwide at this time.

Numerous studies of twins demonstrate that family environment makes no significant separate contribution to these traits. This is not to say that the home environment, parental management abilities, stressful life events, or deviant peer relationships are unimportant or have no influence on individuals having this disorder, as they certainly do. Genetic tendencies are expressed in interaction with the environment. Also, those having ADHD often have other associated disorders and problems, some of which are clearly related to their social environments. But it is to say that the underlying psychological deficits that comprise ADHD itself are not solely or primarily the result of these environmental factors.

This is why leading international scientists, such as the signers below, recognize the mounting evidence of neurological and genetic contributions to this disorder. This evidence, coupled with countless studies on the harm posed by the disorder and hundreds of studies on the effectiveness of medication, buttresses the need in many, though by no means all, cases for management of the disorder with multiple therapies. These include medication combined with educational, family, and other social accommodations. This is in striking contrast to the wholly unscientific views of some social critics in periodic media accounts that ADHD constitutes a fraud, that medicating those afflicted is questionable if not reprehensible, and that any behavior problems associated with ADHD are merely the result of problems in the home, excessive viewing of TV or playing of video games, diet, lack of love and attention, or teacher/school intolerance.

ADHD is not a benign disorder. For those it afflicts, ADHD can cause devastating problems. Follow-up studies of clinical samples suggest that sufferers are far more likely than normal people to drop out of school (32–40%), to rarely complete college (5–10%), to have few or no friends (50–70%), to underperform at work (70–80%), to engage in antisocial activities (40–50%), and to use tobacco or illicit drugs more than normal. Moreover, children growing up with ADHD are more likely to experience teen pregnancy (40%) and sexually transmitted diseases (16%), to speed excessively and have multiple car accidents, to experience depression (20–30%) and personality disorders (18–25%) as adults, and in hundreds of other ways mismanage and endanger their lives.

Yet despite these serious consequences, studies indicate that less than half of those with the disorder are receiving treatment. The media can help substantially to improve these circumstances. It can do so by portraying ADHD and the science about it as accurately and responsibly as possible while not purveying the propaganda of some social critics and fringe doctors whose political agenda would have you and the public believe there is no real disorder here. To publish stories that ADHD is a fictitious disorder or merely a conflict between today's Huckleberry Finns and their caregivers is tantamount to declaring the earth flat, the laws of gravity debatable, and the periodic table in chemistry a fraud. ADHD should be depicted in the media as realistically and accurately as it is depicted in science—as a valid disorder having varied and substantial adverse impact on those who may suffer from it through no fault of their own or their parents and teachers . . .

Sami Timimi et al.

 **NO**

A Critique of the International Consensus Statement on ADHD

Why did a group of eminent psychiatrists and psychologists produce a consensus statement that seeks to forestall debate on the merits of the widespread diagnosis and drug treatment of attention deficit hyperactivity disorder (ADHD)? If the evidence is already that good then no statement is needed. However, the reality is that claims about ADHD being a genuine medical disorder and psychotropics being genuine correctives have been shaken by criticism.

Not only is it completely counter to the spirit and practice of science to cease questioning the validity of ADHD as proposed by the consensus statement, there is an ethical and moral responsibility to do so. History teaches us again and again that one generation's most cherished therapeutic ideas and practices, especially when applied on the powerless, are repudiated by the next, but not without leaving countless victims in their wake. Lack of acknowledgement of the subjective nature of our psychiatric practice leaves it wide open to abuse. For these reasons we, another group of academics and practitioners, feel compelled to respond to this statement.

Merits of the ADHD Diagnosis

The evidence does not support the conclusion that ADHD identifies a group of children who suffer from a common and specific neurobiological disorder. There are no cognitive, metabolic, or neurological markers for ADHD and so there is no such thing as a medical test for this diagnosis. There is obvious uncertainty about how to define this disorder, with definitions changing over the past 30 years depending on what the current favourite theory about underlying aetiology is, and with each revision producing a higher number of potential children deemed to have the disorder. It is hardly surprising that epidemiological studies produce hugely differing prevalence rates from 0.5% to 26% of all children.

Despite attempts at standardising criteria, cross-cultural studies on the rating of symptoms of ADHD show major and significant differences between raters from different countries, rating of children from different cultures, and even within cultures (for example, rates of diagnosis of ADHD have been shown to vary by a factor of 10 from county to county within the same state in the United States.

There are high rates of comorbidity between ADHD and conduct, anxiety, depression, and other disorders, with about three quarters of children diagnosed with ADHD also fulfilling criteria for another psychiatric disorder. Such high rates of comorbidity suggest that the concept of ADHD is inadequate to explain clinical reality.

Neuroimaging research is often cited as "proof" of a biological deficit in those with ADHD, however, after almost 25 years and over 30 studies, researchers have yet to do a simple comparison of unmedicated children diagnosed with ADHD with an age matched control group. The studies have shown nonspecific and inconsistent changes in some children in some studies. However, sample sizes have been small and in none of the studies were the brains considered clinically abnormal; nor has any specific abnormality been convincingly demonstrated. Most worryingly, animal studies suggest that any differences observed in these studies could well be due to the effects of medication that most children in these studies had taken. Even a U.S. federal government report on ADHD concluded that there was no compelling evidence to support the claim that ADHD was a biochemical brain disorder. Research on possible environmental causes of ADHD type behaviors has largely been ignored, despite mounting evidence that psychosocial factors such as exposure to trauma and abuse can cause them.

With regards the claim that ADHD is a genetic condition that is strongly heritable, the evidence is open to interpretation. ADHD shares common genetics with conduct disorder and other externalising behaviors, and so if there is a heritable component it is not specific to ADHD.

Efficacy of Drug Treatment

The relentless growth in the practice of diagnosis of childhood and adolescent psychiatric disorders has also led to a relentless increase in the amount of psychotropic medication being prescribed to children and adolescents. The amount of psychotropic medication prescribed to children in the United States increased nearly threefold between 1987 and 1996, with over 6% of boys between the ages of 6 and 14 taking psychostimulants in 1996, a figure that is likely to be much higher now. There has also been a large increase in prescriptions of psychostimulants to preschoolers (aged 2–4 years). One study in Virginia found that in two school districts, 17% of White boys at primary school were taking psychostimulants. Yet in the international consensus statement the authors still believe that less than half of those with ADHD are receiving treatment. Many of the authors of the consensus statement are well-known advocates of drug treatment for children with AHDH and it is notable that in the statement they do not declare their financial interests and/or their links with pharmaceutical companies.

Despite claims for the miraculous effects of stimulants they are not a specific treatment for ADHD, because they are well known to have similar effects on otherwise normal children and other children regardless of diagnosis. A recent meta-analysis of randomised controlled trials of methylphenidate found that the trials were of poor quality, there was strong evidence of publication bias, short-term effects were inconsistent across different rating scales, side effects were frequent and problematic and long-term effects beyond 4 weeks of treatment were not demonstrated.

The authors of the consensus statement claim that untreated ADHD leads to significant impairment and harm for the afflicted individual; not only do the authors conflate a statistical association with cause but other evidence suggests that drug treatment has at best an inconsequential effect on long-term outcome.

The potential long-term adverse effects of giving psychotropic drugs to children need to cause us more concern than the authors of the consensus statement will allow. Stimulants are potentially addictive drugs with cardiovascular, nervous, digestive, endocrine, and psychiatric side effects. At a psychological level the use of drug treatment scripts a potentially life-long story of disability and deficit that physically healthy children may end up believing. Children may view drug treatment as a punishment for naughty behaviour and may be absorbing the message that they are not able to control or learn to control their own behavior. Drug treatment may also distance all concerned from finding more effective, long-lasting strategies. The children and their carers may be unnecessarily cultured into the attitude of a "pill for life's problems."

A Cultural Perspective on ADHD

Why has ADHD become so popular now resulting in spiralling rates of diagnosis of ADHD and prescription of psychostimulants in the Western world? This question requires us to examine the cultural nature of how we construct what we deem to be normal and abnormal childhoods and child rearing methods. Although the immaturity of children is a biological fact, the ways in which this immaturity is understood and made meaningful is a fact of culture. Differences between cultures and within cultures over time mean that what are considered as desirable practices in one culture are often seen as abusive in another.

In contemporary, Western society children are viewed as individuals who have rights and need to express their opinions as well as being potentially vulnerable and needing protection by the state when parents are deemed not to be adequate. At the same time there has been a growing debate and belief that childhood in modern, Western society has suffered a strange death. Many contemporary observers are concerned about the increase in violence, drug and alcohol abuse, depression, and suicide amongst a generation perceived to have been given the best of everything. Some commentators believe we are witnessing the end of the innocence of childhood, for example, through the greater sexualization and commercialization of childhood interests. It is claimed that childhood is disappearing, through media, such as television, as children have near complete access to the world of adult information leading to a collapse of the moral authority of adults. Coupled with this fear that the boundary between childhood and adulthood is disappearing is a growing sense that children themselves are a risk with some children coming to be viewed as too dangerous for society and needing to be controlled, reshaped and changed.

Thus, in the last few decades of the twentieth century in Western culture, the task of child rearing has become loaded with anxiety. On the one hand, parents and teachers feeling the pressure from the breakdown of adult authority discourse, feel they must act to control unruly children; on the other hand they feel inhibited from doing so for fear of the consequences now that people are aware that families can be ruined and careers destroyed should the state decide to intervene. This cultural anxiety has provided the ideal social context for growth of popularity of the concept of ADHD. The concept of ADHD has helped shift focus away from these social dilemmas and onto the individual child. It has been in the best interests of the pharmaceutical industry to facilitate this change in focus. Drug company strategy for expanding markets for drug treatment of children is not confined to direct drug promotion but includes illness promotion (e.g., funding for parent support groups such as CHADD) and influencing research activities. Thus, the current "epidemic" of ADHD in the West can be understood as a symptom of a profound change in our cultural expectations of children coupled with an unwitting alliance between drug companies and some doctors, that serves to culturally legitimize the practice of dispensing performance enhancing substances in a crude attempt to quell our current anxieties about children's (particularly boys) development.

In their consensus statement, the authors are at pains to point out that it is not the child's, the parent's or the teacher's fault. However, trying to understand the origins and meaning of behaviors labelled, as ADHD does not need to imply blame. What it does require is an attempt to positively engage with the interpersonal realities of human life. This can be done through individualized family counseling and educational approaches, as well as using multiple perspectives to empower children, parents, teachers, and others.

Conclusion

The authors of the consensus statement sell themselves short in stating that questioning the current practice concerning diagnosis and treatment of ADHD is like declaring the earth is flat. It is regrettable that they wish to close down debate prematurely and in a way not becoming of academics. The evidence shows that the debate is far from over.

CHALLENGE QUESTIONS

Does ADHD Exist?

1. What other psychological disorders are commonly treated with medication? Could the existence of these disorders be attributed to the same causes that Timimi and his colleagues attribute to the existence of ADHD? Defend your position.
2. The authors of each selection cannot seem to agree on how to interpret the findings of neuro-imaging studies of ADHD. Look at the available studies yourself and draw your own conclusion.
3. Both selections discuss treating ADHD with medication but only briefly mention other treatments. Research medication treatments for ADHD on your own. Which treatments would you consider to be the most effective? Defend your answer.
4. Find out what the side effects are for current ADHD medications. If you had a particularly hyperactive child who had trouble paying attention, would you medicate him with these drugs? List the pros and cons.
5. If you were a teacher or parent with responsibility for an especially unruly child, how might you help that child change his or her behavior without using medication to alter his or her temperament?

ISSUE 12

Does Taking Antidepressants Lead to Suicide?

YES: David Healy and Chris Whitaker, from "Antidepressants and Suicide: Risk-Benefit Conundrums," *Journal of Psychiatry & Neuroscience* (September 2003)

NO: Yvon D. Lapierre, from "Suicidality With Selective Serotonin Reuptake Inhibitors: Valid Claim?" *Journal of Psychiatry & Neuroscience* (September 2003)

ISSUE SUMMARY

YES: Psychiatrist David Healy and statistician Chris Whitaker argue that psychological research reveals a significant number of suicidal acts by individuals taking antidepressants and, thus, they recommend stricter controls on these drugs.

NO: In response, psychiatrist Yvon D. Lapierre maintains that the research on suicidality and antidepressants is unconvincing, recommending that conclusions from these findings should be severely limited.

Drugs for depression have become so familiar and are used so frequently in our society that their safety has been almost taken for granted. It was surprising, then, when recent research findings seemed to indicate that suicide is a possible effect of a certain class of antidepressants—specifically, selective serotonin reuptake inhibitors, or SSRIs. Almost immediately, the defenders of these drugs offered another explanation: These findings are the result of an increase in the number people with depression and not an effect of antidepressants. In other words, because suicide is a risk for people with depression, an increase in the number of depressed people accounts for the increase in the number of suicides.

The problem is that the Food and Drug Administration (FDA) does not seem to agree with this explanation. Recently, it ordered manufacturers of all antidepressants, not just SSRIs, to include a "black box" warning on their labels—the most serious caution the government can require. This warning alerts people to the increased risk of suicide among children and adolescents taking antidepressant medication. This move by the FDA means the U.S. government believes that current evidence is sufficient to take serious action. Some health professionals fear that people might misinterpret this serious action and resist seeking treatment for depression altogether.

The first article supports the FDA decision. Looking at figures from randomized controlled trials (RCTs)—the gold-standard of research designs—David Healy and Chris Whitaker found too many suicidal acts among people on antidepressants, especially when compared with people using placebos (drugs that have no treatment effect). While the authors agree these studies show that SSRIs do reduce suicidality in some patients, they argue that there is a net increase in suicidal acts associated with their use. In other words, more people are ultimately harmed than helped. Still, Healy and Whitaker do not recommend that people stop taking antidepressants. They do, however, believe that warnings and monitoring of antidepressants are necessary to reduce the overall risk of suicide.

In response, Yvon D. Lapierre disagrees with Healy and Whitakers contention that antidepressants increase the risk of suicide. He notes the number of methodological problems and biases with the studies Healy and Whitaker used to support their conclusions. He also points to other studies that just as strongly indicate that suicidal thoughts are lessened by the same drugs. He admits that the research as a whole has yielded mixed findings. Still, this is all the more reason to avoid hastily concluding that antidepressants lead to suicide. The conclusions of Healy and Whitaker, therefore, are premature.

POINT

- Studies show an increase in suicidal acts when people take antidepressants.

- Studies that claim a reduction of suicidality in some patients ignore how the same treatment can produce suicidality in others.

- Clinicians should be more vigilant and restrict treatment for those most at risk for suicide.

- Consumers and clinicians should be warned about the dangers of antidepressants.

COUNTERPOINT

- The inherent biases of these studies decrease the ability to draw valid conclusions.

- Studies strongly suggest that antidepressants decrease suicidal thoughts in some patients.

- Suicide is already recognized among clinicians as a major risk of depression.

- Because results of clinical studies are inconclusive, more research should be conducted before serious action is taken.

YES

**David Healy and
Chris Whitaker**

Antidepressants and Suicide: Risk–Benefit Conundrums

Introduction

. . . The debate regarding selective serotonin reuptake inhibitors (SSRIs) and suicide started in 1990, when Teicher, Glod and Cole described 6 cases in which intense suicidal preoccupation emerged during fluoxetine treatment. This paper was followed by others, which, combined, provided evidence of dose–response, challenge, dechallenge and rechallenge relations, as well as the emergence of an agreed mechanism by which the effects were mediated and demonstrations that interventions in the process could ameliorate the problems. A subsequent series of reports on the effects of sertraline and paroxetine on suicidality and akathisia pointed to SSRI-induced suicidality being a class effect rather than something confined to fluoxetine.

An induction of suicidality by SSRIs, therefore, had apparently been convincingly demonstrated according to conventional criteria for establishing cause and effect relations between drugs and adverse events, as laid out by clinical trial methodologists, company investigators, medico-legal authorities and the federal courts. Far less consistent evidence led the Medicines Control Agency in Britain in 1988 to state unambiguously that benzodiazepines can trigger suicide.

Specifically designed randomized controlled trials (RCTs) on depression-related suicidality at this time would have established the rates at which this seemingly new phenomenon might be happening. However, no such studies have ever been undertaken. This review, therefore, will in lieu cover the RCT data on newly released antidepressants and suicidal acts, the meta-analyses of efficacy studies in depression that have been brought to bear on the question and relevant epidemiological studies.

Efficacy Studies

In lieu of specifically designed RCTs, the RCTs that formed the basis for the licence application for recent antidepressants are one source of data. Khan and colleagues recently analyzed RCT data to assess whether it was ethical to

From *Journal of Psychiatry & Neuroscience*, vol. 28, no. 5, September 2003, pp. 332–337. Copyright ©
2003 by CMA Management. Reprinted by permission. References omitted.

continue using placebos in antidepresant trials. Although the U.S. Food and Drug Administration (FDA), in general, recommends that data from clinical trials be analyzed both in terms of absolute numbers and patient exposure years (PEY), given that an assessment of the hazards posed by placebo was the object of this study, the investigators appropriately analyzed the figures in terms of PEY only. Khan et al. found an excess of suicidal acts by individuals taking antidepressants compared with placebo, and this was also replicated in another analysis, but the rates of suicidal acts in patients taking antidepressants and those taking placebo were not significantly different in these analyses. Yet, another study reported that rates of suicidal acts of patients taking antidepressants for longer durations may, in fact, fall relative to placebo, which might be expected because longer term studies will select patients suited to the agent being investigated.

Although an analysis in terms of PEYs may be appropriate for an assessment of the risk of exposure to placebo, it is inappropriate for the assessment of a problem that clinical studies had clearly linked to the first weeks of active therapy. An analysis of suicidal acts on the basis of duration of exposure systematically selects patients who do not have the problem under investigation, because those with the problem often drop out of the trial, whereas others who do well are kept on treatment for months or more on grounds of compassionate use.

The data presented by Khan and colleagues has accordingly been modified here in 4 respects (Table 1). First, suicides and suicidal acts are presented in terms of absolute numbers of patients. Second, on the basis of an FDA paroxetine safety review and FDA statistical reviews on sertraline, it is clear that some of the suicides and suicidal acts categorized as occurring while patients were taking placebo actually occurred during a placebo washout period; placebo and washout suicides are therefore distinguished here. Third, data for citalopram, from another article by Khan et al., are included (although no details about the validity of assignments to placebo are available). Fourth, fluoxetine data from public domain documents are presented, again dividing the data into placebo and washout period suicidal acts, along with data for venlafaxine.

When washout and placebo data are separated and analyzed in terms of suicidal acts per patient (excluding missing bupropion data) using an exact Mantel–Haenszel procedure with a 1-tailed test for significance, the odds ratio of a suicide while taking these new antidepressants as a group compared with placebo is 4.40 (95% confidence interval [CI] 1.32–infinity; $p = 0.0125$). The odds ratio for a suicidal act while taking these antidepressants compared with placebo is 2.39 (95% CI 1.66–infinity; $p \leq 0.0001$). The odds ratio for a completed suicide while taking an SSRI antidepressant (including venlafaxine) compared with placebo is 2.46 (95% CI 0.71–infinity; $p = 0.16$), and the odds ratio for a suicidal act while taking SSRIs compared with placebo is 2.22 (95% CI 1.47–infinity; $p \leq 0.001$).

If washout suicidal acts are included with placebo, as the companies appear to have done, but adjusting the denominator appropriately, the relative risk of suicidal acts while taking sertraline, paroxetine or fluoxetine compared with placebo becomes significant, with figures ranging from 3.0 for sertraline to over 10.0 for fluoxetine.

Other data sets yield similar findings. For instance, in Pierre Fabre's clinical trial database of approximately 8000 patients, the rate for suicidal acts by those taking SSRIs appears to be 3 times the rate for other antidepressants. However, these other data sets include a mixture of trials. The current analysis limits the number of studies but ensures that they are roughly comparable, and the selection of studies is based on regulatory requirements rather than individual bias.

Table 1

Incidence of Suicides and Suicide Attempts in Antidepressant Trials from Khan et al. and Kirsch et al.

Treatment	No. of Patients	No. of Suicides	No. of Suicide Attempts	Suicides and Attempts, %
Sertraline hydrochloride*	2053	2	7	0.44
Active comparator	595	0	1	0.17
Placebo	786	0	2	0.25
Placebo washout		0	3	
Paroxetine hydrochloride*	2963	5	40	1.52
Active comparator	1151	3	12	1.30
Placebo	554	0	3	0.54
Placebo washout		2	2	
Nefazodone hydrochloride	3496	9	12	0.60
Active comparator	958	0	6	0.63
Placebo	875	0	1	0.11
Mirtazapine	2425	8	29	1.53
Active comparator	977	2	5	0.72
Placebo	494	0	3	0.61
Bupropion hydrochloride	1942	3	—	
Placebo	370	0	—	
Citalopram*	4168	8	91	2.38
Placebo	691	1	10	1.59
Fluoxetine*	1427	1	12	0.91
Placebo	370	0	0	0
Placebo washout		1	0	
Venlafaxine*	3082	7	36	1.40
Placebo	739	1	2	0.41
All investigational drugs	21556	43	232	1.28
All SSRIs*	13693	23	186	1.53
Active comparators	3681	5	24	0.79
Total placebo	4879	2	21	0.47
SSRI trial placebo	3140	2	16	0.57

*SSRI = selective serotonin reuptake inhibitor.

Meta- and Other Analyses of SSRIs and Suicidal Acts

In addition to the RCT data indicating an excess of suicidal acts by those taking SSRIs, the clinical trials on zimelidine, the first SSRI, suggested there were more suicide attempts by patients taking it than by those taking comparators, but Montgomery and colleagues reported that although this might be the case, zimelidine appeared to do better than comparators in reducing already existing suicidal thoughts. A similar analysis demonstrated lower suicide attempt rates for those taking fluvoxamine than the comparators in clinical trials. Problems with paroxetine led to similar analyses and similar claims.

The best-known analysis of this type was published by Eli Lilly after the controversy with fluoxetine emerged; from the analysis of pooled data from 17 double-blind clinical trials in patients with major depressive disorder, the authors concluded that "data from these trials do not show that fluoxetine is associated with an increased risk of suicidal acts or emergence of substantial suicidal thoughts among depressed patients." There are a number of methodological problems with Lilly's analysis, however, and these apply to some extent to all other such exercises. First, none of the studies in the analysis were designed to test whether fluoxetine could be associated with the emergence of suicidality. In the case of fluoxetine, all of the studies had been conducted before concerns of suicide induction had arisen. Some of the studies used in the analysis had, in fact, been rejected by the FDA. Second, only 3067 patients of the approximately 26,000 patients entered into clinical trials of fluoxetine were included in this meta-analysis. Third, no mention was made of the fact that benzodiazepines had been coprescribed in the clinical trial program to minimize the agitation that Lilly recognized fluoxetine could cause. Fourth, no reference was made to the 5% of patients who dropped out because of anxiety and agitation. Given that this was arguably the very problem that was at the heart of the issue, the handling of this issue was not reassuring. The 5% dropout rate for agitation or akathisia holds true for other SSRIs as well, and the differences between SSRIs and placebo are statistically significant. Given that the *Diagnostic and Statistical Manual of Mental Disorders, fourth edition, text revision* (DSM-IV-TR) has connected akathisia with suicide risk, this point is of importance.

Finally, this and other analyses depend critically on item 3 (i.e., suicide) of the Hamilton Rating Scale for Depression; this approach to the problem is one that FDA officials, Lilly personnel and Lilly's consultants agreed was methodologically unsatisfactory. The argument in these meta-analyses has, broadly speaking, been that in the randomized trials, the SSRI reduced suicidality on item 3 and that there was no emergence of suicidality, as measured by this item. To claim that the prevention of or reduction of suicidality in some patients in some way means that treatment cannot produce suicidality in others is a logical non sequitur. The argument that item 3 would pick up emergent suicidality in studies run by clinicians who are not aware of this possible adverse effect has no evidence to support it.

Despite these methodological caveats, the claim that SSRIs reduce suicidality in some patients appears strong. However, insofar as SSRIs reduce suicidal acts in some, if there is a net increase in suicidal acts associated with SSRI treatment in these same trials, the extent to which SSRIs cause problems for some patients must be greater than is apparent from considering the raw data.

Epidemiological Studies

Epidemiology traditionally involves the study of representative samples of the population and requires a specification of the methods used to make the sample representative. A series of what have been termed epidemiological studies have been appealed to in this debate. The first is a 1-column letter involving no suicides. The second is a selective retrospective postmarketing chart review involving no suicides, which analyzed by the American College of Neuropsychopharmacology, the FDA and others, shows a 3-fold increased relative risk of emergent suicidality for fluoxetine versus other antidepressants.

A third study was conducted by Warshaw and Keller on patients with anxiety disorder, in which the only suicide was committed by a patient taking fluoxetine. However, only 192 of the 654 patients in this study received fluoxetine. This, therefore, was not a study designed to test fluoxetine's capacity to induce suicidality. In a fourth study of 643 patients, conceived 20 years before fluoxetine was launched and instituted 10 years before launch, only 185 patients received fluoxetine at any point. This was clearly not a study designed to establish whether fluoxetine might induce suicidality. None of these studies fit the definition of epidemiology offered above.

Although not properly epidemiological, 2 post-marketing surveillance studies that compared SSRI with non-SSRI antidepressants found a higher rate of induction of suicidal ideation for those taking SSRIs, although not in the rates of suicidal acts or suicides.

In a more standard epidemiological study of 222 suicides, Donovan et al. reported that 41 of those suicides were committed by people who had been taking an antidepressant in the month before their suicide; there was a statistically significant doubling of the relative risk of suicide in those taking SSRIs compared with tricyclic antidepressants. In a further epidemiological study of 2776 acts of deliberate self-harm, Donovan et al. found a doubling of the risk for deliberate self-harm for those taking SSRIs compared with other antidepressants.

A set of post-marketing surveillance studies carried out in primary care in the United Kingdom by the Drug Safety Research Unit (DSRU) recorded 110 suicides in over 50,000 patients being treated by general practitioners in Britain. The DSRU methodology has since been applied to mirtazapine, where there have been 13 suicides reported in a population of 13,554 patients. This permits the comparisons outlined in Table 2.

A further study from British primary care was undertaken by Jick and colleagues, who investigated the rate and means of suicide among people taking common antidepressants. They reported 143 suicides among 172,580 patients taking antidepressants and found a statistically significant doubling

Table 2

Drug Safety Research Unit Studies of Selective Serotonin Reuptake Inhibitors (SSRIs) and Mirtazapine in Primary Care Practice in the United Kingdom

Drug	No. of Patients	No. of Suicides	Suicides/100,000 Patients (and 95% confidence interval)	
Fluoxetine	12692	31	244	(168–340)
Sertraline	12734	22	173	(110–255)
Paroxetine	13741	37	269	(192–365)
Fluvoxamine	10983	20	182	(114–274)
Total SSRIs	**50150**	**110**	**219**	
Mirtazapine	13554	13	96	(53–158)

of the relative risk of suicide with fluoxetine compared with the reference antidepressant, dothiepin, when calculated in terms of patient exposure years. Controlling for confounding factors such as age, sex and previous suicide attempts left the relative risk at 2.1 times greater for fluoxetine than for dothiepin and greater than any other antidepressant studied, although statistical significance was lost in the process. Of further note are the elevated figures for mianserin and trazodone, which are closely related pharmacologically to mirtazapine and nefazodone. Controlling for confounding factors in the case of mianserin and trazodone, however, led to a reduction in the relative risk of these agents compared with dothiepin.

To provide comparability with other figures, I have recalculated these data in terms of absolute numbers and separated the data for fluoxetine (Table 3). The data in the Jick study, however, only allow comparisons between antidepressants. They shed no light on the differences between treatment with antidepressants and non-treatment or on the efficacy of antidepressants in reducing suicide risk in primary care. The traditional figures with which the DSRU studies and the Jick study might be compared are a 15% lifetime risk for suicide for affective disorders. This would be inappropriate, however, because this 15% figure was derived from patients with melancholic depression in hospital in the pre-antidepressant era.

There are very few empirical figures available for suicide rates in primary care depression, the sample from which the Jick et al. and DSRU data come. One study from Sweden reports a suicide rate of 0 per 100,000 patients in non-hospitalized depression. Another primary care study from the Netherlands gives a suicide rate of 33 per 100,000 patient years. Finally, Simon and VonKorff in a study of suicide mortality among individuals treated for depression in Puget Sound, Wash., reported 36 suicides in 62,159 patient years. The suicide risk per 100,000 patient years was 64 among those who received outpatient specialty mental health treatment, 43 among those treated with antidepressant medications in primary care and 0 among those treated in primary care without antidepressants.

Utilizing a database of 2.5 million person years and 212 suicides from North Staffordshire, Boardman and Healy modeled the rate for suicide in treated or untreated depression and found it to be of the order of 68/100,000 patient years for all affective disorders. This rate gives an upper limit on the suicide rate in mood disorders that is compatible with observed national rates of suicide in the United Kingdom. Boardman and Healy estimate a rate of 27 suicides per 100,000 patients per annum for primary care primary affective disorders. Possible relative risks for SSRIs from the DSRU studies set against these figures and the findings from the Jick study for all antidepressants excluding fluoxetine are presented in Table 4.

Table 3

Suicides Rates of Patients Taking Antidepressants in Primary Care Settings in the United Kingdom*

Drug	Suicides/100,000 Patients (and 95% CI)		No. Suicides/No. Patients
Dothiepin	70	(53–91)	52/74 340
Lofepramine	26	(8–61)	4/15 177
Amitriptyline	60	(41–84)	29/48 580
Clomipramine	80	(38–144)	9/11 239
Imipramine	47	(20–90)	7/15 009
Doxepin	69	(17–180)	3/4 329
Flupenthixol	78	(43–129)	13/16 599
Trazodone	99	(31–230)	4/4049
Mianserin	166	(86–285)	11/6609
Fluoxetine	93		11/11 860
Total excluding fluoxetine	67		132/195 931

Note: CI = confidence interval.

* From Jick et al.

Table 4

Relative Risk (RR) of Suicide While Taking SSRIs (from DSRU Studies) Compared with General Risk of Suicide in UK Primary Care Primary Affective Disorders and in UK Primary Care Depression Treated with Non-SSRI Antidepressants

Drug	RR from DSRU Sample Compared with Primary Care Sample	RR from DSRU Sample Compared with Primary Care Depression Sample Treated with Non-SSRI Antidepressants
Sertraline	6.4	2.54
Fluoxetine	9.2	3.59
Paroxetine	10.2	3.96
Total SSRI	**8.3**	**3.44**

Note: DSRU = Drug Safety Research Unit.

Comparing the figures for SSRIs from Table 2 with those for the non-SSRI antidepressants from the Jick study gives a mean figure for non-SSRI antidepressants of 68 suicides per 100,000 patients exposed compared with a figure of 212 suicides for the SSRI group. Based on an analysis of 249,803 exposures to antidepressants, therefore, the broad relative risk on SSRI anti-depressants compared with non-SSRI antidepressants or even non-treatment is 234/68 or 3.44.

There are 2 points of note. First, these low rates for suicide in untreated primary care mood disorder populations are consistent with the rate of 0 suicides in those taking placebo in antidepressant RCTs. Second, correcting the DSRU figures for exposure lengths gives figures for suicides on sertraline and paroxetine comparable to those reported from RCTs by Khan et al.

Conclusion

Since antidepressant drug treatments were introduced, there have been concerns that their use may lead to suicide. Hitherto, there has been a legitimate public health concern that the debate about possible hazards might deter people at risk from suicide from seeking treatment, possibly leading to an increased number of suicides. The data reviewed here, however, suggest that warnings and monitoring are more likely to reduce overall risks or that at least we should adopt a position of clinical equipoise on this issue and resolve it by means of further study rather than on the basis of speculation.

The evidence that antidepressants may reduce suicide risk is strong from both clinical practice and RCTs. An optimal suicide reduction strategy would probably involve the monitored treatment of all patients and some restriction of treatment for those most at risk of suicide. In addition, given evidence that particular personality types suit particular selective agents and that mismatching patients and treatments can cause problems, further exploration of this are a would seem called for.

NO

Yvon D. Lapierre

Suicidality with Selective Serotonin Reuptake Inhibitors: Valid Claim?

Introduction

. . . A plethora of new antidepressants followed the introduction of the selective serotonin reuptake inhibitors (SSRIs) with the associated claims of their relative innocuity compared with the previous generation of tricyclics antidepressants (TCAs) and monoamine oxidase inhibitors. These claims seem to have reached their high point, and SSRIs as well as other antidepressants are now undergoing a second phase of critical review. This reappraisal of antidepressants addresses not only the claims of efficacy but also those related to side effects and to the toxicological profiles of the old as well as of the newer products. These have challenged long-held views and have brought to light new findings that would most likely not have come about otherwise. Invariably, in such circumstances, the pendular shift of attitudes can easily lead to exaggerated claims toward the negative and unwanted effects to the point of discarding previously demonstrated positive findings. It is then necessary to have a critical and balanced expression of opinions and analytic reviews of the available data to arrive at a just appraisal of reality.

The risk of suicide has remained at around 15% in patients with mental disorders, with only a marginal decline of suicide rate since the advent of antidepressants. Over 50% of those who commit suicide have an associated mood disorder, which is usually depression. Long-term follow-up shows that this is more pronounced in unipolar depressives and that treatment lessens the risk somewhat, but it still remains above the norm.

One considerably controversial issue has been the risk of suicide in relation to SSRI antidepressants. The issue arose from a series of case reports of patients who developed intense suicidal preoccupations and intense thoughts of self-harm while taking antidepressants. The initial reports implicated fluoxetine, and this was followed by reports suggesting a similar phenomenon with other SSRIs, thus leading to the speculation of a class effect.

Retrospective analyses of some randomized controlled trials (RCTs) on SSRIs suggest that the incidence of suicide may be higher in patients undergoing

From *Journal of Psychiatry & Neuroscience,* vol. 28, no. 5, September 2003, pp. 340–347. Copyright ©
2003 by CMA Management. Reprinted by permission. References omitted.

treatment with this new class of antidepressant, but any conclusion is still uncertain. This leads to the purpose of this duo of papers (Healy and Whitaker and this one), where facts may be submitted to different views and interpretation. Healy and Whitaker's contention is that SSRIs are conductive to an increased risk of suicide; this author disagrees.

The first question that arises is whether there is a temporal cause–effect relation between the administration of a specific drug and the development of suicidal ideation and of suicide. The order of such a cause and effect relation may then be examined and attributed, if applicable, as either a primary drug effect, a paradoxical drug effect, an expected side effect of the drug or, finally, an action that may be secondary to a side effect of the compound. A second issue to be addressed is whether this effect is drug specific or class specific. The question of validity of any imputed causality must be critically re-evaluated throughout this process. Once these issues are clarified, strategies that would improve the outcome of treatment for patients with depression may arise.

This paper will address the problem by first looking at issues of efficacy and suicide data and then discussing the case for the alleged link between suicide and SSRI and other antidepressant therapies.

Efficacy Issues

The efficacy of a widely used intervention may be evaluated by assessing its impact on the population at large through epidemiological approaches and then on the experiences obtained from clinical trials and clinical practice.

Epidemiological observations suggest that there has been a gradual increase in the incidence of depression in post-World War II generations. There are indications that this illness will become an ever-increasing burden of disability in Western societies. Given that depression is the predominant risk factor for suicide, one would expect that with the increased numbers of depressed individuals, there would be an increase in suicide rates. Furthermore, if there is validity to the claim that SSRIs play a causative role in suicide, there would be an even greater increase in suicide rates since the advent of these drugs. Although this may not have materialized as such, these speculations are not necessarily dismissed as being completely invalid.

Epidemiological studies on the issue of antidepressant treatment and suicide have been conducted in a number of countries. In Italy, there was found to be a possible relation between increased SSRI use from 1988 to 1996 and suicide rate. There was a slight increase in suicide rates for men but a more pronounced decrease for women; however, these changes were not significant. In Sweden, from 1976 to 1996, increased utilization of antidepressants paralleled a decrease in suicide rates. In Finland, the increased use of SSRIs coincided with a decrease in suicide mortality, as well as with an increase in the incidence of fatal overdoses with TCAs. The tricyclics accounted for 82% of suicides by antidepressant overdose.

In the National Institute of Mental Health Collaborative Depression Study, Leon et al. assessed the possibility of an increased suicidal risk associated with the SSRI fluoxetine. In the 185 patients in follow-up, there was a trend for a decrease in the number of suicide attempts compared with patients receiving other treatments. Although this cohort was at higher risk because of a history of repeated suicide attempts, treatment with fluoxetine resulted in a nonsignificant reduction of attempts in these patients.

The findings of these epidemiological studies do not provide any indication that the use of antidepressants, and more specifically SSRIs, contribute to an increased risk of suicide in population bases or in depressed populations.

The main sources of information on psychopharmacological agents are the data from clinical trials. Then, post-marketing studies are intended to provide the alerts on safety and potentially new indications for the drug. Both of these sources have limitations and biases, however, inevitably adding fuel to the present debate.

Given that RCTs are designed to primarily identify clinical efficacy and acute or short-term safety of antidepressants, there are limitations on the gathering of exhaustive data on unwanted side effects. The selection of patients for an RCT generally excludes those who are considered to be at risk for suicide. This is usually determined clinically, and the judgment is based on clinical indicators that have, in past experience, been associated with increased risk. Up to 80% of depressed patients may experience thoughts of suicide, and there is a greater than 15% risk of suicide with depression, making the elucidation of suicidal thoughts and intent increasingly relevant to a valid assessment of risk.

This rationale is based on the premise that suicidal ideation is the precursor to and is likely to lead to suicidal acting out. Suicidal acts in the recent past, as well as a number of other associated factors, contribute to the evaluation of risk and the decision of inclusion or exclusion. This inevitably leads to a skewed population, where those appearing to be most clearly at risk and those more severely depressed are often excluded.

The experimental design most often used is a single-blind placebo-washout phase followed by a double-blind randomized phase with a placebo control, a standard active treatment control and an experimental treatment arm. Because of the pressures against the use of placebo in RCTs, as well as cost considerations, there is a trend toward having unbalanced groups, with fewer subjects in the placebo and control arms. This results in reduced statistical power and the need for more patients in the studies and has contributed to increasing numbers of multicentre trials to meet these and other exigencies.

The end point of an RCT is time limited, and the criteria of successful outcome are based on clinical evaluations that of necessity are quantified using rating scales and focus on the immediate objective. They then have limited retrospective applicability and intrinsic limitations when explored retroactively for other purposes. This does not necessarily invalidate subsequent retrospective studies, but one must consider that there are limits on conclusions that can be reached because of these limitations and other biases. To mention but a few that may be relevant to the issue at hand, patient selection, diagnostic considerations and statistical limitations come to mind.

A similar pattern of biases occurs in post-marketing surveillance studies. The source of data varies from one jurisdiction to the next, as do the methods and obligations to report adverse events. Clinicians are known to adopt different prescribing patterns for patients presenting more severe states of depression and for those considered to be at greater risk for suicide. The former group are more likely to receive a TCA, whereas the latter are more likely to receive a "safer-in-overdose" SSRI. Thus, a significant bias in patient selection arises in the evaluation of suicidal risk under one form of treatment or another.

Suicidality and suicide should be distinguished. Thoughts of suicide are not uncommon in the general population but become problematic if they are too frequent, intense or commanding and lead to greater risk of acting on the ideation. Most suicides are preceded by increases in suicidal ideation. Thus, this becomes an important consideration in the assessment of suicide risk. On the other hand, suicidal ideation as such cannot be totally equated to suicidal behaviour.

Conditions favourable to acting on the ideation, such as increased impulsivity or a high level of anxiety and agitation, increase the risk of suicide. The suicidal tendencies item of the Hamilton Rating Scale for Depression is the instrument for quantification of suicidality in RCTs. It allows for a certain degree of quantification on the seriousness of suicidal tendencies and emphasizes mainly suicidal ideation as such. It is not meant to clearly discriminate and quantify the nuances of suicidality to allow for definitive conclusions to be drawn on the severity of the suicidal risk. However, it is probably the most widely used rating scale for RCTs on depression and has become the standard instrument for the analysis of the many features of this illness and for assessing change at different intervals during a clinical trial.

Meta-analyses of RCTs have yielded conflicting results. The short duration of RCTs, which are the basis of these meta-analyses, may not provide valid long-term data, but they do contribute to an understanding of acute therapeutic effects. There is an inherent deficiency in meta-analyses because of the intrinsic limitations of post hoc analyses. Nevertheless, a few of these reports suggested that fluoxetine was associated with a greater incidence of suicidal thoughts. This was followed by other reports suggesting that sertraline, fluvoxamine paroxetine and citalopram produced similar effects. This led to the speculation of a class effect of SSRIs. On the other hand, there are meta-analytic and other types of studies that just as strongly suggest that emergent suicidal ideation was lessened by these same SSRIs. In the Verkes et al. study, the findings are more convincing because of the high-risk population involved. Others have suggested that, not only do SSRIs reduce suicidal ideation, but the symptom is increased in patients taking norepinephrine reuptake inhibitors.

A meta-analytic study of treatment with fluoxetine, tricyclic antidepressants are placebo in large samples of patients with mood disorders ($n = 5655$) and non-mood disorders ($n = 4959$) did not identify satistically significant differences in emergent suicidal thoughts between groups, and there were no suicides in the non-mood disorder group. These data do not support a suicidogenic effect of SSRIs or TCAs.

Firm conclusions on suicidality and SSRIs based on these findings should be guarded at this point. Suffice it to say that the evidence to suggest that SSRIs generally reduce suicidality is more convincing than that supporting the contrary.

Suicide

The risk of a depressed patient committing suicide with prescribed antidepressants has been a long-standing concern of clinicians treating depressed patients. This was particularly significant with the older generation tricyclics and was one reason to advocate the use of the newer agents (because of their reported lower lethal potential in overdose). On the other hand, it is surprisingly rare for patients to use prescribed antidepressants for suicidal purposes. Data on the agents used for suicide from a number of countries suggest that only about 5% of overdoses are with antidepressants (range 1%–8%). An outlier appears to be the United Kingdom, with reports of 14%. Men commit suicide by overdose much less frequently than women. An important finding in these reports is that patients tend to use previously prescribed, undiscarded antidepressants as their drug of choice. This points to the important role of therapeutic failure in a number of patients who commit suicide.

The advent of the SSRIs brought a renewed impetus in physician and public education on depressive disorders to not only raise professional and public awareness of depression but also publicize the profile of the new antidepressants in their treatment. This, in addition to other factors, has led to many of these educational activities being sponsored by the pharmaceutical industry, with the inevitable ensuing risk of bias. These efforts have certainly contributed to a heightened awareness of depression by professionals and to less reluctance in using antidepressants because of improved safety profiles with equivalent efficacy.

Although antidepressants have been pivotal in the treatment of depression for more than 4 decades, a number of unanswered questions remain. The therapeutic superiority of antidepressants has been taken for granted despite the inconsistent robustness in many controlled studies, where their superiority over placebo is not always clearly demonstrated. Recent data on the latest generation of antidepressants, the SSRIs and serotonin–norepinephrine reuptake inhibitors suggest that only 48% of placebo-controlled studies show a consistent statistically significant superiority of the antidepressant over placebo. This figure may be inferior to the generally accepted greater success rate and emphasizes the need for individualized therapeutic strategies. This becomes critical for poor responders, where the limitations of available treatments become obvious. Depression is the main risk factor for suicide, the final and fatal outcome of non-response to treatment. If, as is suggested by some, the risk of suicide is increased by antidepressants, which are considered to be the cornerstone and most widely accepted treatment for depression, the use of such agents would obviously necessitate a critical re-evaluation.

Suicidality and suicidal actions induced de novo by SSRIs was suggested by a few clinical papers that followed Teicher's initial case report. Because of the paradoxical nature of these observations, a number of retrospective analyses of large cohorts were then conducted. The analyses of the US Food and Drug Administration database by Kahn et al. looked at suicidality and suicide rates in a cohort of 23,201 patients participating in clinical trials of antidepressants.

Overall suicide rates for patients were 627/100,000 compared with a general population rate of 11/100,000. There were no significant differences between rates for placebo, comparator drugs and new-generation investigational drugs. The mortality rates ranged from 0.19% for placebo to 0.14% for the investigational drugs and 0.11% for the active comparators. There were no significant differences in patient exposure years between these 3 groups, although the numerical values were higher for the antidepressant groups. The attempted suicide rate ranged from 0.66% for the investigational drugs to 1.37% for the comparators to 1.39% for placebo (no significant differences). Patient exposure years also did not differ significantly. These findings do not provide information on the duration of exposure to treatment but include the data on all patients who participated in the trials and are thus quite representative of short-term studies. Patient exposure years, which cumulates the duration of treatment and the number of patients treated, did not show differences either. These data do not support the suggestion that SSRIs add to suicide risk.

A similar study was done in the Netherlands by Storosum et al. on data submitted to the Medicines Evaluation Board of the Netherlands for 12,246 patients treated in short-term (<8 wk) clinical trials. Attempts at suicide occurred in 0.4% of patients in both placebo and active drug groups. Completed suicide occurred in 0.1% of patients in both placebo and active treatment groups. In longer-term studies (>8 wk) involving 1949 patients, attempted suicide occurred in 0.7% of patients in both groups, and completed suicides occurred in 0.2% (2 patients) of the active drug group (no significant difference). These results also do not support a suicidogenic effect of these antidepressants.

Donovan et al. reviewed 222 suicides that occurred in a 4-year period in 3 different regions of the United Kingdom. Of these, 83% had been diagnosed with depression in the past and 56% had been prescribed an antidepressants in the previous year; 41 had been prescribed a TCA and 13 an SSRI within 1 month of their suicide, and these formed the main cohort of the study. On the basis of the relative proportion of prescriptions in these regions, the authors concluded that the risk of suicide is greater with SSRIs than with TCAs. An important variable that may have skewed these findings is that those taking SSRIs included most of the patients who had a recent history of deliberate self harm, which in itself is recognized as an important predictor of suicide. It is thus difficult to make any definitive conclusions from these findings because the inherent biases in patient selection for treatment force the results and conclusions.

More recently, Oquendo et al. reported on 136 depressed patients who were discharged from hospital after a major depressive episode and were followed in community settings for 24 months; 15% of patients attempted suicide during the 2 years, and 50% of these attempts occurred during the first 5 months of follow-up. Treatment was in a naturalistic setting and was monitored regularly. The medications administered were mainly the new-generation antidepressants. A critical review of the dosage administered considered it to be adequate in only 9 (43%) of the patients at the time of attempted suicide. Four of these patients had relapsed into a recurrence of depression. These findings elicit a number of questions such as the importance of treatment resistance, history of suicide attempts, components of adequate treatment, adequacy of drug treatment and compliance.

The case put forth in the first of this duo of papers is beguiling. It is indeed seductive to use legal precedents and the court of public opinion to evaluate the scientific merit and withdrawal of a therapeutic agent. However, it remains paramount that methodology not be changed to lead to selective data. For this reason, it is not appropriate in these instances to allow the bias introduced by separating placebo washout out of the trial data, especially if "intent to treat" and last observation carried forward data are to serve as the basis of outcome analyses.

It is not appropriate to agree with the statement that clinicians would not be vigilant to the risk of suicide in antidepressant RCTs, because suicide is universally recognized as the major complication of depression. Although antidepressant RCTs are not designed to evaluate suicide risk, disregarding the data generated is as inappropriate as disregarding the data collected for the study's designed purpose.

Discussion

SSRI antidepressants as a class are among the most frequently prescribed drugs in the Western world. Their applications have broadened from their initial indication in depression to a number of other psychiatric conditions such as obsessive–compulsive disorder, generalized anxiety disorder and, more recently, late luteal phase disorder. This provides a wide spectrum of conditions under which the SSRIs are administered and allows for a much broader clinical experience for the appraisal of the drugs in question. There have not been any reports of suicide in patients taking SSRIs for these other conditions.

Suicide is a leading public health problem in all societies. It is estimated that known suicides account for 1 million deaths worldwide annually. Given that depression is a significant factor in nearly 50% of these cases, the treatment of depression merits critical appraisal, especially if this treatment contributes further to suicidal behaviour, as has been suggested. This partly explains the reaction to the initial reports of increased suicidality during treatment with fluoxetine and then with the other SSRIs. These reports have led to a healthy second look at the available data and to the pursuit of additional studies and observations.

Clinical studies and meta-analyses indicate that an overwhelming number of patients experience a decrease in suicidal ideation while taking SSRIs. The fact that these meta-analyses were based on data collected primarily to demonstrate efficacy does not diminish their validity. Although the method of evaluation has been criticized (i.e., a single item on the HAM-D) and the evidence of decreased suicidality admittedly not highly nuanced, the data still reflect the observed clinical reality. A decrease in suicidality must be considered to reflect an improvement in the depressed condition.

Despite the availability of less toxic antidepressant drugs, the increasing use of antidepressants has not consistently been associated with a significant decline in suicide rates. As the SSRIs gain popularity, the use of the older TCAs as instruments of suicide by overdose has decreased. However, other more violent means are resorted to, thus indirectly reducing the positive safety impact of the SSRIs. It would be simplistic to make conclusions on single causality in suicidal behaviour without recognizing the complexities of the behaviour and circumstances that lead to the outcome.

Although evidence from large studies points to a reduction in suicidal ideation, the few reports of the appearance of intense suicidal thoughts in a few patients must not pass unnoticed. There were sporadic reports of suicidality with zimelidine, the first SSRI. This did not hold up to statistical testing and, because the drug was discontinued shortly after being launched, there was no follow-up. There were no major concerns at this time because most patients experienced an improvement in suicidal thoughts. A sporadic paradoxical effect to a psychotropic agent is a well-known phenomenon. It is well documented with antipsychotic agents such as the phenothiazines, where excitement and even worsening of the psychotic disorder have been observed. These are rare events but must be kept in mind so they will be recognized when they do occur. It is also essential to recognize that the emergence of suicidal thoughts may simply be attributable to underlying psychopathology.

Studies of fluoxetine have reported that this drug, in addition to causing some increase in agitation in some patients, may also cause akathisia. High levels of anxiety and agitation are known to accompany increased suicidal behaviour. In such a situation, the behaviour would be secondary to a side effect of the drug, rather than to its primary action.

Post hoc studies have intrinsic limitations but can shed some light on the understanding of this issue. The findings of Donovan and colleagues suggest that the increased risk of suicide is to a great extent explained by patient selection in some clinical studies. They did not factor in deliberate self-harm in the attribution of patients in their study. The increased risk of suicidality in patients with a history of repeated deliberate self-harm is well known. Even if these patients had been screened as not being actively suicidal at the onset of a trial, they were nevertheless still at higher risk subsequently. This type of susceptibility bias was very much present in the Leon et al. study and in that by Donovan et al.

A common deficiency in many studies of the treatment of depression is a consideration of unipolarity or bipolarity. The latter is readily missed for a number of reasons but, because the condition is not uncommon and requires adapted treatment with mood stabilizers, a greater risk of suicide may appear in these patients than in undertreated patients.

Despite anecdotal reports implicating most of the SSRIs, a drug-specific or class effect is not substantiated. Unfortunately, SSRIs have not been compared critically with other classes of antidepressants. On the other hand, the common pharmacological action of serotonin reuptake inhibition does not explain all of the actions of these drugs. A comparison of fluoxetine with its activating properties and citalopram with its more sedating profile illustrates the different effects SSRIs can have. Fluoxetine is known to occasionally cause some agitation. This may be experienced independently from akathisia which may, albeit rarely, also result from fluoxetine. The combination of the 2 (i.e, akathisia and agitation) has been associated with increased suicidal tendencies in depressed patients, but it is unlikely that this would support a class effect or phenomenon. It is more likely a consequence of a rare side effect of the drug.

A pharmacological explanation for a rare event is difficult to establish because it is, by definition, unpredictable. However, it is not beyond the realm of possibility and merits further exploration, although it is unlikely to attract interest simply because of the rarity of the event and the unpredictability of a host of variables.

Conclusion

Any conclusions based on these few reports of sporadic cases of increased suicidality with SSRIs must be limited and highly tentative. The most these cases can suggest is an individual paradoxical effect, and these can be compared with the large number of patients who experience a diminution of suicidality and an improvement in depression. Another significant factor is that as the use of these antidepressants has broadened, the initial reports have not been followed by an increasing number of cases. Results of clinical studies are inconclusive, with some supporting a link and others refuting one. However, the awareness of the possibility of increased suicidality with SSRI treatment must be taken in the context of the risk of suicide in treating depression with any other antidepressant. Suicide is an inherent risk in the context of depression but this should not deter from adequate treatment.

A review of this issue serves as a reminder of the basic principles of good therapeutics that recommend that the complete profile of the drug be taken into account when selecting a pharmacotherapeutic agent. Once the primary (desired) and secondary (unwanted or not) effects have been fully considered, the total profile of the drug can be tailored to the clinical profile of an individual patient.

The newer SSRI antidepressants were never considered to be superior in efficacy to the TCAs, but their entry into the therapeutics of depression has reduced the risk of iatrogenic intoxication and, most likely, the overall risk of suicidal outcome in adequately treated patients. There is, at this time, insufficient evidence to claim that they lead to suicide.

CHALLENGE QUESTIONS

Does Taking Antidepressants Lead to Suicide?

1. How would you account for the major differences in the results of the studies that Healy/Whitaker and Lapierre present?
2. From the data presented, do you think antidepressants pose a risk for suicide? Support your answer.
3. If you were the parent of a child, under what circumstances would you permit him or her to take antidepressants? Justify your answer with information from the two articles.
4. One of the issues that separates these two sets of authors is whether the data are "sufficient." Interview two faculty members from the psychology department to find out how they would know when the data are sufficient for action, such as the black box warning on antidepressants.
5. There was some discussion about taking SSRI drugs off the market when the potential for suicide was revealed. Why do you think the FDA did not do so? Do you agree? Support your opinion.

ISSUE 13

Is Drug Addiction a Choice?

YES: Jeffrey A. Schaler, from *Addiction Is a Choice* (Open Court, 2000)

NO: Alice M. Young, from "Addictive Drugs and the Brain," *National Forum* (Fall 1999)

ISSUE SUMMARY

YES: Psychotherapist Jeffrey A. Schaler contends that drug addiction is not a disease in the physical sense because that would indicate that addicts have no control or choice over their addictive behaviors, which is not true.

NO: Professor of psychology Alice M. Young describes how addiction to a number of drugs may begin with voluntary usage but end up after repeated use with a physiological tolerance and dependency that is not within one's control or choice.

$\mathbf{N}$o reasonable person would argue that drug addiction is not a major problem, both for those who are addicted and for society in general. However, there is considerable debate about the nature of addiction. Perhaps most pertinent is the question of whether or not drug addiction is a disease like any other physiological or medical disease. In fact, this question brings with it some of the most fascinating and unresolved controversies of psychology.

For example, if drug addition is a medical disease, then addicts are not responsible for their addictive behaviors. Much as any human is not responsible for his or her symptoms of flu or cancer, addicts would not be responsible for the symptoms of their addictions—their addictive behaviors. Does this mean, however, that addicts have no free will, that they cannot make choices about their addictive behaviors? Are these behaviors determined in the same sense as the symptoms of cancer are determined?

If so, then what does this imply about accountability? Should addicts who commit crimes to support their habits be incarcerated if they have no responsibility for their addiction-related actions? How far would this go? Should society refrain from imprisoning alcoholics for alcohol-related criminal activities? Which behaviors are determined and which are not? The self-help group Alcoholics Anonymous (AA) assumes that addicts are "powerless" against their addictions. If addicts do have free will, or choices, regarding their addictive behaviors, does this cast doubt on the AA treatment and way of life?

In the first of the following selections, Jeffrey A. Schaler clarifies a number of these unresolved controversies, partly because he believes that many authorities have assumed too quickly that they have been resolved. He sharpens the main issues to an "ongoing battle" between two models of addiction: the disease model and the free-will model. He then describes what he feels is typically underestimated and misunderstood in the disease model, especially the physical disease model, to demonstrate the problems that it has for a viable understanding of addiction. Perhaps most strikingly, he asserts that a powerful craving for a drug does not itself demonstrate that the person has no choice about whether or not to take the drug. People have plenty of physical cravings that they choose not to indulge.

By contrast, Alice M. Young endorses a more conventional disease approach to addiction in the second selection. She views drug addicts as responding naturally to the reward system of their environment in relation to their neurological processes. Although taking a drug may begin voluntarily, she asserts, the drug taker rapidly develops a physiological dependence due to neural processes. At some point and after repeated dosages, these addictive drugs "hijack" the brain's natural responses to rewards. Eventually, they produce tolerance and dependence and even alter the user's brain chemistry, making a true free will about resulting behaviors almost impossible.

POINT

- If you take away a person's free will (for addicted behaviors), you take away their responsibility and accountability.
- If the disease of addiction is metaphorical rather than physical, then there is no problem with accountability.

- Many experts believe that a physical disease model does more harm than good.

- A powerful craving for a drug does not mean that a person has no choice about whether or not to take it.

COUNTERPOINT

- Drug taking can begin voluntarily but end up with physiological dependencies that cloud judgment and responsibility.
- Repeated dosages of a small number of drugs will produce physical changes and, thus, a physical disease process.
- To be truly addicted to a particular drug is to be physically dependent, so approaching this dependency realistically is important.
- After repeated use, such cravings can become more than cravings; they can become physiological needs.

YES

Jeffrey A. Schaler

Is Addiction Really a Disease?

Being addicted to a melancholy as she is.

—William Shakespeare, *Twelfth Night*

If you watch TV, read the newspaper, or listen to almost any social worker or religious minister, you soon pick up the idea that addiction is a condition in which addicts just physically cannot control themselves, and that this condition is a medical disease.

The federal government views alcohol addiction as a disease characterized by *loss of control,* with a physiological 'etiology' (cause) independent of volition. According to a typical statement of the government's view by Otis R. Bowen, former secretary of health and human services,

> millions of children have a genetic predisposition to alcoholism . . . alcohol use by young people has been found to be a 'gateway' drug preceding other drug use . . . about 1 out of every 15 kids will eventually become an alcoholic. . . . alcoholism is a disease, and this disease is highly treatable. (Bowen 1988, pp. 559, 563)

You may easily conclude that all the experts agree with this kind of thinking. Most people with no special interest in the subject probably never get to hear another point of view.

The true situation is a bit more complicated. Public opinion overwhelmingly accepts the claim that addiction is a disease, but the general public's views are seriously inconsistent. A 1987 study of public views on alcoholism showed that over 85 percent of people believe that alcoholism is a disease, but most of them also believe things that contradict the disease theory. Many people seem to support and reject the disease theory at the same time. For instance, they often say they believe that alcoholism is a disease and also that it is a sign of moral weakness (Caetano 1987, p. 158).

The addiction treatment providers, the many thousands of people who make their living in the addiction treatment industry, mostly accept the disease theory. They are, in fact, for the most part, 'recovered addicts' themselves, redeemed sinners who spend their lives being paid to preach the gospel that social deviants are sick.

Among those psychologists and others who think, write, discuss, and conduct research in this area, however, opinion is much more divided. In this small world, there is an ongoing battle between the 'disease model' and the 'free-will model'.

Biomedical and psychosocial scientists range across both sides of the controversy (Fillmore and Sigvardsson 1988). Some biomedical researchers accept the disease model and assert that genetic and physiological differences account for alcoholism (for example, D.W. Goodwin 1988; F.K. Goodwin 1988; Blum et al. 1990; Tabakoff and Hoffman 1988). Other biomedical researchers have investigated their claims and pronounced them invalid (Lester 1989; Bolos et al. 1990; Billings 1990). Many social scientists reject the idea that alcoholics or other addicts constitute a homogeneous group. They hold that individual differences, personal values, expectations, and environmental factors are key correlates to heavy drinking and drug-taking. Others reject strictly psychological theories (Maltzman 1991; Madsen 1989; Vaillant 1983; Milam and Ketcham 1983; Prince, Glatt, and Pullar-Strecker 1966). Some sociologists regard the disease model of alcoholism as a human construction based on desire for social control (Room 1983; Fillmore 1988). Some embrace the disease model even while agreeing that addiction may not be a real disease—they hold that utility warrants labeling it as such (Kissin 1983; Vaillant 1990). Their opponents believe the disease model does more harm than good (Szasz 1972; Fingarette 1988; Alexander 1990a; 1990b; Crawford et al. 1989; Fillmore and Kelso 1987; Heather, Winton, and Rollnick 1982; Schaler 1996b).

My impression is that the disease model is steadily losing ground. It may not be too much to hope that the notion of addiction as a disease will be completely discredited and abandoned in years to come, perhaps as early as the next 20 years.

If this seems like a fanciful speculation, remember that other recognized 'diseases' have been quite swiftly discredited. The most recent example is homosexuality. Being sexually attracted to members of one's own sex was, overwhelmingly, considered a disease by the psychiatric profession, and therefore by the medical profession as a whole, until the 1960s. Psychiatry and medicine completely reversed themselves on this issue within a few years. Homosexuality was declassified as an illness by the American Psychiatric Association in 1973. It is now officially considered a non-disease, unless the homosexual wishes he were not a homosexual. This doesn't go far enough, but imagine the same principle extended to drug addiction: the addict is not at all sick unless he says he is unhappy being addicted!

Before homosexuality, there were the recognized diseases of masturbation, negritude (having a black skin), Judaism (described as a disease by the German government in the 1930s), and being critical of the Soviet government, which 'treated' political dissidents in mental hospitals (see Rush 1799; Szasz 1970; Robitscher 1980; Lifton 1986; Conrad and Schneider 1992; and Breggin 1993). A similar fate may be in store for the 'disease' of drug addiction.

Many people accept the disease model of addiction on the basis of respect for the messenger. Addiction is a disease because doctors say it's a disease (social psychologists call this peripheral-route processing) rather than critical evaluation of the message itself (central-route processing). Peripheral-route processing has more in common with faith than reason, and research shows that in general its appeal is greatest among the less educated. Reason and faith are not always compatible. Reason requires evidence, faith does not.

Clinical and public policy should not be based on faith, whether the source is drunken anecdote, the proclamations of self-assigned experts, or the measured statements of addiction doctors. Rather, empirical evidence and sound reasoning are required. Both are lacking in the assertion that addiction is a disease.

If it were ever to be shown that there existed a genetic disease causing a powerful craving for a drug, this would not demonstrate that the afflicted person had no choice as to whether to take the drug. Nor would it show that the action of taking the drug was itself a disease.

There are various skin rashes, for example, which often arouse a powerful urge to scratch the inflamed area. It's usually enough to explain the harmful consequences of scratching, and the patient will choose not to scratch. Though scratching may cause diseases (by promoting infection of the area) and is a response to physiological sensations, the activity of scratching is not itself considered a disease.

What Is a Disease?

Is addiction really a disease? Let's clarify a few matters. The classification of behavior as socially unacceptable does not prove its label as a disease. Adherents of the disease model sometimes respond to the claim that addiction is not a disease by emphasizing the terrible problems people create as a result of their addictions, but that is entirely beside the point. The fact that some behavior has horrible consequences does not show that it's a disease.

The 'success' of 'treatment programs' run by people who view addiction as a disease would not demonstrate that addiction was a disease—any more than the success of other religious groups in converting people from vicious practices would prove the theological tenets of these religious groups. However, this possibility need not concern us, since all known treatment programs are, in fact, ineffective.

I will not go into the claims of a genetic basis for 'alcoholism' or other addictions. A genetic predisposition toward some kind of behavior, say, speaking in tongues, would not show that those with the predisposition had a disease. Variations in skin and eye color, for example, are genetically determined, but are not diseases. Fair-skinned people sunburn easily. The fairness of their skin is genetically determined, yet their susceptibility to sunburn is not considered a disease. Neither would a genetic predisposition toward some kind of behavior necessarily show that the predisposed persons could not consciously change their behavior.

With so much commonsense evidence to refute it, why is the view of drug addiction as a disease so prevalent? Incredible as it may seem, because doctors say so. A leading alcoholism researcher once asserted that alcoholism is a disease simply because people go to doctors for it. Undoubtedly, drug 'addicts' seek help from doctors for two reasons. Many addicts have a significant psychological investment in maintaining this view, having been told, and come to believe, that their eventual recovery depends on believing they have a disease. They may even have come to accept that they will die if they question the disease model of addiction. And treatment professionals have a significant economic investment at stake. The more behaviors are diagnosed as diseases, the more they will be paid by health insurance companies for 'treating' these diseases.

When we consider whether drug addiction is a disease we are concerned with what causes the drug to get *into* the body. It's quite irrelevant what the drug does *after* it's in the body. I certainly don't for a moment doubt that the taking of many drugs *causes* disease. Prolonged heavy drinking of alcoholic beverages can cause cirrhosis of the liver. Prolonged smoking of cigarettes somewhat raises the risk of various diseases such as lung cancer. But this uncontroversial fact is quite distinct from any claim that the activity is itself a disease (Szasz 1989b).

Some doctors make a specialty of occupation-linked disorders. For example, there is a pattern of lung and other diseases associated with working down a coal mine. But this does not show that mining coal is itself a disease. Other enterprising physicians specialize in treating diseases arising from sports: there is a pattern of diseases resulting from swimming, another from football, yet another from long-distance running. This does not demonstrate that these sports, or the inclination to pursue these sports, are themselves diseases. So, for instance, the fact that a doctor may be exceptionally knowledgeable about the effects of alcohol on the body, and may therefore be accepted as an expert on 'alcoholism', does nothing to show that alcoholism itself is a legitimate medical concept.

Addiction, a Physical Disease?

If addiction is a disease, then presumably it's either a bodily or a mental disease. What criteria might justify defining addiction as a physical illness? Pathologists use nosology—the classification of diseases—to select, from among the phenomena they study, those that qualify as true diseases. Diseases are listed in standard pathology textbooks because they meet the nosological criteria for disease classification. A simple test of a true physical disease is whether it can be shown to exist in a corpse. There are no bodily signs of addiction itself (as opposed to its effects) that can be identified in a dead body. Addiction is therefore not listed in standard pathology textbooks.

Pathology, as revolutionized by Rudolf Virchow (1821–1902), requires an identifiable alteration in bodily tissue, a change in the cells of the body, for disease classification. No such identifiable pathology has been found in the bodies of heavy drinkers and drug users. This alone justifies the view that addiction is not a physical disease (Szasz 1991; 1994).

A symptom is subjective evidence from the patient: the patient reports certain pains and other sensations. A sign is something that can be identified in the patient's body, irrespective of the patient's reported experiences. In standard medical practice, the diagnosis of disease can be based on signs alone or on a combination of signs and symptoms, but only rarely on symptoms alone. A sign is objective physical evidence such as a lesion or chemical imbalance. Signs may be found through medical tests.

Sometimes a routine physical examination reveals signs of disease when no symptoms are reported. In such cases the disease is said to be 'asymptomatic'—without symptoms. For example, sugar in the urine combined with other signs may lead to a diagnosis of asymptomatic diabetes. Such a diagnosis is made solely on the basis of signs. It is inconceivable that addiction could ever be diagnosed on the basis of bodily signs alone. (The *effects* of heavy alcohol consumption can of course be inferred from bodily signs, but that, remember, is a different matter.) To speak of 'asymptomatic addiction' would be absurd.

True, conditions such as migraine and epilepsy are diagnosed primarily on the basis of symptoms. But, in general, it is not standard medical practice to diagnose disease on the basis of symptoms alone. The putative disease called addiction is diagnosed solely by symptoms in the form of conduct, never by signs, that is, by physical evidence in the patient's body. (A doctor might conclude that someone with cirrhosis of the liver and other bodily signs had partaken of alcoholic beverages heavily over a long period, and might infer that the patient was an 'alcoholic', but actually the doctor would be unable to distinguish this from the hypothetical case of someone who had been kept a prisoner and dosed with alcohol against her will. So, again, strictly speaking, *there cannot possibly be a bodily sign of an addiction.*)

If you visited your physician because of a dull pain in your epigastric region, would you want her to make a diagnosis without confirming it through objective tests? Wouldn't you doubt the validity of a diagnosis of heart disease without at least the results of an EKG? You would want to see reliable evidence of signs. But in the diagnosis of the disease called addiction, there are no signs, only symptoms (Szasz 1987).

We continually hear that 'addiction is a disease just like diabetes'. Yet there is no such thing as asymptomatic addiction, and *logically there could not be*. Moreover, the analogy cannot be turned around. It would be awkward to tell a person with diabetes that his condition was 'just like addiction' and inaccurate too: When a person with diabetes is deprived of insulin he will suffer and in severe cases may even die. When a heavy drinker or other drug user is deprived of alcohol or other drugs his physical health most often improves.

A Mental or Metaphorical Disease?

Mental illnesses are diagnosed on the basis of symptoms, not signs. Perhaps, then, addiction is a mental illness, a psychiatric disease. Where does it fit into the scheme of psychiatric disorders?

Psychiatric disorders can be categorized in three groups: organic disorders, functional disorders, and antisocial behavior (Szasz 1988). Organic disorders include various forms of dementia such as those caused by HIV-1 infection, acute alcohol intoxication, brain tumor or injury, dementia of the Alzheimer's type, general paresis, and multi-infarct dementia. These are physical diseases with identifiable bodily signs. Addiction has no such identifiable signs.

Functional disorders include fears (anxiety disorders), discouragements (mood disorders), and stupidities (cognitive disorders). These are mental in the sense that they involve mental activities. As Szasz has pointed out, they are diseases "only in a metaphorical sense."

Forms of antisocial behavior categorized as psychiatric illness include crime, suicide, personality disorders, and maladaptive and maladjusted behavior. Some people consider these 'disorders' because they vary from the norm and involve danger to self or others. According to Szasz, however, they are "neither 'mental' nor 'diseases'" (Szasz 1988, pp. 249–251). If addiction qualifies as an antisocial behavior, this does not necessarily imply that it is mental or a disease.

Addiction is not listed in the American Psychiatric Association's Diagnostic and Statistical Manual of Mental Disorders IV (DSM-IV). What was once listed as alcoholism is now referred to as alcohol dependence and abuse. These are listed under the category of substance-related disorders. They would not fit the category of organic disorders because they are described in terms of behavior only. They would conceivably fit the functional disorder category but probably would be subordinated to one of the established disorders such as discouragement or anxiety.

Thus, it's difficult to classify addiction as either a physical or a mental disease. Many human problems may be described *metaphorically* as diseases. We hear media pundits speak of a 'sick economy' or 'sick culture'. Declining empires, such as the Ottoman empire at the end of the nineteenth century and the Soviet empire in the 1980s, are said to be 'sick'. There is little harm in resorting to this metaphor, and therefore describing negative addictions as diseases—except that there is the danger that some people will take the metaphor literally.

Today any socially-unacceptable behavior is likely to be diagnosed as an 'addiction'. So we have shopping addiction, videogame addiction, sex addiction, Dungeons and Dragons addiction, running addiction, chocolate addiction, Internet addiction, addiction to abusive relationships, and so forth. This would be fine if it merely represented a return to the traditional, non-medical usage, in which addiction means being given over to some pursuit. However, all of these new 'addictions' are now claimed to be medical illnesses, characterized by self-destructiveness, compulsion, loss of control, and some mysterious, as-yet-unidentified physiological component. This is entirely fanciful.

People become classified as 'addicts' or 'alcoholics' because of their behavior. 'Behavior' in humans refers to intentional conduct. As was pointed out long ago by Wilhelm Dilthey, Max Weber, and Ludwig von Mises, among others, the motions of the human body are either involuntary reflexes or meaningful human action. Human action is governed by the meaning it has for the acting person. The behavior of heavy drinking is not a form of neurological reflex but is the expression of values through action. As Herbert Fingarette puts it:

> A pattern of conduct must be distinguished from a mere sequence of reflex-like reactions. A reflex knee jerk is not conduct. If we regard something as a pattern of conduct . . . we assume that it is mediated by the mind, that it reflects consideration of reasons and preferences, the election of a preferred means to the end, and the election of the end itself from among alternatives. The complex, purposeful, and often ingenious projects with which many an addict may be occupied in his daily hustlings to maintain his drug supply are examples of conduct, not automatic reflex reactions to a singly biological cause. (1975, p. 435)

Thomas Szasz agrees that

> by behavior we mean the person's 'mode of conducting himself' or his 'deportment' . . . the name we attach to a living being's conduct in the daily pursuit of life. . . . bodily movements that are the products of neurophysiological discharges or reflexes are not behavior. . . . behavior implies action, and action implies conduct pursued by an agent seeking to attain a goal. (1987, p. 343)

The term 'alcoholism' has become so loaded with prescriptive intent that it no longer describes any drinking behavior accurately and should be abandoned. 'Heavy drinking' is a more descriptive term (Fingarette 1988). It is imprecise, but so is 'alcoholism'.

If we continue to use the term 'alcoholism', however, we should bear in mind that there is no precisely defined condition, activity, or entity called alcoholism in the way there is a precise condition known as lymphosarcoma of the mesenteric glands, for example. The actual usage of the term 'alcoholism', like 'addiction', has become primarily normative and prescriptive: a derogatory, stigmatizing word applied to people who drink 'too much'. The definition of 'too much' depends on the values of the speaker, which may be different from those of the person doing the drinking.

Calling addiction a 'disease' tells us more about the labeler than the labelee. Diseases are medical conditions. They can be discovered on the basis of bodily signs. They are something people have. They are involuntary. For example, the disease of syphilis was discovered. It is identified by specific signs. It is not a form of activity and is not based in human values. While certain behaviors increase the likelihood of acquiring syphilis, and while the acquisition of syphilis has consequences for subsequent social interaction, the behavior and the disease are separate phenomena. Syphilis meets the nosological criteria for disease classification in a pathology textbook. Unlike addiction, syphilis is a disease that can be diagnosed in a corpse.

Once we recognize that addiction cannot be classified as a literal disease, its nature as an ethical choice becomes clearer. A person starts, moderates, or abstains from drinking because that person wants to. People do the same thing with heroin, cocaine, and tobacco. Such choices reflect the person's values. The person, a moral agent, chooses to use drugs or refrains from using drugs because he or she finds meaning in doing so.

NO

Alice M. Young

Addictive Drugs and the Brain

Thomas De Quincey's 1821 essay, *Confessions of an English Opium-Eater,* vividly captures the psychological power of addictive drugs: " . . . thou hast the keys of Paradise, oh, just, subtle, and mighty opium!" How does opium or its modern relative, heroin, produce the compulsive drug use that we call addiction? Does addictive use of other drugs follow a similar course? Emerging answers to such questions suggest that all addictive drugs may co-opt normal brain processes of learning and emotion.

When De Quincey smoked opium, the smoke delivered morphine and codeine (and numerous other agents contained in opium) into his lungs. These agents moved directly from his lungs into his bloodstream and out through his body. They reached his brain in seconds. Similarly, when a modern user injects, smokes, or snorts heroin, blood carries the drug throughout the body and into the brain. As heroin reaches the brain, it is rapidly metabolized to morphine, which disperses over the surfaces of the brain's nerve cells, or neurons. In some areas of the brain, the morphine encounters small specialized proteins lodged in the outer membranes of certain neurons. These proteins are called opioid receptors ('receptor' for their ability to receive information from the neuron's surroundings, and 'opioid' because they detect opium-like substances). Morphine rapidly attaches and detaches from these opioid receptors. As it does so, it initiates a cascade of actions in the neurons housing the opioid receptors and in the neurons with which they communicate. These actions produce the profound psychological and physiological effects of morphine and other opioids. Some of these actions may underlie addiction.

Current ideas about the brain's role in addiction arise from both psychology and biology. Psychology contributes the concepts of reward and conditioning. These concepts link drug addiction to two important human attributes—our ability to learn and remember through experience and our tendency to repeat actions that had reinforcing consequences in the past. Biology contributes the concept of chemical communication systems in the brain, systems critical to learning and memory.

From Alice M. Young, "Addictive Drugs and the Brain," *National Forum,* vol. 79, no. 4 (Fall 1999). Copyright © 1999 by Alice M. Young. Reprinted by permission of *National Forum: The Phi Kappa Phi Journal.*

Learning Processes Linked to Drug Seeking and Drug Taking

Experimental psychology has shown that, for humans as for other organisms, voluntary behaviors are influenced by their consequences. A voluntary behavior that has a positive consequence today is likely to be repeated in the future. Put another way, we repeatedly engage in behaviors that produce pleasurable feelings and positive reinforcers or rewards. We also repeat behaviors that avoid or escape noxious feelings or negative reinforcers. This fundamental learning process, often called instrumental or operant conditioning, is a primary way that we learn skillful and complex voluntary behaviors.

Our biological, cultural, and social histories have given us normal tendencies to repeat voluntary behaviors that produce a range of natural rewards. These rewards include food, water, sex, social contact, and avoidance of aggressive or painful encounters. Our responsiveness to these natural rewards helps ensure that we engage in behaviors that are critical for our survival as individuals and as a species—behaviors of eating, drinking, procreating, nurturing, and escaping from danger. Neuroscientists are beginning to identify pathways and circuits in the brain that organize our responsiveness to these naturally rewarding activities. Among the chief candidates are circuits involved in behavioral integration, learning, and cognition. These circuits are linked to other circuits that serve perceptual and motor behaviors, and they may be particularly important in forging strong motivations and drives.

We also respond to such artificial rewards as money, consumer goods, and drugs. Artificial rewards engage the same brain circuits as do natural rewards. Addictive drugs may be particularly effective rewards, producing a strong tendency for the user to engage repeatedly in drug seeking and drug use. Indeed, drug rewards can control long sequences of complex and highly directed behaviors that rival activities usually directed at more profitable goals such as strong family ties or professional rewards. Moreover, the effectiveness of addictive drugs as rewards may allow them to compete too effectively with other, more beneficial, rewards, leading to severe disruptions in many areas of a drug abuser's life.

Our natural response to rewards has another element that plays a crucial role in addiction. Over repeated encounters with effective rewards, we begin to associate the reward and the feelings it engenders with the surroundings in which we encounter it. Features or stimuli in those surroundings become associated with rewarding or other effects of drugs by a second fundamental learning process, that of Pavlovian conditioning. With repeated drug use, such conditioning can establish strong memories of drug use or drug effects. These memories can compel strong urges to seek or take the drug itself. Later in an individual's life, these memories can be triggered by encounters with small amounts of the drug or even by the stimuti alone. Such triggered memories probably underlie the cravings and relapses that characterize addictive drug use.

Addictive drugs use multiple strategies to commandeer natural processes and compel strong memories of drug use. Among the most important are their abilities to mimic or modulate brain neurotransmitters and trigger adaptive changes in brain circuits involved in basic learning and emotional processes.

Addictive Drugs and Brain Neurotransmitters

Drugs that have the potential to be addictive for their users actually represent a small minority of the types of drugs we use to affect biological function. The great majority of drugs do not have the ability to establish and reinforce strong behavioral repertoires or compel conditioned memories. The key features of addictive drugs are their special effects on brain chemistry.

The addictive drugs comprise a diverse set of chemicals that differ in their structure and affinity for biological tissues, in their ability to be carried by the body's natural absorption and distribution routes, and in their susceptibility to the body's natural metabolic and excretion systems. It is important to note that the different addictive drugs produce different effects on body systems and markedly different immediate or long-term health consequences. In addition to these differences, however, addictive drugs share a common ability to influence brain chemistry involved in basic processes of reinforcement, learning, and memory.

As a user drinks alcohol, snorts cocaine, or smokes a cigarette, the body's natural systems deliver the chemicals in the drug source throughout the body. The specific drug used and its amount and route of administration will determine its speed of entry into the brain, but most addictive drugs enter the brain very rapidly. Once in the brain, they initiate their actions via the brain's own neurotransmitters. Neurotransmitters are the natural chemicals that neurons use to communicate among themselves and with the rest of the body. Addictive drugs initiate their actions, including those actions that lead to addiction, by mimicking or blocking the brain's neurotransmitters, or by modulating their activity. For example, nicotine (a key addictive component of tobacco products) mimics the natural neurotransmitter acetylcholine. Caffeine, the active drug in coffee, blocks the neurotransmitter adenosine. Cocaine, derived from the coca plant, alters levels of three natural neurotransmitters: dopamine, serotonin, and norepinephrine.

Other addictive drugs influence neurotransmitter systems that were unknown until neuroscientists looked for their targets in the brain. The brain's own opioid neurotransmitters—the endorphins, enkephalins, and dynorphins—were found by researchers investigating how heroin and morphine produce their addictive actions. Avram Goldstein, who spearheaded the discovery of dynorphin, provides a highly readable account of the search for neurotransmitters linked to addictive drugs in his book *Addiction* (W.H. Freeman, 1994). He notes that, "If not for the brain receptors, with their amazing specificity, all the addictive drugs would have the same biologic actions (or more likely, none at all)" (p. 311). The last point is important, because it highlights the fact that the ability of addictive drugs to interact with the brain's normal receptors makes these chemicals 'drugs' rather than poisons or inert agents.

Addictive drugs seem to have a preferential ability to mimic, block, or modulate the neurotransmitters that our brains use to learn and remember highly reinforcing activities. To state the case baldly, addictive drugs may hijack our brains' natural responses to rewards. Drugs such as alcohol, nicotine, heroin, and cocaine may short-circuit the natural reward pathways that have evolved to ensure that we engage in activities critical to our survival.

One working hypothesis in this area suggests that addictive drugs may share a common ability to alter the levels of dopamine in brain areas critical for learning. Although this hypothesis is surely too simplistic, it has guided productive studies that have illuminated how addictive drugs can interact with brain chemistry.

Studies in animals suggest that many addictive drugs change the levels of dopamine in brain pathways linked to the reward circuits described above. One suggested circuit involves areas called the ventral tegmental area (VTA), the nucleus accumbens, and the frontal cortex. The VTA communicates with the nucleus accumbens by releasing the neurotransmitter dopamine, and such release is correlated with activities that animals find highly rewarding. Cocaine and amphetamine powerfully increase the levels of dopamine at the juncture of the VTA and the nucleus accumbens. They do so by blocking the uptake processes that neurons normally use to stop dopamine's actions and, in the case of amphetamine, by causing neurons to release dopamine. The resulting increase in dopamine levels may be critical to the addictive properties of cocaine and amphetamine. Several lines of evidence support this idea. Included in the evidence is the finding that drugs which block the actions of dopamine at its targets can dampen the addictive power of cocaine or amphetamine. Moreover, recent studies suggest that changes in genes that code for receptors for dopamine can produce marked, and unexpected, changes in the avidity with which genetically altered animals seek addictive drugs.

Other addictive drugs also influence the circuit linking the VTA, nucleus accumbens, and frontal cortex. This circuit is rich in neurochemicals, regulating its normal activities via numerous neurotransmitters and their receptors. Its normal neurotransmitters include those targeted by major classes of addictive drugs, including opioids (heroin, morphine, and their relatives), sedatives (alcohol, barbiturates, and benzodiazepines), and nicotine. The working hypothesis described above has been expanded to suggest that these drugs exert addictive actions by regulating the release of dopamine in the circuit, often by complex interlocking mechanisms.

These interactions of drugs with brain reward systems—including the compulsive quality of the behaviors they engender—may be similar to those evoked by other highly reinforcing human activities. Recent imaging studies suggest that the brain areas involved in our reactions to stimuli associated with addictive drugs may be similar to those involved in other compulsive activities such as gambling. More work is required to understand the implications of such similarities.

Changes in Brain Actions With Repeated Drug Use

The interactions among drugs and their brain targets may change when drugs are used repeatedly. At least three different types of change are important for addictive drug use. First, repeated use of a drug can produce tolerance, so that a higher dose must be used to achieve a given level of response. In the case of some drugs, such tolerance occurs because the body begins to break the drug down more efficiently. In the case of many other drugs, tolerance appears to occur at the neurons themselves. For example, when morphine binds to opioid receptors in some brain areas, it initiates a cascade of actions in the neuron. One of these actions slows the activity of an enzyme (adenylate cyclase) that orchestrates the chemical reactions needed for proper neuronal firing. After repeated activation of the opioid receptor by morphine, the enzyme adapts so that the morphine no longer stimulates changes in neuronal firing. Thus, the effect of a given dose of morphine is diminished.

Second, repeated use of some drugs can produce a state of dependence (often called physical dependence), in which nerves in the brain and elsewhere adapt to repeated drug exposure and function normally only in the presence of the drug. If the drug is withdrawn, severe physiological reactions occur. These are often called a 'withdrawal syndrome.' The withdrawal syndrome can be relatively mild (as when I miss my morning cup of coffee), pronounced (as when a high-dose heroin user misses a fix), or life-threatening (as when a severely dependent alcoholic stops drinking suddenly). The brain areas involved in withdrawal reactions may differ from those involved in the rewarding or conditioned effects of drugs, but the psychological reactions to withdrawal can alter these effects.

A third way in which experience alters brain chemistry is in the operation of the reward pathways themselves. With repeated use of cocaine or amphetamine, for example, the neurons in the VTA may decrease their production of dopamine, probably by invoking feedback mechanisms normally used to counter excess production of dopamine. Thus, the cocaine-using individual may begin to have a deficient production of dopamine. If this deficient production is not corrected when cocaine use ceases, the individual may have an altered brain reward system. Such long-term changes in brain chemistry may support conditioning processes that trigger cravings and relapses.

Caveats

Our understanding of the brain's role in addiction is complicated by another feature of addictive drugs. Specifically, patients who use these drugs as clinical medicines usually do not become addicted.

In the case of opioids, the basis for continued medical use was stated succinctly by Sydenham in 1680: "Among the remedies which it has pleased Almighty God to give to man to relieve his sufferings, none is so universal and so efficacious as opium" (Goodman & Gilman. *The Pharmacological Basis of Therapeutics*. MacMillan, 1941, p. 186). Modern opioids, including highly addictive agents, remain a critical therapy for acute and chronic pain. The patient who receives morphine or other opioids for management of severe pain encounters all of the brain actions of opioids discussed above. Indeed, patients receiving opioids for pain may use higher doses, and develop more severe physical dependence, than do opioid addicts. And yet, most of these patients face little risk of addiction. This contrasts with the repetitive drug seeking and drug taking that characterize opioid abusers. What underlies such profound differences in vulnerability to addictive drug use?

It is likely that this question has multiple answers, only some of which can be glimpsed now. First, individuals may differ in their biological or genetic vulnerability to the rewarding or conditioned actions of addictive drugs. Studies in animals suggest that this is true for vulnerability to the rewarding actions of alcohol and opioids, and similar differences may occur in people. Second, the setting and expectancies associated with drug use influence the development of addiction. Third, individuals may differ in learned vulnerability. Individuals who have learned abusive use of one drug may more easily relearn abusive use of the same or a second drug than will an individual who has never abused a drug. Alternatively, other early experiences may increase susceptibility to the rewarding effects of drugs. For example, animal studies suggest that highly stressful experiences may alter susceptibility to drug reward. Finally, voluntary self-administration of a drug may activate chemical systems in the brain different from those activated when the same drug is administered by an outside party. Again, studies in animals suggest that animals which voluntarily seek out and self-administer cocaine or opioids show different changes in neurotransmitter activities than do animals which receive identical doses involuntarily. These differences highlight the importance of individual experience in shaping the neurochemical impact of addictive drugs.

In summary, addictive drugs may be said to capture their users by hijacking brain systems that support reward processes required for survival. On the other hand, the user's individual experience and genetic heritage shape the neurochemical impact of addictive drugs. Thus, addiction is not an inevitable outcome of drug exposure. Addiction requires active interactions among the potential user's brain chemistry, genetic vulnerability, and individual experience. [T]his view of addiction has important implications for our design of prevention and treatment efforts.

CHALLENGE QUESTIONS

Is Drug Addiction a Choice?

1. One of the major points of disagreement between Schaler and Young is the issue of control. How important is it that someone's behaviors, even their addictive ones, are under their control to some degree? What problems might arise if someone lost control over certain sets of behaviors?
2. Describe why Schaler prefers to understand addiction as a metaphoric disease rather than a physical disease.
3. Review some of the psychological literature on the issue of free will and determinism. What role does this issue play in the controversies surrounding the nature of addiction?
4. Young combines knowledge of neuroscience with knowledge of psychology. What schools of psychology does she focus on most, and have there been free will and determinism controversies with regard to them?

PrescribingPsychologist.com

PrescribingPsychologist.com provides information and links regarding the prescription privilege debate.

http://www.prescribingpsychologist.com

National Institute on Drug Abuse

This page of the National Institute on Drug Abuse (NIDA) features an extensive list of links to NIDA constituent organizations, grantees, and government sites of interest. Click on Drug Abuse Treatment Outcome Study (DATOS) for NIDA's third national evaluation of drug abuse treatment effectiveness.

http://www.nida.nih.gov/OtherResources.html

Psychotherapy Links

This directory of psychotherapy Web sites is sponsored by the University of Western Ontario Department of Psychiatry.

http://www.psychiatry.med.uwo.ca/ptherapy/
links.htm

Association for Gray, Lesbian, & Bisexual Issues in Counseling

This is the Web site of the Association for Gay, Lesbian, & Bisexual Issues in Counseling, a division of the American Counseling Association that works toward educating mental health service providers about issues faced by gay, lesbian, bisexual, and transgendered individuals.

http://www.aglbic.org

Sociology & Psychology Queer Links

This QueerByChoice.com page offers links to several organizations and articles related to the social and psychological bases of homosexuality.

http://www.queerbychoice.com/sociolinks.html

PART 6

Psychological Treatment

*P*sychologists have a long history of inventing and testing ways to treat psychological, emotional, and social problems. The problem is that drugs are increasingly being used to treat traditionally psychological disorders, and most psychologists are not permitted to prescribe drugs. Many psychologists believe that they should be able to prescribe medication, especially if they have the appropriate training. However, many other psychologists feel that the move to prescription privileges fundamentally changes the nature of psychology. Psychological treatments have also included controversial procedures, such as changing someone's sexual orientation. Some psychologists argue that homosexuality is not an illness, so there is no need to treat or change it. Indeed, homosexuality is not included in the classification of mental illness in the DSM-IV. Should therapists be allowed to treat something that is not even classified as a mental illness?

- Should Psychologists Be Able to Prescribe Medicine?

- Is Treating Homosexuality Ethical?

ISSUE 14

Should Psychologists Be Able to Prescribe Medicine?

YES: Patrick H. DeLeon and Debra Lina Dunivin, from "The Tide Rises," *Clinical Psychology: Science and Practice* (Fall 2002)

NO: Steven C. Hayes and Grace Chang, from "Invasion of the Body Snatchers: Prescription Privileges, Professional Schools, and the Drive to Create a New Behavioral Health Profession," *Clinical Psychology: Science and Practice* (Fall 2002)

ISSUE SUMMARY

YES: Psychologists Patrick H. DeLeon and Debra Lina Dunivin assert that granting prescription authority to psychologists will improve the quality of psychological care because they will be able to treat both the body and the mind of patients.

NO: Psychologists Steven C. Hayes and Grace Chang fear that prescription authority will fundamentally change psychologists from being experts in human relations to experts in medicine, which we already have.

Medication seems to have emerged recently as a primary treatment not only for physical health but also for mental health. The problem is that psychologists, the traditional experts on mental health, cannot prescribe medications for their patients. Only medical personnel, including psychiatrists, can write prescriptions for medication. As drug treatments are developed and shown to be effective, psychologists could be left out and lose their traditional role. These trends have led to a movement among psychologists for prescription privileges. Why shouldn't they have access to all forms of effective mental health treatment?

A legitimate concern of those who oppose such privileges is that psychologists do not have the necessary training in anatomy and physiology to competently prescribe medication to patients. Those who advocate prescription privileges have attempted to address this concern by requiring extensive training. Still, there are many medical practitioners who contend that psychologists are overstepping their bounds and possibly muscling into the territory of medicine, both professionally and financially. Interestingly, this contention is not unique to medical professionals. Many psychologists are opposed to the prescription movement, with the primary authors of these articles as the long-standing champions of each side of this debate.

As proponents of the prescription movement, psychologists Patrick H. DeLeon and Debra Lina Dunivin strongly believe that granting psychologists prescription authority will benefit society. They argue that many controversial issues in psychology have met with initial resistance only to be widely accepted with time. They attempt to show that the issue of prescription privileges, though not part of psychology's tradition, will nevertheless become an obvious and necessary part of psychological treatment. DeLeon and Dunivin are confident that knowledge of psychopharmacology will enhance a psychologist's ability to provide the highest possible quality of care. They support this assertion by describing several psychologists who have gone through the necessary training and are now functionally prescribing medications.

By contrast, psychologists Steven C. Hayes and Grace Chang contend that prescription authority for psychologists will not benefit society. Because of the proposed shift to a more medical course load, they foresee that the field of psychology will be fundamentally altered. Psychology students, for example, will necessarily spend more time studying topics of medicine and less time on topics related to human relations, the traditional province and role of psychology. As a result, Hayes and Chang predict that psychologists will be more tempted to use medications as a primary form of treatment and less capable of facilitating the psychosocial aspects of therapy. This, they feel, marks a loss of faith in the importance of the psychosocial aspects of therapy, even though there is considerable evidence in support of these aspects. Lastly, they fear psychologists will lose their distinction as specialists in human relations and become just another health professional among the many who prescribe medication.

POINT

- Psychology has a responsibility to society to provide high-quality health care.
- Objective studies demonstrate that nonphysicians can safely utilize medicine.
- Psychopharmacology training will provide a new breed of practitioner who will see his or her patients in a more holistic light.
- Psychology is a growing profession that should not be afraid to change when it benefits clients.
- The key to avoiding an excessive reliance on medication is for psychologists to accurately assess and diagnose a client.

COUNTERPOINT

- There is little evidence that psychologists are less effective because they don't have prescription privileges.
- Prescription authority could create a public health hazard.
- The reach for prescription privileges seems to mark a loss of faith in the importance of the psychological level of analysis.
- Prescription authority will fundamentally alter the field of psychology.
- Psychologists with prescription privileges will be more likely to treat clients with medication.

Patrick H. DeLeon and
Debra Lina Dunivin

 **YES**

The Tide Rises

. . . We must admit that we have genuinely enjoyed watching the maturation of professional psychology's prescriptive authority (RxP-) agenda since U.S. Senator Daniel K. Inouye first raised this issue at the Hawaii Psychological Association annual meeting in November 1984. We say this because in our judgment, the essence of the RxP-movement is providing high quality health care to as many Americans as possible. Psychology is one of the learned professions and, as such, has a societal responsibility to provide proactive vision and programmatic leadership. Since the release of *Healthy People* by the Carter Administration, there has been steadily growing clinical and scientific evidence that the behavioral, environmental, and psychosocial (e.g., psychological) aspects of health care are absolutely critical on both an individual case basis and across populations. As we enter the twenty-first century, it is clear to us that our nation's health care system is embarking upon an era of unprecedented change: educated consumers, the extraordinary impact of technological advances, systemic reliance upon interdisciplinary health care, and growing institutional appreciation for objective (e.g., data-based) practice protocols. We are, of course, acutely aware that change in the status quo is always unsettling and that the specifics of change can never be predicted with any assurance of accuracy.

We maintain that the present prescription privileges movement parallels the professional school movement of 30 years ago. What was then a contentious issue within the profession has now become mainstream. What was then considered by its opponents as a misguided new direction has now become a valuable part of the profession. We fully expect that the same will become true for this new direction taken by proponents of prescriptive authority for psychologists. Other examples of this same phenomenon exist from the beginning of psychology as a discipline—expanding beyond scientific theory into clinical practice, for example, and branching from psychological assessment to psychotherapy. In this brief commentary, we take a closer look at the most recent of these phenomena: the professional school movement and the actual data that have accumulated when members of our profession have incorporated the practice of pharmacotherapy into psychological practice. Taken together, these make the conclusion inevitable. We must take

From *Clinical Psychology: Science and Practice*, vol. 9, no. 3, Fall 2002, pp. 249–255. Copyright © 2002 by Oxford University Press Journals. Reprinted by permission. References omitted.

into account the history of our profession, its tendency to grow and develop in new directions, to incorporate new knowledge and skills into our professional practice, sometimes taking what seems at the time to be a dramatic shift, but always doing it with the highest standards. This is an essential component of what psychology is—a viable, growing profession that isn't afraid to change when it's good for us and the people we serve.

A Historical Perspective

If one reflects upon the history of professional psychology, it soon becomes evident that at every stage in the profession's maturation, psychologists and nonpsychologists expressed grave concern. This was true for the profession's initial efforts to independently diagnose and treat, to be reimbursed for providing clinical services, to administer mental health clinics, to obtain membership on hospital medical staff, and so on. Those who opposed these expansions in psychology's scope of practice frequently expressed the view that these functions were solely reserved for graduates of another profession (i.e., they were medicine's turf). If one wanted to provide care within a hospital ward or be the administrator of a clinic, one should first go to medical school.

Since the establishment of the Task Force on Psychopharmacology by the APA Council of Representatives at the Boston convention, by the overwhelming vote of 118 to 2, in August 1990, the underlying policy issue of psychology prescribing has been thoroughly debated throughout the APA governance. At Council's August 1995 meeting in New York City, obtaining prescriptive privileges for appropriately trained psychologists became formal APA policy. The following year in Toronto, Council adopted a model prescription bill and a model training curriculum. To our knowledge, this is the only time in APA's history that the association's highest elected body (e.g., the Council of Representatives) had ever deemed it appropriate to endorse a particular clinical modality. Accordingly, we were not surprised when in 1997, the American Psychological Association of Graduate Students (APAGS) adopted a formal "resolution of support" for RxP-. It is their future that the RxP- agenda contemplates.

Although the discipline of psychology dates back to the founding of Wundt's laboratory in 1879, on September 21, 1970, classes began at the first independent professional school of psychology: the California School of Professional Psychological (CSPP). This was to become the era of the Doctor of Psychology degree (PsyD), the first program being launched in the Department of Psychology at the University of Illinois at Champaign-Urbana in 1968. There can be little disagreement that the paradigm shift from the traditional research-oriented PhD degree to the professional-oriented PsyD degree represented a fundamental change in psychology's self image and underlying mission, a change that will never be reversed. Today there are 48 accredited PsyD programs, most of which are within professional schools that graduate 58% of all clinical students.

Over the past several decades, professional psychology has done very well in advancing its legislative and administrative agendas. Psychology's clinicians are independently recognized under all federal and private health care (e.g., insurance) programs; psychological expertise is readily utilized throughout the judiciary; and individual psychologists have served at the highest levels of clinical and public policy responsibility. During the 107th Congress, for example, three psychologists were elected to serve in the U.S. House of Representatives. Today there are 155,000 members and affiliates of the American Psychological Association (APA), with APAGS possessing 59,700 members. These are very impressive numbers and they speak well for the future.

The Opposition

If one reflects on the arguments promulgated by those who have consistently opposed psychology obtaining prescriptive authority, they generally fall into several discrete categories. Within the profession, there is a somewhat vocal minority that, from our perspective, may also fundamentally disagree with the underlying tenets of the professional school movement. These are generally academic-based colleagues, housed within traditional social science and educational structures. Some train clinical psychologists. It would admittedly be very difficult for their programs to expand to include psychopharmacology, given the traditional academic pressures involved in allocating constrained teaching resources. The RxP-agenda began with the practitioner community (as, we would note, did the professional school movement). At times, the opposition's apparent lack of respect for those teaching and participating in postdoctoral psychopharmacology training modules seems puzzling at best. They seem to be asserting that psychology's graduates are incapable of learning new materials. Clearly this assertion that psychologists can't learn is contrary to the data: these professionals have spent over two decades in educational pursuit and obtained a least one advanced degree at the doctoral level. Certainly one must conclude that psychologists are not only capable of, but committed to, learning.

Another distinct category of opposition postulates the alleged "public health hazard" argument. These individuals seem to genuinely believe that when psychology's practitioners obtain prescriptive authority, they will affirmatively harm their patients. Over the years, variations on this fundamental theme have been emotionally employed by medical colleagues in efforts to protect their self-proclaimed turf. It has been interesting to observe over the years that organized medicine has used this scare tactic in their efforts to limit consumer access to dental surgery and chiropractic care. Most recently, the anaesthesiologists have questioned the clinical competence of certified nurse anaesthetists in the popular media; notwithstanding the excellent track record of nursing throughout rural American and within federal installations. These physician versus nonphysician battles have been well documented in numerous national health policy reports. Clinical pharmacists, nurse practitioners, optometrists, and podiatrists have had to overcome this scurrilous argument, as they have legislatively succeeded in obtaining prescriptive authority in the various state legislatures and federal agencies. Objective studies over the years demonstrating that nonphysicians (often with considerably less training than psychologists) can safely and cost-effectively utilize medications do not deter these opponents. Nor does the reality that countless psychologists, without any formal psychopharmacology training, have functionally prescribed without adverse consequences under a wide range of conditions.

Accountability to the Public

Traditionally, psychology's practicing clinicians are expected to live up to the standard of functioning within one's scope of competence and keeping up with scientific advances. In addition to this ethical requirement for competent practice, psychologists are also held accountable for competence by state statutes. Under our nation's form of elected constitutional government, it is the fundamental responsibility of the states to establish public agencies (e.g., licensing boards) to protect the public from incompetent or disreputable practitioners. Although there have been increasing calls for national licensure standards over the past several years, with some professions (e.g., professional nursing) rapidly moving toward that objective, within the profession of psychology this responsibility remains at the individual state level. We would remind the readership that within the federal and state systems, professional licensure is generally required, with the specific facility at which the practitioner is employed determining scope of practice issues (within broad agency guidelines). The facility also institutionally provides quality of care oversight, generally through an active peer review process. Similarly, over the years, our nation's educational institutions have established their own formal review procedures for authorizing the establishment of new courses and degrees. Ultimately, the institution's Board of Regents retains final responsibility.

This comprehensive regulatory framework possesses a long and honorable tradition, stretching back over hundreds of years of public disclosure and dialogue. There is every indication that society has been well served by this approach. Accordingly, the efforts of those opposing psychology obtaining prescriptive authority to "debate" the specifics of course content, public licensure board competency, and details of acceptable supervision are not central to this issue. The agencies involved have long demonstrated their competency to resolve these types of matters, changing requirements over time based on practical experiences, and are well-suited to continue in this capacity. One could even suggest that in some instances, the underlying tenor of some of the opponents' arguments are fundamentally anti-intellectual.

The Twenty-First Century

The twenty-first century will be an era of extraordinary reliance on objective, data-driven decision-making processes within the health care arena. Numerous health policy experts have commented on the extent to which, in their judgment, the health care segment of our economy has not yet institutionally incorporated information technological advances. The number of Americans who use the Internet to retrieve health-related information is estimated to be approximately 70–100 million. Currently over half of American homes possess computers, and while information presently doubles every 5 years, it will soon double every 17 days, with traffic on the Web already doubling every 100 days.

At the same time, from a public policy perspective, one can see the process evolving whereby those who are systematically exploring changing definitions of "Quality of Care" are increasingly raising fundamental questions about today's practices. The Institute of Medicine (IOM) was chartered in 1970 by the National Academy of Sciences, acting under the Academy's 1863 congressional charter responsibility to be an advisor to the federal government. The IOM serves as a highly respected health policy think tank for the Congress and various Administrations. In 1999, the IOM released a highly controversial report that found that each year, between 44,000 and 98,000 Americans died in hospitals as a result of medical errors. The report noted that medications are the most frequent medical intervention. Encouraging interdisciplinary collaboration, the report further described how merely by having clinical pharmacists participate during daily hospital rounds, the rate of preventable adverse drug events relating to prescribing decreased significantly (66%) within major teaching facilities. Another IOM report addressed the extent to which the current American health care system lags significantly behind other segments of the economy in utilizing advances in relevant technology and in ensuring that scientific advances are employed in a timely fashion. The American health care delivery system is in need of fundamental change. Americans should be able to count on receiving care that meets their needs and is based on the best scientific knowledge. Yet there is strong evidence that this frequently is not the case. The lag between the discovery of more efficacious forms of treatment and their incorporation into routine patient care is unnecessarily long, in the range of about 15 to 20 years. Even then, adherence of clinical practice to the evidence is highly uneven.

To suggest, as those who employ the fundamental "public health hazard" argument overtly do, that psychology's practitioners will affirmatively harm their patients by prescribing is to ignore not only the realities of today's health care system but also to ignore the data on prescribing psychologists, as discussed in the next section. We are confident that by providing doctoral level psychologists with targeted postdoctoral psychopharmacological training, a highly competent new breed of practitioner will evolve. These will be practitioners who will see their patients in a different (e.g., psychological and holistic) light and who have been extensively trained to value and utilize scientific principles and knowledge in their clinical practices.

Similarly, from an educational perspective, the underlying question should be: what didactic content (that might presently be taught by medicine, nursing, or pharmacy) would effectively complement the extensive psychological knowledge base our colleagues already possess? To draw a visual analogy, the first author's teenage daughter does not need an engineering or computer science degree to effectively utilize the most up-to-date computer software available off the shelf. She does not have to design and build her own computer in order to conduct highly advanced statistical analyses for her high school presentations. Competent educators *can* teach outstanding students; desktop computers *will* provide practitioners of all disciplines (and educated consumers) with helpful input, designed specifically for diagnostic symptom relief. The time has long passed for individual patients to be given a psychiatric diagnosis and placed on a medication for years at a time, without constant monitoring and exploration of less invasive alternative treatment approach.

A Fundamental Public Health Approach

If one reflects on the psychological or public health literature published over the past decade, there is scarcely any specific subpopulation of patients for which a highly reputable source has not proclaimed that its members have been inappropriately medicated. This would include ethnic minority individuals, women, those with serious mental illnesses, those residing in rural America, the elderly, and those residing in long-term care facilities and nursing homes. During the first author's presidency, the APA actively participated in several White House conferences regarding the alleged excessive reliance on medication by those licensed clinicians treating our nation's children. The critical key to effectively utilizing psychotropic medication is, and always has been, an accurate assessment and diagnosis and developing a therapeutic alliance. This has always been the strength of professional psychology.

Psychopharmacology Training Modules

Several different training models in psychopharmacology for psychologists have emerged around the country. Most of these training programs result in enhanced consultation between psychologists and their medical colleagues around the prescription of medications for their mutual patients. In the absence of state laws permitting prescribing of medications by psychologists, those trained in these postdoctoral programs have put their knowledge of psychopharmacology to use in collaborative practice. For some, participation in other training modules results in the practice of clinical psychopharmacology by virtue of another license, for example, prescribing as a nurse practitioner after completing a degree in advanced practice nursing. And participation in one of these programs, the Department of Defense (DoD) Psychopharmacology Demonstration Project (PDP), has resulted in the practice of pharmacotherapy by psychologists *as* psychologists.

In all cases, it is our collective judgment that participation in any one of these programs has resulted in an enhanced scope of clinical competence and practice whether or not that practice includes pharmacotherapy. The Department of Psychology at Eisenhower Army Medical Center (where the second author was stationed) conducted a customer satisfaction survey of all patients seen by her, during her first year after graduation from the DoD psychopharmacology training program. The results indicated "a high level of overall satisfaction with the services she provided. The most common answer to questions regarding satisfaction with Dr. Dunivin, desire to work with her in the future, and willingness to refer a friend to Dr. Dunivin is 'Strongly Agree.'

The percentage of those who agree or strongly agree on these three areas are 94%, 88%, and 86%, respectively."

Although highly visible, the DoD program is not the only one of the training models in clinical psychopharmacology for psychologists that has emerged. Over the past several years, the first author has had the pleasure of serving as the commencement speaker for three separate university-based psychopharmacology postdoctoral training graduations. The graduates have been licensed clinicians (often rather senior) who have subsequently obtained specialized masters degrees, fulfilling the APA model didactic curriculum through special executive track programs targeted toward full-time clinicians. Although clearly considered highly competent professionals by their peers prior to enrolling in the psychopharmacology training, the graduates spoke profusely about how this additional knowledge had subsequently enhanced their clinical skills. They were outstanding clinicians. Now they had become even better with a value-added component. They now tend to gravitate toward different types of patients and to engage in more extensive collaborative practices with relevant medical specialists. Simply stated, they are a new breed of clinicians and still clearly psychologists. Their enthusiasm and successes have become the catalyst for additional training modules (some Web based) to flourish.

The Data on Prescribing Psychologists

A substantial body of data has emerged during the past decade about the practice of pharmacotherapy by psychologists. The conclusions drawn from this data are unequivocal: appropriately trained psychologists can and do provide excellent, high quality psychopharmacological care to their patients. There are dozens of anecdotal reports of psychologists prescribing medications in military and public health service facilities. However, the most extensively evaluated practice of pharmacotherapy by psychologists has occurred within the DoD Psychopharmacology Demonstration Project (PDP). The first two psychopharmacology Fellow psychologists graduated from this program on June 17, 1994, and a total of 10 psychologists have now graduated. Seven of the 10 graduates are still practicing pharmacotherapy within the military health care system. Collectively, they have treated thousands of patients with high quality care. Performance of the Fellows has been subjected to intense evaluation, not only within the military systems in which they worked but also by several outside evaluations over a 7-year period. However, RxP-opponents seem largely to ignore this data. It thus seems appropriate to remind the readership of these findings.

Each of the evaluation reports concluded that the DoD Fellows had been trained to safely and effectively prescribe psychotropic and adjunctive medications through the 2-year postdoctoral fellowship. The investigative arm of the Congress, the General Accounting Office (GAO), surveyed performance of each of the Fellows at their duty stations and concluded that the quality of care provided by them to their patients was well regarded by both their supervisors and other health care providers. The supervisors consistently rated their quality of care as "good to excellent" and had found no evidence of quality problems or adverse outcomes. The GAO further noted that nearly all of the physicians and others interviewed were convinced by the Fellows' performance that they were well trained and knowledgeable, despite the fact that some of the graduates had experienced early resistance at their work sites, particularly among military psychiatrists. The GAO specifically noted that "several physicians also told us that they came to rely on the graduates for information about psychotropic medications."

With respect to the clinical supervision of the Fellows by psychiatrists, the GAO reported: "Without exception, these supervisors—all psychiatrists—stated that the graduates' quality of care was good." Additionally, the report stated: "One supervisor, for example, noted that each of the graduate's patients had improved as a result of the graduate's treatment; another supervisor referred to the quality of care provided by the graduate as 'phenomenal'. The supervisors noted that the graduates are aware of their limitations. . . . Further, the supervisors noted that no adverse patient outcomes have been associated with the treatment provided by the graduates."

By far, the most comprehensive study of the DoD program was the ongoing evaluation performed by the American College of Neuropsychopharmacology, a well-respected professional association of clinical and basic science researchers from the fields of neurology, psychiatry, psychology, and pharmacology. Between 1991 and 1998, the ACNP was contracted to provide DoD with an independent assessment of the psychopharmacology training curriculum and to monitor the ongoing progress of the program's participants, during their fellowship and after graduation. The evaluation process included site visits several times each year; interviews of the participants, their clinical and administrative supervisors, as well as other health care providers; review of clinical records; and conducting written and oral examinations. Despite some early reservations about the feasibility of the project, the final report of the ACNP evaluation panel contained many positive findings, among them the observation that the graduates "filled critical needs, and performed with excellence wherever they served." The ACNP reported that eight of the ten graduates were serving as clinic chiefs or assistant chiefs, and noted that the graduates made valuable contributions to the continuing education of psychologists as well as physicians. As would be expected, the medical knowledge of the graduates was not judged to be comparable to that of psychiatrists; however, as we already noted, it was reported that no adverse effects were associated with the practices of the graduates. Furthermore, they were found to be "medically safe," again providing direct evidence contrary to the public health hazard argument against prescription privileges for appropriately trained psychologists.

Perhaps most important, in our opinion, is the conclusion of the ACNP that those participating in the DoD psychopharmacology program had maintained their professional identities as psychologists, that the program had not produced "mini-psychiatrists" or "psychiatrist-extenders," but rather "extended psychologists with a value added component prescriptive authority provides. They continued to function very much in the traditions of clinical psychology (psychometric tests, psychological therapies) but a body of knowledge and experience was added that extended their range of competence."

The ACNP concluded their executive summary of their final report with what must be considered a ringing endorsement:

> *The PDP graduates have performed and are performing safely and effectively as prescribing psychologists. Without commenting on the social, economic, and political issues of whether a program such as the PDP should be continued or expanded, it seems clear to the evaluation panel that a 2-year program—one year didactic, one year clinical practicum that includes at least a 6 month inpatient rotation—can transform licensed clinical psychologists into prescribing psychologists who can function effectively and safely in the military setting to expand the delivery of mental health treatment to a variety of patients and clients in a cost effective way. We have been impressed with the work of the graduates, their acceptance by psychiatrists (even while they may have disagreed with the concept of prescribing psychologists), and their contribution to the military readiness of the groups they have been assigned to serve. We have been impressed with the commitment and involvement of these prescribing psychologists to their role, their patients, and the military establishment. We are not clear about what functions the individuals can play in the future, but we are convinced that their present roles meet a unique, very professional need of the DoD. As such, we are in agreement that the Psychopharmacology Demonstration Project is a job well done.*

Throughout the course of the DoD Psychopharmacology Fellowship training program, the participants provided regular updates at the APA annual conventions. What comes through in listening to their collective reflections is how differently they view their primary care patients. They approach their patients from a fundamentally psychological orientation, not from an illness-oriented model. They report that there is a real qualitative difference. Patient satisfaction and clinic administration confidence in the DoD Fellows remains high.

Final Comments

We would suggest from our public policy perspective that in the same manner that the establishment of the professional school movement in the 1970s has had a profound impact on all of psychology, the twenty-first century evolution toward prescriptive authority will have a similarly beneficial and monumental impact on the profession and our nation. To conclude otherwise is to ignore the data and professional psychology's history.

NO

Steven C. Hayes and
Grace Chang

Invasion of the Body Snatchers: Prescription Privileges, Professional Schools, and the Drive to Create a New Behavioral Health Profession

. . . It is not too difficult to imagine the following new behavioral health specialty: a doctoral provider with substantial medical training, about the equivalent of existing nurse practitioner's or physician's assistants, with solid training in the delivery of empirically supported psychosocial treatments. This provider would be trained to consume the research literature in both pharmacotherapy and psychotherapy but would be unlikely to produce much research in either area. Consumers accessing such providers could hope to receive empirically supported treatment for behavioral health problems that spanned the range of existing technologies, both psychosocial and pharmacological.

This may sound like a new idea, but it is about as old as modern clinical psychology. In the 1940s Lawrence Kubie argued for this combination of psychological and medical training for an envisioned "Doctorate in Medical Psychology" (DMP) that would be housed in schools of medicine. A similar and more extensive attempt is represented by the efforts to create a licensed "Doctorate in Mental Health" (DMH) in California. The DMH program was launched by psychoanalyst Robert Wallerstein and ran as a formal training program for nearly 15 years in the 1970s and 1980s before being shut down by medical opposition.

Psychiatry cannot fill the niche envisioned by Kubie and Wallerstein, in part because the medical training is so extensive and generalist that the cost of the needed psychosocial training would make this expensive specialty even more expensive. Especially given the reality that the majority of psychoactive prescriptions are not written by psychiatrists and that the prescribing practices of the psychiatrists and general practitioners are similar, this barrier is prohibitive. Indeed, psychiatry has gone in the exact opposite direction, diminishing its role in the psychosocial area.

Now the practice leadership of organized psychology is taking professional doctoral psychology in the direction of the DMP or DMH models. Kubie and Wallerstein, both psychiatrists, were trying to create a new profession, just as

From *Clinical Psychology: Science and Practice*, vol. 9, no. 3, Fall 2002, pp. 264–269. Copyright © 2002 by Oxford University Press Journals. Reprinted by permission. References omitted.

advocates of prescription privileges for psychologists now plan to do in the name of "psychology." For example, Morgan Sammons, one of the graduates of the Department of Defense Psychopharmacology Demonstration program, points to the efforts of Kubie and Wallerstein as antecedents for the goal of the new profession: "blending graduate psychology training with aspects of medicine." This change, done well, could produce an ethically sound and useful new behavioral health profession. The profession will not be psychology as we know it, however, even if that is its name. Like the old science fiction movie, *Invasion of the Body Snatchers,* what will be left in the wake of this transition will look like psychology, but its true nature and substance will be quite different.

The fact that psychology may change its nature, organization and training is not necessarily a concern. If the change is good, it should be embraced. But it is not at all clear that this change will be good, seen from the point of view of a scientific approach to psychological practice. . . .

The Changed Profession

More Drugs for Psychology

To the extent that the prescription privilege movement succeeds in psychology, the field of psychology will be fundamentally altered. At first through post-doctoral training, but inevitably in predoctoral training, psychology students will spend several hundred hours studying medical subjects, and the clients they serve will be much more likely to receive medications as the primary or secondary component of treatment.

It is not clear, however, that this will produce better or less expensive outcomes for the humans psychology serves. In addition to the risks posed by these technologies, the size and source of their beneficial impact are far less clear than is usually supposed, and there is almost no evidence that psychologists are less effective or more expensive because they do not have direct access to these technologies. In the area of antidepressants, for example, the placebo effect is quite similar to the effects found with the major antidepressants, especially when researchers use active placebos (those with similar side effects to the real drug) that better control for penetration of the blind. While the jury is still out, it is not possible to say that antidepressants are clinically superior to active placebos. Antianxiety drugs seem somewhat less controversial, but once again there are profound concerns about the designs of these studies and the meaning of the data. Yet antidepressant and antianxiety drugs constitute a large percentage of the psychoactive drugs likely to be prescribed by those in the new profession.

Advocates of prescription privileges also claim that a major benefit of the new mental health profession will be the ability to take advantage of the known benefits provided by treatments that combine both psychosocial and pharmacological methods. This would be a more persuasive argument if a large body of well-controlled research had proven the benefits of combined treatments. Such is not the case.

As in the area of active placebo controls, the designs used to study combined treatments often have known methodological weaknesses. Consider the most common design containing these four groups: drug placebo, drug psychotherapy, and combined drug and psychotherapy. If a benefit is found for the combined treatment in this design, we still do not know if that benefit comes from biological or entirely psychosocial sources. To determine that, a fifth group needs to be added: combined drug placebo and psychotherapy (ideally using an active drug placebo). When that control is added, the pharmacological basis of benefits that have been found for combined treatments sometimes evaporate. Perhaps present psychologists could not credibly prescribe placebos, but it does not seem worth it to radically change the field of psychology only to be able to administer placebos with a straight face.

Even in the area of cost-effectiveness, the benefits of pharmacotherapy versus psychotherapy are not clear, particularly when the greater durability of psychosocial methods and greater levels of patient acceptability are factored into the equation. Ironically, just when the complex research needed to assess the relative benefits of psychosocial versus pharmaceutical methods is showing that psychosocial methods more than hold their own, the field that leads the way in the production of empirically based psychosocial method is turning away from its own technology toward that of another field. The psychological level of analysis (the interactions of a whole organism with its world, considered both historically and situationally) is a meaningful and important one in the fabric of science. The reach for prescription privileges seems to mark a loss of faith in the importance of that level and in the scientific evidence for its importance.

In addition, it seems likely that the greater involvement of the pharmaceutical industry in psychology would begin to contaminate this new DMH-based form of psychology with its economic considerations, both in research and practice. In medicine and psychiatry, the pharmaceutical industry exerts a clear and known biasing influence both over prescribing practices and even over the integrity of pharmacotherapy research. There seems to be no reason to suppose that the same biasing effects will not be seen in a DMH-based form of psychology.

The combination of this biasing and the reduced amount of psychosocial training could lead to a new profession considerably less sophisticated in the development and dissemination of applied psychological science, and even less connected to the scientific base of psychology. It seems very likely, as has already happened in psychiatry that there would be a gradual reduction both in the delivery of psychosocial treatments and in psychosocial treatment innovation from this new field. The economic contingencies alone seem likely to produce that impact, since practitioners will make more for medication checks than they will for psychotherapy. Doctoral psychologists are the leading producers of new psychosocial technology. Any reduction in their innovative impact would reverberate through the entire field of behavioral health, and through the basic discipline of psychology itself.

More Drugs for All

Advocates of prescription privileges in psychology have emphasized the supposed professional benefits to this new version of psychology. Prescription privileges, so the argument goes, will avoid second-class status for psychology and will reverse or limit the erosion of incomes wrought by managed care. These arguments form the core of the support for the new profession from within the existing practice base. There are multiple reasons to suppose that these outcomes are unlikely, especially over the long term.

For one thing, if prescription privileges quickly spread to other nonmedical behavioral health professions generally considered lower status professions, neither benefit will be realized for long. Ironically the very arguments used by prescription privileges advocates make that sad outcome much more likely. Patrick DeLeon, one of the originators of the prescription privilege movement, has claimed that "prescription privileges is no big deal. It's like learning how to use a desk-top computer." Advocates have claimed that responsible prescribing can be based on just a few weekend workshop.

Psychologists who are advocating for prescription privileges seem unaware that one immediate effect of their movement has been to raise the issue of prescription privileges within social work and mental health counseling. Just as in psychotherapy years ago, organized psychology is blazing a trail that others will readily be able to follow. The only limit to this devolutionary process will be political muscle, once a curriculum for the proper training of nonmedical professionals is agreed on within a given state. It is now fairly easy to imagine how, say, marriage and family therapists or licensed professional counselors will eventually be able to prescribe some of the most powerful and abused drugs known.

Prescribing authority is already housed in nondoctoral professions that take less training than psychology, such as nursing. As the same thing occurs in nonmedical prescribing professions, managed care organizations will have little trouble seeking out the lowest cost provider even of the new "more complete" list of services the new profession hopes to supply. Right now prescribing psychologists could hope to compete with psychiatry, but that situation is not static. Specialty health care is going through a huge downsizing. Psychiatry is being taken over by primary care physicians, and primary care physicians are being replaced by nurse practitioners. Psychologists cannot afford the addition of extensive training in another field only to find themselves competing with nurses. Rather than build on psychology's strength, prescription privileges will take psychology into another area precisely when it is being downsized and turned over to lower-level professionals.

The implications for the existing practice base are not positive. For existing practitioners to access the new profession, the training programs have to be fairly short. Few practitioners would be in a financial or professional position to leave their jobs for a year or more and pay for full-time training. If, however, the door to prescription authority is kept open to the existing practice base by the adoption of a short, weak training model, then a path will have been blazed for social work, counseling and guidance, and other nonmedical professions to follow. Short training models will ultimately greatly increase the number of prescribers, which inevitably will decrease the financial and professional value of prescription privileges.

In other words, in order to give a professional advantage to existing psychologists (and not merely to students trained in this new DMH-based profession), steps must be taken that will ultimately take away that very advantage. These short training models will also, of course, add to the ethical and public health risks raised by the target article. Conversely, if high training barriers are established, it will be obvious that the "benefits" from prescription privileges will accrue not to psychology in its present form, nor to the existing practice base, but solely to students, primarily in professional schools, trained in this new profession. Either way, psychology as a field ultimately will not experience significant professional or economic benefit by allowing itself to be possessed by another professional species.

Weakening of Clinical Science and the Strengthening of Professional Schools

There seems to be a nexus of common interest between opposition to empirically supported treatments, interest in PsyD and professional school training versus university-based PhD training, and advocacy for prescription privileges. A review of the literature on prescription privileges reveals that few of the advocates are faculty in major universities or are known for their scientific research. Leaders of the prescription privilege movement are generally known for their work in practice, politics, and professional schools. The connection is obvious but has rarely been noted and explained.

This nexus is both practical and intellectual. To keep the length of training within reasonable bounds, doctors of mental health cum PhD psychologists will eventually have reduced science training in favor of more technical training, particularly as this training moves to the predoctoral level. This does not seem to bother advocates of prescriptions privileges, since they generally believe, as did designers of the PsyD, the professional school movement, or the DMH program, that "research oriented psychology doctoral programs overemphasized quantitative and statistical sciences at the expense of clinical training."

The same reasoning that supports the importance of general clinical methods over empirically supported treatments seems to lead to the idea that basic biological science training is not that important for prescribing drugs. Thus, former American Psychological Association President Ronald Fox can advocate vigorously for prescription privileges on the one hand yet claim on the other that "psychology practitioners should be helping business understand why they're not well-served by pursuing empirically based treatments" because "psychotherapy . . . works anywhere from 60 to 70 percent of the time and more."

While university-based clinical training programs and clinical science organizations have resisted the call for prescription privileges (see, for example, the resolutions of opposition from Section III of Division 12 or from the Council of University Directors of Clinical Psychology), and the majority of university-based training directors believe that their faculty would be unwilling to make the changes needed to train students to prescribe, professional schools have taken a different attitude. For example, professional schools have eagerly developed model curricula that would help create a new profession. Perhaps in anticipation of this change, PsyD programs and professional schools have already adopted many more required courses from the "Level 3" courses recommended by the American Psychological Association for phar-macotherapy training than have university-based PhD programs.

The proposal to transmogrify psychology along the lines of the DMH model provides a possible competitive opportunity for free standing profes-sional schools vis-à-vis university doctoral programs. Tuition-supported schools are expensive. In the heyday of fee-for-service practice, an adequate flow of qualified students willing to take on the debt burden required was assured, but in the present day of managed care and the proliferation of professions training psychotherapists, these schools are under greater and greater pressure to take poorly qualified students to main the needed student flow. As compared to university-based doctoral clinical training programs, professional schools are perceived to be less prestigious, with higher student to faculty ratios, and (in the majority of cases, but not all) with a training model much less linked to psychology as a science. As a result, graduates of professional schools have had a more difficult time obtaining an internship, competing for some forms of employment, and achieving professionally within clinical psychology.

Prescription privileges promise a partial solution to all of these problems, since it seems obvious that professional schools will be able to move quickly to embrace the new profession. Leaders of free standing professional schools can look forward to the day when graduates from their programs will be able to claim that they are "complete" psychologists, as compared to the "limited" psychologists who graduate from more traditional university-based clinical psychology training programs. These leaders would have reason to expect that this change might attract more and better qualified students, ready to pay even higher tuitions. They might even dream that this change could help solve the irritatingly persistent prestige problem suffered by free standing pro-fessional schools. If the student demand materialized, professional schools would be able to produce thousands of prescribing psychologists quickly.

Much of their immediate success would come through the cannibaliza-tion of the existing psychology practice base. The "body snatching" strategy of the practice leadership ensures that outcome, since prescribing psycholo-gists would be likely to be hired into "psychology" positions or to be placed on "psychology" panels. Prescribing psychologists will obviously describe their training as broader, more comprehensive, or better, *as compared to that of other psychologists*. Psychologists used to being on the short end of the stick with psychiatry will soon find themselves facing that same threat from within. Existing practitioners will face enormous pressures to do whatever it takes to access the new form of training, even though it may means years of disruption of their professional lives.

Conclusions

This then is the dilemma. Although an ethically responsible new profession might be created by following a variant of the DMH model, the political and practical forces that are leading the practice wing of psychology to pursue it make it difficult to achieve that result. Mounting the new profession in a responsible way has unattractive features for the guild leadership. . . . Substantial medical training seems necessary, and yet its substantial nature eliminates the existing practice base as a source of trainees. Commitment to science and to empirically supported treatments seems necessary, but it conflicts with the culture that dominates in many corners of the practice leadership and in some wings of the professional school movement.

The practice leadership of psychology seems determined to transform the PhD in clinical psychology into a "Doctor of Mental Health," through postdoctoral training controlled by practice forces and ultimately predoctorally through professional schools also controlled by these same forces. This fundamental change in the very nature of psychology is to be accomplished in state legislatures one at a time through lobbying by state associations and the APA Practice Directorate, without the agreement or involvement of clinical faculty at research universities and their national associations (e.g., CUDCP). These faculties are being avoided because they are believed to practice "scientism"—the use of supposedly unreasonable and restrictive scientific standards that supposedly harm the profession. Instead, to quote from the title of an article by one of their own, the practice leadership wants to "build a profession that is safe for practitioners." . . . There should be an equally large concern, however: how to build a profession that is safe for the public. Our comments have been oriented toward that issue but also toward an additional concern: how to build a profession that is safe for psychology itself. This is surely not the way.

CHALLENGE QUESTIONS

Should Psychologists Be Able to Prescribe Medicine?

1. DeLeon and Dunivin assert that prescriptive authority will improve a therapist's ability to treat a client. Do you agree? Support your answer.
2. Hayes and Chang feel that prescriptive authority will fundamentally alter the field of psychology. In what ways would psychology be altered?
3. Do you agree with Hayes and Chang that there should be a field like psychology that champions the social and relational aspects of health? Why or why not?
4. Would you want your psychotherapist to have the ability to prescribe medicines? Why or why not?
5. Find three articles on the new prescription privileges in New Mexico and describe how successful this "experiment" seems to be.

ISSUE 15

Is Treating Homosexuality Ethical and Effective?

YES: Warren Throckmorton, from "Efforts to Modify Sexual Orientation: A Review of Outcome Literature and Ethical Issues," *Journal of Mental Health Counseling* (October 1998)

NO: Barry A. Schreier, from "Of Shoes, and Ships, and Sealing Wax: The Faulty and Specious Assumptions of Sexual Reorientation Therapies," *Journal of Mental Health Counseling* (October 1998)

ISSUE SUMMARY

YES: Warren Throckmorton, director of college counseling and an associate professor of psychology at Grove City College, maintains that efforts to assist homosexually oriented individuals to modify their patterns of sexual arousal have been effective and can be conducted in an ethical manner.

NO: Barry A. Schreier, coordinator of training and a psychologist at the Counseling and Psychological Services of Purdue University, counters that homosexuality is not an illness, so there is no need to treat it.

Perhaps no issue in psychology has provoked more intense debate in the surrounding popular culture than that of homosexuality. For nearly 30 years, the governing associations of psychology, psychiatry, and counseling have worked to remove the pathological label from the lifestyles of gay and lesbian individuals. Many professionals assume that empirical research has demonstrated the biological underpinnings of sexual orientation, so many psychologists portray homosexuality as a normal alternative lifestyle and attempt to fight homophobia. Some, however, view these efforts as politically motivated and threatening to traditional religious beliefs. Others resonate with psychology's support of homosexuality as an important protection of minority rights.

One facet of this culture war is the treatment of individuals who are dissatisfied with their sexual orientation. Reorientation, or conversion therapy, as it is sometimes called, was regularly practiced before the 1970s. However, many people currently feel that it is an unethical and unproven brand of treatment.

They argue that gay individuals can internalize society's pervasive homophobia and, thus, express the desire to leave the homosexual lifestyle. Others counter that no one should stand in the way of an individual's desire and that psychotherapists have an obligation to honor this desire. Of course, honoring the desire to change sexual orientation presumes that such change is possible, which is another issue in dispute.

In the following selection, Warren Throckmorton expresses discomfort with the American Counseling Association's (ACA) recent resolution against conversion therapy. He reviews the effectiveness and appropriateness of therapeutic efforts to change sexual orientation and finds several successful efforts to modify patterns of sexual arousal from multiple perspectives. Although he contends that the concept of sexual orientation has limited clinical use because it is not well defined, Throckmorton discusses the ethical obligations of psychotherapists to allow clients the choice of conversion therapy.

In the second selection, Barry A. Schreier asks why some therapists continue to insist, in the face of disconfirming scientific research, that homosexuality is an illness that needs to be cured. Schreier defends the concept of sexual orientation and states that studies supporting conversion therapy have been heavily criticized for their methodological flaws. In response to Throckmorton's ethical defense of conversion therapy, Schreier reviews the phenomenon of minority groups' struggling to accept their identities and illuminates ways in which Throckmorton's bias may underlie and skew his ethics.

POINT

- The issue of conversion therapy needs more examination before psychology's governing bodies reject them out of hand.
- The concept of sexual orientation is unclear and subjective, and it has not been tested in longitudinal research.
- Efforts to assist homosexually oriented individuals who wish to modify their patterns of sexual arousal have been shown to be empirically effective.
- Individuals who wish to modify their patterns of sexual arousal should be allowed the option of conversion therapy.

- Religious freedom may be denied if the freedom to choose conversion therapy is not affirmed.

COUNTERPOINT

- The American Psychological Association (APA) and the ACA have a long history of justified opposition to labeling homosexuality a pathology.
- Sexual orientation is a valid concept, descriptive of a natural and long-occurring characteristic.
- Research that seemingly demonstrates modified sexual orientation is methodologically flawed.

- Individuals who wish to modify their patterns of sexual arousal may have internalized society's prejudices and need help feeling validated in a minority identity.
- If conversion therapy is ineffective or damaging, then no religous freedom is denied.

YES

Warren Throckmorton

Efforts to Modify Sexual Orientation

In light of the American Counseling Association's (ACA) recent resolution expressing concerns about conversion therapy, this article reviews the effectiveness and appropriateness of therapeutic efforts to change sexual orientation. The concept of sexual orientation is briefly reviewed and found to be of limited clinical use. The article reviews successful efforts to modify patterns of sexual arousal from psychoanalytic, behavioral, cognitive, group, and religious perspectives. An ethical analysis of the ACA resolution is presented. The author concludes that efforts to assist homosexually oriented individuals who wish to modify their patterns of sexual arousal have been effective, can be conducted in an ethical manner, and should be available to those clients requesting such assistance.

Since 1972, the mental health professions have been assessing and reassessing the status of homosexuality in mental health. During the last three decades, homosexuality has been conceptualized as a disorder, a possible disorder in the case of the *DSM-III* [Diagnostic and Statistical Manual of Mental Disorders III] ego-dystonic homosexuality, and most recently, as neutral as it relates to the mental status of an individual (Rubinstein, 1995).

One impact of this openness to diverse sexual identities is the emergence of opposition to any form of counseling to modify or to attempt to change the sexual orientation of a client from homosexual to heterosexual. Davison (1976), Martin (1984), and Haldeman (1994) suggest that psychotherapeutic efforts to change sexual orientation are unethical. In 1997, after nearly 2 years of debate and study, the American Psychological Association (APA) passed a resolution expressing concern that clients may request conversion therapy due to "societal ignorance and prejudice about same gender sexual orientation" and "family or social coercion and/or lack of information" (APA, 1997; Sleek, 1997). In March 1998, the American Counseling Association (ACA) passed a similar resolution at its annual convention in Indianapolis (ACA, 1998).

The ACA resolution was proposed by the association's Human Rights Committee and the motion to accept was made by the representative of the Association for Gay, Lesbian, and Bisexual Issues in Counseling (AGLBIC). The resolution was titled, "On Appropriate Counseling Responses to Sexual

Orientation" and proposed to place the ACA in opposition to any form of conversion therapy. The proposed resolution originally read "be it further resolved that the American Counseling Association *opposes the use of so-called 'conversion or reparative' therapies in counseling individuals having a same gender sexual orientation;* opposes portrayals of lesbian, gay, and bisexual youth as mentally ill due to their sexual orientation; and supports the dissemination of accurate information about sexual orientation, mental health, and appropriate interventions in order to counteract bias that is based in ignorance or unfounded beliefs about same-gender sexual orientation." (ACA, 1998, p. 1–2). During debate over the resolution, the association's governing council deleted the phrase in italics above concerning opposition to conversion therapies (ACA, 1998). Thus, the ACA's opposition was maintained if the conversion therapy portrays "gay, lesbian or bisexual youth as mentally ill," or a counselor spreads inaccurate information or has "unfounded beliefs" about sexual orientation (ACA, 1998, p. 1–2).

As it stands, the resolution's impact is difficult to gauge. The resolution seems to discourage efforts to promote a shift from homosexual to heterosexual orientation but comes short of clear opposition. If passed as originally proposed, the resolution would have had enormous impact on practice. Mental health counselors would have been constrained to tell clients who want to modify their sexual arousal patterns that such an objective is faulty. Mental health counselors who believe homosexuality can be modified would be in danger of being charged with a violation of the ethics code. Even mental health counselors outside of the membership of ACA would be at risk, since most states adopt the ACA Code of Ethics in their counselor licensing statutes. Since most states automatically adopt subsequent revisions of that code, mental health counselors performing activities deemed unethical based on a reading of the code would be in danger of review by state licensing authorities.

This ACA resolution, along with a companion resolution supporting same-gender marriage, created immediate controversy (Lee, 1998). The association's Western Regional Assembly voted to request that the governing council rescind the motions and the Southern Regional Assembly requested the issue be reexamined (Gerst, 1998). Given the impact on counselors practicing conversion techniques and the controversy surrounding the issue, an examination of the major issues raised by the resolution is needed. The ACA resolution opposed conversion therapy on the grounds that such therapy is both ineffective and unethical. This article examines the effectiveness and ethicality of helping clients redirect their sexual orientation. First I examine the concept of sexual orientation, followed by a [brief] review of the literature concerning the modification of sexual orientation. Finally, I present an ethical analysis of the ACA resolution concerning conversion therapy. . . .

A Word About Sexual Orientation

Haldeman (1994) suggests that before questions of change in sexual orientation are considered, clinicians and researchers should examine "the complex nature of sexual orientation and its development in the individual" (p. 222).

I agree with this caution and submit that before opponents of conversion therapies attempt to eliminate sexual reorientation as an acceptable therapeutic goal, they must confront the same issue.

As Haldeman (1994) asserts, sexual orientation is not a well-defined concept. There are many suggestions in the literature concerning the proper method of defining sexual orientation. The point of departure for defining sexual orientation is often the work of Kinsey (Kinsey, Pomeroy, & Gebhard, 1948). Kinsey suggests that sexual orientation ranges along a continuum from exclusively homosexual (Kinsey rating "6") to exclusively heterosexual (Kinsey rating "0") (House & Miller, 1997). Gonsiorek, Sell, and Weinrich (1995) recommend assessing "same- and opposite-sex orientations separately, not as one continuous variable." (p. 47). They suggest treating each orientation as a continuous variable. For clinical purposes, such scales would be interesting but not terribly helpful to assess the impact of efforts to modify sexual orientation. Why? There are no norms or points along each continuum where clinicians may designate a given sexual orientation. Since researchers are mixed as to where on the continuum to declare a client truly gay or straight, how can counselors know if they are aiding clients to change from one sexual orientation to another?

Gonsiorek et al. (1995) note that the most common means of assessing sexual orientation is via self-report. However, they also note that "there are significant limitations to this method." (Gonsiorek et al., 1995, p. 44). The most obvious problem is the subjective nature of self-assessment. Being gay, lesbian, or bisexual means different things to different people. Some define their sexual orientation by their behavior or attractions or fantasies or some combination of each dimension. After summarizing the difficulties in defining sexual orientation, Gonsiorek et al. (1995) state, "Given such significant measurement problems, one could conclude there is serious doubt whether sexual orientation is a valid concept at all." (p. 46). Years earlier, Birk (1980) expressed a similar view saying "there is in fact no such unitary thing as 'homosexuality' . . . instead . . . there are many, many different homosexuals who collectively defy rigid characterization." (p. 376).

Concerning the potential for assessing change of orientation, Gonsiorek et al. (1995) note, "Perhaps the most dramatic limitation of current conceptualizations is change over time. There is essentially no research on the longitudinal stability of sexual orientation over the adult life span." (p. 46). If there is no research concerning change, how can professional associations be certain that sexual orientation cannot change? Thus, defining sexual orientation is a work in progress. Counselors ought to articulate to clients this lack of certainty in an unbiased manner.

In the absence of any sure way to define sexual orientation, assistance for questioning individuals should not be limited. Even if one accepts the presumption that sexual orientation cannot be changed, how does one know when a client's sexual orientation is settled? Without a more certain way to objectively determine sexual orientation, perhaps we should place considerable weight on the self-assessment of clients. Clients who want to change cannot reliably be told that they cannot change, since we cannot say with certainty that they have settled on a fixed trait. If any conclusions can be drawn from the literature, it is that change in sexual orientation is possible. For instance, in their review of the literature on once-married lesbians, Bridges and Croteau (1994) found that 25% to 50% of lesbians in various reports had once been in heterosexual marriages. While heterosexual marriage alone may not be a complete gauge of sexual orientation, the reasons for the marriage should offer some insight into the sexual identity of the women at the time. Kirkpatrick (1988) reports that once-married lesbian women often married because they were in love with their husbands. In examining the reasons for the shift in sexual expression, Charbonneau and Lander (1991) find two broad explanations. One group felt they had always been lesbian and were becoming true to themselves. However, another group viewed their change as a choice among sexual options. If counselors are not to assist clients in their wishes for a shift in sexual orientation, how would ACA's governing council wish for counselors to respond to such women wanting to become more settled in their choice of a lesbian identity?

More practically, I do not know with certainty if I have ever been successful in "changing" a person's sexual orientation, since I do not know how to precisely define sexual orientation or if it is even a valid clinical concept. However, I have assisted clients who were, in the beginning of mental health counseling, primarily attracted to those of the same gender but who declare they are now primarily attracted to the opposite gender. I fear that resolutions such as passed by APA and ACA will prevent such outcomes, which are viewed quite positively by the clients who have experienced them.

Efforts to Modify Sexual Orientation

Broadly, opponents of shifting sexual orientation as a therapeutic goal express doubts that sexual orientation can be changed by any means. From a gay-affirming perspective, Martin (1984) and Haldeman (1994) review studies that claimed to demonstrate change in sexual orientation. Their view is that there were no empirical studies that supported the idea that conversion therapy can change sexual orientation. However, they omitted a number of significant reports and failed to examine the outcomes of many studies that have demonstrated change.

Narrowly, the question to be addressed is: Do conversion therapy techniques work to change unwanted sexual arousal? . . . The available evidence supports the observation of many counselors—that many individuals with a same-gender sexual orientation have been able to change through a variety of counseling approaches. [Some of this evidence will be briefly addressed below, with references to additional research included.]

> *[The following text summarizes a lengthy section of the original article that is not included here—Ed.]*
>
> *Psychoanalytic approaches report rates of change to exclusive heterosexuality ranging from 18% to 44% of clients. (Bieber et al., 1962; Hatterer, 1970; Socarides, 1979; MacIntosh, 1994; Nicolosi, 1991, 1993). Rates for less dramatic shifts in sexual orientation are even higher in some of the reports. None*

of the reports document negative side effects of such efforts and, indeed, seem to show positive results for a significant number of participants, even those who do not change sexual orientation. Nicolosi, Byrd, and Potts (1998) report the results of a national survey of 882 clients engaged in sexual reorientation therapy. At the beginning of therapy, 318 of the sample rated themselves as having an exclusive same-gender sexual orientation. Posttreatment, 18% of the 318 rated themselves exclusively heterosexual, 17% rated themselves as "almost entirely heterosexual" and 12% viewed themselves as more heterosexual than gay or lesbian. Of the entire 882, only 13% remained either exclusively or almost exclusively gay or lesbian after treatment. Countering claims that reorientation therapies are harmful, the survey also asked clients concerning psychological and interpersonal adjustments both before and after therapy. The survey respondents reported significant improvements in such areas as self-acceptance, personal power, self-esteem, emotional stability, depression, and spirituality (Nicolosi et al., 1998).

Behavioral approaches to the modification of sexual orientation progressed from a reliance on aversive approaches to the use of sophisticated multimodal approaches which attempt to extinguish same-gender attraction and then provide a variety of behavioral and supportive counseling techniques to facilitate heterosexual responsiveness. (Greenspoon & Lamal, 1987; Tarlow, 1989; Barlow & Durand, 1995). Generally, the cases reported in the behavioral counseling literature support the efficacy of efforts to modify sexual orientation. (McCrady, 1973; Barlow and Agras, 1973, Phillips, Fischer, Groves & Singh, 1976)

Birk (1980) reports probably the highest success rates of any therapist. Using a combination of behavioral group and individual counseling, he reports that 100% of exclusively gay men beginning therapy with the intent to change sexual arousal were able to attain a heterosexual adaptation. Contrary to Haldeman's supposition that the men in Birk's treatment group may have had "preexisting heteroerotic tendencies" (Haldeman, 1994, p. 223), one of Birk's criteria for inclusion in this analysis is that these clients had not experienced heterosexual intercourse (Birk, 1980). Birk points to pretreatment motivation as a major key in understanding the results. Of these 14 clients who had shifted, 10 of the 14 (71%) were satisfactorily married at follow-up.

Albert Ellis, founder of Rational-Emotive Behavior Therapy (REBT), wrote in 1992 that people are free to "try a particular sexual pathway, such as homosexuality, for a time and then decide to practically abandon it for another mode, such as heterosexuality" (Ellis, 1992, p. 34). While not believing that same-gender sexual orientation is a sign of inherent emotional disturbance, Ellis recently evidenced his belief that client options should not be abridged by joining the Committee of Concerned Psychologists (CCP) (CCP, 1995). When the APA first considered a resolution to discourage the use of conversion therapies in 1995, an ad hoc group of psychologists opposed the motion. Ellis was one of more than 40 psychologists who signed a letter which urged the rejection of the motion and branded it as "illegal, unethical, unscientific, and totalitarian" (CCP, 1995, p. 4).

Finally, a number of clients report change through religiously based interventions in groups such as OneByOne, Exodus International, and Transformation Ministries. While, as Haldeman (1994) documents, it is true that some ex-gays have become ex-ex-gays, the stories and research reports of individuals changing through religious interventions should not be minimized (see Pattison and Pattison 1980; Davies & Rentzel, 1994; Saia, 1988).

Ethical Principles and Conversion Therapies: Another Look

The psychological literature seems unclear about the ethics of conversion therapy. While Haldeman (1994) portrays such therapies as unethical, Garnets, Hancock, Cochran, Goodchilds, and Peplau, (1991) in the *American Psychologist* specify "biased, inadequate and inappropriate practice" and "exemplary practice" when clients present with sexual orientation issues. As an example of an exemplary response, Garnets et al. (1991) include this theme: "A therapist does not attempt to change the sexual orientation of the client without strong evidence that this is the appropriate course of action and that change is desired by the client" (p. 968). They presented as an exemplar of this theme the following comments by a survey respondent, "I had a male client who expressed a strong desire to 'go straight.' After a careful psychological assessment, his wish to become heterosexual seemed to be clearly indicated and I assisted him in that process" (Garnets et al., 1991, p. 968). This course is at odds with the proposed APA and ACA resolutions, which originally sought to deem conversion therapy unethical and therefore clinically inappropriate.

The ACA resolution begins by affirming ten principles concerning treatments to alter sexual orientation. The first is that homosexuality is not a mental disorder. While some writers who practice reparative therapy believe homosexuality is a developmental deficit (Nicolosi, 1991), it does not seem necessary to believe homosexuality is a disorder in order to offer counseling to modify sexual feelings. In fact, counseling as a profession has traditionally held that one does not need to have a disorder in order to profit from counseling. Thus, if a client requested such counseling, offering it would not require the counselor to view the client as mentally ill.

Even if one asserts that offering a mode of treatment implies a disorder, there is a condition in the *DSM-IV* that would be the proper object of conversion therapies—Sexual Disorder, Not Otherwise Specified (NOS) (American Psychiatric Association, 1994). Though the diagnosis of ego-dystonic homosexuality was removed from the *DSM-III*, Sexual Disorder, NOS remains in the *DSM-IV* with several descriptors, one of which is "persistent and marked distress about sexual orientation" (American Psychiatric Association, 1994, p. 538). Certainly, many individuals who seek conversion therapy could be described in this manner.

The second principle is that counselors should not discriminate against clients due to their sexual orientation. Contrary to this principle, banning efforts to modify sexual orientation would require the ACA to discriminate against those clients who want to change.

The third principle is that counselors will "actively attempt to understand the diverse cultural backgrounds of the clients with whom they work" (ACA, 1998). Nothing in conversion therapy negates this principle. Those requesting conversion therapy often do so because of a conflict between their homosexual feelings and the culture with which they identify. When such conflicts occur, what makes one set of loyalties more important than another set? If professional associations discredit efforts to modify sexual orientation, they may be implying that sexual arousal is more vital than any conflicting personality variables or moral convictions. The prohibition desired by proponents of the ACA resolution is an absolute one. A client's moral objection to same-gender attraction is not acknowledged by efforts to prohibit conversion approaches. On this point, I believe mental health counselors who practice conversion therapy do attempt to understand the cultural background of a client who presents in deep conflict over sexual impulses and deeply held moral convictions.

Principle four requires the counselor to inform clients concerning the "purposes, goals, techniques, procedures, limitations and potential risks and benefits of services to be performed." Nothing in this principle prohibits conversion therapy. As the above review of the literature demonstrates, it would be a violation of this point to say that there is no empirical evidence of efficacy of various conversion therapies.

The fifth principle states that "clients have the right to refuse any recommended service and be advised of the consequences of such refusal." The consensus of those finding success in shifting sexual orientation is that client's desire to change is necessary to be successful. This is true of nearly all mental health treatments.

The sixth principle supports the availability of conversion therapies. The resolution quotes the ACA Code of Ethics, section A.3.b, which states that counselors "offer clients freedom to choose whether to enter into a counseling relationship" (ACA, 1998). It is my experience that clients ask for assistance with unwanted homosexual feelings. Clients should have the freedom to choose the approaches that help them meet their goals.

The seventh principle states "when counseling minors or persons unable to give voluntary informed consent, counselors act in these clients' best interests" (ACA, 1998). Mental health counselors engaging in counseling to modify sexual orientation have a duty to act in the client's best interests whether a minor or an adult. Since it has not been shown that such counseling is intrinsically harmful, assisting a minor client who wishes to engage in such counseling does not violate this principle. When a parent's and child's counseling objectives differ, achieving a working alliance with the family requires skill in conflict resolution and family interventions no matter what kind of problem is presented.

In the eighth principle, counselors are reminded to be "aware of their own values, attitudes, beliefs, and behaviors and these apply in a diverse society and avoid imposing their values on clients" (ACA, 1998). Apparently, this point assumes that the availability of conversion therapy is an imposition of values on clients everywhere. What does the opposition to conversion therapy say? To conflicted clients who want to explore the possibility of change to a hetero sexual orientation, it means that their wish is diminished, not to be taken seriously. For individuals who are morally opposed to homosexuality as a lifestyle, it means that the professions have denigrated their moral convictions. For individuals who have successfully changed, who now are heterosexual, it means that the professions have criticized their accomplishments. The existence of conversion therapy for people who want it does not require the conversion therapist to force it on someone who does not. The most appropriate response when the client's goals and the mental health counselor's skills do not match is to refer to another mental health counselor.

The ninth principle, related to the above point, is the statement from the ACA Code of Ethics (section A.6.a) that counselors "are aware of their influential positions with respect to clients, and they avoid exploiting the trust and dependency of clients." The counseling profession has been oblivious to a double standard concerning sexual orientation and religious conviction. While the ACA has opposed the modification or questioning of an individual's homosexual feelings, there has been no movement to avoid the disruption of an individual's religious convictions. For instance, Barret and Barzan (1996), in their article concerning spirituality and the gay experience, suggest that "assisting gay men and lesbians to step away from external religious authority may challenge the counselor's own acceptance of religious teachings" (p. 8). According to Barret and Barzan (1996), "most counselors will benefit from a model that helps them understand the difference between spiritual and religious authority" (p. 8). . . .

The last principle requires counselors to "report research accurately and in a manner that minimizes the possibility that results will be misleading." As noted above, evidence exists for the efficacy of conversion therapies. However, these findings have not been consistently reported in the counseling and psychological literature over the last two decades. A search of the *Journal of Mental Health Counseling, Journal of Counseling and Development, Counseling and Values* and the *Journal of Multicultural Counseling and Development* reveals no articles on conversion therapy. All articles concerning homosexuality espouse the gay-affirming approach to therapy. I think the information given in this article, previously unreported in counseling journals, should be widely distributed to address the issue raised in the tenth principle of the ACA resolution. . . .

Discussion

The purpose of this review is to demonstrate that therapeutic efforts to help clients modify patterns of sexual arousal have been successful and should be available to clients wishing such assistance. I believe the available literature leaves no doubt that some degree of change is possible for some clients who wish to pursue it. The literature on therapeutic assistance for unwanted same-gender sexual arousal suddenly came to a near halt in the early 1970s, but clients wishing assistance did not cease to come to counseling. I personally have experience with clients who have wanted assistance to change their pattern of sexual arousal and due to their reports believe such change is possible.

Sexual orientation as a concept has limited clinical utility. Since the categorization of sexual orientation is somewhat arbitrary, I submit it is inappropriate to tell a client that it cannot be changed or modified. Bell and Weinberg (1978) in their large study of homosexuality in the San Francisco area, define a homosexual as anyone with a Kinsey rating of four or higher. In the literature cited above, rates of change for individuals with Kinsey ratings of 4 and 5 were in the 57% to 78% range (Feldman, MacCulloch, & Orford,

1971; Hatterer, 1970; Mayerson & Lief, 1965). Thus, defined in the manner of the Bell and Weinberg study, an impressive majority of clients were able to change sexual orientation. Whether one can say that sexual orientation is being changed depends on how narrowly one defines sexual orientation or if it can be defined at all.

Proposed Guidelines

So what should mental health counselors do when confronted with clients who request sexual reorientation? I propose the following guidelines.

1. Neither gay-affirmative nor conversion therapy should be assumed to be the preferred approach. Generally, gay-affirmative therapy or referral to such a practitioner should be offered to those clients who want to become more satisfied with a same-gender sexual orientation. Conversion therapy or referral should be offered to clients who decide they want to modify or overcome same-gender patterns of sexual arousal. Assessment should be conducted to help clarify the strength and persistence of the client's wishes.
2. For those clients who are in distress concerning their sexual orientation and are undecided concerning reorientation, mental health counselors should not assume what approach is best. They should inform clients that many mental health professionals believe same-gender sexual orientation cannot be changed but that others believe change is possible. Clients should be informed that some mental health professionals and researchers dispute the concept of an immutable sexual orientation. Mental health counselors should explain that not all clients who participate in gay-affirming therapy are able to find satisfaction in a gay adjustment nor are all clients who seek sexual reorientation successful. When clients cannot decide which therapeutic course to pursue, mental health counselors can suggest that clients choose consistent with their values, personal convictions, and/or religious beliefs (Nicolosi et al., 1998).
3. Since religion is one of the client attributes that mental health counselors are ethically bound to respect, counselors should take great care in advising those clients dissatisfied with same-gender sexual orientation due to their religious beliefs. To accommodate such clients, counselors should develop expertise in methods of sexual reorientation or develop appropriate referral resources.

Finally, mental health counselors have an obligation to respect the dignity and wishes of all clients. ACA and other mental health associations should not attempt to limit the choices of gays and lesbians who want to change.

References

American Counseling Association. (1998, March). *On appropriate counseling responses to sexual orientation.* Adopted by the American Counseling Association Governing Council, March 27, 1998.

American Psychiatric Association. (1994). *Diagnostic and statistical manual of mental disorders* (4th ed.). Washington, DC: Author.

American Psychological Association. (1997, August). *Resolution on appropriate therapeutic responses to sexual orientation.* Adopted by the American Psychological Association Council of Representatives, August 14, 1997.

Barlow, D., & Agras, W. S. (1973). Fading to increase heterosexual responsiveness in homosexuals. *Journal of Applied Behavior Analysis, 6,* 355–366.

Barlow, D., & Durand, V. M. (1995). *Abnormal psychology: An integrative approach.* New York: Brooks/Cole Publishing.

Barret, R., & Barzan, R. (1996). Spiritual experiences of gay men and lesbians. *Counseling and Values, 41,* 4–15.

Bell, A. P., & Weinberg, M. S. (1978). *Homosexualities: A study of diversity among men and women.* New York: Simon & Schuster.

Bieber, I., Dain, H. J., Dince, P. R., Drellich, M. G., Grand, H. G., Gundlach, R. H., Kremer, M. W., Rifkin, A. H., Wilbur, C. B., & Bieber, T. B. (1962). *Homosexuality.* New York: Basic Books.

Birk, L. (1980). The myth of classical homosexuality: Views of a behavioral psychotherapist. In J. Marmor (Ed.), *Homosexual Behavior* (pp. 376–390). New York: Basic Books.

Bridges, K. L., & Croteau, J. M. (1994). Once-married lesbians: Facilitating changing life patterns. *Journal of Counseling and Development, 73,* 134–140.

Charbonneau, C., & Lander, P. S. (1991). Redefining sexuality: Women becoming lesbian in mid-life. In B. Sang, J. Warshow, & A. J. Smith (Eds.), *Lesbians at midlife: The creative transition* (pp. 35–43). San Francisco, CA: Spinsters Book Co.

Committee of Concerned Psychologists. (1995). Letter to the American Psychological Association Council of Representatives. Quoted in *North Bulletin, 3*(2), 4–5.

Davies, B., & Rentzel, L. (1994). *Coming out of homosexuality.* Downers Grove, IL: InterVarsity Press.

Davison, G. C. (1976). Homosexuality: The ethical challenge. *Journal of Consulting and Clinical Psychology, 44,* 157–162.

Ellis, A. (1992, September/October). Are gays and lesbians emotionally disturbed? *The Humanist,* 33–35.

Feldman, M. P., MacCulloch, M. J., & Orford, J. F. (1971). Conclusions and speculations. In M. P. Feldman & M. J. MacCulloch, *Homosexual behaviour: Therapy and assessment* (pp. 156–188), New York: Pergamon Press.

Garnets, L., Hancock, K., Cochran, S., Goodchilds, J., & Peplau, L. (1991). Issues in psychotherapy with lesbians and gay men. *American Psychologist, 46,* 964–972.

Gerst, R. (1998, May). Letter to the editor. *Counseling Today,* 4.

Gold, S., & Neufeld, I. L. (1965). A learning approach to the treatment of homosexuality. *Behavior Research and Therapy, 2,* 201–204.

Gonsiorek, J. C., Sell, R. L., & Weinrich, J. D. (1995). Definition and measurement of sexual orientation. *Suicide and Life Threatening Behavior, 25*(Supplement), 40–51.

Greenspoon, J., & Lamal, P. (1987). A behavioristic approach. In L. Diamant (Ed.), *Male and female homosexuality: Psychological approaches.* (pp. 109–127). New York: Hemisphere Publishing.

Haldeman, D. (1994). The practice and ethics of sexual orientation conversion therapy. *Journal of Consulting and Clinical Psychology, 62,* 221–227.

Hatterer, L. (1970). *Changing homosexuality in the male.* New York: McGraw-Hill.

House, R. M., & Miller, J. L. (1997). Counseling gay, lesbian and bisexual clients. In D. Capuzzi & D. Gross (Eds.), *Introduction to the counseling profession* (2nd ed.) (pp. 397–432). Boston, MA: Allyn & Bacon.

Kinsey, A., Pomeroy, W. B., & Gebhard, P. H. (1948). *Sexual behavior in the human male.* Philadelphia: Saunders.

Kirkpatrick, M. (1988). Clinical implications of lesbian mother studies. In E. Coleman (Ed.). *Integrated identity for gay men and lesbians: Psychotherapeutic approaches for emotional well-being* (pp. 201–211). New York: Harrington Park Press.

Lee, C. (1998, May). Promoting a healthy dialogue. *Counseling Today, 5.*

McCrady, R. (1973). A forward-fading technique for increasing heterosexual responsiveness in male homosexuals. *Journal of Behavioral Therapy and Experimental Psychiatry, 4,* 257–261.

MacIntosh, H. (1994). Attitudes and experiences of psychoanalysts in analyzing homosexual patients. *Journal of the American Psychoanalytic Association, 42,* 1183–1206.

Martin, A. D. (1984). The emperor's new clothes: Modern attempts to change sexual orientation. In E. S. Hetrick & T. S. Stein (Eds.), *Psychotherapy with homosexuals* (pp. 59–74). Washington, DC: American Psychiatric Association.

Mayerson, P., & Lief, H. I. (1965). Psychotherapy of homosexuals: A follow-up study of nineteen cases. In J. Marmor (Ed.), *Sexual inversion* (pp. 302–344). New York: Basic Books.

Nicolosi, J. (1991). *Reparative therapy of male homosexuality.* Northvale, NJ: Jason Aronson.

Nicolosi, J. (1993). *Healing homosexuality.* Northvale, NJ: Jason Aronson.

Nicolosi, J., Byrd, A. D., & Potts, R. W. (1998). *Towards the ethical and effective treatment of homosexuality.* Unpublished manuscript.

Pattison, E. M., & Pattison, M. L. (1980). "Ex-gays": Religiously mediated change in homosexuals. *American Journal of Psychiatry, 137,* 1553–1562.

Phillips, D., Fischer, S. C., Groves, G. A., & Singh, R. (1976). Alternative behavioral approaches to the treatment of homosexuality. *Archives of Sexual Behavior, 5,* 223–228.

Rubinstein, G. (1995). The decision to remove homosexuality from the DSM: Twenty years later. *American Journal of Psychotherapy, 49,* 416–427.

Saia, M. R. (1988). *Counseling the homosexual.* Minneapolis, MN: Bethany House Publishers.

Sleek, S. (1997, October). Resolution raises concerns about conversion therapy. *Monitor,* 16.

Socarides, C. (1979). The psychoanalytic theory of homosexuality: With special reference to therapy. In I. Rosen (Ed.), *Sexual deviation* (2nd ed.) (pp. 243–277). New York: Oxford University Press.

Tarlow, G. (1989). *Clinical handbook of behavior therapy: Adult psychological disorders.* Brookline, MA: Brookline Books, Inc.

Barry A. Schreier

 **NO**

Of Shoes, and Ships, and Sealing Wax

Warren Throckmorton's assumption in his article "Efforts to Modify Sexual Orientation: A Review of Outcome Literature and Ethical Issues" is that there is pathology inherent in same-sex orientations, and thus there is treatment for it. Throckmorton makes the proposal that since there is viability to this type of treatment, The American Counseling Association's (ACA) resolution "On Appropriate Counseling Responses to Sexual Orientation" (ACA, 1998) is a restriction of trade and service. This paper presents a counter position on Throckmorton's article and demonstrates why organizations such as ACA and the American Psychological Association (APA) are correctly declaring these "reorientation therapies" unethical practice. It is ethically questionable to practice treatments that are not based in empirical methodologies, that cause harm, that are based on faulty and specious assumptions, and that incorporate societal prejudice.

No Illness, No Cure

In 1998, the American Psychological Association reiterated the "long-standing official position that homosexuality and bisexuality are not mental disorders" (APA, 1998). Dr. Bryant Welch, APA's Executive Director for Professional Practice, stated, "no scientific evidence exists to support the effectiveness of any of the conversion therapies that try to change one's sexual orientation" and that "research findings suggest that efforts to 'repair' homosexuals are nothing more than social prejudice garbed in psychological accouterments" (Welch, 1990; see also Buie, 1990). The American Counseling Association's recent resolution puts ACA ethically on par with APA as well as other national health organizations including the American Psychiatric Association (1973). Even the 101st United States Congress did not include homosexuality into the Americans With Disabilities Act as it does not constitute an illness and thus cannot constitute a disability (Morin & Rothblum, 1991).

All of these organizations have adopted these policies affirming the inherent worth, dignity, and validity of same-sex orientations. These organizations

From Barry A. Schreier, "Of Shoes, and Ships, and Sealing Wax: The Faulty and Specious Assumptions of Sexual Reorientation Therapies," *Journal of Mental Health Counseling*, vol. 20 (October 1998). Copyright © 1998 by *Journal of Mental Health Counseling*. Reprinted by permission of The American Mental Health Counselors Association.

have made this move because of the lack of conclusive empirical evidence supporting that same-sex orientations are any more or less mentally and physically healthy than a heterosexual orientation (Schüklenk & Ristow, 1996). In fact, the research literature has so extensively supported the nonpathological nature of same-sex orientations that the aforementioned organizations could do nothing but declassify them (Gonsiorek, 1991). And yet, some continue to insist that same-sex orientations are something of a "less than" nature and claim that if they are not desired, they can be eliminated. Hobo personality disorder was part of *Diagnostic and Statistical Manual of Mental Disorders* (American Psychiatric Association, 1952). Although it is no longer a recognized diagnosis, there do not remain advocates who are forming national associations of research and therapy for people with hobo personality disorder. Homosexuality is also no longer a diagnosis and has not been for almost 30 years (with each year bringing a further resolve and stronger evidence that it is not pathological). Yet, there continue to be those who advocate for its cure. Richard Socarides stated that "almost half of those who engage in homosexual practices have a concomitant schizophrenia, paranoia, or latent pseudoneurotic schizophrenia" (Bayer, 1987). A tremendous statement to make in light of the empirical evidence countering this and the official positions of APA and ACA.

The primary goal in responding to Throckmorton's article is to explain the logical fallacies that serve as the ground work for Throckmorton's claims. Since many of the claims are laid on untruths, the claims themselves are untruths. For instance, reorientation necessarily assumes a bipolarity in sexual orientation. This is an antiquated view of sexual orientation (Leck, 1994; Schreier, 1998; Suppe, 1985) dating back before the 1940s. Even the original American work in this area by Kinsey, Pomeroy, and Martin (1948) found that sexual orientation fell across a continuum. Sexual reorientation therapies are based on a limited understanding of sexual orientation and one that assumes a reductionistic bipolarity; one is either exclusively same-sex oriented or opposite-sex oriented.

Faulty Assumptions of Reorientation Therapy

A primary assumption Throckmorton makes is that sexual orientation is a behavioral act. Claiming that reorientation can occur by behaviorally modifying sexual arousal, as Throckmorton does, is negligent of the plethora of evidence which connotes the multimodality of sexual orientation. Sexual orientation is inclusive of behavior, cognitions, fantasy, and emotions (Golden, 1987; Isay, 1985). Even at the basic definitional level, the APA *Publication Manual* (APA, 1994) states the following, "Sexual behavior should be distinguished from sexual orientation" (p. 51). Throckmorton's behavioral definition of sexual reorientation presents a limited understanding of sexual orientation. Gonsiorek, Sell, and Weinrich (1995) define sexual orientation as an "erotic and/or affectional disposition to the same or opposite sex" (p. 41). Troiden (1989) claims a developmental model approach to defining sexual orientation. Troiden also defines a multidimensional approach that includes sexual orientation as an identity. Rothblum (1994) calls for clearer definition by the scientific community for sexual orientation and makes this call to provide more affirming mental health services for people working with sexual orientation. Throckmorton does not address this body of literature.

A further assumption Throckmorton makes is that sexual orientation may not be a valid clinical concept. Same-sex orientation is a valid concept descriptive of a naturally and long-occurring phenomenon (Ford & Beach, 1951; Gonsiorek et al., 1995; Shively & DeCecco, 1977; Stein & Cohen, 1986). If Throckmorton validly uses the word *reorientation* to denote the therapy, then Throckmorton must necessarily assume the validity of the concept of sexual orientation. How can reorientation occur if orientation is not a valid concept? To support the point that sexual orientation is not a valid concept, however, Throckmorton quotes Gonsiorek et al. (1995) where they state that due to measurement problems there is doubt whether sexual orientation is a valid concept. If one reads the actual article, it is clear that Throckmorton has taken this quote out of context. The rest of the paragraph in which the quote is found discusses social constructionist and essentialism perspectives and then concludes that regardless of this debate, a predominate number of people adhere to self-definitions that clearly and distinctly conceptualize sexual orientation. Gonsiorek et al. also goes on to make the point that "there has been an increase recently in 'disinformation' about sexual orientation in the service of some political agendas, which specifically distorts measurement and definition of sexual orientation" (p. 40). This is a more accurate portrayal of the position of Gonsiorek et al. than the out-of-context quote misused by Throckmorton. Throckmorton is again negligent of the body of literature that describes the multimodality of sexual orientation. A further questioning of the validity of sexual orientation as a phenomenon has become an exercise in polemics and not a discussion of science.

The spirit of Throckmorton's argument about sexual orientation posits it as something that only people who are gay and lesbian have. The author does not discuss what heterosexuals have. It is assumed that heterosexuals have a sexual orientation, otherwise, heterosexuality too would be made as meaningless as Throckmorton has attempted to do with same-sex orientations. If heterosexuality is an orientation, is it not as "variable and unfixed" as he proposes heterosexuality to be? It would be curious to note if the author simply considers heterosexuality above discussion as a target of reorientation therapies. Throckmorton demonstrates bias by also not advocating for reorientation therapy for people who are heterosexual and are not satisfied. Throckmorton is critical about an article by Wolpe (1973) where Wolpe chose to offer religious reorientation rather than sexual reorientation. If sexual orientation is variable and fluid, is not religion as well? We know for sure that religion is a choice. Perhaps instead of sexual reorientation, individuals could seek religious reorientation to any number of major U.S. religions that are affirming of people with same-sex orientations (e.g., American Baptist Churches, Disciples of Christ, Episcopal Church, Metropolitan Community Churches, Presbyterian Church, U.S.A., Reform Judaism, Society of Friends, Unitarian Universalist Church). Not all religions are judgmental and condemning. Advocating for sexual reorientation while being critical of religious reorientation again demonstrates nothing more than bias.

Another assumption Throckmorton makes is that numerous successful reorientations are documented in the literature. Unfortunately, these outcomes, too, are erroneously based. The author uses several studies to denote the efficacy of reorientation therapies by denoting percentages of clients who have had reorientation therapy and have "successfully and happily" changed. Articles supporting this position are rife with methodological problems that limit their generalizability and call into question their outcomes (Bieber et al., 1962; Birk, 1980; Cautela, 1967; Feldman & MacCulloch, 1965; Hadden, 1966; McConaghy, 1976; Mayerson & Lief, 1965; Mintz, 1966; and others). It is space consuming to reiterate again what many other authors have already discovered about the research supportive of reorientation therapies. As a result, the limits of this paper do not allow the space needed to delineate the problematic methodologies, participant selection criteria, statistical analyses, and outcome measures. For a detailed explanation of this, however, see Haldeman (1994); Herek (1998); Martin (1984); and Morin (1977).

Throckmorton also denotes religious-based studies demonstrating exceptional success in reorientation. Again, there are no empirical bases for these claims and many of the practices are fraught with unethical behavior, sexual abuse, deception, theological malpractice, and other highly questionable activities (see Blair, 1982; Haldeman, 1994; Lawson, 1987). Despite clear evidence time and time again that these studies are "bad science" or no science at all, Throckmorton and others continue to make use of these same studies as conclusive proof of the efficacy of reorientation studies.

A further faulty assumption is that there is only a single psychoanalytic interpretation of homosexuality. There are numerous interpretations of psychoanalytic thought some of which view same-sex orientations as healthy variations in human sexuality. Throckmorton relies on works of Nicolosi (1991; 1993) and Socarides (1979). These two authors base their work on a unitary belief in the pathology of the gay "lifestyle" (again a reductionistic term where in reality there are as many lifestyle variations as there are people with same-sex orientations). A broad review of the psychoanalytic literature reveals a rainbow of interpretations that homosexuality is a regular occurring variation in the spectrum of human sexuality. Nicolosi's National Association for Research and Therapy of Homosexuality presents a majority of work based largely on methodological ambiguities and questionable results (Haldeman, 1991) that are not supported by any empirical evidence (Edwards, 1996) nor published in refereed journals. Their theoretical suppositions are easy to make and impossible to disprove because of their tautological nature. It would be just as easy to use their interpretation of psychoanalytic theory to state that those who advocate for reorientation therapies are latent homosexuals. And because of this latency and inadequate ego strength, they must sublimate and reaction from their own same-sex orientation into advocacy for reorientation therapies. Theorists like Nicolosi ignore the lack of empirical support for their illness model and ignore the wide breadth of literature that consistently validates the nonpathological view of same-sex orientations (Haldeman, 1994; Gonsiorek, 1991). Ferguson (1994) and Isay (1985) state that many psychoanalysts are simply biased toward homosexuality and guide their analyses via their personally held value systems. These psychoanalysts appear unable to factor out their own values. Their value bias aids their claims of success in reorientation therapy because of their countertransferences that prey on the "transference manifestation of wanting to be loved, the need to acquiesce, and the patient's passive longings" (p. 248). Even Freud noted that homosexuality cannot be classified as an illness (Freud, 1950). Furthermore, Freud noted that "to undertake to convert a fully developed homosexual into a heterosexual does not offer much more prospect of success than the reverse, except that for good practical reasons the latter is never attempted" (Freud, 1955, p. 151). Despite these admonitions from the founder of psychoanalysis, this minority of practitioners maintain their biases.

An additional faulty assumption of these psychoanalysts is that people with same-sex orientations need help because of their inability to have successful intimate relationships. The assumption that problematic intimate relationships are a marker for the need for reorientation is faulty. These types of problems are no more true for people with same sex-orientations than they are for heterosexuals. Throckmorton uses Nicolosi (1991) as proof of this argument. In his 1991 work, Nicolosi states that "researchers were unable to find a single male couple that was able to maintain sexual fidelity for more than five years" (p. 111). Nicolosi uses this statement to denote the inability for people with same-sex orientations to have fulfilling or lasting relationships due to the regressed and fixated nature of this sexual orientation. Simple logic informs us that heterosexual people are responsible for 100% of all divorces. Heterosexuals have also experienced divorce rates as high as 50% rate across heterosexual relationships (Peck, 1993). One only has to watch something such as TV's Jerry Springer Show to see heterosexuality continually and consistently displayed as a failed experiment. Throckmorton does not mention any inherent problems with heterosexuality in terms of relationship difficulties. It is a specious argument that when people with same-sex orientations have problems it is due to their sexual orientation. On the other hand, reorientationists indicate that when heterosexuals have problems it is due to something else. Weiss reported that many homosexuals "did not reveal unrealistic, immature traits or neurotic symptoms, whereas many heterosexuals did" (Panel, 1960, p. 560). Empirical evidence has existed since Evelyn Hooker's landmark study in 1957 that there are few discernible differences between the mental and physical health of people who are homosexual or heterosexual (see a replication of Hooker, 1957 in Freedman, 1971; also see Hart et al., 1978; Hopkins, 1969; Morin & Rothblum, 1991; Reiss, 1980; Ross, Paulsen, & Salstrom, 1988; Thompson, McCandless, & Strickland, 1971).

A final faulty assumption is that these practitioners continue their work without the idea that their treatment can caused harm—a dangerous ethical precipice for any practitioner to stand on! Throckmorton makes the statement that "Since it has not been shown that such counseling is intrinsically harmful" (p. 297). There is empirically based evidence that reorientation therapies have caused harm. Throckmorton makes his statement with no empirical support and again demonstrates the myopic view inherent in bias. Liddle (1996) surveyed 392 lesbians and gay men who reported on 923 therapy experiences.

In an additional analyses, Liddle found that of these 923 therapists, only a small minority ($n = 64$) discounted, argued against, or pushed their clients to renounce their same-sex orientations. When clients reported this behavior, 58% reported that that particular therapist was "destructive" and 22% reported the therapist was "not at all helpful"—a powerful indictment of both the futility and potential harm of reorientation therapies. Isay (1985) noted that reorientation therapy can cause symptomatic depression and social problems later in life by contributing to an already damaged self-esteem. Sleek (1997), quoting Linda Garnets, Ph.D., Chair of APA's Board for the Advancement of Psychology in the Public Interest, states that reorientation therapies "feed upon society's prejudice towards gays and may exacerbate a client's problems with poor self-esteem, shame, and guilt." Haldeman (1994) noted that religious-based programs are "possibly exacerbating the harm to naive, shame-ridden counselees" (p. 224). Throckmorton notes, but then discounts, the ever-burgeoning "Ex-Ex-Gay Movement." This movement strongly demonstrates that people are feeling harmed by the activities of reorientationists.

Furthermore, Throckmorton does not make note in any way of the minority identity development literature (Helms, 1995; Pederson, 1988; Sue, Arredondo, & McDavis, 1992). This literature alerts mental health practitioners to this vital point: the typical period of self-loathing that occurs as individuals try to come to terms emotionally and cognitively with their minority status in a context that does not necessarily value them (Coleman, Butcher, & Carson, 1984). This is a time when social prejudice can easily become internalized (Cass, 1979; Myers et al., 1991). Working with clients to continue the internalization of this injurious and biased process is contrary to the ethical practices of counselors and psychologists (ACA, 1998; APA, 1998). Herr and Cramer (1988) state that counselors must work with client groups to reduce the "stereotypes, discrimination, and environmental barriers that impeded the development of such groups" (p. 154). By ignoring this body of research, reorientation counselors can easily engage in harmful practices with clients. They do so by colluding with them in accepting prejudicially based beliefs and attitudes. To say there is no harm caused by reorientation therapies is dangerous!

Conclusions

The main purpose of this article is to provide a different stance to Throckmorton's article. This stance shows that reorientation therapies are based on bias and logical fallacies stemming from faulty assumptions and lack of awareness of the wide breadth of knowledge available on same-sex orientation. This stance also shows that the problems underlying reorientation therapies are being passed off to the consumer public not as problems, but as good science. ACA has followed suit with other major mental health organizations such as the APA and the American Psychiatric Association by stating that when there is no illness, there is no cure. A minority of practitioners continue, however, to feel propelled to offer a cure. An explanation for this is that certain practitioners possess a cultural and personal bias (Ferguson, 1994). Garnets, Hancock, Cochran, Goodchilds, and Peplau (1991) have documented biased, inappropriate, and inadequate practice when it came to understanding people with same-sex orientations, their identity developments, relationships, and parenting practices.

It is time for the field of mental health to finally come to the conclusion that reorientation counselors act out of bias though they pass their work off as science. An examination of the faulty logic, lack of good empirical support, specious arguments, and ignorance of vast bodies of multicultural theory leads to this conclusion. A review of Throckmorton's article reveals only an extensive literature review, but it does not lead to a convincing conclusion that ACA has taken a position that is anything less than ethical.

References

American Counseling Association, (1998). *ACA code of ethics and standards of practice.* Alexandria, VA: Author.

American Psychiatric Association, (1973). *Diagnostic and statistical manual of mental disorders* (2nd ed.) Washington, DC: Author.

American Psychiatric Association, (1952). *Diagnostic and statistical manual of mental disorders.* Washington, DC: Author.

American Psychological Association, (1998). *Resolution of therapeutic responses to sexual orientation.* Washington, DC: Author.

American Psychological Association, (1994). *Publication Manual* (4th ed.). Washington, DC: Author.

Bayer, R. (1987). *Homosexuality and the practice of psychiatry* (2nd ed.), Princeton, NJ: Princeton University Press.

Bieber, I., Dain, H. J., Dince, P. R., Drellich, M. G., Grand, H. G., Gundlach, R. H., Kremer, M. W., Rifkin, A. H., Wilbur, C. B., & Bieber, T. B. (1962). *Homosexuality.* New York: Basic Books.

Birk, L. (1980). The myth of classical homosexuality: View of a behavioral psychotherapist. In J. Marmor (Ed.), *Homosexual behavior.* New York: Basic Books.

Blair, R. (1982). *Ex-gay.* New York: Homosexual Counseling Center.

Buie, J. (1990, March). 'Heterosexual ethic' mentality is decried. *APA Monitor,* 20.

Cass, V. C. (1979). Homosexual identity formation: A theoretical model. *Journal of Homosexuality, 4,* 219–235.

Cautela, J. R. (1967). Covert sensitization. *Psychological Report, 20,* 459–468.

Coleman, J. C., Butcher, J. N., & Carson, R. C. (1984). *Abnormal psychology and modern life* (7th ed.), Glenview, IL: Scott, Foresman.

Edwards, R. (1996, September). Can sexual orientation change with therapy? *APA Monitor, 27* 49.

Feldman, M. P., & MacCulloch, M. J. (1965). The application of anticipatory avoidance learning to the treatment of homosexuality: Theory, techniques, and preliminary results. *Behavior Research and Therapy, 3,* 165–183.

Ferguson, M. (1994). Fixation and regression in the psychoanalytic theory of homosexuality: A critical evaluation. *Journal of Homosexuality, 27,* 309–327.

Ford, C. S., & Beach, F. A. (1951). *Patterns of sexual behavior.* New York: Harper & Row.

Freedman, M. (1971). *Homosexuality and psychological functioning.* Belmont, CA: Brooks/Cole.

Freud, S. (1950). A letter from Freud. *American Journal of Psychiatry, 107,* 786–787.

Freud, S. (1955). Psychogenesis of a case of homosexuality in a woman. In J. Strachey (Ed. & trans.) *Standard edition of the complete works of Sigmund Freud,* (Vol. 18). London: Hogarth Press.

Garnets, L., Hancock, K. A., Cochran, S. D., Goodchilds, J., & Peplau, L. A. (1991). Issues in psychotherapy with lesbians and gay men. *American Psychologist, 46,* 964–972.

Golden, C. (1987). Diversity and variability in women's sexual identities. In the Boston Lesbian Psychologies Collective (Eds.), *Lesbian psychologies: Exploration and challenges* (pp. 18–34). Urbana, IL: University of Illinois Press.

Gonsiorek, J. (1991). The empirical basis for the demise of the illness model of homosexuality. In J. Gonsiorek & J. Weinrich (Eds.), *Homosexuality: Research implications for public policy* (pp. 115–136). Newbury Park, CA: Sage.

Gonsiorek, J. C., Sell, R. L., & Weinrich, J. D. (1995). Definition and measurement of sexual orientation. *Suicide and Life Threatening Behavior, 25* (Suppl), 40–51.

Hadden, S. B. (1966). Treatment of male homosexuals in group. *International Journal of Group Psychotherapy, 16,* 13–22.

Haldeman, D. C. (1991). Conversion therapy for gay men and lesbians: A scientific examination. In J. Gonsiorek & J. Weinrich (Eds.), *Homosexuality: Research implications for public policy* (pp. 149–160). Newbury Park, CA: Sage.

Haldeman, D. C. (1994). The practice and ethics of sexual orientation conversion therapies. *Journal of Consulting and Clinical Psychology, 62,* 221–227.

Hart, M., Roback, H., Tittler, B., Weitz, L., Walston, B., & McKee, E. (1978). Psychological adjustment of nonpatient homosexuals: Critical review of the research literature. *Journal of Clinical Psychiatry, 39,* 604–608.

Helms, J. E. (1995). An update of Helm's white and people of color racial identity models. In J. G. Ponterotto, J. M. Casas, L. A. Suzuki, & C. M. Alexander (Eds.), *Handbook of multicultural counseling* (pp. 181–198). Thousand Oaks, CA: Sage.

Herek, G. (1998). Stigma and sexual orientation: Understanding prejudice against lesbians, gay men, and bisexuals. *Psychological Perspectives on Lesbian and Gay Issues, 4,* 223–255.

Herr, E., & Cramer, S. (1988). *Career guidance: Counseling through the lifespan* (3rd ed.). Glenview, IL: Scott, Foresman.

Hooker, E. (1957). Male homosexuality in the Rorschach. *Journal of Projective Techniques, 22,* 33–54.

Hopkins, J. (1969). The lesbian personality. *British Journal of Psychiatry, 115,* 1433–1436.

Isay, R. A. (1985). On the analytic treatment of homosexual men. *Psychoanalytic Study of the Child, 40,* 235–254.

Kinsey, A. C., Pomeroy, W. B., & Martin, C. E. (1948). *Sexual behavior in the human male.* Philadelphia: W. B. Saunders.

Lawson, R. (1987, June). *Scandal in the Adventist-funded program to 'heal' homosexuals: Failure, sexual exploitation, official silence, and attempts to rehabilitate the exploiter and his methods.* Paper presented at the annual convention of the American Sociological Association, Chicago, IL.

Leck, G. (1994). Politics of adolescent sexual identity and queer responses. *The High School Journal, 77,* 186–192.

Liddle, B. J. (1996). Therapist sexual orientation, gender, and counseling practices as they relate to ratings of helpfulness by gay and lesbian clients. *Journal of Counseling Psychology, 43,* 394–401.

McConaghy, N. (1976). Is a homosexual orientation irreversible? *British Journal of Psychiatry, 129,* 556–563.

Martin, A. D. (1984). The emperor's new clothes: Modern attempts to change sexual orientation. In T. Stein & E. Hetrick (Eds.), *Innovations in psychotherapy with homosexuals* (pp. 24–57). Washington, DC: American Psychiatric Press.

Mayerson, P., & Lief, H. I. (1965). Psychotherapy of homosexuals: A follow-up study of nineteen cases. In J. Marmor (Ed.), *Sexual inversion* (pp. 302–344). New York: Basic Books.

Mintz, E. E. (1966). Overt male homosexuals in combined group and individual treatment. *Journal of Consulting Psychology, 30,* 193–198.

Morin, S. F. (1977). Heterosexual bias in research on lesbianism and male homosexuality. *American Psychologist, 32,* 629–637.

Morin, S. F., & Rothblum, E. D. (1991). Removing stigma: Fifteen years of progress. *American Psychologist, 46,* 947–949.

Myers, L. J., Speight, S. L., Highlen, P. S., Cox, C. I., Reynolds, A. L., Adams, E. M., & Hanley, C. P. (1991). Identity development and world view: Toward an optimal conceptualization. *Journal of Counseling and Development, 70,* 54–63.

Nicolosi, J. (1991). *Reparative therapy for male homosexuality.* Northvale, NJ: Jason Aronson.

Nicolosi, J. (1993). *Healing homosexuality.* Northvale, NJ: Jason Aronson.

Panel (1960). Theoretical and clinical aspects of male homosexuality. *American Psychoanalytic Association, 8,* 552–566.

Peck, D. L. (1993). The fifty-percent divorce rate: Deconstructing a myth. Special issue: Focus on family issues. *Journal of Sociology and Social Welfare, 20*(3), 135–144.

Pederson, P. (1988). *A handbook for development of multicultural awareness.* Alexandria, VA: American Counseling Association.

Reiss, B. F. (1980). Psychological tests in homosexuality. In J. Marmor (Ed.), *Homosexual behavior: A modern reappraisal* (pp. 296–311). New York: Basic Books.

Ross, M. W., Paulsen, J. A., & Salstrom, O. W. (1988). Homosexuality and mental health: A cross-cultural review. *Journal of Homosexuality, 15,* 131–152.

Rothblum, E. (1994). I only read about myself on bathroom walls: The need for research on the mental health of lesbians and gay men. *Journal of Consulting and Clinical Psychology, 62,* 213–220.

Schreier, B. A. (1998). Talking 'bout my generation: Responding to bisexual and transgendered student identities. *Commission VII: Counseling and Psychological Services, 24*(2), 4–5.

Schüklenk, U., & Ristow, M. (1996). The ethics of research into the causes of homosexuality. *The Journal of Homosexuality, 31*(3), 5–30.

Shively, M. G., & DeCecco, J. P. (1977). Components of sexual identity. *Journal of Homosexuality, 2,* 41–48.

Sleek, S. (1997, October). Concerns about conversion therapy. *APA Monitor, 28,* 15.

Socarides, C. (1979). The psychoanalytic theory of homosexuality: With special reference to therapy. In I. Rosen (Ed.), *Sexual deviation* (2nd ed. pp. 243–277). New York: Oxford University Press.

Stein. T. S., & Cohen, C. J. (1986). Introduction. In T. S. Stein & C. J. Cohen (Eds.), *Contemporary perspectives on psychotherapy with lesbians and gay men.* New York: Plenum Press.

Sue, D. W., Arredondo, P., & McDavis, R. J. (1992). Multicultural counseling competencies and standards: A call to the profession. *Journal of Counseling and Development, 70,* 477–786.

Suppe, F. (1985). In defense of a multimodal approach to sexual identity. *Journal of Homosexuality, 103*–4), 7–14.

Thompson, N. L., McCandless, B. R., & Strickland, B. R. (1971). Personal adjustment of male and female homosexual. *Journal of Abnormal Psychology, 78,* 237–240.

Troiden, R. R. (1989). The formation of homosexual identities. *Journal of Homosexuality, 17*(1/2), 43–73.

Welch, B. L. (1990, January 26). Statement. Washington, DC: American Psychological Association.

Wolpe, J. (1973). *The practice of behavior therapy* (2nd ed.), New York: Pergamon Press.

CHALLENGE QUESTIONS

Is Treating Homosexuality Ethical and Effective?

1. What message does providing assistance to individuals who are dissatisfied with their homosexual orientation convey to satisfied gay and lesbian individuals? Does the potential threat to a minority's identity outweigh some individuals' right to choose to reject that identity?
2. Why have some people argued that there is no empirical evidence supporting conversion therapy's effectiveness? What do they say are the problems with the research literature? Illustrate the supposed problems with a description of a real study.
3. The values of each author are a major issue in this debate. Is it possible to escape one's values? Can one value be proven to be truer than another?
4. In what ways does the surrounding political and religious dialogue about homosexuality influence the debate over conversion therapy?

CRETV: Center for Research on the Effects of Television

Based at Ithaca College, the Center for Research on the Effects of Television has an archive of television content and a research lab conducting studies of the content of television and its effects on viewers.

http://www.ithaca.edu/cretv/

libertus.net:Studies & Research

This libertus.net page contains links to studies and research on the effects of portrayals of violence in the electronic media, as well as reviews, analyses, and commentaries on that research.

http://libertus.net/censor/studies.html

Journal of Personality and Social Psychology

This site contains a description of the *Journal of Personality and Social Psychology,* the current issue's table of contents (with abstracts), past tables of contents, and selected online articles from the journal. Looking over the tables of contents should provide you with an overview of current topics of interest to social psychologists.

http://www.apa.org/journals/psp.html

The Society for the Psychological Study of Social Issues

This home page of the Society for the Psychological Study of Social Issues (SPSSI) provides information about current research in social psychology as well as abstracts of issues of the *Journal of Social Issues.*

http://www.spssi.org

Feminists for Free Expression

This page features the position statement on pornography of Feminists for Free Expression (FFE), as well as other position statements, further reading, and related links.

http://www.ffeusa.org/pornography.html

PART 7

Social Psychology

*S*ocial psychology is the study of humans in their social environments. A central concern of social psychologists is how aspects of society affect the individual. For example, does media violence, such as in video games, harm children? Does playing violent video games make children more aggressive? Another potentially destructive social influence is pornography. More people than ever have ready access to sexually explicit materials through the Internet. Do such materials negatively influence how men treat women? What about other aspects of the Internet? Does this relatively new technology help or hurt users' psychological and emotional well-being?

- Do Video Games Lead to Violence?

- Does the Internet Have Psychological Benefits?

- Is Pornography Harmful?

ISSUE 16

Do Video Games Lead to Violence?

YES: Douglas A. Gentile and Craig A. Anderson, from "Violent Video Games: The Newest Media Violence Hazard," in Douglas A. Gentile, ed., *Media Violence and Children: A Complete Guide for Parents and Professionals* (Praeger, 2003)

NO: Cheryl K. Olson, from "Media Violence Research and Youth Violence Data: Why Do They Conflict?" *Academic Psychiatry* (Summer 2004)

ISSUE SUMMARY

YES: Developmental psychologist Douglas A. Gentile and department of psychology chair Craig A. Anderson assert that violent video games cause several physiological and psychological changes in children that lead to aggressive and violent behavior.

NO: Cheryl K. Olson, a professor of psychiatry, contends that further research is needed because there is so little current evidence of a substantial connection between exposure to violent video games and serious real-life violence.

The nation was horrified when Eric Harris and Dylan Klebold brutally murdered 13 students and a teacher at their high school in Littleton, Colorado. What could have caused these teenagers to commit such merciless acts of violence? As authorities investigated, they discovered that Harris and Klebold spent much of their time playing violent video games. Could exposure to such games lead to this kind of violent behavior?

Almost 30 years have past since the first violent video game was released. Debate about the effects of violent games on children's behavior has filled the last 20 of those 30 years. Many scholars have concluded from this debate that playing violent video games increases a child's violent behavior. They contend that by being involved in this kind of interactive, violent stimuli, children essentially train themselves to act in violent ways. This is especially true of those children who are notably aggressive prior to their experience with violent games. As graphics improve and game-play becomes more and more realistic, these scholars and some parents worry that these unhealthy effects will only increase.

In the first selection, Douglas A. Gentile and Craig A. Anderson address what they feel recent research has made very clear: playing violent video games leads to violent behavior. Gentile and Anderson claim that several things happen while a child is playing violent video games: an increase in physiological arousal, aggressive cognitions and emotions, aggressive behaviors, and decreased prosocial behaviors. These researchers also take on some of the more popular criticisms facing video game research. For instance, some say violent video games affect only a select few who are already abnormally aggressive. However, Gentile and Anderson argue that this criticism is illegitimate because no group has ever been discovered to be totally immune to the effects of violent video games.

In the second selection, Cheryl K. Olson suggests there might not be as strong a connection between violent video games and violent behavior as researchers like Gentile and Anderson depict. She points to a lack of definitive consensus on what is meant by "violence" and "aggression." How can we be so sure about these findings, Olson seems to say, when we cannot even define the main concepts involved? Moreover, she insists violent behavior and playing violent video games are not as connected as the popular media likes to portray. While she does not deny the possibility that violent video games could affect kids in some way, Olson feels current research is inadequate and cannot be generalized to situations outside a laboratory setting due to small, nonrandom, and unrepresentative sampling.

POINT

- Research shows that playing violent video games increases aggressive thoughts and emotions.
- Experiments with violent video games demonstrate increases in aggressive behaviors.
- The validity and generalization of these studies are widely acknowledged.
- More realistic video games increases physiological arousal.
- Because violent video games are interactive, what children learn comes quickly and is deeply absorbed.

COUNTERPOINT

- Vague definitions of aggression and violence undermine the credibility of such studies.
- There is little evidence of a substantial link between exposure to violent video games and serious, real-life violence.
- Test conditions are difficult to generalize to the real world and the results are often erroneously interpreted.
- National data show no correlation between the recent rise in violent video game usage and violent juvenile crime.
- Researchers have not considered video game violence alongside recognized causes of violent behavior.

Douglas A. Gentile
and Craig A. Anderson

 **YES**

Violent Video Games: The Newest Media Violence Hazard

. . . Time Spent with Video Games

Video games have become one of the dominant entertainment media for children in a very short time. In the mid-1980s, children averaged about four hours a week playing video games, including time spent playing at home and in arcades. By the early 1990s, home video game use had increased and arcade play had decreased. The average amount was still fairly low, averaging about two hours of home play per week for girls, and about four hours of home play per week for boys. By the mid 1990s, home use had increased for fourth grade girls to 4.5 hours per week, and to 7.1 hours per week for fourth grade boys. In recent national surveys of parents, school-age children (boys and girls combined) devote an average of about seven hours per week playing video games. In a recent survey of over 600 eighth and ninth grade students, children averaged 9 hours per week of video game play overall, with boys averaging 13 hours per week and girls averaging 5 hours per week. Thus, while sex-correlated differences in the amount of time committed to playing video games continue to exist, the rising tide has floated all boats.

Even very young children are playing video games. Gentile & Walsh found that children aged two to seven play an average of 43 minutes per day (by parent report), and Woodard and Gridina found that even preschoolers aged two to five average 28 minutes of video game play per day. Although few studies have documented how the amount of time devoted to playing video games changes with development, some studies have suggested that video game play may peak in early school-age children. Buchman & Funk found the amount of time was highest for fourth grade children and decreased steadily through eighth grade. Others have suggested that play is highest between ages 9 and 12, decreases between ages 12 and 14, and increases again between ages 15 and 18. Surprisingly, the amount of time children devote to television has remained remarkably stable even as the amount of time devoted to video and computer games has increased.

Although the research evidence is still limited, amount of video game play has been linked with a number of risk factors for maladaptive development,

From *Media Violence and Children: A Complete Guide for Parents and Professionsals,* 2003, pp. 131–133, 135–136, 139–140, 141–142, 147–150. Copyright © 2003 by Greenwood Publishing Group. Reprinted by permission. References and notes omitted.

including smoking, obesity, and poorer academic performance. These results parallel those showing that greater use of television is correlated with poorer grades in school. . . .

Preferences for Violent Video Games

Although video games are designed to be entertaining, challenging, and sometimes educational, most include violent content. Recent content analyses of video games show that as many as 89 percent of games contain some violent content, and that about half of the games include violent content toward other game characters that would result in serious injuries or death.

Many children prefer to play violent games. Of course, what constitutes a "violent" game varies depending upon who is classifying them. The video game industry and its ratings board (Entertainment Software Rating Board) claim to see much less violence in their games than do parents and other researchers. Even within the research community there is some inconsistency in definition of what constitutes a violent video game. Generally, however, researchers consider as "violent" those games in which the player can harm other characters in the game. In many popular video games, harming other characters is the main activity. It is these games, in which killing occurs at a high rate, that are of most concern to media violence researchers, child advocacy groups, and parents. . . . In studies of fourth through eighth grade children, more than half of the children state preferences for games in which the main action is predominantly human violence or fantasy violence. In surveys of children and their parents, about two-thirds of children named violent games as their favorites. Only about one-third of parents were able to correctly name their child's favorite game, and in 70 percent of the incorrect matches, children described their favorite game as violent. A preference for violent games has been linked with hostile attribution biases, increased arguments with teachers, lower self-perceptions of behavioral conduct, and increased physical fights. . . .

Why Violent Video Games May Have a Greater Effect Than Violent TV

The public health community has concluded from the preponderance of evidence that violent television leads to "increases in aggressive attitudes, values, and behavior, particularly in children." Although the research on violent video games is still growing, there are at least six reasons why we should expect violent video games to have an even greater impact than violent television. These reasons are based on what we already know from the television and educational literatures.

1. *Identification with an aggressor increases imitation of the aggressor.* It is known from research on violent television that children will imitate aggressive actions more readily if they identify with an aggressive character in some way. On television, it is hard to predict with which characters, if any, a person will identify. One might identify most

closely with the victim, in which case the viewer would be less likely to be aggressive after watching. In many violent video games, however, one is required to take the point of view of one particular character. This is most noticeable in "first-person shooter" games, in which the players "see" what their character would see as if they were inside the video game. Thus, the player is forced to identify with a violent character. In fact, in many games, players have a choice of characters to play and can upload photographs of their faces onto their character. This identification with the aggressive character is likely to increase the likelihood of imitating the aggressive acts.

2. *Active participation increases learning.* Research on learning shows that when one becomes actively involved in something, one learns much more than if one only watches it. This is one reason computer technology in the classroom has been considered to be educationally beneficial. Educational video games are theorized to be effective partly because they require active participation. With regard to violent entertainment, viewers of violent content on television are passive observers of the aggressive acts. In contrast, violent video games by their very nature require active participation in the violent acts.

3. *Practicing an entire behavioral sequence is more effective than practicing only a part.* If one wanted to learn how to kill someone, one would quickly realize that there are many steps involved. At a minimum, one needs to decide whom to kill, get a weapon, get ammunition, load the weapon, stalk the victim, aim the weapon, and pull the trigger. It is rare for television shows or movies to display all of these steps. Yet, violent video games regularly require players to practice each of these steps repeatedly. This helps teach the necessary steps to commit a successful act of aggression. In fact, some video games are so successful at training whole sequences of aggressive behaviors that the U.S. Army has licensed them to train their forces. For example, the popular violent video game series *Rainbow Six* is so good at teaching all of the steps necessary to plan and conduct a successful special operations mission that the U.S. Army has licensed the game engine to train their special operations soldiers. Furthermore, the U.S. Army has created their own violent video game as a recruitment tool.

4. *Violence is continuous.* Research with violent television and movies has shown that the effects on viewers are greater if the violence is unrelieved and uninterrupted. However, in both television programs and movies, violent content is rarely sustained for more than a few minutes before changing pace, changing scenes, or going to commercials. In contrast, the violence in violent video games is often continuous. Players must constantly be alert for hostile enemies, and must constantly choose and enact aggressive behaviors. These behaviors expose players to a continual stream of violent (and often gory) scenes accompanied by screams of pain and suffering in a context that is incompatible with feelings of empathy or guilt.

5. *Repetition increases learning.* If one wishes to learn a new phone number by memory, one often will repeat it over and over to aid memory. This simple mnemonic device has been shown to be an effective learning technique. With few exceptions (e.g., *Blue's Clues*), children rarely see the same television shows over and over. In a violent video

game, however, players often spend a great deal of time doing the same aggressive actions (e.g., shooting things) over and over. Furthermore, the games are usually played repeatedly, thus giving a great deal of practice repeating the violent game actions. This increases the odds that not only will children learn from them, but they will make these actions habitual to the point of automaticity.

6. *Rewards increase imitation.* There are at least three different processes involved. First, rewarding aggressive behavior in a video game (e.g., winning extra points and lives) increases the frequency of behaving aggressively in that game (see number 5, above). Second, rewarding aggressive behavior in a video game teaches more positive attitudes toward the use of force as a means of solving conflicts. Television programs rarely provide a reward structure for the viewer, and it would be rarer still to have those rewards dependent on violent acts. In contrast, video games often reward players for participating. Third, the reward patterns involved in video games increase the player's motivation to persist at the game. Interestingly, all three of these processes help educational games be more effective. The last process can make the games somewhat addictive.

The Effects of Violent Video Games

Over the past 20 years, a number of scholars have expressed concern over the potential negative impact of exposing youth to violent video games. . . .

Meta-Analytic Summary of Violent Video Game Effects

Narrative reviews of a research literature, such as that by Dill and Dill, are very useful ways of examining prior studies. Typically, the researchers try to find an organizing scheme that makes sense of the varied results that typically occur in any research domain. However, as useful as such reviews of the literature are, meta-analyses (studies of studies) are a much more powerful technique to find the common effects of violent video games across multiple studies. Specifically, a meta-analysis uses statistical techniques to combine the results of various studies of the same basic hypothesis, and provides an objective answer to the questions of whether or not the key independent variable has a reliable effect on the key dependent variable, and if so, what the magnitude of that effect is. Only recently have there been enough studies on violent video games to make meta-analysis a useful technique. In 2001, the first comprehensive meta-analysis of the effects of violent video games was conducted. A more recent update to that meta-analysis produced the same basic findings. A consistent pattern of the effects of playing violent games was documented in five areas.

1. *Playing violent video games increases physiological arousal.* Studies measuring the effects of playing violent video games tend to show larger increases in heart rate and systolic and diastolic blood pressure compared to playing nonviolent video games. The average effect size across studies between violent game play and physiological arousal was 0.22.[1]

For example, Ballard and West showed that a violent game (*Mortal Kombat* with the blood "turned on") resulted in higher systolic blood pressure responses than either a nonviolent game or a less graphically violent game (*Mortal Kombat* with the blood "turned off"). . . .

2. *Playing violent video games increases aggressive cognitions.* Studies measuring cognitive responses to playing violent video games have shown that aggressive thoughts are increased compared to playing nonviolent video games. The average effect size across studies between violent game play and aggressive cognitions was 0.27. These effects have been found in children and adults, in males and females, and in experimental and nonexperimental studies. . . .

3. *Playing violent video games increases aggressive emotions.* Studies measuring emotional responses to playing violent video games have shown that aggressive emotions are increased compared to playing nonviolent video games. The average effect size across studies between violent game play and aggressive emotions was 0.18. These effects have been found in children and adults, in males and females, and in experimental and nonexperimental studies. In one study, adults' state hostility and anxiety levels were increased after playing a violent game compared to controls. In a study of third through fifth grade children, playing a violent game increased frustration levels more than playing a nonviolent game.

4. *Playing violent video games increases aggressive behaviors.* Studies measuring aggressive behaviors after playing violent video games have shown that aggressive behaviors are increased compared to playing nonviolent video games. The average effect size across studies between violent game play and aggressive behaviors was 0.19. These effects have been found in children and adults, in males and females, and in experimental and nonexperimental studies. . . .

5. *Playing violent video games decreases prosocial behaviors.* Studies measuring responses to playing violent video games have shown that prosocial behaviors are decreased compared to playing nonviolent video games. The average effect size across studies between violent game play and prosocial behaviors was –0.16. These effects have been found in both experimental and nonexperimental studies. In one study of 278 seventh and eighth graders, children who named violent games as their favorite games to play were rated by their peers as exhibiting fewer prosocial behaviors and more aggressive behaviors in the classroom. . . .

Critiques of the Video Game Research Literature

Any new research domain has strengths and weaknesses. If all goes well, over time the researchers identify the weaknesses and address them in a variety of ways. When the new research domain appears to threaten the profits of some large industry, there is a tendency for that industry to deny the threatening research and to mount campaigns designed to highlight the weaknesses, obfuscate the legitimate findings, and cast doubt on the quality of the research. The history of the tobacco industry's attempt to ridicule, deny, and obfuscate research linking smoking to lung cancer is the prototype of such efforts. The TV and movie industries have had considerable success in their 40-year campaign against the media violence research community. The same type of effort has now been mounted by the video game industry. We do not claim that there are no weaknesses in the video game research literature. Indeed, we have highlighted some of them in our own prior writings. In this final section, we focus on two types of criticisms, legitimate ones (usually raised by researchers) and illegitimate ones (usually raised by the video game industry and their supporters in the scholarly community).

Illegitimate Criticisms

1. *There are too few studies to warrant any conclusions about possible negative effects.*

This can be a legitimate concern if the small number of studies yields a lack of power to detect small effects. However, it is an illegitimate argument when it is used to claim that the current set of video game studies do not warrant serious concern about exposure to violent video games. If anything, it is remarkable that such reliable effects have emerged from such a relatively small number of studies (compared to TV and movie violence studies), and that the studies that vary so much in method, sample population, and video game stimuli.

2. *There are problems with the external validity of lab experiments due to demand characteristics, participant suspicion and compliance problems, trivial measures, artificial settings, and unrepresentative participants.*

These old arguments against laboratory studies in the behavioral sciences have been successfully debunked many times, in many contexts, and in several different ways. Both logical and empirical analyses of such broad-based attacks on lab experiments have found little cause for concern. Furthermore, more specific examination of these issues in the aggression domain have consistently found evidence of high external validity, and have done so in several very different ways.

3. *Complete dismissal of correlational studies: "Correlation is not causation."*

This is an overly simplistic view of how modern science is conducted. Psychology instructors teach this mantra to introductory psychology students, and hope that they will gain a much more sophisticated view of methods and scientific inference by the time they are seniors. Whole fields of science are based on correlational data (e.g., astronomy). Correlational studies are used to test causal theories, and thus provide falsification opportunities. A well-conducted correlational design, one which attempts to control for likely "third variable" factors, can provide much useful information. To be sure, correlational studies are generally (but not always) less informative about causality than experimental ones. What is most important is the whole pattern of results across studies that differ in design, procedure, and measures. And the existing research on violent video games yields consistent results.

4. *Arousal accounts for all video game effects on aggressive behavior.*

Physiological arousal dissipates fairly quickly. Therefore, the arousal claim does not apply to studies that measure aggressive behavior more than 30 minutes after game play has occurred, or studies in which aggression is measured by a retrospective report. For example, this criticism generally doesn't apply to correlational studies, but correlational studies show a significant link between violent video game exposure and aggression. Furthermore, there are a few experimental studies in which the violent and nonviolent game conditions were equated on arousal, and significant violent-content effects still occurred.

5. *There are no studies linking violent video game play to "serious" or actual aggression.*

This criticism is simply not true. A number of correlational studies have linked repeated violent video game play to serious aggression. For example, Anderson and Dill showed that college-student reports of violent video game play in prior years were positively related to aggression that would be considered criminal (e.g., assault, robbery) if known to police. Similarly, Gentile et al. found significant links between violent game play and physical fights.

6. *Violent media affect only a few who are already disturbed.*

As discussed earlier, there are reasons (some theoretical, some empirical) to believe that some populations will be more negatively affected than others. However, no totally "immune" population has ever been identified, and populations sometimes thought to be at low risk have nonetheless yielded significant violent video game exposure effects.

7. *Effects of media violence are trivially small.*

Once again, this is simply not true. Violent video game effects are bigger than: (a) effects of passive tobacco smoke and lung cancer; (b) exposure to lead and IQ scores in children; (c) calcium intake and bone mass.

Note that the critics use these seven illegitimate criticisms to basically dismiss all research on violent video games. Once one has dismissed all correlational studies (number 3, above) and all experiments that use laboratory or other "trivial" measures of aggression (number 2, above), the only potential type of study left is clearly unethical: an experimental field study in which violent crime is the measure of aggression. Such a study would require randomly assigning children to high versus low video game violence conditions for a period of years and then following up on their rates of violent criminal activity over the course of their lives. It is not an accident that all ethically feasible types of studies are dismissed by the industry and its supporters.

Legitimate Criticisms

1. *Sample sizes tend to be too small in many studies.*

If the average effect size is about r = 0.20, then N (the number of study participants) should be at least 200 for 0.80 power (power is the likelihood of being able to find a legitimate difference between groups). When N is too small, individual studies will *appear* inconsistent even if they are all accurate samples of the true r = 0.20 effect. For this reason, the best way of summarizing the results of a set of too-small studies is to combine the results via meta-analysis, rather than using the more traditional narrative review. When this is done, we see that the video game studies yield consistent results.

2. *Some studies do not have "violent" and "nonviolent" games that are sufficiently different in actual violent content.*

This problem was noted earlier in this chapter in the discussion of how early studies might find weaker effects because the "violent" video games in the early years were not very violent by contemporary standards. . . . Future studies need to do a better job of assessing the violent content of the video games being compared.

3. *Some experimental studies have used a "control" or "nonviolent game" condition that was more boring, annoying, or frustrating than the violent game.*

The obvious solution for future studies is to do more pilot testing or manipulation checks on such aggression-relevant dimensions. In trying to summarize past research, one can sometimes find a more appropriate comparison condition within the same experiment.

4. *Some studies did not report sufficient results to enable calculation of an effect size for participants who actually played a video game.*

This problem arose in several cases in which half of the participants played a video game while the other half merely observed. Reported means then collapsed across this play versus observe dimension. Future reports should include the individual means.

5. *Some studies that purportedly study aggressive behavior have used dependent variables that are not true aggressive behavior.*

A surprising number of past studies have used trait or personality aggression scales as measures of aggressive behavior in short-term experiments. This is a problem because there is no way that a short-term manipulation of exposure to violent versus nonviolent video games (e.g., 20 minutes) can influence one's past frequency of aggression. In this short-term context, such a trait measure might possibly be conceived as a measure of cognitive priming, but clearly it is not a measure of aggressive behavior.

A related problem is that some studies have included hitting an inanimate object as a measure of aggressive behavior. Most modern definitions of aggression restrict its application to behaviors that are intended to harm another person.

The obvious solution for future studies is to use better measures of aggression. In the analysis of past research one can sometimes disaggregate the reported composite measure to get a cleaner measure of aggression.

6. *There are no longitudinal studies.*

This is true. Major funding is needed to conduct a large-scale longitudinal study of video game effects. To date, such funding has not been forthcoming. Thus, one must rely on longitudinal studies in the TV/movie violence domain to get a reasonable guess as to the likely long-term effects. . . .

Summary

Although there is less research on the effects of violent video games than there is on television and movies, the preponderance of evidence looks very similar to the research on violent television. In particular, violent video games appear to increase aggressive thoughts and feelings, physiological arousal, and aggressive behaviors, as well as to decrease prosocial behaviors. There are many theoretical reasons why one would expect violent video games to have a greater effect than violent television, and most of the reasons why one would expect them to have a lesser effect are no longer true because violent video games have become so realistic, particularly since the late 1990s. . . .

Note

1. All effect sizes reported in the chapter are scaled as correlation coefficients, regardless of whether the study was experimental or correlational in design. See Comstock and Scharrer (this volume) for a discussion of how to interpret effect sizes.

NO

Cheryl K. Olson

Media Violence Research and Youth Violence Data: Why Do They Conflict?

. . . It's almost an American tradition to blame the corruption of youth on violent mass media, from the lurid "half-dime" novels of the 19th century to 1930s gangster films and 1950s horror/crime comics. In 1972, a report to the U.S. Surgeon General addressed then-growing concerns about violent television. Its authors pondered how television content and programming practices could be changed to reduce the risk of increasing aggression without causing other social harms. They concluded: "The state of present knowledge does not permit an agreed answer."

Violent video games are the most recent medium to be decried by researchers, politicians, and the popular press as contributing to society's ills. In particular, they were implicated in a series of notorious shootings:

> Although it is impossible to know exactly what caused these teens to attack their own classmates and teachers . . . one possible contributing factor is violent video games. Harris and Klebold enjoyed playing the bloody, shoot-'em-up video game *Doom,* a game licensed by the U.S. Army to train soldiers to effectively kill.

(Anderson and Dill did not cite a source for the use of *Doom* by the military. However, according to the web site of the U.S. Army Corps of Engineers Topographic Engineering Center, *Doom II* was indeed licensed in 1996 and transformed into *Marine Doom,* which "teaches concepts such as mutual fire team support, protection of the automatic rifleman, proper sequencing of an attack, ammunition discipline and succession of command" [see www.tec.army.mil/ TD/tvd/survey/Marine_Doom.html]).

> "We've been seeing a whole rash of shootings throughout this country and in Europe that relate back to kids who obsessively play violent video games. The kids involved as shooters in Columbine were obsessively playing violent video games. We know after the Beltway sniper incident where

From *Academic Psychiatry*, Summer 2004, pp. 144–149. Copyright © 2004 as conveyed via the Copyright Clearance Center. Reprinted by permission. References omitted.

the 17-year-old was a fairly good shot, but Mr. Muhammad, the police tell us, got him to practice on an ultra-violent video game in sniper mode to break down his hesitancy to kill."

—Washington State Rep. Mary Lou Dickerson, on *The NewsHour with Jim Lehrer,* July 7, 2003. (She co-sponsored legislation to ban the sale or rental of games that portray violence against police to children under 17.)

The series of random shootings by Lee Malvo and John Muhammad created panic in the Washington, DC area. News headlines repeated claims by Malvo's defense team that the youth had been brainwashed and trained to kill while playing video games with sniper shooting modes such as *Halo, Tom Clancy's Ghost Recon,* and *Tom Clancy's Rainbow Six: Covert Ops.* The jury was shown clips of these games and of the film *The Matrix.* A psychologist testified that exposure to this kind of entertainment makes violence seem more acceptable and promotes violent thoughts and actions. In response, the prosecutor simply asked, "What about the millions and millions of young American males who play video games and don't go out and kill random people on the street?"

Certainly, the stealing, beating, strangling, and hacking depicted in games such as *Grand Theft Auto III, Manhunt,* and *Mortal Kombat: Deadly Alliance* are shocking to many adults. It seems reasonable to assume that wielding virtual guns and chainsaws must be bad for our children. However, the potential of gangster movies to trigger violence or teach criminal methods to the young seemed just as real to previous generations. Local censorship boards in New York and Chicago edited out hundreds of scenes that "glorified gangsters or outlaws" or "showed disrespect for law enforcement."

In that place and time, it's possible that cinema criminals such as James Cagney and Edward G. Robinson were bad influences on some young people. This can't be proved or disproved. Today, however, most of us view these films as quaint entertainment classics. Before we make sweeping assumptions about the effects of media content, we must examine the data.

School Shootings and Video Games

In response to the outcry that followed deadly shootings in Colorado, Oregon, Kentucky, and Arkansas, the U.S. Secret Service and the U.S. Department of Education began a study called the Safe School Initiative. This involved an intensive review of the 37 incidents of "targeted" school violence, aimed at a specific person, group, type (such as "jocks" or "geeks"), or at an entire school, that took place between 1974 and 2000. The goal was to look for commonalities and create a profile of potential attackers in order to prevent future tragedies.

The conclusion: There was no useful profile. Along with male gender, the most common shared trait was a history of suicide attempts or suicidal thoughts, often with a documented history of extreme depressed feelings. If all schools instituted programs to identify and refer depressed and suicidal youth, more would receive treatment and promising futures could be saved. But using those methods to detect potential killers would result in overwhelming numbers of false positives and the stigmatization of thousands.

Moreover, there is no evidence that targeted violence has increased in America's schools. While such attacks have occurred in the past, they were and are extremely rare events. The odds that a child will die in school through murder or suicide are less than one in one million. What *has* dramatically increased is our exposure to local and national news about the "recent trend" in school shootings. Research has shown that crime-saturated local and national television news reports increase viewers' perception of both personal and societal risk, regardless of actual danger.

Constant news coverage leaves the impression that youthful crime is increasing. Some have referred to a "wave of violence gripping America's youth," fueled by exposure to violent media. Using data supplied to the FBI by local law enforcement agencies, the U.S. Office of Juvenile Justice and Delinquency Prevention reported that the rate of juvenile arrests increased in the late 1980s, peaking in 1994. At the time, this seemed to be a worrisome trend, but it proved to be an anomaly. Juvenile arrests declined in each of the next 7 years. Between 1994 and 2001, arrests for murder, forcible rape, robbery, and aggravated assaults fell 44%, resulting in the lowest juvenile arrest rate for violent crimes since 1983. Murder arrests, which reached a high of 3,800 in 1993, fell to 1,400 in 2001.

Interestingly, the sharp temporary rise in juvenile murders from 1983 to 1993 has been attributed to a rapid rise in gun use, concentrated among black male adolescents. We have no evidence that black male adolescents' use of violent media differed significantly from that of other young people, though there is ample evidence that as a group, they have greater exposure to other risk factors for violence. And what of juvenile arrests for property crimes? In 2001, these achieved their lowest level in over 30 years. In other words, there's no indication that violence rose in lockstep with the spread of violent games. Of course, this is not proof of lack of harm.

Could violent media have played some role in the rare but horrifying mass murders in our schools? This can't be ruled out, but evidence is scant. According to the Secret Service review, one in eight perpetrators showed some interest in violent video games, one-fourth in violent movies, and one-fourth in violent books, but there was no obvious pattern. Instead of interactive games, their interactive medium of choice was pen and paper. Thirty seven percent expressed violent thoughts and imagery through poems, essays, and journal entries.

Trends in Violent Game Use

The rapid spread of video games among the young, including violent games, has surprised and unnerved many parents. Games with violent content and "Mature" ratings are available for computers, all three major game consoles (PlayStation 2, Xbox, and GameCube), and portable handhelds such as Game Boy.

According to a 1999 survey by the Kaiser Family Foundation, 83% of children ages 8 to 18 reported having at least one video game console in their home, and 45% had one in their bedroom. In addition, 74% have at least one computer at home. Fifty-five percent of boys and 23% of girls said they played video games on a typical day, with nearly 20%, primarily boys, playing an "action or combat [game], (i.e., *Duke Nukem, Doom*)."

These figures have probably increased since that time. According to the Entertainment Software Association (formerly called the Interactive Digital Software Association), sales of video and computer games in the United States have grown steadily, from $3.2 billion in 1995 to $7 billion in 2003. The industry group is coy about how many children are actually playing, stating only that among the "most frequent" computer and video game players, 30% and 38%, respectively, are under age 18. Citing market research data from 2000, an IDSA report states that 61% of game users are 18 or older (suggesting that 39% are *under* 18).

Violent games are also widely sold. It is possible to find even gore-laden games such as *BloodRayne* (named for its bustier-clad vampire spy heroine and described on the maker's web site as "an intense third-person action/horror experience") at child-friendly outlets such as Toys R Us. Similar to R-rated movie restrictions, retailers are supposed to prevent sales of M-rated games to youth under age 17. However, "mystery shopper" studies by the U.S. Federal Trade Commission found that young teens ages 13 to 16 were able to purchase M-rated games 85% of the time. This number declined to 69% in a follow-up survey released in October 2003. In sum, playing video and computer games—including games with violent content—is now a routine activity for American youth, particularly boys.

Video Game Research and Public Policy

How has this spurt in electronic game play affected our youth? Along with the Washington, D.C. snipers and school shooters, several academic studies (primarily experiments) have received broad coverage in the popular media and are cited by the press and some advocacy groups as evidence that video games create dangerous, aggressive thoughts, feelings, and behaviors. Local, state, and federal legislation, including criminal penalties for selling or renting certain games to minors, have been introduced based on these studies, as have private lawsuits.

Many of these studies provide useful insights into the potential for harm (and sometimes benefit) from violent interactive games. But problems arise when the customary discussion of limitations falls by the wayside. Ideas are taken out of context and repeated in the media echo chamber, creating a false sense of certainty. Here are some of the limitations of current studies as a basis for policy making, with illustrative examples.

Vague Definitions of Aggression

Some researchers use "aggression" and "violence" almost interchangeably, implying that one inevitably leads to the other. Aggressive play that follows exposure to games or cartoons containing violence is not distinguished from aggressive behavior intended to harm. Aggressive thoughts, feelings, and behaviors may be presented as equivalent in importance and treated as valid surrogates for real-life violence, with the assumption that reducing these factors will reduce harm. The muddled terminology and unspoken assumptions can undermine the credibility of studies. After all, most parents of whining toddlers have occasional aggressive thoughts and feelings, but that's a far cry from actual child abuse.

Use of Violent Media Is Not Put Into Context With Other Known Contributors to Aggression or Violence

Lee Malvo, for example, had a history of antisocial and criminal behavior. He reportedly hunted and killed perhaps 20 cats with a slingshot and marbles. Compared to playing violent video games, animal torture is both more unusual and directly related to harming humans. According to public health and juvenile justice research, the strongest childhood predictors of youth violence are involvement in crime (not necessarily violent crime), male gender, illegal substance use, physical aggressiveness, family poverty, and antisocial parents. As children grow older, peer relationships become important predictors: associating with antisocial or delinquent peers, gang membership, and lack of ties with prosocial peers and groups.

A final problem with using aggression as a surrogate for violence is that most children who are aggressive or engage in antisocial behavior do not grow up to be violent adolescents or adults, and most violent adolescents were not notably aggressive as children.

Test Conditions That Are Difficult to Generalize to the Real World

Experimental settings are not only artificial, but turn game play into game "work." Subjects may have only 10 minutes to learn and play a game before results are measured and cannot choose when to start or stop playing. Most experiments involve a single game exposure, which cannot reasonably represent the effects of playing an array of games in real life. Additionally, young people commonly play games with others. In the Kaiser Family Foundation survey, virtually all children played their video games with friends, siblings, or other relatives. (By contrast, the majority of computer games were played alone, although some children played with a friend in the room or with someone over the Internet.) Effects of the social context of games, be they positive or negative, have received little attention to date.

Small, Nonrandom, or Nonrepresentative Samples

This is another barrier to broad generalization of research results. While it is not uncommon to recruit college undergraduates in psychology courses for experimental studies, those students differ in numerous ways from the typical young American teen—the population of greatest interest to most researchers and policy makers. Other studies use samples that are very narrow in age or geography (e.g., 10- and 11-year-old Flemish children).

A Blinkered View of Causality

Some (but not all) experimental studies have found that aggressive thoughts or behavior increase after playing a particular video game. It has been postulated that experimental studies prove causality by ruling out other plausible explanations. In the real world, however, this could be a very complex relationship. That is, aggressive children may seek out violent games, and violent games may reinforce aggressive behavior. This may be a two-way relationship or the result of other factors such as lack of parental supervision or connection. Additionally, effects of moderating variables, such as the nature and context of violence in a given game, or subject age or developmental stage are often not considered.

Study Findings Are Combined in Ways Not Appropriate for Policy Use

"Meta-analysis" and related techniques, for example, may be used to merge study findings for a more robust result. A 2004 meta-analysis of the effects of playing violent video games combined studies with subjects of varying age and gender who were exposed to different types and amounts of game violence in a variety of environments (experiments and correlational studies), with varying outcomes—a range of behavioral, cognitive, affective, and arousal measures. Results were represented only in terms of average effect size. Given the different study types, exposures, populations, and outcome measures, this goes well beyond the prohibition against "comparing apples and oranges" in meta-analyses.

Again, however, the primary problem is the way these findings are interpreted. The size and representativeness of study samples were not considered in assessing study quality, and the outcome of concern—real-world violence or related harm—was never directly studied. Despite this, the results were viewed as important evidence that violent game exposure leads to major societal harm.

Current Thinking on Game Violence Effects

The research community is sharply divided on whether violent games are harmful, and if so, for whom and to what degree. Several well-regarded reviews have concluded that the current body of research is unable to support the argument that the fantasy violence of games leads to real-life violence—although this could change as evidence accumulates or games become more realistic.

In an appendix to its chapter on risk factors, the Surgeon General's 2001 report on youth violence reviewed effects of exposure to violent media. The report noted that there is evidence for a small to moderate short-term increase in physically and verbally aggressive behavior. However, the sum of findings from cross-sectional, experimental, and longitudinal studies "suggest that media violence has a relatively small impact on violence" and that "the impact of video games on violent behavior remains to be determined."

Potential Effects of Games on "Below the Radar" Violence

This does not mean that we should put research on media violence on the back burner. Instead, we need to put it in context. First, many known risk factors for violence aren't amenable to change, while exposure to media (content and dose) is potentially alterable. Second, while they may not play a starring role in headline-grabbing crimes, video games and other violent media could have less visible but significant harmful effects on children's lives. For example, it's feasible that certain types or amounts of video game play could affect emotions, cognitions, perceptions, and behaviors in ways that promote bullying and victimization.

In recent years, we have become increasingly aware of bullying as a threat to healthy development and well being. A large United States survey of children in grades 6 through 10 found that nearly 30% reported occasional or frequent (at least once a week) involvement as a bully, victim, or both. The most recent government report on school crime and safety found that the percentage of children ages 12 to 18 who reported being bullied increased from 1999 (5%) to 2001 (8%). According to the latest National Youth Risk Behavior Survey, the percentage of high school students who felt too unsafe to go to school at least once in the previous 30 days increased significantly from 1997 to 2001 (from 4% to 6.6%). In 2001, fewer adolescents reported carrying weapons on school property (which could reflect aggressive intent or a fear-based need for self-protection), but the risk of being threatened or injured with a gun, club, or knife on school property has not decreased, as 8.9% of students reported this had happened to them at least once in the previous 12 months.

Suggestions for Future Research

In summary, it's very difficult to document whether and how violent video and computer games contribute to serious violence such as criminal assault or murder. (Practically speaking, this would require a massive and expensive study because game playing is common, and murder is rare.) It is feasible, however, to study how violent games may contribute to some types of everyday violence and aggression and to the beliefs, attitudes, and interpretations of behavior that support them. For example, are heavy players of violent games more likely to view aggression as a first-choice solution to problems instead of a last resort (e.g., instead of talking or seeking mediation first), to see violence as easily justified, to feel less empathy for others, or to interpret ambiguous behavior (e.g., a bump in the school hallway) as deliberately hostile, threatening, or disrespectful? Another issue is whether and how the effects of video game violence might be compounded by exposure to violence in other media. Cautious interpretation is necessary, since there is always the risk of confusing cause and effect or correlation with causation.

To make intervention efforts more effective and cost-efficient, it's important to focus on which children are at risk. Risk factors for violence tend to occur in clusters. Violent game play may disproportionately affect children who lack protective factors such as a nurturing relationship with at least one adult and connection to and relative success in school. A child's stage of emotional or cognitive development may also be important.

The amount of time spent playing games is also worthy of study. Given the ubiquity of violent game play among boys, we might see a J-shaped curve, similar to common findings in research on adult alcohol use: a little is healthy, but a lot becomes a health risk. In other words, a moderate amount of interactive game play may be associated with a healthier social life, while increasing amounts of play (or solitary play) may correlate with poor adjustment or emotional difficulties.

Few researchers have asked children *why* they play games and what meaning games have for them. While most probably play for fun or sociability, some children seem to use games to vent anger or distract themselves from problems. This could be functional or unhealthy, depending on the child's mental health and the amount and type of game play. We know almost nothing about the differential effects of games on depressed or anxious children or those with attention deficit-hyperactivity disorder.

There is also a need for research on the effects of different types of games, going beyond the gore level. Does violence that serves a worthy end (e.g., a SWAT team rescuing hostages) or violence that is ultimately punished (e.g., a criminal protagonist ends up dead or in jail) have different effects than violence that is rewarded, even if the games are equally bloody? Do children who enjoy violent games with story lines differ from those who prefer bouts of fighting? Do violent games that make use of irony and sarcasm, such as *Grand Theft Auto: Vice City,* have differential effects on children who are not cognitively able to detect that irony and sarcasm?

We need to learn more about what activities are displaced by game play. A teenager who spends hours playing games over the Internet might miss key opportunities to build social skills with real people or lose opportunities for healthy physical activity.

Finally, researchers must acknowledge that electronic games are a moving target. The technology is constantly advancing. Studies conducted 5 or even 2 years ago may have limited relevance given improvements in graphics, the rise of Internet gaming, the introduction of games controlled by voice of body movements, and the potential for increased tactile feedback via "haptics" technology to create the sense of immersion in a virtual world.

We might take a lesson from America's history of media hysteria. It's time to move beyond blanket condemnations and frightening anecdotes and focus on developing targeted educational and policy interventions based on solid data. As with the entertainment media of earlier generations, we may look back on some of today's games with nostalgia, and our grandchildren may wonder what the fuss was about.

CHALLENGE QUESTIONS

Do Video Games Lead to Violence?

1. Is Olson's criticism of the research on video game violence—that the test conditions are difficult to generalize to real-world settings—a criticism that could be made of other areas of psychological research? If so, describe one such area.
2. Gentile and Anderson list several reasons why violent video games may have a greater effect on kids than violent television. Which do you think has the greater effect? Defend your position.
3. What is the difference between correlation and causation? How does this difference pertain to Olson's critique of violent video game research?
4. Based on what you have learned from the two selections, what kinds of restrictions, if any, do you think parents should place on their children's exposure to violent video games? Defend your answer with information from both selections.
5. Olson cites a Web site where she learned of the U.S. Army's use of violent video games to train its troops. Find examples of other organizations that use video games to educate their personnel. Are they using violent video games? Why or why not?

ISSUE 17

Does the Internet Have Psychological Benefits?

YES: James E. Katz and Philip Aspden, from "A Nation of Strangers?" *Communications of the ACM* (December 1997)

NO: Robert Kraut et al., from "Internet Paradox: A Social Technology That Reduces Social Involvement and Psychological Well-Being?" *American Psychologist* (September 1998)

ISSUE SUMMARY

YES: Research scientist James E. Katz and Philip Aspden, executive director of the Center for Research on the Information Society, contend that the Internet has positive effects on the lives of its users. They also maintain that the Internet creates more opportunities for people to foster relationships with people, regardless of their location.

NO: Robert Kraut, a professor of social psychology and human computer interaction, and his colleagues at Carnegie Mellon University question how beneficial Internet use really is. They argue that Internet use reduces the number and quality of interpersonal relationships that one has.

Not long ago, phrases like "surfing the Web" were understood by only the most technologically advanced. Now the Internet is accessible by almost anyone from almost anywhere, including classrooms, homes, and businesses. People can even check their e-mail in some malls. People spend increasing amounts of time on the Internet and use it for an increasing number of things. With the touch of a button, people can gain access to oceans of information and all sorts of new activities. What effects does the explosion of Internet access have on the psychological well-being of Internet users? Is it beneficial or harmful?

Many people feel that the Internet gives them greater opportunities to meet new friends in chat rooms and through other forms of Internet communication. The Internet offers the potential for thousands of new relationships and the protection of relative anonymity. No one knows if a user is attractive, has a particular ethnicity, or has a good job. All that an individual's chat room companions know is what she or he tells them. The problem is that Internet relationships require people to spend time in relative isolation—time in front of a machine. This has spurred some to predict that the Internet will decrease community and family involvement. They feel that the time spent in front of a computer monitor, communicating with people who cannot be seen, greatly detracts from more healthy relationships. Instead of talking to immediate family members or friends, the Internet user spends hours talking to people who require little from the user. Critics maintain that Internet relationships are largely superficial and that some are even deceptive.

In the following selection, James E. Katz and Philip Aspden contend that the Internet is anything but harmful. They indicate that the Internet is, in fact, beneficial to the psychological health of its users. Internet use merely adds to traditional forms of social ties, they argue, and users of the Internet are just as active in social organizations as nonusers. Rather than shrinking a person's social contacts, the Internet expands social opportunities. Katz and Aspden also argue that Internet use does not negatively influence the quantity or quality of time spent with family and friends.

In the second selection, Robert Kraut et al. hold that Internet use not only decreases family communication but also increases depression and loneliness. Although they acknowledge that the Internet does allow for a greater number of friendships, they argue that the kinds of friendships gained on the Internet are of a poorer quality than more traditional friendships. They suggest that "people are substituting poorer quality social relationships for better relationships, that is, substituting weak ties for strong ones." Kraut et al. maintain that Internet use should be carefully balanced with real-life social involvement in order to curtail the negative psychological effects of reliance on Web friends.

POINT

- Internet use leads to more relationships, regardless of geography or convenience.

- Internet use does not have a significant effect on time spent with friends and family.

- The number one use of the Internet is interpersonal communication.

- Sixty percent of the people who have met friends on the Internet also went on to meet them face-to-face.

COUNTERPOINT

- Relationships gained on the Internet block people from "real," more satisfying relationships and reduces social involvement.

- Greater use of the Internet causes declines in family communication as well as increased rates of depression and loneliness.

- Internet use is associated with physical inactivity and less face-to-face contact.

- Only 22 percent of people who have used the Internet for at least two years have ever made a new friend on the Internet.

319

A Nation of Strangers?

Readers of New York tabloid newspapers may have been shocked [in 1997] by a front-page photograph showing a local computer expert being led away in handcuffs, having been arrested on charges of raping a woman he had met via the Internet. But troubles with Internet acquaintances are by no means unique. Stories appear in the news media with disturbing frequency about young boys or girls running away from their homes with adults they met through computer bulletin boards or chat groups. . . . As similar stories arise about Internet friendships going awry, or even of these "friendships" being malicious cons in the first place, concerns over the Internet's social impact will increase. Of course the concern is by no means limited to the one-on-one level of interpersonal friendships. National and international bodies are grappling with questions about what to do about various extremist political or religious groups who are aiming to suborn or recruit large groups of people. The mass suicide of the Heaven's Gate cult, which had a presence on the Internet, was a ready target for those who fear the way the Internet is changing society.

But the Internet situation is not unique. Every new technology finds dour critics (as well as ebullient proponents). Communication technologies in particular can be seen as opening the doors to all varieties of social ills. When the telegraph, telephone and the automobile were in their infancy, each of these three earlier "communication" technologies found vitriolic critics who said these "instruments of the devil" would drastically alter society (which they did) with disastrous consequences for the quality of life and the moral order (readers may judge for themselves about this point). The Internet is no exception to this rule. Indeed, it has stimulated so many commentators that not even the most indefatigable reader can stay abreast of the flood of speculation and opinion. Yet, as might be expected in light of the conflicts, difficulties, and tragedies associated with the Internet mentioned previously, one area in particular has been singled out for comment: the way the Internet affects social relationships generally and participation in community life in particular. Among those who have criticized the Internet are MIT's Sherry Turkle, who claims that it leads to the destruction of meaningful community and social integration, and Berkeley's Cliff Stoll, who says it reduces people's commitment to and enjoyment of real friendships. . . .

From James E. Katz and Philip Aspden, "A Nation of Strangers?" *Communications of the ACM*, vol. 40, no. 12 (December 1997). Copyright © 1997 by The Association for Computing Machinery. Reprinted by permission. References omitted.

By contrast, optimists argue that genuinely meaningful communities can be established in cyberspace, and indeed even fostered via online communications. Rheingold holds that since virtual interfacing obscures social categories we ordinarily use to sift our relationships (race, sex, age, location), the possibility of new relationships and hence new communities is multiplied. An even more utopian argument is that new, powerful communities will arise in cyberspace, supplanting physical ones of the past, and becoming to an unprecedented extent cohesive, democratic, and meaningful for its members. Indeed, Internet pioneer and Lotus Corporation cofounder Mitch Kapor sees virtual communities ringing in at last the Jeffersonian ideal of community. "Life in cyberspace seems to be shaping up exactly like Thomas Jefferson would have wanted: founded on the primacy of individual liberty and a commitment to pluralism, diversity, and community."

But all these theories have been based on personal impressions, anecdotal evidence or case studies rather than systematic investigation. We wanted to get a broader, more objective picture of what is going on in terms of friendship formation and community involvement for the denizens of the Internet. (We use the term Internet to encompass such aspects of cyberspace as networked computers, computer bulletin boards, and email). Hence in late 1995 we carried out a national random telephone survey which had among its objectives to: compare "real-world" participation for Internet users and non-users, and to examine friendship creation via the Internet.

Our approach was to consider the perspectives of five different Internet awareness/usage groups:

- Those not aware of the Internet,
- Non-users who were aware of the Internet,
- Former users,
- Recent users—those who started using the Internet in 1995,
- Longtime users—those who started using the Internet prior to 1995.

By comparing those who were on the Internet versus those who were not, and controlling statistically for demonstrable demographic differences among user categories, we would be in a position to see if, on average, Internet users were less likely to belong to various voluntary organizations, thus strengthening the hand of those who see the Internet as socially pernicious. Of course if they belonged to more organizations than their non-Internet-using counterparts, the celebrationists would be supported. Likewise, by getting a representative sample of Internet users to speak about their experiences with friendship formation, we would also have some more reliable views of what the typical or majority experiences have been in this regard, without having our understanding biased by a few extraordinary reports.

Our October 1995 survey yielded 2,500 respondents—8% reported being Internet users, 8% reported being former Internet users, 68% reported being aware of the Internet but not being users, and 16% reported not being aware of the Internet. The sample of Internet users was augmented by a national random telephone sample of 400 Internet users. Of the total of

600 Internet users, 49% reported being longtime Internet users. As a whole, our survey of 2,500 respondents closely matches socioeconomic patterns of the U.S. population on key variables: compared to 1990/91 U.S. Census data, our sample reflects national averages in gender, ethnic mix, and age, and is slightly wealthier and better educated.

No Evidence of Internet Users Dropping Out of Real Life

We explored respondents' community involvement in the real world by asking them how many religious, leisure, and community organizations they belonged to.

Religious organizations.   Our survey showed no statistically significant differences across the five awareness/usage categories in membership rates of religious organizations. Fifty-six percent of respondents reported belonging to one religious organization, while a further 8% reported belonging to two or more religious organizations. . . .

Leisure organizations.   Here we found that non-users reported belonging to fewer organizations than users, both former and current. Non-users who were not aware of the Internet reported being members of fewest leisure organizations—11% reported belonging to one leisure organization and a further 13% belonged to two or more leisure organizations. Non-users who were aware of the Internet reported belonging to significantly more leisure organizations—21% reported belonging to one leisure organization and a further 19% belonged to two or more leisure organizations.

Reported membership rates for former and current users were much higher—21% of former users reported belonging to one leisure organization and 28% to two or more; 24% of recent users reported belonging to one leisure organization and 25% to two or more; and 24% of longtime users reported belonging to one leisure organization and 29% to two or more. However when we statistically controlled for demographic variables, these differences disappeared.

Community organizations.   The aggregate responses to the question about membership of community organizations did not appear to display a pattern relating to the awareness/usage categories. Those who were not aware of the Internet and recent users appeared to belong to the fewest community organizations. . . .

Non-users who were aware of the Internet and former users belonged to more community organizations. . . .

Longtime Internet users reported belonging to most community organizations—27% reported belonging to one organization and a further 22% to two or more. Overall, the survey results provide no evidence that Internet users belong to fewer community organizations. . . .

The Internet Is Augmenting Involvement in Existing Communities

. . . Contact with family members.   An area where the Internet appeared to have a significant impact on social involvement was communications with family members where just under half the users reported contacting family members at least once or twice. Longtime users reported contacting family members more often than recent members. Thirty-five percent of longtime users reported contacting family members at least several times a month, twice the proportion of recent users.

Participation in Internet communities.   We also asked users the extent they participated in Internet communities. Again we found a significant degree of participation—31% of longtime users and 17% of recent users reported doing so. The distribution of the number of communities belonged to for both long-time and recent users was not statistically different (Chi square = 3.6, sig. = 0.6, with 5 degrees of freedom). Of those who reported participating in various Internet communities, 58% participated in one or two communities, 28% participated in three or four communities, and 14% participated in five or more communities.

Change in face-to-face/phone communications.   For the vast majority of both longtime and recent users, use of the Internet did not appear to have much impact on the time spent with friends and family. The two groups' views were not statistically different. Eighty-eight percent of users reported that the time spent with friends and family face-to-face or by phone since they started using Internet had not changed. The same proportions (6%) of users reported they spent more time with friends and family face-to-face or by phone, as those who spent less time.

The Internet Is Emerging as a Medium for Friendship Creation

Friendship formation.   As part of our survey, we asked Internet users whether they knew people only through the Internet whom they considered their friends. Of our 601 Internet users, a significant minority (82 respondents, 14% of our sample of Internet users) reported knowing people in this way.

Propensity to form friendships through the Internet appeared to relate more strongly to general measures of Internet usage and experience, rather than demographic variables. For example, those with self-identified higher Internet skill levels appeared more likely to make Internet friends. Nine percent of novices, 13% of those with average skill levels, 22% of those with above average skill levels, and 27% of those with excellent skill levels reported making Internet friendships.

Somewhat surprisingly, we found no statistical relationships between propensity to make friends and a wide range of measures of traditional forms of social connectedness and measures of personality attributes. . . . This perhaps points to the Internet deemphasizing the importance of sociability and personality differences.

Number of friendships formed.   For the 81 users who reported establishing friendships via the Internet, a substantial proportion said they had made numerous friendships. Thirty percent of the group (24 respondents) reported having established friendships with 1 to 3 people, 40% (32 respondents) with 4 to 10 people, 22% (18 respondents) with 11 to 30 people, and 9% (7 respondents) with 31 or more people. The best predictor of the number of friends made was again a general measure of Internet usage. Longtime users reported making more friends. . . .

Internet friendships leading to meetings.   A majority of people who reported making friends through the Internet met one or more of them. Of the 81 respondents who reported making friends via the Internet, 60% reported meeting one or more of these friends. Those reporting higher numbers of Internet friends were more likely to have met at least one of them. . . .

Number of friends met.   For the 49 users who reported meeting Internet friends, a substantial number of meetings were reported. Thirty-seven percent of the group (18 respondents) reported meeting with 1 to 3 Internet friends, 29% (14 respondents) with 4 to 10 Internet friends, 22% (11 respondents) with 11 to 30 Internet friends, and 12% (6 respondents) met with 31 or more Internet friends. . . .

Although it is always dangerous to extrapolate, we will do so nonetheless. Based on the data, it would be our guess that perhaps two million new face-to-face meetings have taken place due to participation on the Internet. We do not know, since we did not ask, what the purpose of these meetings might have been (dating services, support groups, hobbyists, political activism?). We hope to explore questions along these lines in our future work.

Pessimism for Pessimistic Theories

Based on our national snapshot, we found no support for the pessimistic theories of the effects of cyberspace on community involvement. When controlling for demographic differences between users and non-users, we found no statistical differences in participation rates in religious, leisure, and community organizations.

Moreover, the Internet appeared to augment existing traditional social connectivity. Just under half of Internet users reported contacting family members at least once or twice via the Internet. A significant minority of users also reported participating in Internet communities. In addition, the vast majority of both longtime and recent users reported that time spent with friends and family in face-to-face contact or by phone had not changed since they started using the Internet.

Further, our survey suggests that the Internet is emerging as a medium for cultivating friendships which, in a majority of cases, lead to meetings in the real world. The Internet is currently a medium where Internet skills appear to be the most important determinant of friendship formation, eclipsing personality characteristics such as sociability, extroversion, and willingness to take risks.

. . . We also found—due to people's Internet activities, the formation of many new friendships, the creation of senses of community, and reports of voluminous contact with family members. In sum, although the "Jeffersonian ideal" may not be realized, a high proportion of Internet users are engaging in lots of social contact and communication with friends and family. Many family members are keeping in touch and new friendships are being formed. Far from creating a nation of strangers, the Internet is creating a nation richer in friendships and social relationships.

 **NO**

Internet Paradox

Fifteen years ago, computers were mainly the province of science, engineering, and business. By 1998, approximately 40% of all U.S. households owned a personal computer; roughly one third of these homes had access to the Internet. Many scholars, technologists, and social critics believe that these changes and the Internet, in particular, are transforming economic and social life (e.g., Anderson, Bikson, Law, & Mitchell, 1995; Attewell & Rule, 1984; King & Kraemer, 1995). However, analysts disagree as to the nature of these changes and whether the changes are for the better or worse. Some scholars argue that the Internet is causing people to become socially isolated and cut off from genuine social relationships, as they hunker alone over their terminals or communicate with anonymous strangers through a socially impoverished medium (e.g., Stoll, 1995; Turkle, 1996). Others argue that the Internet leads to more and better social relationships by freeing people from the constraints of geography or isolation brought on by stigma, illness, or schedule. According to them, the Internet allows people to join groups on the basis of common interests rather than convenience (e.g., Katz & Aspden, 1997; Rheingold, 1993). . . .

Whether the Internet is increasing or decreasing social involvement could have enormous consequences for society and for people's personal well-being. In an influential article, Putnam (1995) documented a broad decline in civic engagement and social participation in the United States over the past 35 years. Citizens vote less, go to church less, discuss government with their neighbors less, are members of fewer voluntary organizations, have fewer dinner parties, and generally get together less for civic and social purposes. Putnam argued that this social disengagement is having major consequences for the social fabric and for individual lives. At the societal level, social disengagement is associated with more corrupt, less efficient government and more crime. When citizens are involved in civic life, their schools run better, their politicians are more responsive, and their streets are safer. At the individual level, social disengagement is associated with poor quality of life and diminished physical and psychological health. When people have more social contact, they are happier and healthier, both physically and mentally (e.g., S. Cohen & Wills, 1985; Gove & Geerken, 1977).

From Robert Kraut, Michael Patterson, Vicki Lundmark, Sara Kiesler, Tridas Mukopadhyay, and William Scherlis, "Internet Paradox: A Social Technology That Reduces Social Involvement and Psychological Well-Being?" *American Psychologist*, vol. 53, no. 9 (September 1998). Copyright © 1998 by The American Psychological Association. Reprinted by permission. References omitted.

Although changes in the labor force participation of women and marital breakup may account for some of the declines in social participation and increase in depression since the 1960s, technological change may also play a role. Television, an earlier technology similar to the Internet in some respects, may have reduced social participation as it kept people home watching the set. By contrast, other household technologies, in particular, the telephone, are used to enhance social participation, not discourage it (Fischer, 1992). The home computer and the Internet are too new and, until recently, were too thinly diffused into American households to explain social trends that originated over 35 years, but, now, they could either exacerbate or ameliorate these trends, depending on how they are used. . . .

Internet for Entertainment, Information, and Commerce

If people use the Internet primarily for entertainment and information, the Internet's social effects might resemble those of television. Most research on the social impact of television has focused on its content; this research has investigated the effects of TV violence, educational content, gender stereotypes, racial stereotypes, advertising, and portrayals of family life, among other topics (Huston et al., 1992). Some social critics have argued that television reinforces sociability and social bonds (Beniger, 1987, pp. 356–362; McLuhan, 1964, p. 304). One study comparing Australian towns before and after television became available suggests that the arrival of television led to increases in social activity (Murray & Kippax, 1978). However most empirical work has indicated that television watching reduces social involvement (Brody, 1990; Jackson-Beeck & Robinson, 1981; Neuman, 1991; Maccoby, 1951). Recent epidemiological research has linked television watching with reduced physical activity and diminished physical and mental health (Anderson, Crespo, Bartlett, Cheskin, & Pratt, 1998; Sidney et al., 1998). . . .

Like watching television, using a home computer and the Internet generally imply physical inactivity and limited face-to-face social interaction. Some studies, including our own, have indicated that using a home computer and the Internet can lead to increased skills and confidence with computers (Lundmark, Kiesler, Kraut, Scherlis, & Mukopadhyay, 1998). However, when people use these technologies intensively for learning new software, playing computer games, or retrieving electronic information, they consume time and may spend more time alone (Vitalari, Venkatesh, & Gronhaug, 1985). Some cross-sectional research suggests that home computing may be displacing television watching itself (Danko & McLachlan, 1983; Kohut, 1994) as well as reducing leisure time with the family (Vitalari et al., 1985).

Internet for Interpersonal Communication

The Internet, like its network predecessors (Sproull & Kiesler, 1991), has turned out to be far more social than television, and in this respect, the impact of the Internet may be more like that of the telephone than of TV. Our research has shown that interpersonal communication is the dominant use of the Internet at home (Kraut, Mukhopadhyay, Szczypula, Kiesler, & Scherlis, 1998). That people use the Internet mainly for interpersonal communication, however, does not imply that their social interactions and relationships on the Internet are the same as their traditional social interactions and relationships (Sproull & Kiesler, 1991), or that their social uses of the Internet will have effects comparable to traditional social activity.

. . . Strong ties are relationships associated with frequent contact, deep feelings of affection and obligation, and application to a broad content domain, whereas weak ties are relationships with superficial and easily broken bonds, infrequent contact, and narrow focus. Strong and weak ties alike provide people with social support. Weak ties (Granovetter, 1973), including weak on-line ties (Constant, Sproull, & Kiesler, 1996), are especially useful for linking people to information and social resources unavailable in people's closest, local groups. Nonetheless, strong social ties are the relationships that generally buffer people from life's stresses and that lead to better social and psychological outcomes (S. Cohen & Wills, 1985; Krackhardt, 1994). People receive most of their social support from people with whom they are in most frequent contact, and bigger favors come from those with stronger ties (Wellman & Wortley, 1990).

Generally, strong personal ties are supported by physical proximity. The Internet potentially reduces the importance of physical proximity in creating and maintaining networks of strong social ties. Unlike face-to-face interaction or even the telephone, the Internet offers opportunities for social interaction that do not depend on the distance between parties. People often use the Internet to keep up with those whom they have preexisting relationships (Kraut et al., 1998). But they also develop new relationships on-line. Most of these new relationships are weak. . . .

Whether a typical relationship developed on-line becomes as strong as a typical traditional relationship and whether having on-line relationships changes the number or quality of a person's total social involvements are open questions. . . .

Current Data

Katz and Aspden's national survey (1997) is one of the few empirical studies that has compared the social participation of Internet users with nonusers. Controlling statistically for education, race, and other demographic variables, these researchers found no differences between Internet users' and nonusers' memberships in religious, leisure, and community organizations or in the amount of time users and nonusers reported spending communicating with family and friends. From these data, Katz and Aspden concluded that "[f]ar from creating a nation of strangers, the Internet is creating a nation richer in friendships and social relationships" (p. 86).

Katz and Aspden's (1997) conclusions may be premature because they used potentially inaccurate, self-report measures of Internet usage and social participation that are probably too insensitive to detect gradual changes over time. Furthermore, their observation that people have friendships on-line does not necessarily lead to the inference that using the Internet increases the people's social participation or psychological well-being; to draw such a conclusion, one needs to know more about the quality of their on-line relationships and the impact on their off-line relationships. Many studies show unequivocally that people can and do form on-line social relationships (e.g., Parks & Floyd, 1995). However, these data do not speak to the frequency, depth, and impact of on-line relationships compared with traditional ones or whether the existence of on-line relationships changes traditional relationships or the balance of people's strong and weak ties.

Even if a cross-sectional survey were to convincingly demonstrate that Internet use is associated with greater social involvement, it would not establish the causal direction of this relationship. In many cases, it is as plausible to assume that social involvement causes Internet use as the reverse. For example, many people buy a home computer to keep in touch with children in college or with retired parents. People who use the Internet differ substantially from those who do not in their demographics, skills, values, and attitudes. Statistical tests often under-control for the influence of these factors, which in turn can be associated with social involvement (Anderson et al., 1995; Kraut, Scherlis, Mukhopadhyay, Manning, & Kiesler, 1996; Kohut, 1994).

A Longitudinal Study of Internet Use

The research described here uses longitudinal data to examine the causal relationship between people's use of the Internet, their social involvement, and certain likely psychological consequences of social involvement. The data come from a field trial of Internet use, in which we tracked the behavior of 169 participants over their first one or two years of Internet use. It improves on earlier research by using accurate measures of Internet use and a panel research design. Measures of Internet use were recorded automatically, and measures of social involvement and psychological well-being were collected twice, using reliable self-report scales. Because we tracked people over time, we can observe change and control statistically for social involvement, psychological states, and demographic attributes of the trial participants that existed prior to their use of the Internet. With these statistical controls and measures of change, we can draw stronger causal conclusions than is possible in research in which the data are collected once.

Method

Sample

The HomeNet study consists of a sample of 93 families from eight diverse neighborhoods in Pittsburgh, Pennsylvania. . . . Children younger than 10 and uninterested members of the households are not included in the sample. . . .

Families received a computer and software, a free telephone line, and free access to the Internet in exchange for permitting the researchers to automatically track their Internet usage and services, for answering periodic questionnaires, and for agreeing to an in-home interview. . . .

Data Collection

We measured demographic characteristics, social involvement, and psychological well-being of participants in the HomeNet trial on a pretest questionnaire, before the participants were given access to the Internet. After 12 to 24 months, participants completed a follow-up questionnaire containing the measures of social involvement and psychological well-being. During this interval, we automatically recorded their Internet usage using custom-designed logging programs. The data reported here encompass the first 104 weeks of use after a HomeNet family's Internet account was first operational for the 1995 subsample and 52 weeks of use for the 1996 subsample. . . .

Internet usage   Software recorded the total hours in a week in which a participant connected to the Internet. Electronic mail and the World Wide Web were the major applications that participants used on the Internet and account for most of their time on-line. Internet hours also included time that participants read distribution lists such as listservs or Usenet newsgroups and participated in real-time communication using the Web chat lines, MUDs, and Internet Relay Chat. For the analyses we report here, we averaged weekly Internet hours over the period in which each participant had access to the Internet, from the pretest up to the time he or she completed the follow-up questionnaire. Our analyses use the log of the variable to normalize the distribution.

Social Involvement

Family communication   . . . The analysis of family communication showed that teenagers used the Internet more hours than did adults, but Whites did not differ from minorities, and female participants did not differ from male participants in their average hours of use. Different families varied in their use of the Internet . . . but the amount of communication that an individual family member had with other members of the family did not predict subsequent Internet use. . . . For our purposes, the most important finding is that greater use of the Internet was associated with subsequent declines in family communication.

Size of participants' social networks   . . . Greater social extroversion and having a larger local social circle predicted less use of the Internet during the next 12 to 24 months. Whites reported increasing their distant social circles more than minorities did, and teens reported increasing their distant circles more than adults did; these groups did not differ in changes to their local circles. Holding constant these control variables and the initial sizes of participants' social circles, greater use of the Internet was associated with subsequent declines in the size of both the local social circles ($p < .05$) and, marginally, the size of the distant social circle ($p < .07$). . . .

Psychological Well-Being

Loneliness   . . . Note that initial loneliness did not predict subsequent Internet use. Loneliness was stable over time. People from richer households increased loneliness more than did those from poorer households, men increased loneliness more than did women, and minorities increased loneliness more than did Whites. Controlling for these personal characteristics and initial loneliness, people who used the Internet more subsequently reported larger increases in loneliness. The association of Internet use with subsequent loneliness was comparable to the associations of income, gender, and race with subsequent loneliness. . . .

Depression   . . . Initial depression did not predict subsequent Internet use. Minorities reported more increases in depression than did Whites, and those with higher initial stress also reported greater increases in depression. For the purposes of this analysis, the important finding is that greater use of the Internet was associated with increased depression at a subsequent period, even holding constant initial depression and demographic, stress, and support variables that are often associated with depression. This negative association between Internet use and depression is consistent with the interpretation that use of the Internet caused an increase in depression. Again, it is noteworthy that depression . . . did not predict using the Internet subsequently.

Discussion

Evaluating the Causal Claim

The findings of this research provide a surprisingly consistent picture of the consequences of using the Internet. Greater use of the Internet was associated with small, but statistically significant declines in social involvement as measured by communication within the family and the size of people's local social networks, and with increases in loneliness, a psychological state associated with social involvement. Greater use of the Internet was also associated with increases in depression. Other effects on the size of the distant social circle, social support, and stress did not reach standard significance levels but were consistently negative.

Our analyses are consistent with the hypothesis that using the Internet adversely affects social involvement and psychological well-being. The panel research design gives us substantial leverage in inferring causation, leading us to believe that in this case, correlation does indeed imply causation. Initial Internet use and initial social involvement and psychological well-being were included in all of the models assessing the effects of Internet use on subsequent social and psychological outcomes. Therefore, our analysis is equivalent to an analysis of change scores, controlling for regression toward the mean, unreliability, contemporaneous covariation between the outcome and the predictor variables, and other statistical artifacts (J. Cohen & Cohen, 1983). Because initial social involvement and psychological well-being were generally not associated with subsequent use of the Internet, these findings imply that the direction of causation is more likely to run from use of the Internet to declines in social involvement and psychological well-being, rather than the reverse. The only exception to this generalization was a marginal finding that people who initially had larger local social circles were lighter users of the Internet.

The major threat to the causal claim would arise if some unmeasured factor varying over time within individuals were to simultaneously cause increases in their use of the Internet and declines in their normal levels of social involvement and psychological well-being. One such factor might be developmental changes in adolescence, which could cause teenagers to withdraw from social contact (at least from members of their families) and to use the Internet as an escape. Our data are mixed regarding this interpretation. In analyses not reported . . . , statistical interactions of Internet use with age showed that increases in Internet use were associated with larger increases in loneliness ($\beta = -.16$, $p < .02$) and larger declines in social support ($\beta = -.13$, $p < .05$) for teenagers than for adults. On the other hand, increases in Internet use were associated with smaller increases in daily stress for teenagers than adults ($\beta = -.16$, $p < .02$). There were no statistical interactions between Internet use and age for family communication, depression, or size of social circle. . . .

Finally, we can generalize our results only to outcomes related to social behavior. In particular, we are not reporting effects of the Internet on educational outcomes or on self-esteem related to computer skill learning. Participants gained computer skills with more Internet usage. Several parents of teenagers who had spent many hours on-line judged that their children's positive educational outcomes from using the Internet outweighed possible declines in their children's social interaction. Future research will be needed to evaluate whether such trade-offs exist. . . .

Displacing social activity   The time that people devote to using the Internet might substitute for time that they had previously spent engaged in social activities. According to this explanation, the Internet is similar to other passive, nonsocial entertainment activities, such as watching TV, reading, or listening to music. Use of the Internet, like watching TV, may represent a privatization of entertainment, which could lead to social withdrawal and to declines in psychological well-being. Putnam (1995) made a similar claim about television viewing.

The problem with this explanation is that a major use of the Internet is explicitly social. People use the Internet to keep up with family and friends through electronic mail and on-line chats and to make new acquaintances through MUDs, chats, Usenet newsgroups, and listservs. Our previous analyses showed that interpersonal communication was the dominant use of the Internet among the sample studied in this research (Kraut et al., 1998). They used the Internet more frequently for exchanging electronic mail than for surfing the World Wide Web and, within a session, typically checked their mail before looking at the Web; their use of electronic mail was more stable over time than their use of the World Wide Web; and greater use of e-mail relative to the Web led them to use the Internet more intensively and over a longer period (Kraut et al., 1998). Other analyses, not reported here, show that even social uses of the Internet were associated with negative outcomes. For example, greater use of electronic mail was associated with increases in depression.

Displacing strong ties   The paradox we observe, then, is that the Internet is a social technology used for communication with individuals and groups, but it is associated with declines in social involvement and the psychological well-being that goes with social involvement. Perhaps, by using the Internet, people are substituting poorer quality social relationships for better relationships, that is, substituting weak ties for strong ones (e.g., Granovetter, 1973; Krackhardt, 1994). People can support strong ties electronically. Indeed, interviews with this sample revealed numerous instances in which participants kept up with physically distant parents or siblings, corresponded with children when they went off to college, rediscovered roommates from the past, consoled distant friends who had suffered tragedy, or exchanged messages with high school classmates after school.

However, many of the on-line relationships in our sample, and especially the new ones, represented weak ties rather than strong ones. Examples include a woman who exchanged mittens with a stranger she met on a knitting listserv, a man who exchanged jokes and Scottish trivia with a colleague he met through an on-line tourist website, and an adolescent who exchanged (fictional) stories about his underwater exploits to other members of a scuba diving chat service. A few participants met new people on-line and had friendships with them. For instance, one teenager met his prom date on-line, and another woman met a couple in Canada whom she subsequently visited during her summer vacation. However, interviews with participants in this trial suggest that making new friends on-line was rare. Even though it was welcomed when it occurred, it did not counteract overall declines in real-world communication with family and friends. Our conclusions resonate with Katz and Aspden's (1997) national survey data showing that only 22% of the respondents who had been using the Internet for two or more years had ever made a new friend on the Internet. Although neither we nor Katz and Aspden provide comparison data, we wonder whether, in the real world, only a fifth of the population make a friend over a two-year period.

On-line friendships are likely to be more limited than friendships supported by physical proximity. On-line friends are less likely than friends developed at school, work, church, or in the neighborhood to be available for help with tangible favors, such as offering small loans, rides, or baby-sitting. Because on-line friends are not embedded in the same day-to-day environment, they will be less likely to understand the context for conversation, making discussion more difficult (Clark, 1996) and rendering support less applicable. Even strong ties maintained at a distance through electronic communication are likely to be different in kind and perhaps diminished in strength compared with strong ties supported by physical proximity (Wellman & Wortley, 1990). Both frequently of contact and the nature of the medium may contribute to this difference. For example, one of our participants who said that she appreciated the e-mail correspondence she had with her college-aged daughter also noted that when her daughter was homesick or depressed, she reverted to telephone calls to provide support. Although a clergyman in the sample used e-mail to exchange sermon ideas with other clergy, he phoned them when he needed advice about negotiating his contract. Like that mother and clergyman, many participants in our sample loved the convenience of the Internet. However, this convenience may induce people to substitute less involving electronic interactions for more involving real-world ones. The clergyman in the sample reported that his involvement with his listserv came at the expense of time with his wife. . . .

Both as a nation and as individual consumers, we must balance the value of the Internet for information, communication, and commerce with its costs. Use of the Internet can be both highly entertaining and useful, but if it causes too much disengagement from real life, it can also be harmful. Until the technology evolves to be more beneficial, people should moderate how much they use the Internet and monitor the uses to which they put it.

CHALLENGE QUESTIONS

Does the Internet Have Psychological Benefits?

1. Do you use the Internet? Discuss how it has increased or decreased your ability to create and sustain relationships. Integrate your experiences with current research.
2. One of the issues embedded in this controversy is the importance of face-to-face contact. How significant are a body, nonverbal communication, and the environment of communication in such contact?
3. Are there benefits of the Internet other than social? Review the research on this, and discuss it in light of the social relationship issue.
4. Take a survey of at least 20 people who use the Internet. Ask them questions about how and why they use the Internet. Use your results to support or disprove a hypothesis that you might have regarding social relationships.

ISSUE 18

Is Pornography Harmful?

YES: Diana E. H. Russell, from *Dangerous Relationships: Pornography, Misogyny, and Rape* (Sage, 1998)

NO: Michael C. Seto, Alexandra Maric, and Howard E. Barbaree, from "The Role of Pornography in the Etiology of Sexual Aggression," *Aggression and Violent Behavior* (January–February 2001)

ISSUE SUMMARY

YES: Sociology professor Diana E. H. Russell argues that pornography is profoundly harmful because it predisposes men to want to rape women and undermines social inhibitions against acting out rape fantasies.

NO: Michael C. Seto, Alexandra Maric, and Howard E. Barbaree, of the Centre for Addiction and Mental Health, contend that evidence for a causal link between pornography use and sexual offense remains equivocal.

The United States has some of the highest rates of violence in the world, particularly among advanced societies. Of special concern are the high rates of violence against women. What causes this? Finding the answer to this question has led numerous psychological researchers to investigate the relationship between pornography, especially violent pornography, and actual violence.

Results from these investigations have led to two basic conclusions. Those who view pornography as a prime cause of violence against women contend that pornography depicts women as objects to be degraded and abused. As they see it, continual exposure to such degradation and abuse eventually leads viewers to engage in the same kind of behavior. Researchers who hold this opinion look to *social learning theory,* a prominent psychological explanation of behavior, as a rationale for their arguments: What people see is eventually what people do. Other psychologists contend that pornography does not negatively affect viewers' attitudes and actions toward women. They consider pornography to be a scapegoat for society's ills, and they maintain that the research does not bear out the direct effect that many people believe exists.

In the following selection, Diana E. H. Russell minces no words in indicting pornography for much of the violence that men perpetrate against women. She contends that pornography predisposes some males to want to rape women and undermines some males' internal and social inhibitions against acting out their desire to rape. According to Russell, pornography objectifies and dehumanizes women, perpetuates the myth that women enjoy rape, and desensitizes males to rape.

Michael C. Seto, Alexandra Maric, and Howard E. Barbaree disagree with Russell's interpretation of pornography research. In the second selection, they point to difficulties in defining pornography and in measuring aggression, and they contend that an individual's predisposition to sexual aggression plays a larger role than many suspect. Indeed, Seto et al. argue that individuals who are not predisposed to violence are unlikely to show an effect of pornography exposure. That is, perpetrators of sexual violence are not predisposed *by* the pornography but predisposed *before* the pornography, which merely accentuates this predisposition.

POINT

- Pornography exposure predisposes individuals to rape in many different ways.
- By demonstrating and reinforcing violence, pornography nurtures a violent tendency where none existed before.

- Research shows that pornography undermines internal inhibitions by objectifying women, teaching rape myths, and trivializing the act of rape.

- Although many things ultimately "cause" sexual violence, there exists abundant evidence to implicate pornography as a major factor.

COUNTERPOINT

- People who rape are predisposed to violence before they are exposed to pornography.
- Although pornography may accentuate a tendency to aggress in those who are already prone to violence, pornography is unlikely to elicit sexual aggression in those who are not prone to violence.
- Pornography research has been seriously limited by subjective definitions of pornography, disputed measures of sexual offending, and experimenter demand effects.
- More research needs to be conducted to understand the extent of pornography's role in sexual violence.

Diana E. H. Russell  **YES**

Pornography as a Cause of Rape

Sociologist David Finkelhor has developed a very useful multicausal theory to explain the occurrence of child sexual abuse. According to Finkelhor's (1984) model, in order for child sexual abuse to occur, four conditions have to be met. First, someone has to *want* to abuse a child sexually. Second, this person's internal inhibitions against acting out this desire have to be undermined. Third, this person's social inhibitions against acting out this desire (e.g., fear of being caught and punished) have to be undermined. Fourth, the would-be perpetrator has to undermine or overcome his or her chosen victim's capacity to avoid or resist the sexual abuse.

According to my theory, these four conditions also have to be met in order for rape, battery, and other forms of sexual assault on adult women to occur (Russell, 1984). Although my theory can be applied to other forms of sexual abuse and violence against women besides rape, this formulation of it will focus on rape because most of the research relevant to my theory has been limited to this form of sexual assault.

In *Sexual Exploitation* (1984), I suggest many factors that may predispose a large number of males in the United States to want to rape or assault women sexually. Some examples discussed in that book are (a) biological factors, (b) childhood experiences of sexual abuse, (c) male sex-role socialization, (d) exposure to mass media that encourage rape, and (e) exposure to pornography. Here I will discuss only the role of pornography.

Although women have been known to rape both males and females, males are by far the predominant perpetrators of sexual assault as well as the biggest consumers of pornography. Hence, my theory will focus on male perpetrators.

. . . As previously noted, in order for rape to occur, a man must not only be predisposed to rape, but his internal and social inhibitions against acting out his rape desires must be undermined. My theory, in a nutshell, is that pornography (a) predisposes some males to want to rape women and intensifies the predisposition in other males already so predisposed; (b) undermines some males' internal inhibitions against acting out their desire to rape; and (c) undermines some males' social inhibitions against acting out their desire to rape.

The Meaning of "Cause"

Given the intense debate about whether or not pornography plays a causal role in rape, it is surprising that so few of those engaged in it ever state what they mean by "cause." . . .

[P]ornography clearly does not cause rape, as it seems safe to assume that some pornography consumers do not rape women and that many rapes are unrelated to pornography. However, the concept of *multiple causation* (defined below) *is* applicable to the relationship between pornography and rape.

> With the conception of MULTIPLE CAUSATION, various possible causes may be seen for a given event, any one of which may be a sufficient but not necessary condition for the occurrence of the effect, or a necessary but not sufficient condition. . . .

This section will provide the evidence for the . . . different ways in which pornography can induce this predisposition.

1. Predisposes by pairing of sexually arousing stimuli with portrayals of rape. The laws of social learning (e.g., classical conditioning, instrumental conditioning, and social modeling), about which there is now considerable consensus among psychologists, apply to all the mass media, including pornography. As Donnerstein (1983) testified at the hearings in Minneapolis: "If you assume that your child can learn from Sesame Street how to count one, two, three, four, five, believe me, they can learn how to pick up a gun" (p. 11). Presumably, males can learn equally well how to rape, beat, sexually abuse, and degrade females.

A simple application of the laws of social learning suggests that viewers of pornography can develop arousal responses to depictions of rape, murder, child sexual abuse, or other assaultive behavior. Researcher S. Rachman of the Institute of Psychiatry, Maudsley Hospital, London, has demonstrated that male subjects can learn to become sexually aroused by seeing a picture of a woman's boot after repeatedly seeing women's boots in association with sexually arousing slides of nude females (Rachman & Hodgson, 1968). The laws of learning that operated in the acquisition of the boot fetish can also teach males who were not previously aroused by depictions of rape to become so. . . .

2. Predisposes by generating rape fantasies. Further evidence that exposure to pornography can create in males a predisposition to rape where none existed before is provided by an experiment conducted by Malamuth. Malamuth (1981a) classified 29 male students as sexually force-oriented or non-force-oriented on the basis of their responses to a questionnaire. These students were then randomly assigned to view either a rape version of a slide-audio presentation or a mutually consenting version. The account of rape and the pictures illustrating it were based on a story in a popular pornographic magazine, which Malamuth describes as follows:

> The man in this story finds an attractive woman on a deserted road. When he approaches her, she faints with fear. In the rape version, the

man ties her up and forcibly undresses her. The accompanying narrative is as follows: "You take her into the car. Though this experience is new to you, there is a temptation too powerful to resist. When she awakens, you tell her she had better do exactly as you say or she'll be sorry. With terrified eyes she agrees. She is undressed and she is willing to succumb to whatever you want. You kiss her and she returns the kiss." Portrayal of the man and woman in sexual acts follows; intercourse is implied rather than explicit. (p. 38)

In the mutually consenting version of the story the victim was not tied up or threatened. Instead, on her awakening in the car, the man told her that she was safe and "that no one will do her any harm. She seems to like you and you begin to kiss." The rest of the story is identical to the rape version (Malamuth, 1981a, p. 38).

All subjects were then exposed to the same audio description of a rape read by a female. This rape involved threats with a knife, beatings, and physical restraint. The victim was portrayed as pleading, crying, screaming, and fighting against the rapist (Abel, Barlow, Blanchard, & Guild, 1977, p. 898). Malamuth (1981a) reports that measures of penile tumescence as well as self-reported arousal "indicated that relatively high levels of sexual arousal were generated by all the experimental stimuli" (p. 33).

After the 29 male students had been exposed to the rape audio tape, they were asked to try to reach as high a level of sexual arousal as possible by fantasizing about whatever they wanted but without any direct stimulation of the penis (Malamuth, 1981a, p. 40). Self-reported sexual arousal during the fantasy period indicated that those students who had been exposed to the rape version of the first slide-audio presentation created more violent sexual fantasies than those exposed to the mutually consenting version *irrespective of whether they had been [previously] classified as force-oriented or non-force oriented* (p. 33).

As the rape version of the slide-audio presentation is typical of what is seen in pornography, the results of this experiment suggest that similar pornographic depictions are likely to generate rape fantasies even in previously non-force-oriented male consumers. As Edna Einsiedel (1986) points out,

> Current evidence suggests a high correlation between deviant fantasies and deviant behaviors. . . . Some treatment methods are also predicated on the link between fantasies and behavior by attempting to alter fantasy patterns in order to change the deviant behaviors. (1986, p. 60)

Because so many people resist the idea that a desire to rape may develop as a result of viewing pornography, let us focus for a moment on behavior other than rape. There is abundant testimonial evidence that at least some males decide they would like to perform certain sex acts on women after seeing pornography portraying such sex acts. For example, one of the men who answered Shere Hite's (1981) question on pornography wrote: "It's great for me. *It gives me new ideas to try and see,* and it's always sexually exciting" (p. 780;

emphasis added). Of course, there's nothing wrong with getting new ideas from pornography or anywhere else, nor with trying them out, as long as they are not actions that subordinate or violate others. Unfortunately, many of the behaviors modeled in pornography *do* subordinate and violate women, sometimes viciously.

The following statements about men imitating abusive sexual acts that they had seen in pornography were made by women testifying at the pornography hearings in Minneapolis, Minnesota, in 1983 (Russell, Part 1, 1993b). Ms. M testified that

> I agreed to act out in private a lot of the scenarios that my husband read to me. These depicted bondage and different sexual acts that I found very humiliating to do. . . . He read the pornography like a textbook, like a journal. When he finally convinced me to be bound, he read in the magazine how to tie the knots and bind me in a way that I couldn't escape. Most of the scenes where I had to dress up or go through different fantasies were the exact same scenes that he had read in the magazines.

Ms. O described a case in which a man

> brought pornographic magazines, books, and paraphernalia into the bedroom with him and told her that if she did not perform the sexual acts in the "dirty" books and magazines, he would beat her and kill her.

Ms. S testified about the experiences of a group of women prostitutes who, she said,

> were forced constantly to enact specific scenes that men had witnessed in pornography. . . . These men . . . would set up scenarios, usually with more than one woman, to copy scenes that they had seen portrayed in magazines and books.

For example, Ms. S quoted a woman in her group as saying,

> He held up a porn magazine with a picture of a beaten woman and said, "I want you to look like that. I want you to hurt." He then began beating me. When I did not cry fast enough, he lit a cigarette and held it right above my breast for a long time before he burned me.

Ms. S also described what three men did to a nude woman prostitute. They first tied her up while she was seated on a chair, then,

> They burned her with cigarettes and attached nipple clips to her breasts. They had many S and M magazines with them and showed her many pictures of women appearing to consent, enjoy, and encourage this abuse. She was held for twelve hours while she was continuously raped and beaten.

Ms. S also cited the following example of men imitating pornography:

> They [several johns] forced the women to act simultaneously with the movie. In the movie at this point, a group of men were urinating on a naked woman. All the men in the room were able to perform this task, so they all started urinating on the woman who was now naked. . . .

3. Predisposes by creating an appetite for increasingly stronger material.   . . . Zillmann and Bryant (1984) report that as a result of massive exposure to pornography, "consumers graduate from common to less common forms" (p. 127), including pornography portraying "some degree of pseudoviolence or violence" (p. 154). These researchers suggest that this change may be "because familiar material becomes unexciting as a result of habituation" (p. 127).

According to Zillmann and Bryant's research, then, pornography can transform a male who was not previously interested in the more abusive types of pornography into one who *is* turned on by such material. This is consistent with Malamuth's findings . . . that males who did not previously find rape sexually arousing generate such fantasies after being exposed to a typical example of violent pornography.

The Role of Pornography in Undermining Some Males' *Internal* Inhibitions Against Acting Out Their Desire to Rape

. . . Evidence has [shown] that 25% to 30% of males admit that there is some likelihood that they would rape a woman if they could be assured that they would get away with it. It is reasonable to assume that a substantially higher percentage of males would *like* to rape a woman but would refrain from doing so because of their internal inhibitions against these coercive acts. Presumably, the strength of these males' motivation to rape as well as their internal inhibitions against raping range from very weak to very strong, and also fluctuate in the same individual over time.

[There are] seven ways in which pornography can undermine some males' internal inhibitions against acting out rape desires. . . .

1. Objectifying women.   Feminists have been emphasizing the role of objectification (treating females as sex objects) in the occurrence of rape for many years (e.g., Medea & Thompson, 1974; Russell, 1975). Males' tendency to objectify females makes it easier for them to rape girls and women. Check and Guloien (1989) note that other psychologists (e.g., Philip Zimbardo, H. C. Kelman) have observed that "dehumanization of victims is an important disinhibitor of cruelty toward others" (p. 161). The rapists quoted in the following passages demonstrate the link between objectification and rape behavior.

> It was difficult for me to admit that I was dealing with a human being when I was talking to a woman, because, if you read men's magazines, you hear about your stereo, your car, your chick. (Russell, 1975, pp. 249–250)

After this rapist had hit his victim several times in the face, she stopped resisting and begged him not to hurt her.

> When she said that, all of a sudden it came into my head, "My God, this is a human being!" I came to my senses and saw that I was hurting this person. (p. 249)

Another rapist said of his victim, "I wanted this beautiful fine *thing* and I got it" (Russell, 1975, p. 245; emphasis added). . . .

2. Rape myths. If males believe that women enjoy rape and find it sexually exciting, this belief is likely to undermine the inhibitions of some of those who would like to rape women. Sociologists Diana Scully (1985) and Martha Burt (1980) have reported that rapists are particularly apt to believe rape myths. Scully, for example, found that 65% of the rapists in her study believed that "women cause their own rape by the way they act and the clothes they wear"; and 69% agreed that "most men accused of rape are really innocent." However, as Scully points out, it is not possible to know if their beliefs preceded their behavior or constitute an attempt to rationalize it. Hence, findings from the experimental data are more telling for our purposes than these interviews with rapists.

Since the myth that women enjoy rape is widely held, the argument that consumers of pornography realize that such portrayals are false is totally unconvincing (Brownmiller, 1975; Burt, 1980; Russell, 1975). Indeed, several studies have shown that portrayals of women enjoying rape and other kinds of sexual violence can lead to increased acceptance of rape myths in both males and females. In an experiment conducted by Neil Malamuth and James Check (1985), for example, one group of college students saw a pornographic depiction in which a woman was portrayed as sexually aroused by sexual violence, and a second group was exposed to control materials. Subsequently, all subjects were shown a second rape portrayal. The students who had been exposed to the pornographic depiction of rape were significantly more likely than the students in the control group:

1. to perceive the second rape victim as suffering less trauma;
2. to believe that she actually enjoyed being raped; and
3. to believe that women in general enjoy rape and forced sexual acts. (Check & Malamuth, 1985, p. 419)

Other examples of the rape myths that male subjects in these studies are more apt to believe after viewing pornography are as follows:

- A woman who goes to the home or the apartment of a man on their first date implies that she is willing to have sex;
- Any healthy woman can successfully resist a rapist if she really wants to;
- Many women have an unconscious wish to be raped, and may then unconsciously set up a situation in which they are likely to be attacked;

- If a girl engages in necking or petting and she lets things get out of hand, it is her own fault if her partner forces sex on her. (Briere, Malamuth, & Check, 1985, p. 400)

In Maxwell and Check's 1992 study of 247 high school students (described above), they found very high rates of what they called "rape supportive beliefs," that is, acceptance of rape myths and violence against women. . . .

A quarter of girls and 57% of boys expressed the belief that it was at least "maybe okay" for a boy to hold a girl down and force her to have intercourse in one or more of the situations described by the researchers. In addition, only 21% of the boys and 57% of the girls believed that forced intercourse was "definitely not okay" in any of the situations. The situation in which forced intercourse was most accepted was when the girl had sexually excited her date. In this case, 43% of the boys and 16% of the girls stated that it was at least "maybe okay" for the boy to force intercourse on her (Maxwell & Check, 1992).

According to Donnerstein (1983), "After only 10 minutes of exposure to aggressive pornography, particularly material in which women are shown being aggressed against, you find male subjects are much more willing to accept these particular [rape] myths" (p. 6). These males are also more inclined to believe that 25% of the women they know would enjoy being raped (p. 6).

3. Acceptance of interpersonal violence.   Males' internal inhibitions against acting out their desire to rape can also be undermined if they consider male violence against women to be acceptable behavior. Studies have shown that when male subjects view portrayals of sexual violence that have positive consequences—as they often do in pornography—it increases their acceptance of violence against women. Examples of some of the beliefs used to measure acceptance of interpersonal violence include the following:

- Being roughed up is sexually stimulating to many women;
- Sometimes the only way a man can get a cold woman turned on is to use force;
- Many times a woman will pretend she doesn't want to have intercourse because she doesn't want to seem loose, but she's really hoping the man will force her. (Briere et al., 1985, p. 401) . . .

4. Trivializing rape.   According to Donnerstein (1985), in most studies on the effects of pornography, "subjects have been exposed to only a few minutes of pornographic material" (p. 341). In contrast, Zillmann and Bryant (1984) examined the impact on male subjects of what they refer to as "massive exposure" to nonviolent pornography (4 hours and 48 minutes per week over a period of 6 weeks . . .). After 3 weeks the subjects were told that they were participating in an American Bar Association study that required them to evaluate a trial in which a man was prosecuted for the rape of a female hitchhiker. At the end of this mock trial, various measures were taken of the subjects' opinions about the trial and about rape in general. For example, they were asked to recommend the prison term they thought most fair.

Zillmann and Bryant (1984) found that the male subjects who had been exposed to the massive amounts of pornography considered rape a less serious crime than they had before they were exposed to it; they thought that prison sentences for rape should be shorter; and they perceived sexual aggression and abuse as causing less suffering for the victims, even in the case of an adult male having sexual intercourse with a 12-year-old girl (p. 132). The researchers concluded that "heavy exposure to common nonviolent pornography trivialized rape as a criminal offense" (p. 117). . . .

5. Sex callousness toward females.   In the same experiment on massive exposure, Zillmann and Bryant (1984) found that "males' sex callousness toward women was significantly enhanced" by prolonged exposure to pornography (p. 117). These male subjects, for example, became increasingly accepting of statements such as, "A woman doesn't mean 'no' until she slaps you"; "A man should find them, fool them, fuck them, and forget them"; and "If they are old enough to bleed, they are old enough to butcher." However, judging by these statements, it is difficult to distinguish sex callousness from a general hostility toward women. . . .

6. Acceptance of male dominance in intimate relationships.   A marked increase in males' acceptance of male dominance in intimate relationships was yet another result of the massive exposure to pornography (Zillmann & Bryant, 1984, p. 121). The notion that women are, or ought to be, equal in intimate relationships was more likely to be abandoned by these male subjects (p. 122). Finally, their support of the women's liberation movement also declined sharply (p. 134).

These findings demonstrate that pornography increases the acceptability of sexism. As Van White (1984) points out, "by using pornography, by looking at other human beings as a lower form of life, they [the pornographers] are perpetuating the same kind of hatred that brings racism to society" (p. 186).

For example, Ms. O testified about the ex-husband of a woman friend and next-door neighbor: "When he looked at the magazines, he made hateful, obscene, violent remarks about women in general and about me. He told me that because I am female I am here to be used and abused by him, and that because he is a male he is the master and I am his slave" (Russell, 1993b, p. 51). . . .

7. Desensitizing males to rape.   In an experiment specifically designed to study desensitization, Donnerstein and Linz showed 10 hours of R-rated or X-rated movies over a period of 5 days to male subjects (Donnerstein & Linz, 1985, p. 34A). Some students saw X-rated movies depicting sexual assault; others saw X-rated movies depicting only consenting sex; and a third group saw R-rated sexually violent movies. . . .

By the fifth day, the subjects rated the movies as less graphic and less gory and estimated fewer violent or offensive scenes than after the first day of viewing. They also rated the films as significantly less debasing and degrading to women, more humorous, and more enjoyable, and reported a greater willingness to see this type of film again (Donnerstein & Linz, 1985, p. 34F). Their sexual arousal to this material, however, did not decrease over this 5-day period (Donnerstein, 1983, p. 10).

On the last day, the subjects went to a law school, where they saw a documentary reenactment of a real rape trial. A control group of subjects who had never seen the films also participated in this part of the experiment. Subjects who had seen the R-rated movies: (a) rated the rape victim as significantly more worthless, (b) rated her injury as significantly less severe, and (c) assigned greater blame to her for being raped than did the subjects who had not seen the films. In contrast, these effects were not observed for the X-rated nonviolent films. However, the results were much the same for the violent X-rated films, despite the fact that the R-rated material was "much more graphically violent" (Donnerstein, 1985, pp. 12–13).

Donnerstein and Linz (1985) point out that critics of media violence research believe "that only those who are *already* predisposed toward violence are influenced by exposure to media violence" (p. 34F). This view is contradicted by the fact that Donnerstein and Linz actually preselected their subjects to ensure that they were not psychotic, hostile, or anxious; that is, they were not predisposed toward violence prior to the research. . . .

In summary: I have presented only a small portion of the research evidence for seven different effects of pornography, all of which probably contribute to the undermining of some males' internal inhibitions against acting out their rape desires. This list is not intended to be comprehensive.

NO

Michael C. Seto, Alexandra Maric, and Howard E. Barbaree

The Role of Pornography in the Etiology of Sexual Aggression

Abstract. Despite the public and scientific attention the topic has received, the evidence for a causal link between pornography use and sexual offending remains equivocal. This article critically examines the research literature on the association of pornography and sexual offending, focusing on relevant experimental work. The difficulty of this research is highlighted in a discussion of operational definitions of the term *pornography*, the choice of proxy measures for sexual offending in experimental research, and the emphasis given sexual assault of adult females over other kinds of criminal sexual behavior such as child molestation, exhibitionism, and voyeurism. We also review the major theoretical perspectives—conditioning, excitation transfer, feminist, and social learning—and some of the hypotheses that can be derived from them. From the existing evidence, we argue that individuals who are already predisposed to sexually offend are the most likely to show an effect of pornography exposure and are the most likely to show the strongest effects. Men who are not predisposed are unlikely to show an effect; if there actually is an effect, it is likely to be transient because these men would not normally seek violent pornography. . . .

Introduction

Extent of the Problem

Since the first large-scale public inquiry into pornography by the U.S. Commission on Obscenity and Pornography (1970), there has been vociferous debate about the potentially harmful effects of pornography. Over a quarter of a century later, after at least five other major government inquiries,[1] as well as many scientific studies, the evidence for a causal link between pornography and sexually aggressive behavior remains equivocal.

The debate is profound because of public and professional concern about sexual assaults committed against women or children.[2] Sexual victimization is a major social problem: over 160,000 rapes and 152,000 attempted rapes were reported to police in the United States in 1993, resulting in a

Abridged from Michael C. Seto, Alexandra Maric, and Howard E. Barbaree, "The Role of Pornography in the Etiology of Sexual Aggression," *Aggression and Violent Behavior,* vol. 6 (2001). Copyright © 2001 by Elsevier Science Ltd. Reprinted by permission of Elsevier and Michael C. Seto.

combined incidence rate for rape and attempted rape of approximately 750 per 100,000 American women (Bastian, 1995).[3] It is widely acknowledged that sexual assaults are underreported to police. Estimates of the lifetime prevalence of sexual coercion experienced by females range from 14 to 25% in the majority of studies (see review by Koss, 1993). A large-scale survey in the United States suggests that approximately 27% of females and 16% of males have experienced some form of sexual abuse as children (Finkelhor et al., 1990). The correlates of sexual victimization can be very serious, resembling the symptoms of posttraumatic stress disorder (see reviews by Beitchman et al., 1992; Hanson, 1990; but see also Rind, Tromovitch, & Bauserman, 1998).

At the same time, the pornography industry has been growing rapidly. *Adult Video News*, one of the major trade publications, found in their 1997 survey of retailers that sales and rentals of adult videos doubled in the previous 5 years, with a current annual review of approximately $4.2 billion (Adult Video News, 1998). This estimate obviously does not include other forms of pornography, such as magazines, telephone sex services, CD-ROMs, and Internet services. A finding that pornography use causes sexually aggressive behavior would have important implications for public policy.

Overview

This article will critically evaluate the research literature on the association between pornography and sexual aggression, focusing on relevant experimental work. . . . [T]he difficulty of this research is highlighted in a discussion of operational definitions of the term *pornography*, the choice of proxy measures for sexual offending, and the emphasis given sexual assault of adult females over other kinds of criminal sexual behavior (child molestation, paraphilic behaviors such as exhibitionism and voyeurism). . . .

Operational Definitions

In the eighth edition of the *Concise Oxford Dictionary of Current English*, pornography is defined as "the explicit description or exhibition of sexual activity in literature, films, etc., intended to stimulate erotic rather than aesthetic or emotional feelings" (R.E. Allen, 1990). The word pornography derives from the Greek word *pornographos*, typically translated as "the writing of harlots." According to the annotated *Criminal Code of Canada*, Section 163(8), "For the purposes of this definition, the court referred to three categories of pornography: (1) explicit sex with violence; (2) explicit sex without violence but which subjects people to treatment that is degrading or dehumanizing; and (3) explicit sex without violence that is neither degrading nor dehumanizing" (Martin's Annual Criminal Code, 1996). The definition depends on a judgment of the degree of harm and degradation, and requires a test of community standards of acceptability. The obvious difficulty with these definitions is the subjective and relative nature of community standards of aesthetic value, morality, and acceptability.

A distinction has sometimes been made between erotica and pornography. Erotica can be described as sexually explicit material that depicts adult men and women consensually involved in pleasurable, nonviolent, nondegrading, sexual interactions (Fisher & Barak, 1989; Marshall & Barrett, 1990). In contrast, pornography can be described as depictions of sexual activity where one of the participants is objectified or portrayed as powerless or nonconsenting (Marshall & Barrett, 1990). Pornography can be further divided into two broad categories, based on the presence or absence of physical violence or threat of violence against an actor. Violent pornography refers to sexually explicit material portraying sexual aggression, typically enacted by men against women (see also Donnerstein & Berkowitz, 1981; Fisher & Barak, 1989, 1991; Malamuth, 1984; Marshall & Barrett, 1990; Zillmann & Bryant, 1986). Degrading pornography can refer to sexually explicit material that depicts people (usually women) as submissive or hypersexual beings who experience sexual pleasure despite being in degrading or humiliating circumstances (see Fisher & Barak, 1991; Linz et al., 1987). Both violent and degrading pornography depict sexual interactions that are impersonal, without affection or consideration of the actors as individuals (see Marshall & Barrett, 1990).

The identification of degrading pornography is difficult because of the central role of subjective judgment in the definition. Although cues of violence, threat, or nonconsent can be reliably identified in violent pornography because they can be defined in terms of overt behavior, judgments of degradation, depersonalization, and affection are likely to depend on the context of interactions between actors (e.g., affectionate partners engaging in bondage role-play), observer characteristics, and observer inferences about the mental states of the actors. Observer characteristics that may be relevant include gender, age, previous exposure to sexually explicit materials, and attitudes regarding sexuality and depictions of sexuality. However, we believe it is possible to make a valid distinction between violent and nonviolent pornography, where pornography is simply defined as any material depicting sexually explicit activities. . . .

Causal Models

Each of the theories [linking pornography and aggression] can be subsumed under one of the following causal statements: (a) use of pornography causes sexual offending, through such mediating variables as antisocial personality, physical aggressiveness, offense-supportive attitudes and beliefs, or conditioned sexual responding to cues of nonconsent; (b) use of pornography and sexual offending are both caused by third factors such as antisocial personality, hypermasculinity, offense-supportive attitudes and beliefs, or paraphilic interests; or (c) sexual offending is caused by a third factor in conjunction with the use of pornography (e.g., the effect of sexual deviance is potentiated by exposure to arousing pornography).

These causal models are not mutually exclusive, as noted by Seto and Barbaree (1995) in their discussion of the role of alcohol in sexual aggression.

Pornography may have both direct and indirect effects on sexual offending, require the presence of an additional "catalyst" factor to have these effects, and may be at least partly related because of common predispositional or situational factors. Regardless of its role, it is also important to recognize that pornography use can be neither a necessary nor sufficient cause of sexual offending, because sexual offenses have been committed by individuals with little or no exposure to pornography, and many users of pornography have not committed sexual offenses.

Review of the Literature

Correlational Studies

Population Level
This method of investigation relies on correlational analyses between changes in pornography consumption and fluctuations in official reports of rape or sexual assault. If pornography consumption increases the likelihood that its consumer will be sexually aggressive, then the incidence of sex crimes as measured by arrest or conviction rates should increase during periods of greater availability of pornography (e.g., liberalized censorship laws). Kutchinsky's (1991) work is a good example of this type of investigation. He examined the prevalence of sex crimes in Denmark, West Germany, Sweden, and the United States during periods when censorship of pornography decreased. Kutchinsky demonstrated that during the 20-year period between 1964 and 1984, as pornography laws became less and less restrictive, the number of reported incidents of rape did not increase more than the number of reported incidents of nonsexually violent crimes in any of these countries. In contrast, Court (1976) found a positive association between availability of pornography and sex crime rate in a study using data from seven countries, and Jaffee and Strauss (1987) found a positive association between sex magazine readership and rates of reported rape across the American states.

A strength of this kind of approach is that structural factors are considered, permitting a test of feminist and other sociocultural hypotheses regarding the effects of pornography. A serious limitation is the imprecision of the level of analysis. A positive association with aggregate data does not actually demonstrate that sexually aggressive men consume more pornography, usually differentiate between types of pornography, distinguish between effects at the individual level (men exposed to pornography are more likely to sexually offend) and at the social level (the prevalence of pornography reflects or promotes a climate that tolerates sexual offending), or provide control over factors such as changes in the pattern of criminal prosecution for sexual offenses.

Individual Level
Another approach is to look at the association of pornography use with the likelihood of sex aggression within individuals. For example, many studies have examined the use of pornography by detected sex offenders. These

studies use retrospective self-report and typically find no difference between sex offenders and relevant comparison groups (e.g., Condron & Nutter, 1988; Goldstein et al., 1971; Langevin et al., 1988; Marshall, 1988). Cook et al. (1971) found that sex offenders reported less frequent exposure to pornography and exposure to less sexually explicit content than a comparison group of non-sex offenders. Interestingly, Carter and colleagues found that, as adults, their sample of 26 child molesters used more pornography than their sample of 38 rapists, and were more likely to incorporate pornography in their sexual offending, for example, viewing photographs before having contact with the victims (Carter et al., 1987). Finally, 160 adolescent sex offenders surveyed by J. V. Becker and Stein (1991) reported that sexually explicit materials played no role in their crimes.

A strength of the individual level approach is its ecological validity, because actual pornography use is assessed and related to the dependent measures of interest. Problems include the possibility of self-report biases (e.g., denying use of pornography so as to appear less sexually deviant) and the generalizability from identified sex offenders (usually incarcerated or involved in the criminal justice system in some way) to the population of sexually aggressive men. Finally, as with other correlation studies, these types of studies do not directly address the question of causality. Pornography use may cause sexual offending, or men who are already predisposed to sexual offending may seek out pornography. One plausible explanation is that men who are sexually deviant, such as pedophiles, may preferentially seek out pornography that depicts content that is highly arousing for them (e.g., materials depicting nude children or children engaged in sexual activities). The analogous argument is that heterosexual men interested in viewing pornography seek out materials that are highly arousing to them, and are therefore unlikely to seek out depictions of homosexual male activity.

Experimental Studies

Laboratory studies are the main mode of empirical investigation into the potential causal role of pornography. Experimental research has focused mostly on either attitudes, beliefs, and cognitions of the participants, or on laboratory analogs of physical aggression against female targets. Studies that examine the effects of pornography exposure on attitudes, beliefs, and cognitions typically use paper-and-pencil measures (e.g., Check, 1985; Linz et al., 1988; Malamuth et al., 1980; Padgett et al., 1989). In contrast, studies that examine the effects of pornography exposure on laboratory analogs of aggression typically use a version of the Buss shock paradigm (e.g., Donnerstein & Berkowitz, 1981; Goldstein, 1973; Langevin et al., 1988; Malamuth & Ceniti, 1986; Marshall, 1988).

A conventional laboratory paradigm entails exposing male university students to violent, coercive, or degrading pornography. A common manipulation in these types of experiments is to have the female confederate anger or treat the male participant unfairly before he is exposed to pornography and given the opportunity to electrically shock the female when she ostensibly makes mistakes on a learning task. Strengths of the experimental approach include high internal validity (because of control over extraneous factors) and the ability to directly test the possibility of a causal relationship. Weaknesses include limits to external validity because of the contrived situations and settings and the possibility of experimental demand. . . .

Effects on Attitudes, Beliefs, and Cognitions

In their meta-analysis of 24 studies with a total of 4,268 participants, M. Allen et al. (1995) concluded that nonexperimental studies (i.e., studies in which participants are questioned about their previous exposure to sexually explicit material and their endorsement of rape myths) showed almost no relationship, while experimental studies (i.e., participants exposed to sexually explicit materials and then asked about their endorsement of rape myths) showed a small positive effect. Specifically, the meta-analysis showed that exposure to pornography, with or without depictions of violence, increased acceptance of rape myths.

However, these findings need to be qualified by the critical issue of whether attitudes, beliefs, or cognitions are good proxy measures of sexual aggression. Although some models suggest antisocial and anti-women attitudes, beliefs, and cognitions play an important role in sexual aggression, they also recognize that other factors are required (Malamuth et al., 1993). For example, Demarè et al. (1993) surveyed 383 males using measures of anti-women attitudes, pornography use, likelihood of sexual aggression, and actual sexual aggression. The measure of sexual aggression included items regarding verbal coercion (lying, persistent arguments) and a potentially ambiguous item about "getting carried away" during sexual activity. In this sample, 86% of the participants had previously used nonviolent pornography, 36% had viewed pornography that depicted forced sexual acts on women, and 25% had viewed pornography depicting rape. Moreover, 16% of the men had been coercive and 12% had previously used force to obtain sex (including the ambiguous item). Demarè et al. found that self-reported likelihood of raping was not related to actual behavior. An obvious potential problem with using self-reported likelihood of using force of committing rape is report bias. Other studies find that negative attitudes toward women do not distinguish rapists from non-sex offenders (Marolla & Scully, 1986; Scott & Tetreault, 1987). . . .

Effects on Sexual Arousal to Rape

Marshall et al. (1991) found that pre-exposure to videotaped depictions of rape increased sexual arousal to rape in a subsequent experimental session, while pre-exposure to videotaped depictions of consenting sex did not. Malamuth and colleagues have found that prior exposure to violent pornography increased subsequent sexual arousal; in a subset of nonoffender controls, prior exposure to depictions of rape increased sexual arousal to rape, while prior exposure to consenting sex did not (Malamuth & Check, 1980; Malamuth et al., 1980). . . . A particularly noteworthy finding is that showing stimuli that depict the female victim as aroused during the forced sexual interaction appears to potentiate the effect of pornography on sexual arousal to rape. Malamuth and Check (1985) found that depicting the victim as aroused by the forced sexual interaction increased men's beliefs in rape myths, particularly those men who were more inclined to be aggressive toward women, while an earlier study of theirs found an increase in both acceptance of interpersonal violence and rape myths (Malamuth & Check, 1981).

Methodological Issues

The Laboratory Analog for Aggression

It is not clear that the Buss shock paradigm provides a good laboratory analog for sexual aggression (see Tedeschi & Quigley, 1996). For example, to support the assumption that delivering an electric shock is a specific analog for sexual aggression, it would be necessary to demonstrate that the effects of pornography increases aggression against female, but not male, targets in heterosexual subjects. However, M. Allen et al. (1995a) found no difference between aggression against female targets versus aggression against male targets, and no difference in effect size for male compared to female participants. This finding suggests that the effect of pornography on aggression is not gender-specific. . . . It also suggests that there is no direct causal link between pornography use and sexual aggression.

A common criticism of the Buss shock paradigm is that aggressive behavior can occur in the absence of negative consequences or a nonaggressive alternative. The findings from these experiments do not necessarily indicate how men may respond to being angered in a "real world" setting where there are potentially serious consequences for their actions, and nonaggressive responses are available (e.g., leaving the potentially aggressive situation). Fisher and Grenier (1994) examined how male participants would choose to handle a situation in which they were angered by a female confederate, exposed to violent pornography, and then given the choice of nonaggressive and aggressive options. The participants were given the following options: (a) speak with the confederate through an intercom, (b) shock her, or (c) proceed directly to the debriefing phase of the experiment (akin to removing themselves from the potentially aggressive situation). Of the 14 participants in the study, Fisher and Grenier found that nine of the participants chose to proceed to the debriefing phase of the experiment, three chose to speak with the confederate via the intercom, and only two chose to be aggressive and sent an electric shock to the confederate. The authors noted that these last two participants had expressed considerable interest and eagerness to use the Buss apparatus when they were shown it, well before viewing the sexually violent stimulus; one of these two subjects tried to use the Buss apparatus prior to the commencement of the experiment. Fisher and Grenier concluded that, when given a nonaggressive option, provocation and exposure to violent pornography did not result in physical aggression by most male subjects against the female confederate. Although the sample size was small, this finding is important to consider in interpreting findings from the shock paradigm.

Finally, participants are often angered or treated unfairly by a female confederate before being exposed to pornography and participating in the shock paradigm (e.g., Donnerstein, 1984; Donnerstein & Berkowitz, 1981). The effect of the experimental manipulation may represent an interaction between provocation (situational factor) and individual differences (person factor). It is possible that only participants who are high in hostility, irritability, or aggressiveness will exhibit aggressive behavior when provoked. Given this possibility, it is not clear how often pornography use is associated with provocation in natural settings. The influence of moderators, such as hostility and aggressive disposition have been explored in the literature on the effects of alcohol on aggression (Bushman & Cooper, 1990; Seto & Barbaree, 1995).

Sample Composition

In a study examining individual differences in sexual arousal to rape depictions, Malamuth and Check (1983) found that university students who chose to volunteer for studies involving sexually explicit stimuli differed significantly from their peers who chose not to volunteer. Volunteers were more oriented toward unconventional sexual activities (e.g., more likely than their nonvolunteer counterparts to engage in anal intercourse or group sex) and less restricted, a priori, in their willingness to use force.

Fisher and Grenier (1994) drew attention to selective attrition in pornography research. They described a study by Check and Guloien (1989) in which participants were repeatedly exposed to violent pornography and compared to a no-exposure group in terms of changes in self-reported likelihood of raping. Check and Guloien found that repeated exposure to violent pornography increased the subject's self-reported likelihood of raping a female when compared to a no-exposure condition. However, Fisher and Grenier (1994) noted that, while the control condition did not lose any subjects, the repeated exposure to violent pornography condition suffered from a 14% attrition rate. Subjects who did not endorse violence against women may have prematurely removed themselves from the experimental condition, providing an alternative explanation for the difference that was found.

Experimental Design

Linz et al. (1987) observed that laboratory studies are limited in that they may be susceptible to an "experimenter demand effect," in which the subjects may try to guess the experimental hypothesis and attempt to confirm it. This indicates a need for manipulation checks and open-ended questions at the end of the study session to see if participants have guessed the researchers' hypotheses.

Length of exposure to the stimulus material in pornography research is also an important methodological issue. Pornography research can be divided into studies that have provided "short-term" exposure to the stimulus material versus studies that have provided "long-term" exposure. In a review of the literature on pornography's effects on attitudes toward rape, Linz (1989) suggested that short-term exposure consisted of less than an hour, while long-term exposure was an hour or more. But pornography use in the real world may continue for weeks, months, even years. The fact that some studies find effects of short-term exposure to pornography in the laboratory suggests that the effects of prolonged exposure in the real world should be very large if additional exposure has an incremental effect. . . . If so, it is surprising that the experimental findings are not more consistent. It is also interesting to note that another meta-analysis by Allen and his colleagues finds that a short debriefing after participation in pornography research is sufficient to defuse any negative effects of short-term exposure to pornography (M. Allen et al., 1996). . . .

A lot of the existing pornography research assumes that pornography can have a large effect on attitudes or behavior toward women. This research, therefore, does not control for predisposing factors or the role of other determinants. Candidates include personality factors, such as hypermasculinity (Malamuth et al., 1993), authoritarianism (Walker et al., 1993), and erotophilia (M.A. Becker & Byrne, 1985); attitudes about sex roles (Check & Malamuth, 1983); and the acceptability of interpersonal violence (Malamuth et al., 1986). For example, Lopez and George (1995) found that erotophilic male subjects liked deviant-explicit stimuli better and viewed these stimuli longer than erotophobic subjects. However, males viewed the deviant-explicit stimuli for a shorter period of time if a female confederate was present; this confederate effect was attenuated if the female was portrayed as "curious" about pornography rather than "uncomfortable" with it. This finding suggests that there is a role for normative cues, that is, whether the material is condoned or censured (Sinclair et al., 1995). One way in which experimenter demand could have an effect is the implicit suggestion that the pornographic material chosen by the research is "acceptable" for consumption.

Finally, almost all the reviewed studies have examined the effects of pornography, with or without violent content, on proxy measures of rape (i.e., offense-supportive attitudes on beliefs, aggression). This article, reflecting the research literature, has also focused on the potential effects of pornography on proxy measures of rape. The role of pornography in other kinds of sexually inappropriate behavior, such as child molestation, exhibitionism, and voyeurism, is much less studied. Research is needed to examine whether there are crossover effects in terms of pornography content; for example, does watching violent or degrading pornography involving adults increase an individual's likelihood of offending against children? If so, how can this kind of effect be explained?

Discussion

Overall, there is little support for a direct causal link between pornography use and sexual aggression. The recent meta-analytic reviews by M. Allen and colleagues concluded that exposure to pornography has a reliable effect on proxy measures of sexual aggression, such as rape myth acceptance and physical aggression (Allen et al., 1995a,b). However, many of these studies did not consider the possibility of interactions between individual characteristics and pornography exposure. We argue that individuals who are already predisposed to sexually offend are the most likely to show an effect of pornography exposure and are the most likely to show the strongest effects. Men who are not predis-posed are unlikely to show an effect; if there actually is an effect, it is likely to be transient because these men would not normally expose themselves to vio-lent pornography. This question can be addressed only by looking at historical consumption of pornography in participants volunteering for this kind of research, and comparing naive participants with participants reporting a great deal of previous exposure.

Consistent with this view, Mould (1988) has argued that "Donnerstein and Berkowitz's research has relevance only in circumstances in which an already angry individual views a sexually violent depiction and subsequently has access to, and circumstances that permit, aggression against the anger-instigating individual [italics in original]." (p. 339). Similarly, Mosher (1988) has suggested that subjective response to pornography depends on how well the depicted content matches the individual's existing, preferred sexual scripts. Individuals who do not like pornography in general, or who do not like particular kinds of content, are unlikely to seek it out in the real world.

Notes

1. U.S. Attorney General's Committee on Pornography (U.S. Department of Justice, 1986); Surgeon General's Workshop on Pornography and Public Health (Mulvey & Haugaard, 1986); Canada's Special Committee on Pornog-raphy and Prostitution (1988); the Australian Joint Select Committee on Video Material (1988); and New Zealand's Ministerial Committee of Inquiry into Pornography (1989).

2. Some sexual assaults are committed against adult males, but they represent a small proportion of sexual assault victims and less is known about them. Also, we focus on male perpetrators because much more empirical research is available.

3. The terms *rape, sexual aggression, sexual assault,* and *sexual coercion* will be used interchangeably here. Rape and sexual assault represent extreme forms of sex-ual coercion. Sexual coercion can range from psychological pressure or the administration of alcohol or drugs to violent physical assault.

References

Adult Video News. (1998). The 1998 annual entertainment guide. Van Nuys, CA: Author.

Allen, M., D'Alessio, D., & Brezgel, K. (1995a). A meta-analysis summarizing the effects of pornography. II: Aggression after exposure. *Human Communications Research, 22,* 258–283.

Allen, M., Emmers, T., Gebhardt, L., & Giery, M. A. (1995b). Exposure to pornogra-phy and acceptance of rape myths. *Journal of Communication, 45,* 5–26.

Allen, M., D'Alessio, D., Emmers, T. M., & Gebhardt, L. (1996). The role of educa-tional briefings in mitigating effects of experimental exposure to violent sexually explicit material: A meta-analysis. *Journal of Sex Research, 33,* 135–141.

Allen, R. E. (Ed.). (1990). *Concise Oxford Dictionary of Current English* (8th edn). Oxford: Clarendon Press.

Australian Joint Selection Committee on Video Material. (1988). *Report of the Joint Select Committee on Video Material.* Canberra: Australian Government Publishing Service.

Bastian, L. (1995). National crime victimization survey: Criminal victimization 1993. *Bureau of Justice Statistics Bulletin.* Rockville, MD: Bureau of Justice Statistics Clearinghouse.

Becker, J. V., & Stein, R. M. (1991). Is sexual erotica associated with sexual deviance in adolescent males? *International Journal of Law and Psychiatry, 14,* 85–95.

Becker, M. A., & Byrne, D. (1985). Self-regulated exposure to erotica, recall errors, and subjective reactions as a function of erotophobia and type A coronary-prone behavior. *Journal of Personality and Social Psychology, 48,* 760–767.

Beitchman, J. H., Zucker, K. J., Hood, J. E., DaCosta, G. A., Akman, D., & Cassavia, E. (1992). A review of the long-term effects of child sexual abuse. *Child Abuse and Neglect, 16,* 101–118.

Bushman, B. J., & Cooper, H. M. (1990). Effects of alcohol on human aggression: An integrative research review. *Psychological Bulletin, 107,* 341–354.

Canada's Special Committee on Pornography and Prostitution. (1988). *Pornography in Canada: Report of the Special Committee: Response to the Victimization of Women and Children, 9,* 16–20.

Carter, D. L., Prentky, R. A., Knight, R. A., Vanderveer, P. L., & Boucher, R. J. (1987). Use of pornography in the criminal and developmental histories of sexual offenders. *Journal of Interpersonal Violence, 2,* 196–211.

Check, J. V. P. (1985). The effects of violent and nonviolent pornography. Report to the Department of Justice. Department of Justice, Department of Supply and Services Contract 05SV. (1920) 0–3–0899.

Check, J. V. P., & Guloien, T. H. (1989). Reported proclivity for coercive sex following repeated exposure to sexually violent pornography, nonviolent dehumanizing pornography, and erotica. In D. Zillmann & J. Bryant (Eds.), *Pornography: Research advances and policy considerations* (pp. 159–184). Hillsdale, NJ: Lawrence Erlbaum Associates.

Check, J. V. P., & Malamuth, N. M. (1983). Sex role stereotyping and reactions to depictions of stranger versus acquaintance rape. *Journal of Personality and Social Psychology, 45,* 344–356.

Condron, M. K., & Nutter, D. E. (1988). A preliminary examination of the pornography experience of sex offenders, paraphiliacs, sexual dysfunction patients, and controls based on Meese Commission recommendations. *Journal of Sex and Marital Therapy, 14,* 285–298.

Cook, R. E., Fosen, R. H., & Pacht, A. (1971). Pornography and the sex offender: Patterns of previous exposure and arousal effects of pornographic stimuli. *Journal of Applied Psychology, 55,* 503–511.

Court, J. H. (1976). Pornography and sex-crimes: A re-evaluation in the light of recent trends around the world. *International Journal of Criminology and Penology, 5,* 129–157.

Demarè, D., Lips, H. M., & Briere, J. (1993). Sexually violent pornography, anti-women attitudes, and sexual aggression: A structural equation model. *Journal of Research in Personality, 27,* 285–300.

Donnerstein, E. (1984). Pornography: Its effect on violence against women. In N. M. Malamuth & E. Donnerstein (Eds.), *Pornography and Sexual Aggression* (pp. 53–84). Orlando, FL: Academic Press.

Donnerstein, E., & Berkowitz, L. (1981). Victim reactions in aggressive erotic films as a factor in violence against women. *Journal of Personality and Social Psychology, 41,* 710–724.

Finkelhor, D., Hotaling, G., Lewis, I. A., & Smith, C. (1990). Sexual abuse in a national sample of adult men and women: Prevalence, characteristics, and risk factors. *Child Abuse and Neglect, 14,* 19–28.

Fisher, W. A., & Barak, A. (1989). Sex education as a corrective: Immunizing against possible effects of pornography. In D. Zillmann & J. Bryant (Eds.), *Pornography: Recent Research, Interpretations, and Policy Considerations* (pp. 289–320). Hillsdale, NJ: Erlbaum.

Fisher, W. A., & Barak, A. (1991). Pornography, erotica, and behavior: More questions than answers. *International Journal of Law and Psychiatry, 14,* 65–83.

Fisher, W. A., & Grenier, G. (1994). Violent pornography, antiwoman thoughts, and antiwoman acts: In search of reliable effects. *Journal of Sex Research, 31,* 23–38.

Goldstein, M. J. (1973). Exposure to erotic stimuli and sexual deviance. *Journal of Social Issues, 29,* 197–219.

Goldstein, M. J., Kant, H., Judd, L., & Green, R. (1971). Experience with pornography: Rapists, pedophiles, homosexuals, transsexuals, and controls. *Archives of Sexual Behavior, 1,* 1–15.

Hanson, R. K. (1990). The psychological impact of sexual assault on women and children: A review. *Annals of Sex Research, 3,* 187–232.

Jaffee, D., & Straus, M. A. (1987). Sexual climate and reported rape: A state-level analysis. *Archives of Sexual Behavior, 16,* 107–123.

Koss, M. P. (1993). Detecting the scope of rape: A review of prevalence research methods. *Journal of Interpersonal Violence, 8,* 198–222.

Kutchinsky, B. (1991). Pornography and rape: Theory and practice? *International Journal of Law and Psychiatry, 14,* 47–64.

Langevin, R., Lang, R. A., Wright, P., Handy, L., Frenzel, R. R., & Black, E. L. (1988). Pornography and sexual offences. *Annals of Sex Research, 1,* 335–362.

Linz, D., Donnerstein, E., & Penrod, S. (1987). The findings and recommendations of the Attorney General's Commission on Pornography: Do the psychological "facts" fit the political fury? *American Psychologist, 42,* 946–953.

Linz, D., Donnerstein, E., & Penrod, S. (1988). The effects of long-term exposure to violent and sexually degrading depictions of women. *Journal of Personality and Social Psychology, 55,* 758–768.

Lopez, P. A., & George, W. H. (1995). Attitudes and gender-specific attitudes and gender-specific norms. *Journal of Sex Research, 32,* 275–288.

Malamuth, N. M. (1984). Aggression against women: Cultural and individual causes. In N. M. Malamuth & E. Donnerstein (Eds.), *Pornography and Sexual Aggression* (pp. 19–52). Orlando, FL: Academic Press.

Malamuth, N. M., & Ceniti, J. (1986). Repeated exposure to violent and nonviolent pornography: Likelihood of raping ratings and laboratory aggression against women. *Aggressive Behavior, 12,* 129–137.

Malamuth, N. M., & Check, J. V. P. (1980). Penile tumescence and perceptual responses to rape as a function of victim's perceived reactions. *Journal of Applied Social Psychology, 10,* 528–547.

Malamuth, N. M., & Check, J. V. P. (1981). The effects of mass media exposure on acceptance of violence against women: A field experiment. *Journal of Research in Personality, 15,* 436–446.

Malamuth, N. M., & Check, J. V. P. (1983). Sexual arousal to rape depictions: Individual differences. *Journal of Abnormal Psychology, 92,* 55–67.

Malamuth, N. M., & Check, J. V. P. (1985). The effects of aggressive pornography on beliefs in rape myths: Individual differences. *Journal of Research in Personality, 19,* 299–320.

Malamuth, N. M., Check, J. V. P., & Briere, J. (1986). Sexual arousal in response to aggression: Ideological, aggressive, and sexual correlates. *Journal of Personality and Social Psychology, 50,* 330–340.

Malamuth, N. M., Haber, S., & Feshbach, S. (1980). Testing hypotheses regarding rape: Exposure to sexual violence, sex differences, and the "normality" of rapists. *Journal of Research in Personality, 14,* 121–137.

Malamuth, N. M., Heavey, C. L., & Linz, D. (1993). Predicting men's antisocial behavior against women: The interaction model of sexual aggression. In G. C. N. Hall, R. Hirschman, J. R. Graham, & M. S. Zaragoza (Eds.), *Sexual aggression: Issues in etiology, assessment, and treatment* (pp. 63–97). Washington, DC: Taylor and Francis.

Marolla, J., & Scully, D. (1986). Attitudes toward women, violence, and rape: A comparison of convicted rapists and other felons. *Deviant Behavior, 7,* 337–355.

Marshall, W. L. (1988). The use of sexually explicit stimuli by rapists, child molesters, and nonoffenders. *Journal of Sex Research, 25,* 267–288.

Marshall, W. L., & Barrett, S. (1990). *Criminal neglect: Why sex offenders go free.* Toronto: Doubleday.

Marshall, W. L., Seidman, B. T., & Barbaree, H. E. (1991). The effects of prior exposure to erotic and nonerotic stimuli on the rape index. *Annals of Sex Research, 4,* 209–220.

Martin's Annual Criminal Code. (1996). Aurora, ON: Canada Law Book.

Mosher, D. L. (1988). Pornography defined: Sexual involvement theory, narrative context, and goodness-of-fit. *Journal of Psychology and Human Sexuality, 1,* 67–85.

Mould, D. E., (1988). A critical analysis of recent research on violent erotica. *Journal of Sex Research, 24,* 326–340.

Mulvey, E. P., & Haugaard, J. L. (1986). *Report of the Surgeon General's Workshop on Pornography and Public Health.* Washington, DC: U.S. Department of Health and Human Services, Office of the Surgeon General.

New Zealand's Ministerial Committee of Inquiry into Pornography. (1989). Report of the Ministerial Committee of Inquiry into Pornography. Wellington, New Zealand: Crown Copyright.

Padgett, V. R., Brislin-Slutz, J. A., & Neal, J. A. (1989). Pornography, erotica, and attitudes toward women: The effects of repeated exposure. *Journal of Sex Research, 26,* 479–491.

Rind, B., Tromovitch, P., & Bauserman, R. (1998). A meta-analytic examination of assumed properties of child sexual abuse using college samples. *Psychological Bulletin, 124,* 22–53.

Scott, R. L., & Tetreault, L. A. (1987). Attitudes of rapists and other violent offenders toward women. *Journal of Social Psychology, 127,* 375–380.

Seto, M. C., & Barbaree, H. E. (1995). The role of alcohol in sexual aggression. *Clinical Psychology Review, 15,* 545–566.

Sinclair, R. C., Lee, T., & Johnson, T. E. (1995). The effect of social-comparison feedback on aggressive responses to erotic and aggressive films. *Journal of Applied Social Psychology, 25,* 818–837.

Tedeschi, J. T., & Quigley, B. M. (1996). Limitations of laboratory paradigms for studying aggression. *Aggression and Violent Behavior, 1,* 163–177.

U.S. Commission on Obscenity and Pornography. (1970). *Report of the Commission on Obscenity and Pornography.* Washington, DC: Government Printing Office.

U.S. Department of Justice. (1986). *Attorney General's Commission on Pornography: Final report.* Washington, DC: Author.

Walker, W. D., Rowe, R. C., & Quinsey, V. L. (1993). Authoritarianism and sexual aggression. *Journal of Personality and Social Psychology, 65,* 1036–1045.

Zillmann, D., & Bryant, J. (1986). Shifting preferences in pornography consumption. *Communication Research, 13,* 560–578.

CHALLENGE QUESTIONS

Is Pornography Harmful?

1. Why do both authors shy away from the notion of a "direct cause"? What is the difference between pornography predisposing individuals to rape and pornography being a direct and sufficient cause of an individual's rape? How might this distinction affect this issue?
2. If pornography does cause men to be violent toward women, what might this imply about other types of media and other types of behavior?
3. Do the methodological problems that Seto and his colleagues note invalidate the research that Russell reviews? How serious are these research limitations in drawing conclusions about pornography's effects?
4. If an aggressive nature, rather than pornography, is to blame for sexual violence, will avoiding pornography help to reduce rape? If so, why? If pornography avoidance will *not* help, what will?

Contributors to This Volume

EDITOR

BRENT SLIFE is currently professor of psychology at Brigham Young University, where he chairs the doctoral program in theoretical and philosophical psychology and serves as a member of the doctoral program in clinical psychology. He has been honored recently with several awards for his scholarship and teaching, including the Eliza R. Snow Award (for research on the interface of science and religion), the Karl G. Maeser Award (Top Researcher at BYU), Circle of Honor Award (Student Honor Association), and both "Teacher of the Year" by the university and "Most Outstanding Professor" by the psychology student honorary, Psi Chi. Dr. Slife moved from Baylor University where he served as director of clinical training for many years and was honored there as "Outstanding Research Professor" as well as the "Circle of Achievement" award for his teaching. The recipient of numerous grants, he is also listed in *Who's Who in the World, America, Science and Engineering, and Health and Medicine.* As a fellow of several professional organizations, including the American Psychological Association, he recently served as the president of the Society of Theoretical and Philosophical Psychology and on the editorial boards of five journals: *Journal of Mind and Behavior, Journal of Theoretical and Philosophical Psychology, Qualitative Research in Psychology, Methods,* and *International Journal of Existential Psychology and Psychotherapy.* He has authored over 120 articles and books, with the most recent books: *Critical Thinking About Psychology: Hidden Assumptions and Plausible Alternatives* (APA Books) and *Critical Issues in Psychotherapy: Translating New Ideas into Practice* (Sage Publications). Dr. Slife also continues his psychotherapy practice of over 20 years, where he specializes in marital and family therapies.

STAFF

Larry Loeppke	Managing Editor
Jill Peter	Senior Developmental Editor
Nichole Altman	Developmental Editor
Beth Kundert	Production Manager
Jane Mohr	Project Manager
Tara McDermott	Design Coordinator
Bonnie Coakley	Editorial Assistant
Lori Church	Permissions

AUTHORS

CRAIG A. ANDERSON received his Ph.D. in psychology from Stanford University and is currently a professor and chair of the Department of Psychology at Iowa State University.

PHILIP ASPDEN is executive director of the Center for Research on the Information Society (CRIS) in Pennington, New Jersey. He has consulted in telecommunications and technology-based economic development for a wide range of high-tech firms, public bodies, and foundations in both the United States and Europe. He has also been a research scholar at the International Institute for Applied Systems Analysis.

HOWARD E. BARBAREE is clinical director of the Law and Mental Health Program at the Centre for Addiction and Mental Health and a professor in the Department of Psychiatry at the University of Toronto. He is also founding director of the Warkworth Sexual Behaviour Clinic, a Canadian Federal Penitentiary treatment program for sex offenders. Dr. Barbaree has published numerous journal articles and book chapters on the topic, and he is coeditor, with William L. Marshall and Stephen M. Hudson, of *The Juvenile Sex Offender* (Guilford, 1993).

JOHN A. BARGH is a professor of psychology at Yale University. In 1989, he received the American Psychological Association (APA) Early Career Award for contributions to psychology. His research interests include attitudes; close relationships; ethics and morality; motivation and goal setting; person perception; prejudice and stereotyping; and social cognition.

RUSSELL A. BARKLEY is currently professor of psychiatry at the Medical University of South Carolina. The recipient of numerous awards for his research on ADHD, Dr. Barkley has authored, co-authored, or co-edited 15 books and clinical manuals and has published more than 170 scientific articles and book chapters on ADHD and related disorders.

DIANA BAUMRIND is a research psychologist and the principal investigator for the Family Socialization and Developmental Competence Project of the University of California's Institute for Human Development in Berkeley, California. She has contributed numerous articles to professional journals and books, and she is on the editorial board of *Developmental Psychology.* She is also the author of *Child Maltreatment and Optimal Caregiving in Social Contexts* (Garland, 1995).

JOSEPH BIEDERMAN is chief of the Joint Program in Pediatric Psychopharmacology at the Massachusetts General and McLean Hospitals in Boston, Massachusetts, and a professor of psychiatry at Harvard Medical School. He is board certified in general and child psychiatry. His clinical program treats more than 2,000 children, adolescents, and adults, and evaluates more than 300 new patients every year. Dr. Biederman's research focus is on attention deficit hyperactivity disorder, juvenile mood and anxiety disorders, and studies of children at risk.

ARTHUR C. BOHART is a professor of psychology at California State University in Dominguez Hills. He is also affiliated with Saybrook Graduate

School and Research Center in San Francisco, CA. He has published extensively on the client's active role in psychotherapy. He is the author of several books, including *How Clients Make Therapy Work: The Process of Active Self-Healing* (with Karen Tallman; APA, 1999) and *Foundations of Clinical and Counseling Psychology* (with Judith Todd; Waveland Press, 3rd edition, 2002).

JEANNE BROOKS-GUNN is the Virginia and Leonard Marx Professor of Child Development and Education at Teacher's College, Columbia University. She assesses parental contributions to cognitive development and studies the impact of poverty on child outcomes. She earned her Ed.M. from Harvard University and her Ph.D. from the University of Pennsylvania. She has published over 300 articles and 15 books, including *Conflict and Cohesion in Families: Causes and Consequences,* coedited with Martha J. Cox (Lawrence Erlbaum, 1999).

GRACE CHANG is currently a doctoral student in the clinical psychology program at the University of Nebraska.

TANYA L. CHARTRAND is an associate professor of marketing and psychology in the Fuqua School of Business at Duke University. Her research interests include consumer behavior, social psychology, social cognition, automaticity and nonconscious processes, and research methods.

PATRICK H. DELEON is a former president of the American Psychological Association. He received a Ph.D. in Clinical Psychology at Purdue University, a Master of Public Health at the University of Hawaii, and a JD at the Columbus School of Law. He is currently using his training and skills as a clinical psychologist by working on Capital Hill. He helps shape policy and legislation that best reflects both the science and application of clinical psychology.

DEBRA LINA DUNIVIN was a 1992–1994 APA Congressional Fellow. Currently, she is a major in the U.S. Army and is a Department of Defense Psychopharmacology Fellow in Washington, D.C.

STEPHEN V. FARAONE, a clinical psychologist, is an associate professor in the Department of Psychiatry at Harvard Medical School at the Massachusetts Mental Health Center and director of Pediatric Psychopharmacology Research at Massachusetts General Hospital. He is coeditor of the journal *Neuropsychiatric Genetics* and statistical section editor of the *Journal of Child and Adolescent Psychopharmacology.* The author or coauthor of over 300 journal articles, editorials, chapters, and books, he was the eighth highest producer of high-impact papers in psychiatry from 1990 to 1999, as determined by the Institute for Scientific Information.

R. G. FREY, a professor of philosophy at Bowling Green State University, is a senior research fellow of the Social Philosophy and Policy Center in Bowling Green, of the Kennedy Institute of Ethics, and of the Westminster Institute of Ethics and Public Policy at the University of Ontario, Canada. He is the author of numerous articles and books on ethical theory, applied ethics, the history of ethics, and social/political theory. And he is coauthor, with Gerald Dworkin and Sissela Bok, of *Euthanasia and Physician-Assisted Suicide* (Cambridge University Press, 1988).

HOWARD GARDNER is the John H. and Elisabeth A. Hobbs Professor in Cognition and Education at the Harvard Graduate School of Education. He also holds positions as adjunct professor of psychology at Harvard, adjunct professor of neurology at the Boston University School of Medicine, and codirector of Harvard Project Zero. He is the author of several hundred articles and 18 books, including *Extraordinary Minds* (Basic Books, 1997) and *The Disciplined Mind: What All Students Should Understand* (Simon & Schuster, 1999).

DOUGLAS A. GENTILE received his doctorate in child psychology from the Institute of Child Development at the University of Minnesota. He is a developmental psychologist and the director of research for the National Institute on Media and the Family. He is currently a member of the psychology department faculty at Iowa State University.

LINDA S. GOTTFREDSON is a professor of educational studies at the University of Delaware, where she has been teaching since 1986, and codirector of the Delaware–Johns Hopkins Project for the Study of Intelligence and Society. She earned her Ph.D. in sociology from the Johns Hopkins University in 1977 and won the Mensa Research Foundation Award for Excellence in Research, 1999–2000. Her research interests include intelligence and social inequality, employment testing and job aptitude demands, and affirmative action and multicultural diversity.

WEN-JUI HAN is an assistant professor of social work in the School of Social Work at Columbia University. Her professional interests include social welfare policy, with an emphasis on children and families, and child care issues facing immigrant families. She earned her M.S.W. from the University of California, Los Angeles, and her Ph.D. from Columbia University.

STEVEN C. HAYES is a professor in the Department of Psychology at the University of Nevada. An author of 25 books and 340 scientific articles, his career has focused on an analysis of the nature of human language and cognition and the application of this to the understanding and alleviation of human suffering. In 1992, the Institute for Scientific Information listed him as the 30th "highest impact" psychologist in the world during 1986–1990. Dr. Hayes has also been President of Division 25 of the American Psychological Association, of the American Association of Applied and Preventive Psychology, and of the Association for Advancement of Behavior Therapy.

DAVID HEALY is a psychiatrist at Cardiff University in Wales. He has authored 13 books on various aspects of psychopharmaceuticals as well as 110 peer-reviewed papers and approximately 100 other publications. Nine of these books are on the area of the history of psychopharmacology, for which Healy has a leading role worldwide. His other research interests include cognitive functioning in affective disorders and psychoses, and circadian rhythms in affective disorders.

E. MAVIS HETHERINGTON is an emeritus professor in the Department of Psychology at the University of Virginia. She is also a former president of Division 7, the Developmental Psychology Division of the American Psychological Association, and of the Society for Research in Child Development in Adolescence. She has authored and edited many books in the area of child development, including *Child Psychology: A Contemporary Viewpoint,* updated 5th ed., coauthored with Virginia Otis Locke and Ross D. Parke (McGraw-Hill, 2002). She earned her Ph.D. in psychology from the University of California, Berkeley.

GAIL E. JOSEPH is an assistant professor in educational psychology at the University of Colorado at Denver. She has been involved in national projects designed to help professionals work with children who have challenging behaviors.

JAY JOSEPH is a registered clinical psychologist doing a postdoctoral internship at a psychotherapy clinic.

JAMES E. KATZ is a professor of communication at Rutgers University and a senior scientist at Bellcore (Bell Communications Research) in New Jersey. He has examined a variety of issues concerning the Internet and its societal consequences, and he is an expert in privacy policy. He has also been involved in the World Wide Web Consortium and U.S. National Science Foundation planning exercises for research on knowledge networks.

JOHN KELLY is a freelance journalist and coauthor of a number of books, including *Stepfamilies: Love, Marriage, and Parenting in the First Decade* (Broadway Books, 1999).

ALFIE KOHN is a popular lecturer and the author of several books on education and human behavior. He is often viewed as the leading critic of competition and his works fly in the face of traditional wisdom about motivation and compensation. Kohn was educated at Brown University and the University of Chicago.

ROBERT KRAUT is a professor of social psychology and human computer interaction at Carnegie Mellon University, with joint appointments in the Department of Social and Decision Sciences, the Human Computer Interaction Institute, and the Graduate School of Industrial Administration. His current research focuses on the design and social impacts of information technologies in small groups, in the home, and between organizations. He is coauthor of *Research Recommendations to Facilitate Distributed Work* (National Academy Press, 1994).

GEORGIOS K. LAMPROPOULOS has a Master's Degree in Clinical Psychology and is currently a Ph.D. candidate in Counseling Psychology at Ball State University. He is also a practitioner and a clinical researcher with primary interests in the process and outcome of psychotherapy. He has guest-edited three special issues in psychology journals (e.g., *Journal of Clinical Psychology*) and has published over 20 peer-reviewed journal articles on psychotherapy practice, research, and training.

YVON D. LAPIERRE is the founder and former Director General of the University of Ottawa Institute of Mental Health Research and is an internationally recognized clinical researcher in biological psychiatry and psychopharmacology. He has collaborated with the pharmaceutical industry in the development of new therapeutic agents for the treatment of major mental disorders, and with other leading investigators in the study of the relationship between pharmacologic treatment options and clinical response. His expertise has placed him in high demand as a consultant for many other national and international organizations. Dr. Lapierre has also authored or co-authored over 300 scientific publications.

JULIA M. LEWIS is a professor of psychology at San Francisco State University. Her area of expertise is divorce and its effect on children, and she hold a Ph.D. in psychology from the University of California, Los Angeles.

ALEXANDRA MARIC is affiliated with the Forensic Division of the Clarke Institute of Psychiatry, which is part of the University of Toronto's Centre for Addiction and Mental Health.

STANLEY MILGRAM (1933–1984) was an experimental social psychologist and a professor of psychology at the Graduate School and University Center of the City University of New York. He is especially well known for his series of controversial investigations regarding obedience to authority, which were performed at Yale University from 1960 to 1963. His publications include *Obedience to Authority: An Experimental View* (Harper & Row, 1975).

CHERYL K. OLSON is a professor of psychiatry at the Harvard Medical School Center for Mental Health and Media and has been recognized nationally as an expert in health communications and behavior change.

DIANA E. H. RUSSELL is a professor emeritus of sociology at Mills College in Oakland, California. A leading authority on sexual violence against women and girls, she has performed research and written articles and books on rape, incest, the misogynist murder of women, and pornography for 25 years. Her publications include *Against Pornography: The Evidence of Harm* (Russell, 1994) and *Making Violence Sexy: Feminist Views on Pornography* (Teachers College Press, 1993).

JEFFREY A. SCHALER has been a psychologist and therapist in private practice since 1973. He is also an adjunct professor of justice, law, and society at American University's School of Public Affairs, where he has taught courses on drugs, psychiatry, liberty, justice, law, and public policy since 1990. He writes a regular column for *The Interpsych Newsletter,* and he is the author of *Smoking: Who Has the Right?* (Prometheus Books, 1998).

BARRY A. SCHREIER is coordinator of training for Counseling and Psychological Services at Purdue University in West Lafayette, Indiana. His areas of interest include gay, lesbian, bisexual, and transgendered issues; interpersonal supervision and training; and clinical ethics. He earned his Ph.D. in counseling psychology from the University of Missouri at Kansas City.

MICHAEL C. SETO is a research psychologist in the Law and Mental health Program at the Centre for Addiction and Mental Health in Toronto, Ontario, Canada. He earned his Ph.D. from Queen's University in 1997.

PETER SINGER is the DeCamp Professor of Bioethics in the University Center for Human Values at Princeton University. He was foundation president of the International Association of Bioethics, and he is currently a member of its board of directors. He is coeditor of the journal *Bioethics*, and he is the author of *One World: The Ethics of Globalization* (Yale University Press, 2002).

AMY FISHER SMITH is an assistant professor of psychology at the University of Dallas. She is a licensed clinical psychologist, and her most current research interests include the role and management of values—particularly therapist values—in psychotherapy.

PHILLIP S. STRAIN is a professor in educational psychology at the University of Colorado at Denver. Some of his work includes the development of comprehensive early-intervention programs for children with autism or severe problem behaviors.

ROBERT W. SUSSMAN is a professor of physical anthropology at Washington University in St. Louis, Missouri, and editor emeritus of *American Anthropologist*. He is the author of *The Biological Basis of Human Behavior: A Critical Review*, 2d ed. (Prentice Hall, 1998) and *Primate Ecology and Social Structure, Vol. 2: New World Monkeys*, 2d ed. (Pearson Higher Education, 2003). He earned his Ph.D. from Duke University in 1972.

WARREN THROCKMORTON is director of College Counseling and an associate professor of psychology at Grove City College in Grove City, Pennsylvania. He holds an M.A. from Central Michigan University and a Ph.D. from Ohio University.

SAMI TIMIMI is a consultant child and adolescent psychiatrist who works for the National Health Service in the United Kingdom. Timimi has published on several topics, including cross-cultural psychiatry, psychotherapy, eating disorders, and Attention Deficit Hyperactivity Disorder (ADHD).

THOMAS M. VANDER VEN is an assistant professor in the Department of Sociology and Anthropology at Ohio University. His areas of specialization include crime and delinquency and links between work, family, and crime. His articles have appeared in such journals as *Criminology* and *Social Problems*, and he is the author of *Working Mothers and Juvenile Delinquency* (LFB Scholarly Pub LLC, 2003).

JANE WALDFOGEL is a professor of social work in the School of Social Work at Columbia University. Her professional interests focus on social policy, including the impact of public policies on child and family well-being, Comparative Social Welfare policy, and child protective services and child welfare policy. She earned her M.Ed. and Ph.D. from Harvard University, and she is coeditor, with Sheldon Danziger, of *Securing the Future: Investing in Children From Birth to Adulthood* (Russell Sage Foundation, 2000).

JUDITH S. WALLERSTEIN is an internationally recognized authority on the effects of divorce on children and their parents. She has been executive director of the Center for the Family in Transition and a senior lecturer in the School of Social Welfare at the University of California, Berkeley. She is the author of *The Good Marriage: How and Why Love Lasts* (Warner Books, 1996) and coauthor, with Sandra Blakeslee, of *What About the Kids? Raising Your Children Before, During, and After Divorce* (Hyperion Press, 2003).

CHRIS WHITAKER is a statistician in the department of psychology at the University of Wales, Bangor.

MICHAEL L. WILSON has been studying primates in East Africa since 1992, starting with baboons in Kenya (1992–1993) and continuing with chimpanzees in Uganda (1996–1998) and Tanzania (2001–present). He received his Ph.D. in anthropology at Harvard University and is currently the director of field research for Gombe Stream Research Centre, Jane Goodall Institute—Tanzania.

RICHARD WRANGHAM is a professor of anthropology at Harvard University. His main research interests are primate behavioral ecology and human evolutionary ecology. He earned his Ph.D. in zoology from Cambridge University in 1975, and he is coeditor of *Chimpanzee Cultures* (Harvard University Press, 1994).

ALICE M. YOUNG is a professor of psychology and of psychiatry and behavioral neurosciences at Wayne State University, where she also serves as associate dean of the College of Science. Her research interests include behavioral and brain processes involved in opioid tolerance and dependence.

Index